BRINGING GOD TO MEN

BRINGING
God to Men

American Military Chaplains
and the Vietnam War

JACQUELINE E. WHITT

THE UNIVERSITY OF NORTH CAROLINA PRESS | *Chapel Hill*

*This book was published with the assistance of the
Anniversary Endowment Fund of the University of North Carolina Press.*

© 2014 THE UNIVERSITY OF NORTH CAROLINA PRESS

Library of Congress Cataloging-in-Publication Data
Whitt, Jacqueline E.
Bringing God to men : American military chaplains and the
Vietnam War / Jacqueline E. Whitt.
pages cm
Includes bibliographical references and index.
ISBN 978-1-4696-1294-2 (paperback : alkaline paper)
ISBN 978-1-4696-1295-9 (E-book)
1. Vietnam War, 1961–1975—Chaplains. 2. Vietnam War, 1961–1975—Religious
aspects. 3. Military chaplains—United States—Attitudes—History—20th
century. 4. Military chaplains—Vietnam—Attitudes—History—20th century.
5. United States—Armed Forces—Chaplains—History—20th century.
6. Reconciliation—Social aspects—United States—History—20th century.
7. Vietnam War, 1961–1975—Social aspects—United States. 8. Social
conflict—United States—History—20th century. 9. Social change—
United States—History—20th century. I. Title.
DS559.64.W47 2014
959.704'37—dc23
2013031253

18 17 16 15 14   5 4 3 2 1

This work expresses the opinions of the author, and does not represent
the views of the Department of Defense, the Department of the Army,
the Department of the Air Force, the Department of the Navy,
the Air War College, or the Air University.

TO MY GRANDMOTHERS,

Ruth "Jackie" Whitt and Earline Harris Edwards

War Zone Communion

some knelt
some stood
some held out hands
some extended tongues
others just
wanted whatever
it was I was
giving away

—CHAPLAIN JAMES F. HARRIS, 1972

CONTENTS

Tables

ACKNOWLEDGMENTS

By now it seems we should have fully abandoned the image of a solitary author locked away in a dusty archive or library, scribbling (or typing) furiously and revising in solitude until a finished product emerges. Surely, we know better: research and writing are rarely solitary undertakings. This book is no exception.

The journey to this point began at Hollins University under the careful direction of Peter Coogan, Andre Spies, Ruth Doan, and Joe Leedom. Forming a small but formidable department, they taught me about history, writing, and community, and they didn't laugh when I said I wanted to be a historian (though they did warn me about graduate school and the job market). In a more immediate way, I must thank my Ph.D. adviser and mentor, Richard Kohn, for enthusiastic support during my graduate career, for a careful eye for detail and style, and for consistently pushing me to refine my arguments and explanations. Yaakov Ariel, Donald Mathews, Jerma Jackson, and Alex Roland likewise provided stimulating conversation about the project and indispensable critiques and suggestions. Three colleagues from Duke and UNC, Seth Dowland, Elesha Coffman, and Matt Harper, provided critical feedback, commiseration, and encouragement as our writing group transcended the Tobacco Road rivalry to read and comment on one another's work. Further, colleagues in four research seminars read drafts carefully and thoughtfully and entertained my more than occasional ramblings on the connections between military and religious history.

Laura Lumb, an outstanding undergraduate student at UNC, carefully transcribed two oral history interviews. My friend and colleague Maren Wood was an able and cheerful research assistant, as I could not travel to find some last critical sources. Others who I am lucky to call colleagues and friends, Robert Citino, Greg Daddis, Josiah Grover, Waitman Beorn, and Kevin Benish, each read all or parts of the manuscript at critical points when I needed an outside set of eyes to continue making progress on revisions. Anonymous reviewers for the University of North Carolina Press provided insightful critique and suggestions for revision. The editorial staff at UNC Press, especially David Perry, Mark Simpson-Vos, and Mary Caviness, deserve highest praise for their handling of the manuscript and publication process. The manuscript is immeasurably better because of their work.

Historical research and writing also does not happen without institutional and financial support. The Faherty Fund for research in military history and the Mowry Grant at the University of North Carolina at Chapel Hill provided critical funds for research and travel. The United States Army Center of Military History provided a generous writing grant, which enabled me to finish the first draft of the manuscript. I also owe a debt of gratitude to the historians and librarians at the Army Chaplain School and Center at Fort Jackson, South Carolina, especially historian John Brinsfield and librarian Donna Dellinger. They graciously provided access to documents, work space, and thought-provoking conversations about my project. After I completed graduate school, the United States Military Academy at West Point and the Air War College in Montgomery, Alabama, provided me intellectual and physical spaces in which to refine my arguments and continue work on the manuscript.

It may go without saying, but this project would have been impossible without the chaplains who are the subjects of the book. For their experiences, writings, survey responses, reports, and reflections, I have utmost respect. Many of them also helped in a direct way: their generous correspondence and willingness to send information and out-of-print books was invaluable. Special thanks are due to James Johnson, Jackson Day, and Joseph Beasley, who generously agreed to be interviewed.

My UNC Writing Center friends and colleagues bridged the gap between those who commented and read my work and those who kept me sane in the process. The Writing Center was a supportive and friendly environment, and working there made me a more critical reader and a more careful writer. To my AMUN family—the family I choose—thanks for sticking with me as this project came into being, hit some rocky spots, and was finally finished. Miraculously, you all managed to figure out when to ask how it was going and when to stay quiet, and provided me with plenty of other-than-manuscript projects to make me feel accomplished when progress on the book seemed to stall out. Finally, the family I was lucky enough to be born into deserves my sincerest gratitude and humble thanks. To Alta and Steve, Jessica, Jenna, Joshua, Jeff, Jacob, Josiah, Carter, and Stella: You all—and the clean laundry, hot meals, SNATH activities, sympathetic phone calls, hugs, and support you have given me in the past decade—are quite possibly the reason this is actually finished.

I could not hope to repay the debts I have incurred, but as always, the mistakes, omissions, and oversights that remain are entirely my own.

ABBREVIATIONS

ACLU American Civil Liberties Union
AFSC American Friends Service Committee
AO area of operations
AOG Assemblies of God
AR Army Regulation
ARVN Army of the Republic of Vietnam
AUSCS Americans United for Separation of Church and State
AVF all-volunteer force
AWOL absent without leave
CALCAV Clergy and Laymen Concerned about Vietnam
CAP civic action program
CO conscientious objector/ion
CONARC Continental Army Command
DAB Dependents Assistance Board
FM Field Manual
FRSA Fleet Religious Support Activities
GCCAFP General Commission on Chaplains and Armed Forces Personnel
HUAC House on Un-American Activities Committee
KIA killed in action
LDS Church of Jesus Christ of Latter-day Saints
MAAG-V Military Assistance Advisory Group – Vietnam
MACV Military Assistance Command, Vietnam
MIA missing in action
MSTS Military Sea Transport Service
NAE National Association of Evangelicals
NJWB National Jewish Welfare Board
NLF National Liberation Front
NVA North Vietnamese Army
OCCH Office of the Chief of Chaplains (Army)
PCUSA Presbyterian Church in the United States of America
POW prisoner of war
PTSD post-traumatic stress disorder
SBC Southern Baptist Convention
SDI Strategic Defense Initiative

UMT Unit Ministry Team
UMT universal military training
USARV United States Army Vietnam
VC Viet Cong
WELS Wisconsin Evangelical Lutheran Synod

BRINGING GOD TO MEN

INTRODUCTION

God and country. Peace and war. Civilian and military. Sacred and secular. American and foreign national. Officer and enlisted. At every turn, American military chaplains inhabit these liminal spaces at the intersections of religion and war. First, they occupy a space somewhere between military and civilian life: they are full-fledged members of the military, but they are also responsible to their various religious communities. Second, they often mediate between the more clearly defined categories of officers and enlisted personnel, an intermediary position symbolized by their title of "Chaplain" rather than their rank. Third, they fall somewhere between their own religious denominations and a broader religious community—for example, a Methodist chaplain must not only uphold and practice his individual faith and provide spiritual support to his coreligionists but also provide access to the same support for Muslim or Mormon soldiers. Chaplains cross cultural boundaries, working both with American service members and with foreign nationals, and they also cross service boundaries—Army chaplains provide for the spiritual needs of Navy, Marine, and Air Force personnel, and Navy and Air Force chaplains are similarly flexible. Finally, the chaplain lives between the sacred and the secular. The chaplain is concerned with the spiritual, the other-worldly, the moral, the tenets and practice of faith; at the same time, the chaplain must operate in a secular environment, in an organization governed by hierarchy and orders, which exists as the violent arm of a secular state. By institutional design and personal choice, military chaplains are fundamentally people in the middle.[1]

Chaplains' fundamental ambiguity and disorientation of identity and position are, ultimately, their most important qualities because they allow chaplains flexibility in responding to the various moral, theological, and political questions raised by war and their participation in it. During the Vietnam War, their liminal position is precisely what produced chaplains' diverse range of experiences in the war, provided complex strategies for resolving conflict, enabled the institutional chaplaincy to fulfill its mission, and prompted chaplains to interpret the Vietnam War in ways fundamentally different from nonchaplain military members and their civilian clergy counterparts. During and after the war, the chaplains' position in the middle of various communities shaped public discourse about religion and war and guided postwar institutional changes.

The crucible of the Vietnam War intensified these potentially conflicting spaces and highlighted the chaplain's ambiguous and problematic position. As the nation waged literal war in Vietnam, it also came apart over a war of words and actions about the war in Vietnam. While conservative and liberal voices clashed over the morality of the Vietnam War and argued about a chaplain's prophetic responsibility to support or criticize the war effort from the inside, chaplains themselves remained focused on providing pastoral care for their military constituency.[2] These competing views came to a head after the war ended and resulted in a fundamentally changed organizational culture within the military chaplaincy. The experience of Vietnam often compounded or complicated moral, political, religious, and social divisions for chaplains and soldiers. Vietnam raised a host of doubts and created a range of conflicts not only for individuals and religious communities but also for the nation as a whole as "Vietnam" came to represent both a failure of American foreign policy and of a certain vision of American identity and destiny.

Yet chaplains' institutional affiliations and personal attributes prompted them to bridge divides that separated various communities. They served as mediators between religious and military cultures in situations that demanded explanation and reconciliation, though their resolutions of these tensions and conflicts were often morally complex. Those who served in Vietnam faced fierce moral and religious dilemmas during the war, and personal faith did not always provide satisfactory answers—nor did it alleviate the stress of combat. Yet the evidence suggests that most chaplains did not buckle under the pressure of their ambiguous positions, nor did they abandon their religious values and beliefs in favor of military ones. Instead, chaplains' actions and interpretations of the war in Vietnam complicate and add nuance to the dominant narrative about the nature and practice of religion in a time of war.

In sociological studies of chaplains, "role conflict" is the dominant paradigm for explaining military chaplains' experiences and behaviors. Role conflict suggests that situations with competing demands, values, and systems create conflict that must somehow be resolved, either by compartmentalization, by privileging one role over another, or through cognitive dissonance, that is, bringing conflicting actions and beliefs into alignment. For chaplains, the conventional wisdom goes, the primary conflict comes from competing "military" and "religious" worldviews, and in the final analysis, the military almost always wins out over religion as the chaplain cleaves more closely to the martial than the spiritual.[3] This rendering is an unfortunately simplistic view of the problem and the outcome. Logically, it makes little sense to posit "religious" as the opposite of "military"—centuries of crusades, jihad, holy war, and religiously-motivated violence would clearly suggest otherwise. I argue, instead, that chaplains recognized and worked in the middle of *several* potentially conflicting spaces, and while full reconciliation between the chaplains' many worlds was rare, so was simply forsaking one set of values for the other. More often, conflict and tension emerged within a certain value system, where religious values competed with each other, or the military ideal was internally inconsistent. Chaplains' ability to operate in these multiple worlds, then, gave them a broader tool kit for interpreting and dealing with the experience, aftermath, and interpretation of war. Their resolutions to these tensions were often complex and morally ambiguous, but they were not fundamentally irreligious.

And so, in the midst of a war, and heated discussion about that war, chaplains served as vital links between diverse communities, sometimes working to reconcile—both personally and publicly—apparently conflicting worldviews. As the military found itself embroiled in conflict in Southeast Asia, and as religious communities responded to this intervention, chaplains were critical connectors in networks of both individuals and organizations. They occupied this ambiguous space as they stood astride many different but intimately connected worlds. They were challenged by the implications of their actions within each group, by their resistance to or participation in war fighting, and by the necessity of maintaining their credibility among diverse audiences. Ultimately, chaplains occupied space in between and on the margins of several communities: civilian and military, officer and enlisted, denominational and faith groups, and the sacred and secular. They were positioned in these liminal spaces for structural reasons and because of their specific cultural knowledge and skills, but this position allowed them to interpret their experiences from military and religious perspectives alike. Chaplains' access to various religious, secular, civilian, and military communities afforded them significant flexibility when they faced moral, theological, pastoral, or identity-related conflicts in war.

Military Chaplains in Popular and Scholarly Imagination

There have been three persistent and predictable archetypes of military chaplains in the twentieth century: the saint, the militarist, and the incompetent. Though rarely at the forefront of depictions of war in popular culture, chaplains appeared frequently in the background, signifying larger cultural and political issues. In each category, a few examples are instructive.

First, there are self-sacrificing chaplains, paragons of military virtue and valor on the battlefield. Chaplains in this image include the four chaplains of the World War II troop transport ship USS *Dorchester* who, according to eyewitness accounts died holding hands, praying, and singing as the ship went down. Since then, they have been memorialized on stamps and medals and numerous chapels and foundations have been named for them.[4] Other chaplains, like Medal of Honor recipient Vincent Capodanno, received military awards for their actions in war as well as religious accolades. In 2006, the Military Ordinate of the Catholic Church began the process to beatify and canonize Father Capodanno, with Rome officially declaring him a Servant of God. In May 2007, the Investigation of the Cause of Canonization was inaugurated.[5] These chaplains, under the protection and direction of God, faced death and battle with religious serenity combined with steely resolve and are the preferred archetype for chaplain advocates and supporters.

Second, there is the gung ho, gun-toting, militarist chaplain—such as the one described by Gunnery Sergeant Hartman in the film *Full Metal Jacket*: "There will be a magic show at zero-nine-thirty! Chaplain Charlie will tell you about how the free world will conquer Communism with the aid of God and a few Marines! God has a hard-on for Marines because we kill everything we see! He plays His games, we play ours! To show our appreciation for so much power, we keep Heaven packed with fresh souls! God was here before the Marine Corps! So you can give your heart to Jesus, but your ass belongs to the Corps! Do you ladies understand?"[6] Or take the example from Pearl Harbor, where a Navy chaplain, according to legend, took control of a machine gun, shot an enemy airplane, and shouted, "Praise the Lord, and Pass the Ammunition"; his actions were later immortalized and revered in the song of the same name.[7] Just as easily in this vein is this (in)famous prayer written by the chaplain with General George Patton's Third Army at Bastogne in 1944: "Almighty and most merciful Father, we humbly beseech Thee, of Thy great goodness, to restrain these immoderate rains with which we have had to contend. Grant us fair weather for Battle. Graciously hearken to us as soldiers who call upon Thee that, armed with Thy power, we may advance from victory to victory, and crush the oppression and wickedness of our enemies and establish Thy justice among men and nations."[8] This image of chaplains is most often called forth by critics of the chaplaincy who fear an excessively intimate relationship between church and state or between religion and warfare more generally.

Finally, there is the chaplain who is generally a nice guy but can't seem to get anything done. He is physically and spiritually disconnected from the soldiers he serves, and the consequences of his ineffectiveness range from benign to catastrophic. On one end of the spectrum might lie Father Francis Mulcahy from the film *M*A*S*H*, who, unable to stop the dentist's suicide attempt, earns neither admiration nor contempt from his flock. In the middle of this range we might find the chaplain character in Alfredo Vea's dystopian novel *Gods Go Begging* who loses his mind in the fog and blood of war, eventually going AWOL (absent without leave) and abandoning both his post and flock. Finally on the other, more problematic, end of this spectrum is the case of the chaplain whose ineffectiveness leads to deadly consequence. In Herman Melville's *Billy Budd*, for example, the chaplain is too concerned with Billy's eternal salvation to notice or do anything to stop a grave miscarriage of earthly justice.[9] Chaplains in this mold are either inconsequential or potentially dangerous—but the image is not a positive one.

Ultimately, all these depictions of chaplains are caricatures rather than historically accurate representations, but they serve as an important starting point for uncovering how chaplains' roles and identities have been understood and how the relationship between religion, war, and the military has evolved over time. Most of the writing on American military chaplains is polemical, agenda-driven, and anecdotal. Consequently, the pop cultural archetypes of chaplains are reinforced in the limited scholarship that does exist.

Contemporary military chaplains have been neglected by historians of both the military and religion. This considerable gap in scholarship has two sources: the combat-oriented focus of military history, despite the advent of social and cultural historical methodologies, and the generally liberal, antiwar roots of religious studies programs founded in the post-Vietnam period. Both of these trends mean that military chaplains, despite their presence in military organizations across time and space, and despite their clear vocational connection to the practice of religion in a unique institutional environment, are generally left out of conversations in either field. Nevertheless, Doris Bergen, in the introduction to a general essay collection about military chaplains, identified three major themes that have appeared consistently within the existing scholarship: the relationship between chaplains and those they served; the relationship of chaplains to their military and religious superiors; and the moral and theological dilemmas of the chaplaincy.[10] In addition, the existing scholarship, including many of the excellent essays in Bergen's collection, responds primarily to what Michael Snape, historian of the British Royal Army Chaplains' Department, has called the "pacifist critique" of military chaplains, which assumes there are fundamental conflicts between (Judeo-Christian) faith and the military mission.[11] This book not only engages the themes that Bergen identifies but also confronts the pacifist critique of chaplains and the chaplaincy head on. Finally, this study places chaplains' experiences and interpretations of war into the broader historical context of late-twentieth-century America and the war in Vietnam.

Collectively, chaplains did not emerge from Vietnam as battlefield heroes or martyrs, as having displayed the best qualities of soldiers and clergy while bringing spiritual clarity and solace to chaos, as uncritical supporters of the chaplaincy suggest. Nor were they simply militant legitimizers of what many believed to be an unjust war, carrying weapons and encouraging soldiers to "kill a Commie for Christ," sacrificing their religious ideals and identities for military ones, as those critical of the chaplaincy and of the war have implied. Neither were they all well-intentioned but bumbling, ineffective ministers caught between and paralyzed by both the demands of religious conviction and military necessity. To be sure, there were some of each of these sorts of chaplains, but just as stereotypes and popular images of soldiers and officers fall apart under scrutiny, so do those of chaplains. For most chaplains, the Vietnam War tested both their faith and character, and most of them left the war with their faith and commitment to ministry strengthened. Rather than entrenching or exacerbating tensions between chaplains' multiple roles, or cementing the binary division between "faith" and "war," the Vietnam experience induced most of these chaplains to resolve such tensions by engaging both the material and spiritual realms, and the spaces in between.

The Problem of Religion and the Vietnam War

From accounts in Deuteronomy of Jewish priests inspiring and blessing soldiers before battle, to the furor in 2003–4 over charges that a Muslim chaplain committed espionage at the U.S. military detention center at Guantanamo Bay, chaplains represent both the sympathies and tensions between religious and military communities.[12] Though the Latin word *capellanus* (from which the French *chapelain* and the English "chaplain" are derived) did not appear until the ninth century, modern military chaplaincies trace their historical antecedents back much further: the Canadian Chaplain Corps looks back to the Assyrian army; the British chaplaincy to the Roman army; and the American Chaplain Corps to the clerics of ancient Israel, Egypt, and Rome.[13] By claiming such long historical roots, institutional chaplaincies assert their significance to the military and religious life of their societies.[14] Although chaplains' actions seldom, if ever, directly influenced the outcomes of war, they were a constant feature in battle for the twentieth-century American military. As such, their wartime experiences and connections to broader military and religious institutions illuminate well some of the connections between religion and war in a given society.

In the United States, ministers serving with troops have been part of every major conflict since the Pequot War in the 1630s, and George Washington himself frequently asked the Continental Congress to make allowances for chaplains and repeatedly emphasized their importance for improving troop morale and securing God's blessing on the Army before battle.[15] Chaplains continued to participate in American wars at various levels and in different ways through the Civil War, the Spanish-American-Philippine War, the two World Wars, and the Korean conflict.

A brief survey of the literature suggests that the relationship between American religion and the American military—including military chaplains—has been well covered through the end of the nineteenth century. There is excellent scholarship on the place and function of religion particularly in the American Revolution and American Civil War, and in the intervening years.[16] Then, for the twentieth century, the close examination of religion and military affairs drops off, reflective of a more general pattern within the history of the modern United States.[17] Existing scholarship suggests that religion was a generally positive force within American history. For example, religion comforted and motivated soldiers in the First World War, and progressive foreign policy-makers often infused the language of democratization and liberalism with religious references, specifically Christian ones.[18] This examination of the lived religion of soldiers and progressive religion was balanced by the study of a robust religious pacifist movement (also labeled "progressive" in some accounts) in the same period, but neither interpretive viewpoint tended to question the fundamental goodness or righteousness of the American project, however defined. Indeed, Americans, especially, remembered World War II as a quintessentially "good" war in which the American religious tradition was a source of national strength and pride.[19] Religious dissent against World War II in the United States ebbed, though support for the war effort was not as full-throated as it had been in the First World War. Religious communities broadly supported the national objective but remained somewhat cautious. American politicians did face critique, particularly about humanitarian issues and the treatment of civilians, for example on the issue of Japanese internment, the plight of Jewish refugees, and the development and use of atomic weapons and strategic bombing.[20] Then the immediate postwar period saw a marked increase in religious commitment in the United States. This upswing in religiosity was strengthened by the Cold War, as Americans envisioned themselves as a Judeo-Christian bulwark against godless Communism.[21]

This narrative, which merged mutually reinforcing religious, patriotic, and martial themes continued until it hit a concrete wall in the form of Vietnam, a war that shattered visions of an American consensus as well as a certain providential vision of an American identity. But in this failed, unpopular war, what role did American religious communities play? In answering this question, the story of religion in the Vietnam War shifted away from the established historiographical tradition. Religious Studies programs became the provenance for scholarship exploring the role of religion in the Vietnam War. These departments were largely formed in the post-Vietnam era of anti-military backlash within the academy, and their political and analytical sympathies lay primarily with the religious motives of some antiwar activists; they dismissed the brand of American religiosity that supported and even fueled Cold War anti-Communism and patriotism as politically pernicious and religiously misguided. Even as scholars advocate for more research on the connections between foreign policy and religion, however, there exists a mistaken assumption that the Vietnam War era has been well covered.[22] Scholars have privileged the religious motives of the antiwar movement without taking seriously the religious responses and motivations of either those who supported the war or those who were ambivalent about it. Especially evocative are biographical profiles of nationally prominent religious leaders or groups, such as Yale University chaplain William Sloane Coffin or the National Council of Churches, as well as the well-known antiwar Catholic priests Daniel and Philip Berrigan.[23] For many, the idea of "religion" during the Vietnam War has come primarily to mean religious protest against the war.[24] Though an important and illuminating narrative that begins connecting war to society, religion, and politics in the years following World War II, it is incomplete and oversimplifies the role of religious belief and practice in modern America, particularly in respect to war and foreign policy.

The origins and assumptions behind this argument about the fundamental incompatibility between religion and war, notably the same one used to critique the chaplaincy as a perversion of true religious expression, are easy enough to decipher. After all, fragments of the Judeo-Christian scriptural tradition are clear: thou shalt not kill; love your neighbor; you cannot serve two masters; blessed are the peacemakers; God is love. (The fact that these are, at best, incomplete summations of scripture, theology, and doctrine, much less practice, figures little into the discussion.) How could chaplains proclaim these truths and still serve in the military, especially in what was largely considered to be an unjust war of choice and hubris, where the failures of the American military and political system were made plain? Surely, they would have to be confronted by extreme role conflict—forced to compartmentalize their roles or privilege one identity over the other. The tensions between religion and warfare seem so obvious, and the cataclysm of Vietnam the perfect case for exploring the problem.

Partly as a result of these ideas, critics of the military chaplaincy assume that, conceptually and practically, the American chaplaincy system was and remains rife with contradictions, ironies, and conflicts. Scholars and casual observers have assumed that the intersection of religion and the military in such a specific institution must *necessarily* involve some level of conflict between church and state, a Judeo-Christian tradition and war, and military and clerical professionalism. As these ideas coalesced in the 1980s, much of the scholarship at the time argued that chaplains experienced conflict because of their multiple roles as military officers and clergymen and were thus confronted by the "two masters" dilemma—the idea that religious and military values and expectations were mutually incompatible, forcing chaplains to choose one identity over another.[25] These observations often culminated in cries to eliminate or civilianize the chaplaincy, suggesting there is limited, if any, space for official religious participation in the prosecution of war or even in the peacetime military.

Yet in the United States, given the complex history of the tension between the First Amendment's free exercise clause and the restrictive establishment clause, a host of considerations must be made to determine the proper relationship between religion, war, and the military. These considerations include not only the constitutionality and legality of religious programs within the military but also the requirements and conditions of religious orthodoxy and orthopraxy, as well as the pragmatic and prosaic requirements for religious observation within a military setting.

Based on these historiographical trends and the existing scholarship on military chaplains, the story that played out in Vietnam should have been quite simple. The historical record should show signs of this obvious conflict and spiritual torment for chaplains during the Vietnam War. Military chaplains, living and working in this mess of competing ideals and values and expectations, should be torn between two fundamentally and irreconcilably incompatible worlds—or they should show clear signs of having forsaken one identity and world (usually the religious one) in favor of the other. The argument would write itself with evidence of the tortured logic of chaplains forsaking their religious roles and identities for military ones. Such a study should tell a story about chaplains, the Vietnam War, and the falling apart of American religion, the American military, and American society—a veritable crisis of faith.

The emblematic chaplain in this rendering would be Angelo J. Liteky, a Catholic chaplain who served in Vietnam in 1967. In December of that year, he was caught with part of the 199th Light Infantry Brigade in an intense firefight. Over the course of the battle, Liteky, himself wounded, evacuated more than twenty wounded and dead soldiers to a landing zone and directed several medevac choppers in and out of the area. Liteky's citation for the Medal of Honor told of heroic deeds in the face of danger. In addition to evacuating many men to safety, he prayed with dying men and observed last rites for the dead while bullets flew fewer than fifteen feet away. He showed pastoral concern for his men even as he was intimately involved in the military's mission. In a 2000 interview, Liteky recalled, "I was 100 percent behind going over there and putting those Communists in their place. . . . I had no problems with that. I thought I was going there doing God's work."[26]

Liteky's story of battlefield heroism and religious practice in war grows more complicated when extended beyond the battlefield and into the post-Vietnam era. He left the chaplaincy in 1971 and the priesthood in 1975, in his words, "mainly because of celibacy." In subsequent years, Liteky took up the cause of human rights abuses in Central America, vociferously protesting American foreign policy there, especially the Reagan administration's support for Nicaraguan Contra rebels. In July 1986, Liteky renounced his Medal of Honor and its attendant benefits; he placed the medal, along with a letter to Ronald Reagan, in a paper bag and left it at the Vietnam Veterans' Memorial Wall in Washington, D.C.

As he grew older, Liteky continued to protest U.S. operation of the School of the Americas, and said in a 2001 interview, "The reason I do what I do now is basically the same" as the reason he cited for his actions in Vietnam: "to save lives." He explained, "In the case of the School of the Americas, it's to stop training the military from the Third World, who take the training back and employ it in the oppression of their people." In Vietnam, Liteky said, "the situation was more immediate. People were getting blown up, shot and killed all around me. I didn't get hit, and there was nothing for me to do but help them. Some were dead. One young man died in my arms, breathing his last breath and just gasping for air. I held him for a bit, then I gave him last rites. Then I moved on because there were other people crying for help."[27] Liteky understood his role vis-à-vis the United States military as a life-saving one, regardless of whether that positioned him to act in concert with U.S. military goals or in opposition to them.

Yet while Liteky could justify his own actions in the war as having redemptive value, his overall interpretation of the war in Vietnam was damning. In 2003, in an open letter to American forces in Iraq—in a military engagement that he vocally opposed—he wrote, "In depth study of the Vietnam War revealed political and military liars insensitive to the value of human life, inclusive of their own countrymen."[28] In the letter, he positioned himself as "a veteran of an ill-fated war, in the waning years of [his] life," and ultimately concluded, "this letter . . . is not meant to cast blame for an attack on Iraq on U.S. military personnel. I'm sure you believe that what you are a part of is right and just. I once believed the same of my participation in the Vietnam War. . . . God be with you in your search for truth, your quest for justice, and your efforts to help a beautiful people."[29] Liteky's journey from soldier and supporter of war to an antiwar activist was long and deeply connected to his experiences in Vietnam and to his religious training.

Although Liteky's later protests did not emerge directly from an evaluation of his participation in the Vietnam War, the place he chose to return and renounce the medal demonstrated the significance of his Vietnam experience. In order to honor his values and beliefs about American militarism and intervention in Central America, he returned to the site established to honor those who had died in Vietnam. For Liteky, the wall symbolized the place where those same values and beliefs had been first tested. Liteky's actions in Vietnam and his changed interpretations of war after the fact may be reassuring: in war, the chaplain displayed selfless sacrifice and courage to minister to men under fire, but upon his return home and reflection on the evils of war, he denounced militarism and violence in favor of a more pacifist—perhaps a more "Christian"—existence.

As it usually is, the historical record is much more complicated. Liteky's story is not typical or generalizable. In fact, it turns out to be rather *atypical* when analyzed alongside other chaplains' stories. Instead, what emerges from the evidence, and what follows in this book, is a more complex story not only about chaplains as individuals but also about the institutional chaplaincy, American religious culture, and the place of religion in the modern American military.

Uncovering the Religious History of the Military

How to deal with cultural approaches to the study of war has been an ongoing question in the field of military history, as has the question of how to deal with the discourse created by, in, and about war. Though historians of the American military have come to accept, if not embrace, cultural history approaches and methodologies as important aspects of military history, they have struggled to articulate its significance to the field and incorporate fully such approaches and methods into their work. In a 1993 article, John Shy suggested that historians were apt to use "cultural approaches" to the study of war only when their explanations of events could not rely on rationality.[30] A decade later, John Lynn proposed a model by which historians could understand the relationship between the "discourse" of war and the "reality" of war, arguing that the two were closely and dialogically related to one another. His work suggested that understanding culture was most helpful for figuring out why and where discourse departed from the reality of war, but it neglects to consider that the "reality of war" may be itself culturally determined.[31] These two works represented a concerted effort to retain military history's traditional focus on battle and the explanation of military outcomes while recognizing other historical perspectives and methodologies.

Additionally, the "home front" emerged as an obvious place to understand the cultural dimension of warfare. The most robust discussions of the home front have been in the realm of "war and society" studies, which Wayne Lee defined as "those that emphasize the connections between social organization, political institutions, and military activity."[32] Yet, as Jeremy Black has noted, such studies almost always cleave "more to society than to war in both methodology and fundamental concerns."[33] Lee also suggested that historians may take into account "societal culture," which "encompasses not only the silent assumptions that common soldiers bring with them from society into the military . . . but also the public's expectations and values about war that form the environment in which decision makers operate."[34] Combining these two categories of study may lead to fruitful discoveries about the relationship between home front attitudes, cultures, and institutions and battlefield actions, attitudes, and realities.

Thus this study engages the growing base of cultural studies about the military by analyzing the discourse and cultural expectations surrounding chaplains and the relationship between warfare and religion during and after the Vietnam War. Archival records, including those from the Army Office of the Chief of Chaplains and the Military Assistance Command, Vietnam (MACV), provide narrative context and a chronological framework that enables an analysis of bureaucratic and organizational issues. The Air Force archival record for the period 1960–67 is fragmentary at best; materials were not handled correctly, and there was no central repository or guidance for collecting materials related to the chaplaincy. During the Vietnam War era, materials were collected on an informal basis and eventually archived at the Air Force Archives at Maxwell Air Force Base in Alabama with the appropriate unit reports. Given the fragmentary nature of the records and the dispersal throughout the Air Force historical collection, most of the Air Force information in this study comes instead from the official history studies completed under the direction of the Office of the Air Force chief of chaplains. Even this, however, is of limited use, as most of the materials that were collected were from bases in the United States; the overwhelming focus of the official history and the archival record is on stateside chaplain activities and, secondarily, on activities in Europe and Korea. Like the Air Force records, most of the U.S. Navy's archival sources are specific to activities within the continental United States, though, again, official histories provide information about naval chaplain activities during the Vietnam War. Ultimately, Army chaplains outnumbered Air Force and Navy chaplains in Vietnam by at least two to one at any given time, and in the early and late years, the imbalance was far greater. And throughout the war, most chaplains serving in-country fell under the operational command of MACV. In practice, then, the Chaplain Corps was somewhat immune to some of the intense interservice rivalries and coordination challenges that plagued the war effort in Vietnam, again making its story unique among Vietnam-era narratives. With this in mind, only when a service distinction is merited is it noted in the text. In addition to military records, published sources from national and religious media provide an entry point to understanding the interaction between society, bureaucracies, and the individual. Additionally, first-person accounts balance out the official and structural view from the archives; these sources include chaplains' memoirs, diaries, letters, survey responses, personal websites, oral history interviews, and personal accounts in published and online forums.

Chaplains' self-presentations of their wartime experiences are central to the analysis of chaplains' beliefs, actions, and roles during and after the war. They wrote and published reflections on the war in specific historical contexts and for specific reasons—both stated explicitly and constructed implicitly. Such sources, however, present significant challenges for the historian. Even though chaplains enjoyed significant credibility and authority, especially among religious audiences, their first-person accounts are certainly not immune to the persistent "problem of memory" so readily identified by cultural historians.[35] Memory is fallible, and published personal accounts, given the interplay of memory, selectivity, authorial intent, and editorial decisions, provide only a relatively narrow view of a chaplain's experience. What chaplains wrote about their experiences in Vietnam is, almost certainly, riddled with factual error, exaggeration, and hyperbole. Their accounts require the historian to move beyond simple narrative and factual claims and enter the mental world of others.[36] Ultimately, memoirs, diaries, and interviews provide compelling evidence of what chaplains believed and did and how they interpreted the war and their role in it. How chaplains chose to recount their experiences is at least as important as what actually happened.

The narrative presented here traces the evolution of the American military chaplaincy from an ecumenical Judeo-Christian organization in the post–World War II era through a period of conflict for individual chaplains and the chaplaincy as a whole during the Vietnam War to the emergence of a generally conservative, evangelical Chaplain Corps in the post-Vietnam era. Thus, it is a story which parallels that of American religious and military culture during the second half of the twentieth century.

Chapter 1 examines the broad religious, cultural, political, and international setting of the early Cold War. Beginning with larger cultural forces in the years preceding American intervention in Vietnam, the origins of the deep ideological and philosophical divisions that emerged during and after the Vietnam War are made clear. In the 1940s and 1950s, conflicts between two predominant sectors of American religious culture—one conservative and evangelical, the other with a liberal-progressive bent—simmered just below the surface and sometimes boiled over, as during McCarthyism and the concomitant attack on the "pink" religious fringe. Usually, though, the tropes of religious consensus and civil religion provided Americans a common language through which to understand diverse religious and political ideas, but these ties were insufficient to mask deep divisions that would fracture American communities during the Vietnam War.

In the next four chapters, the focus shifts to the decade of direct American involvement in Vietnam, roughly from 1962 to 1973. This central part of the book examines how chaplains negotiated their positions and roles within military and religious communities as they took part in the war. During the war years, the categories of difference that seemed so sharp in the 1950s and early 1960s faded under the intense pressure of combat. In fact, it seems that denominational, service, and racial distinctions that may have been quite important "back in the world" (Vietnam-era slang for the United States) had little effect on chaplains' actions during the war. When conflict existed, it centered around the pragmatic and immediate rather than the philosophical or theological.

Chapter 2 explores how chaplains managed their dual identities as clergy and officers and operated within bureaucratic and institutional restraints to build networks of religious support for American service personnel and to form relationships with Vietnamese nationals. All the while, chaplains maintained professional, personal, and pastoral relationships with individual enlisted personnel and officers, highlighting the structural and cultural ambiguities of the chaplain's position. Chapter 3 examines the concept of role conflict in some depth, and explores five topical cases—conscientious objection, the drug problem and chaplains' noncombatant status, participation in civic action programs, and personal morality related to alcohol, cursing, and sex—to understand how chaplains responded to situations that could produce tension between various roles and identities. In each case, chaplains demonstrated their ability to resolve role tension using pragmatic approaches that allowed for them to retain both a military and religious identity. The chapter then explores the question of chaplains' anemic responses to war crimes and atrocities in light of the role conflict model, the instances where it seems most obvious that chaplains may have abandoned their religious identities and values for military ones. Even here, however, I argue that chaplains' religious values were on display and that the role conflict model is insufficient to explain their behavior.

As chaplains involved themselves in the military life of their units, they encountered serious questions about the morality of the Vietnam War and religious practice in wartime; this is the focus of Chapter 4. Chaplains responded creatively as they worked out practical solutions to wartime dilemmas. At the same time, they, along with the soldiers and officers they served, created distinct and dynamic liturgies of war that involved reinterpreting traditional religious practices to fit a wartime setting. These reinterpretations demonstrated the intense ecumenism of combat, a development distinct from the ever-increasing divides over religious faith and practice on the home front.

Chaplains were relatively isolated from religious and political debates at home, yet they did enter these discussions, occasionally as participants and often as symbols, about the Vietnam War in both religious and secular communities. Chapter 5 explores how chaplains' positions as people in the middle allowed them to address a wide variety of audiences to offer experientially grounded analysis of the Vietnam War but also situated them as living symbols of a long-standing philosophical debate about the proper role of chaplains in war and a policy-oriented discussion about civilianizing the military chaplaincy. While the debate over chaplains never dominated, or even became central to, debates about the Vietnam War, it was indicative of theological and doctrinal fissures within the American religious community.

After the withdrawal of combat forces from Vietnam, chaplains and others were left to interpret the war's meaning and to reshape the chaplain's role and identity within the American military. Chapter 6 explores how chaplains worked out many of the theological, moral, and identity-related conflicts of the war in written first-person accounts that overwhelmingly offered a redemptive narrative for their Vietnam experience. In this way, chaplain narratives are well-situated in the traditions of combat memoirs, spiritual autobiography, and trauma writing, but, again, their conclusions offer an obvious counternarrative to the more traditional one of desolation and defeat that emerges in nonchaplain first-person memoirs and accounts of the Vietnam War. Chapter 7 then examines the institutional chaplaincy and how it changed in the post-Vietnam period. In the 1970s, the American military chaplaincy came under nearly continuous attack from liberal and mainline religious groups and from secular critics even as it worked to increase the demographic diversity within the Chaplain Corps. Yet, in the end, liberals and mainliners within the chaplaincy lost out, as they slowly ceded ground and stopped participating in the institutional shaping of the chaplaincy.

The war in Vietnam reduced the utility of the Cold War's consensus-based language about religion and instead brought division to the forefront of public debate. Yet military chaplains serving in Vietnam remained largely divorced from these debates. In the midst of war, chaplains tended to make pastoral and pragmatic decisions—thorny theological and liturgical issues were often pushed aside in favor of changed, but very immediate and very real, religious faith and practice. They privileged their priestly role over their prophetic one, learning to negotiate conflicting institutional interests as well as conflicts within their own belief systems about the proper role and right practice of faithful people in war. After the war, they, like other soldiers, underwent a process of reintegration into the world and reflection on their Vietnam experience, yet, unlike many other Vietnam veterans, chaplains read the Vietnam War as a redemptive narrative. By virtue of their training and vocation, they had access to psychological resources and a religious idiom that eased their transition back to the world as they worked out for themselves and others the meaning of the war and their participation in it. And just as chaplains' experiences in Vietnam informed their interpretations of faith and civic duty, these same experiences on a corporate level influenced the organizational culture and institutional mission of the military chaplaincy by bringing about changes that paralleled developments within the broader American religious culture after Vietnam. In the midst of and wake of the Vietnam War, the chaplaincy became more demographically diverse, introducing for the first time female chaplains and increasing the number of denominations represented in the chaplaincy. By the mid-1980s, the effects of these cultural crosscurrents—declining liberal support for the chaplaincy and rising power of conservative religious groups—demonstrated that the ecumenism of combat had given way to aggressive sectarianism and evangelicalism in peace.

The most accurate generalization about military chaplains during the Vietnam War may, in fact, be the most apt for all those who served in Vietnam: most of them just wanted to make it out alive. Military chaplains, like others who served in Southeast Asia, had a variety of experiences in the war and exhibited the full range of human responses to the war, and, though their religious affiliations, beliefs, and training did not dictate how they would respond to or interpret the war, religion surely affected their behavior. Depending on who you ask and where you look, there were brave chaplains and cowardly ones; chaplains who supported the war effort and others who did not; some chaplains never left headquarters, while others patrolled in the jungles of Southeast Asia. Some chaplains suffered from post-traumatic stress disorder (PTSD), and others counseled veterans with it. Chaplains died and were wounded and were decorated for their actions;

some kept short-timers' calendars; others used drugs and some drank too much to escape the trauma of war. Religious faith and formal training did not turn chaplains into otherworldly saints in the midst of war, but neither did war destroy, or even cause most of them to question, their faith.

Chaplains' experiences in Vietnam, their postwar reflections about those experiences, and changes in the institutional chaplaincy reveal both deep-seated tensions and compatibilities between the realms of faith and war. Chaplains followed a religious calling to enter vocational ministry, and most reported a special pull toward ministry with military personnel. Yet this very calling involved them in one of the most divisive wars in American history. Many mainline and liberal religious leaders led intense protests against American actions in Vietnam, while more conservative ones trumpeted the cause of the Christian United States against a godless Communist enemy. Chaplains, from both conservative and liberal camps, frequently found themselves caught in the middle of these debates as they were ostensibly full members of both church and military (though their acceptance in each community was often qualified and granted only with some suspicion). These two institutions shaped nearly every aspect of an adherent's life, and chaplains lived and worked at the intersections of these two worlds and had to define for themselves, the chaplaincy, and their religious communities exactly what "Vietnam" meant.

Understanding chaplains to be fundamentally part of the American story about religion, the Vietnam War, and its legacy provides a broader and more accurate view of the ways in which religious people, including clergy, experienced and interpreted that war. While chaplains' actions in and responses to the war in Vietnam were far from uniform, many adopted a moderate view of the conflict, one that accommodated religiously oriented tension over the morality and conduct of the war without necessitating an all-out denunciation of the war—an untenable position for many religious Americans at the time. It would be easy to write off these views as only quasi-religious—merely examples of the military's power to co-opt religious language and ideals—or even as perversions of religious truth, but such a view plainly ignores the long history of religion and warfare complementing and reinforcing each other. The pages that follow counter this conventional thinking by using chaplains' experiences to demonstrate the diversity and complexity of religious responses to American involvement in Vietnam.

CHAPTER ONE

Consensus and Civil Religion

By most measures, the decade following World War II was a period of renewed religious commitment. According to polls, church membership and attendance rose, as did financial support of religious institutions, and charismatic evangelical leaders left their mark on a mass audience using advances in media and technology to increase their reach. The religious atmosphere that emerged was simultaneously theistic and civic. It owed much of its character to mainline Protestantism with a smattering of other beliefs mixed in. In the civic realm, it encouraged loyalty to the nation, in some cases substituting the ideals of patriotism and nationalism for common religious doctrines. Responding to both World War II and the Cold War, Americans redefined their religious heritage as "Judeo-Christian," recognizing the contributions of at least one non-Christian minority to the development of the United States while still marginalizing Islam and non-Abrahamic religious traditions.[1]

Religion entered public discourse frequently and urgently, and theologians such as Reinhold Niebuhr and religious leaders such as Billy Graham were truly public men who exercised considerable influence on American politics. Politicians also entered the discourse by declaring the United States' religious foundations and consistently invoking religious imagery in political contexts. As the Cold War came to dominate thinking about America's relationship to the world, America's religious culture often assumed a martial character, planting itself firmly in the way of a godless Soviet empire. Civil religion employed both clergy and politicians as priests and prophets.

As the state mobilized to confront the Soviet Union, military leadership integrated the dominant religious and political cultures of the day into policy, most notably in the military chaplaincy and "character guidance" programs. Designed to build up the character and fighting effectiveness of American troops, chaplains and character guidance programs identified religious beliefs as essential components of American identity and connected civil society, military service, and religious faith.

Nevertheless, many religious groups, especially liberal ones, kept a distance, retaining a critical edge in their dealings with and commentary on the government. In addition to the religious left's and the black church's participation in the civil rights movement, left-leaning religious responses to the use of the atomic bomb, proposals calling for universal military training (UMT) and peacetime conscription, and the U.N. action in Korea complicated conversations between military and religious interests during the 1950s. These episodes of disagreement and divergence within the American religious community were bellwethers of some of the controversies about religious and military matters that emerged during the Vietnam War. The "religious community" did not speak with a unified voice even in the 1950s, not that it ever had, but it is important to note that religious dissent against government policies did not begin in the 1960s, and the war in Vietnam was not the first political issue to fracture American religious communities.

In fact, "Vietnam" had long been a site for American discussions about democracy, colonialism, and America's role in the world. Since Woodrow Wilson's internationalist and idealist calls for self-determination in the 1910s and another move toward decolonization in the years following World War II, American policy-makers had been acutely aware of the French colonies in Southeast Asia, and in both cases, postwar rhetoric indicated that the United States favored independence over colonialism for the Vietnamese. Yet this rhetoric did not produce convergent expectations or actions.[2] In the second half of the 1940s, growing Cold War tensions deepened the connections between the United States and Western Europe that had been forged in World War II. The Chinese Communist victory in 1949 and the subsequent outbreak of war in Korea led many to believe that other East Asian nations formed critical points along a containment line, and American politicians crafted policies to counteract the manpower and influence of China and to prop up former colonial powers, thereby strengthening European democracies.[3]

Early on, American policy-makers and journalists were well aware of the Communist foundations of the Viet Minh, the underground revolutionaries who resisted French rule in Southeast Asia.[4] Between 1945 and 1954, French military officers referred to Vietnam as the "last rampart against Communism in Southeast Asia," and the Central Intelligence Agency warned that if the South Vietnamese government fell, "the forces of International Communism would acquire a staging area from which military operations could be launched against other countries in Southeast Asia."[5]

The French Far East Expeditionary Corps fought against the Viet Minh between 1941 and 1954 but had little success in stabilizing the regime of Bao Dai, the nominal emperor of Vietnam, or in subduing terrorist attacks on military and civilian installations. French involvement in Vietnam culminated at the disastrous battle at Dien Bien Phu in May 1954.[6] Though the United States offered limited and covert military assistance to the French before and during the battle, both American politicians and military leaders agreed that direct intervention was unwise: militarily, they deemed the situation hopeless, and politically, it could be considered an act of war.

After the French defeat at Dien Bien Phu in 1954, American policy-makers started the country down the long road of extended entanglement with Vietnam. In addition to religious overtones to policy rhetoric in the United States, the presence of a small but significant minority of Catholics in Vietnam and close ties between American and Vietnamese Catholics such as John F. Kennedy and Ngo Dinh Diem served only to enhance the significance of Vietnam for American political objectives.[7] As a result, religious groups' responses to early American forays into Vietnam were generally supportive, though not uncritical, and official American policy statements about Vietnam frequently had religious themes. By the time the first chaplains arrived in Vietnam in 1962, the stage had been set for a decade-long struggle to define the proper role of religion in the American military, the religious nature of America's Cold War mission, and the character of the American military chaplaincy.

Cold War civil religion, early debates over religious programs within the U.S. military, and initial American involvement in Vietnam all pointed to the contested atmosphere in which chaplains in Vietnam eventually operated. The early Cold War and an American religious revival again injected religious and civil-religious language into public discourse and public space, suggesting a distinct "public theology" during the 1950s and early 1960s. As this theological language entered the public imagination, the military responded to and used the dominant religious culture of the day to shape policies, specifically those regarding the chaplaincy and character guidance programs. Eventually, American involvement in Vietnam and long-standing ties to the Catholic community there prompted responses from religious communities that were wrapped in the language of civil religion.

The convergences and divergences in American military and religious cultures during the early Cold War not only illuminated trends within each realm but also highlighted the extent to which the two existed in a dialogic relationship with one another. Religious communities and military ones borrowed freely and frequently from the lexicons and cultures of the other, producing in the early Cold War period a common language with which to express and understand religiosity and patriotism. Yet theological and doctrinal differences did not disappear with the construction of common tropes and rhetorical patterns, even as the fear of confrontation with the Soviet Union demanded that religious communities and civic communities emphasize unity over difference for the collective good of the nation. These ideological and theological differences, buried beneath a common language, emerged in full force in the 1960s, especially as American involvement in Vietnam expanded; the foundations of civil religion that provided a patina of consensus in the early Cold War crumbled, setting up American religious and political communities for intense political and religious debates and division that would define the Vietnam and post-Vietnam eras.[8]

An American Way of Life and Civil Religion

Since the 1967 publication of Robert Bellah's essay "Civil Religion in America," scholars, clergy, politicians, and social commentators have debated the substance and utility of such an idea, which suggests an intimate relationship between American religion and American civil society.[9] Because the essay appeared near the height of the war in Vietnam and was sharply critical of U.S. involvement there, it is rightly considered a primary source for studies on the Cold War and religion; it helps to establish the tenor and content of public religious and civil debates. Yet, since the 1970s, "civil religion" has also become a key analytical tool for understanding the nature of American religion, particularly in the public sphere. Civil religion is thus both an idea that emerged in a specific historical context as well as an analytical category that can help elucidate the relationship between the military, politics, and religion during the Cold War.

In the years following World War II, civil, military, and religious themes in American life were sometimes integrated, and often considered in close proximity to one another. Yet the matches were imperfect and the inconsistencies were indicative of tension between these topics. For example, in one poll in *Ladies' Home Journal*, Americans responded to a question about how they should treat their neighbors by saying that they believed they needed to follow the "law of love" toward their fellow human beings—except those who were the nation's enemies or of suspect political orientation.[10] Both religion and ideology shaped American responses, leading sometimes to contradictory trends in Americans' worldviews and behaviors. American behaviors and attitudes, as well as presidential statements, sermons from religious leaders, and the addition of "under God" to the pledge of allegiance in 1954 by a joint resolution of Congress, emphasized that the lines between church and state were blurry indeed.

To be sure, the lines had never been clear. Historians have been well attuned to the intricacies of the theocratic New England colonies, to the establishment of churches across the colonial and republican United States, to the relationship between ecclesiastical and political divisions in the Civil War, and to the religious bent of the southern Lost Cause.[11] As the United States entered the twentieth century, instances such as these continued to suggest an intimate relationship between the American state, the American people, and God. But the nature of that relationship was always under discussion.[12]

Bellah proposed that the concept of civil religion clarified the complicated relationship between religion and politics in the United States.[13] Rather than understanding this pattern as evidence that civil society had co-opted religious beliefs or that religious people had abdicated true religion for civic consensus, Bellah believed American civil religion to be a kind of hybrid, related to but separate from either the church or the state. He wrote, "There are . . . certain common elements of religious orientation that the great majority of Americans share. These have played a crucial role in the development of American institutions and still provide a religious dimension for the whole fabric of American life, including the political sphere."[14]

Will Herberg's earlier formulation of the "American Way of Life" served as an important foundation for Bellah's concept. He argued that in the twentieth-century United States, the broad categories of "Protestant," "Catholic," and "Jew" had created spaces in which ethnic differences among white Americans were subsumed by religious denomination.[15] The results of this tripartite melting pot, Herberg argued, were significant: "With the religious community as the primary context of self-identification and social location, and with Protestantism, Catholicism, and Judaism as three culturally diverse representations of the same 'spiritual values,' it becomes virtually mandatory for the American to place himself in one or another of these groups" because such identification "is understood as the specific way, and increasingly perhaps the only way, of being an American and locating oneself in American society."[16] Herberg and others have since suggested this correlation may have prompted people who did not identify with one of these traditions, or who in fact did not believe in God at all, to respond otherwise in polls and profess otherwise in public. This theme reemerged with significant force within the context of the military, where identification with a broad religious tradition became the norm, and especially in combat as particular religious beliefs and practices were often shed in favor of more communal, less-specific variations.

Herberg asserted that the "American Way of Life" supplied "American society with an 'overarching sense of unity' amid conflict."[17] For Herberg, the concept was, essentially, "a spiritual structure of ideas and ideals, of aspirations and values, of beliefs and standards; it synthesized all that commends itself to the American as the right, the good, and the true in actual life. It embraced such seemingly incongruous elements as sanitary plumbing and freedom of opportunity, Coca-Cola and an intense faith in education."[18] Furthermore, the American Way of Life was peculiarly democratic, individualistic, dynamic, pragmatic, humanitarian, and idealistic. This "common denominator" religion allowed Americans with diverse political and theological views to coalesce against the Communist enemy around shared language and basic ideas without having to agree on the specifics of motive and policy.[19]

Yet this watered-down version of mainline Protestantism, which according to some united the American people, also meant that the great center of American sociability and organization in the 1950s was founded on shaky ground. Ultimately, the major social and cultural ruptures of the 1960s and 1970s should not be surprising. Although the conflict and trauma of combat proved to be a remarkably ecumenical space, the political divisions and relative isolation of the home front from the war itself may have intensified politico-religious conflict at home. The unpopularity and uncertainty of the war in Vietnam proved too heavy a burden for an apparently broad religious consensus built around ideals of anti-Communism, civility, and tolerance.

Though Bellah's overall assessment of civil religion was more positive than Herberg's, Bellah, too, found himself deeply worried about the prospects for civil religion in the late 1960s. He believed it a short leap from practicing the positive, unifying brand of civil religion to using the rhetoric of civil religion to support morally reprehensible ideas and actions. Bellah warned, "It can be overtly or implicitly linked to the idea of manifest destiny which has been used to legitimate several adventures in imperialism since the early nineteenth century." And he believed the danger continued

into the turbulent years of the late 1960s, when the issue was not imperial expansion, but instead the "tendency to assimilate all governments
or parties in the world which support our immediate policies or call upon
our help by invoking the notion of free institutions and democratic values. Those nations that are for the moment 'on our side' become 'the free
world,'" and thus a "repressive and unstable military dictatorship in South
Vietnam" could become "the free people of South Vietnam and their government." Government and military leaders could use the language of civil
religion to sacralize the war effort, so when soldiers died, it would allow
the state "to consecrate the struggle further by invoking the great theme
of sacrifice." These were precisely the dangers that many on the Left, and
especially critics of the military chaplaincy, cited during the Vietnam War
and that framed the debate about the proper religious response to war.

The civil religion that emerged during this period obscured important
differences in political and theological interpretations under a common
language, which often served to mask differences rather than illuminate
them. Despite the patina of consensus on the spiritual and religious foundation of the country, significant theological and philosophical differences
divided Americans. Though various groups and individuals had different
concerns and interests, civil-religious rhetoric provided religious liberals
and conservatives, as well as more universalist or nationalist thinkers, a
way to participate in the public discourse of the Cold War.[20] Politicians and
citizens, clergy and laymen participated in conversations that assumed a
common religious heritage, or at least a common religious language, with
potentially disastrous results.

Public Theology and the Cold War

In 1955, 42 percent of Americans reported to Gallup that they had attended
religious services at least once in the past week, and between 96 and 98
percent consistently reported that they "believed in God." Using aggregate
poll numbers from 1939 to 1958, Jonathan Herzog has suggested this represents a 10–15 percent increase in self-reported religious attendance.[21] In
1952, Dwight Eisenhower declared, "Our government makes no sense unless
it's founded on a deeply felt religious faith, and I don't care what it is."[22]
Belief itself was the important thing—the content of that belief (though
assumed to be vaguely Judeo-Christian) was less important. Eisenhower
himself was perhaps the best embodiment of this idea. Adlai Stevenson,
Eisenhower's opponent in the 1952 presidential election, spoke regularly

of his specific religious values and with theological specificity during the campaign, but he was nonetheless stymied by his Unitarian affiliation and his status as a divorcee.[23] Eisenhower, on the other hand, often spoke of religion in vague terms and joined a Presbyterian church (at the suggestion of Billy Graham) only after his electoral victory. Martin Marty has suggested that Americans knew nothing about Eisenhower's personal creed beyond the first two words "I Believe" yet seemed entirely willing to accept Eisenhower's version of spirituality as a legitimate one.[24] Eisenhower's language was specific enough to invoke civil religion but vague enough to appeal to a diverse audience.

Between 1955 and 1965, most religious denominations' membership grew significantly. Even mainline churches experienced moderate growth, though evangelical, fundamentalist, and Pentecostal churches grew more rapidly. During that decade, only the United Church of Christ saw its numbers decline. The United Methodist Church had the slowest rate of increase at 10.5 percent, while the Assemblies of God grew a total of 43 percent during the same time.[25] Church attendance varied according to religious affiliation. Catholics were the most consistent attendees, averaging around 70–75 percent weekly attendance at Mass. Protestant attendance declined slowly during the period, but averaged around 42 percent, while Jewish attendance was significantly lower, staying between 18 and 27 percent, depending on the poll.[26]

But widespread belief in "God" and even increased church membership did not translate directly into heightened piety or observable religious practice. In the 1950s, when over nine million copies of the Bible were sold each year, over half of American adults could not name a single one of the first four books of the New Testament, the Gospels. Similarly, polling numbers on church attendance in any given week were likely false, the over-reporting a reflection more of what people had hoped to do or planned to do in the future than an accurate representation of their actions in the past week.[27] Overwhelmingly, in polls on religious faith and practice, Americans said they embraced some version of the Golden Rule as the primary means for salvation, rather than citing specific religious doctrines of sin, repentance, or sacrifice.[28]

Thus, the ways in which religion entered public discourse and public space in the 1950s reflected both the substance and the effects of this religious renewal on the United States. This "public theology" differed significantly from private theologies or institutional doctrines, but it facilitated the intertwining of civic and religious language during the Cold War. But men and women did not have to be theological or political giants to influence, use, and sustain this public theology; indeed it suffused the halls of Congress, the courts, schools, the military, and other public spaces. In addition to the sustained public debate, Christian communities also vigorously debated the Cold War among themselves in the texts of ecumenical, nondenominational, and denominational publications.[29]

Religion offered Americans concrete reasons for joining the anti-Communist struggle. Though not all Americans were traditionally religious, the "American Way of Life" and civil-religious beliefs clearly valued the First Amendment protection of free religious exercise. Communism, by denying the existence of God and suppressing religious practice, threatened not only religious Americans' worldviews but also one of the United States' founding principles. Even conservative Christians, who historically had supported disengagement from the political sphere, spoke out for the moral imperative of protecting Christians' rights abroad, essentially entangling political and religious goals.[30] Additionally, religion acted as a socially conservative force, encouraging unity and the status quo. As a social institution, religion offered American communities a form of "social sacralization," by which they legitimated themselves against another society. In this case, the perception of a common religious heritage allowed the United States to define itself against the Soviet Union.[31]

While religious anti-Communism united many Americans in principle, in practice, the ways in which American religious groups expressed their anti-Communist ideas varied greatly.[32] Political scientist Kenneth Wald, seeing both the traditional tripartite grouping of American religious adherents into "Protestant, Catholic, Jew" and more specific denominational groups as problematic for understanding the basic cleavages between religious people on political issues, has suggested that scholars move toward analyzing religious "worldviews." He defined two dominant ones—"liberal-progressive" and "conservative-orthodox"—as better indicators of religious response to political and social issues.[33]

In Wald's analysis, conservatives generally "supported a strongly nationalistic line which portrayed communism as a moral enemy to be resisted wherever it appeared." They "stressed active opposition, endorsed military action taken in the cause of anticommunism, and expressed skepticism about the prospects of negotiation with communist states." On the other side, progressives and liberals believed Communism could best be resisted by building more just societies and relying on the framework of international law to lessen tension and prevent war. They believed that "military action, when unavoidable, should be pursued defensively and only in service of limited goals. . . . To the extent Christianity had a role to play, the task of church representatives was to promote the social and economic development of poor countries and so diminish the attractiveness of radical solutions to desperate people." The foreign policy positions of these worldviews were not foreordained; in fact, both groups had essentially the same goal—to defeat Communism—but for different reasons and advocated different methods for accomplishing it.

Both religious liberals and conservatives in the United States routinely labeled themselves anti-Communist; only a small minority of religious groups, most notably Dorothy Day and her associates at the *Catholic Worker*, openly supported Communism.[34] During the early Cold War, several theologians and ministers alike enjoyed a national public status that allowed them to articulate their religious and political viewpoints. Though many religious perspectives fell under the rubric of anti-Communism, there were significant differences in the specific rhetoric of religious liberals and conservatives. Theologian Reinhold Niebuhr expressed the liberal viewpoint, whereas evangelical minister Billy Graham best articulated the conservative position. As religion and the politics of the Cold War merged in public discourse, these two men embodied the essence of public theology.[35]

Reinhold Niebuhr began his intellectual life as a socialist, and although he became disenchanted with socialism's political program, he continued to be attracted to its fundamental criticism of capitalism and its reliance on class as an explanatory factor in history. He was the primary figure behind the concept of Christian Realism, which advocated a "tough" stance on complicated issues of the day—for example, he derided Social Gospel–style liberalism for being "too soft," and for its mistaken belief that human action could actually change the dominant social and economic systems. Niebuhr instead advocated a different type of human agency and a religious philosophy that would take into account various evils in the world such as Communism.

Though a prolific writer in the years of the Depression and the Second World War, not until the postwar period did Niebuhr gain his widest public audience with the publication of his 1952 work, *The Irony of American History*.[36] In it, Russell Sizemore argues, Niebuhr "argued for the centrality of power in order to advocate an expanded, morally sensitive conception of power. . . . [He] militantly espoused liberal measures to counter the conservative militarists of his time and offered a realistic rationale for exercising moral restraint."[37] As a result, Niebuhr often found himself between competing camps, neither of which was wholly comfortable with his analysis. Democratic Party liberals were uncomfortable with Niebuhr's wholehearted endorsement of the Cold War, and though Niebuhr's support precipitated a crisis for many liberals, more than a few eventually chose to follow his lead, which paved the way for the mainstream American Left's endorsement of Harry Truman's foreign policy.[38] Later, Niebuhr would roll back some of his early proclamations, especially with the advent of mutual assured destruction and the Vietnam War, but his early support for Cold War initiatives helped secure both political and religious liberal support.

Niebuhr's initial support for the Cold War and by extension some American involvement in Vietnam is significant because it highlights the importance of the long time horizon of American involvement in Vietnam. American involvement developed slowly over time, and the initial period of assistance to the French and South Vietnamese, followed by the advisory period, followed by the committal of U.S. ground forces, escalation, and eventual Vietnamization and drawdown, meant that views often changed over the course of the war and according to the strategic aims and operational specifics of the war at any given time. Thus, objecting to U.S. policy toward Vietnam in the 1950s or even in the early 1960s was fundamentally different from protesting the war effort in 1968. Early on, American policy toward Vietnam garnered wide support, but as the war grew increasingly contentious, so too did the rhetoric employed by religious groups on the right and left.

On the conservative side of the religious spectrum stood Billy Graham and other likeminded religious leaders. Whereas Niebuhr's anti-Communism had been cautious and he advocated military engagement as a last resort, Graham's was strident and often militant in tone. In one pamphlet, titled "Christianism and Communism," Graham claimed, "Communism is far more than just an economic and philosophical interpretation of life. Communism is a fanatical religion that has declared war upon the Christian God. To a striking degree this atheistic philosophy is paralleling and counterfeiting Christianity."[39] Graham defined the world and the threats to it in ways that echoed the U.S. government's position. It was a fight between good and evil, and the United States needed to fortify both its faith and its military in order to overcome the Soviet menace. Using clear millennial and dispensational Christian referents, Graham wrote, "Communism *could* be only a shadow of a greater movement that is yet to come. However, it carries with it all the indications of anti-Christ."[40] Faith alone, however, would be insufficient; he called for a religious war, perhaps a crusade:

"Christianity needs a show of strength and force" and must "maintain the strongest military establishment on earth."[41]

Other conservative theologians and ministers were less charitable to their coreligionists and found liberal religion, particularly liberal Protestantism, to be insidious forces in the Cold War. Concerned that liberal Protestantism relied on principles of collective salvation, a holdover from the era of the Social Gospel, J. B. Matthews, a conservative commentator and the director of research for House Un-American Activities Committee (HUAC) excoriated liberal Protestant clergy for being on the wrong side of the global struggle. In an article titled "Reds and Our Churches"—inflammatory to be sure—Matthews warned, "The largest single group supporting the Communist apparatus in the United States today is composed of Protestant clergymen." Citing the People's Institute of Applied Religion, a southern organization involved with the labor movement and with Communist ties, Matthews charged that in the past seventeen years, thousands of professors and more than 7,000 clergymen had supported the Communist Party either as members, fellow travelers, spies, or dupes.[42] An ultraconservative Lutheran publication titled "How Red is the National Council of Churches?" suggested that the national ecumenical group was in cahoots with the Soviet Union.[43] These were not accusations to be taken lightly, made as they were in the midst of Joseph McCarthy's senate hearings and general national anti-Communist hysteria. Clearly, there were significant fissures within American Christianity on the issue of the Cold War and domestic politics, but civil religious language obscured many of these differences, especially for a public not well-versed in either theology or foreign policy.

Military and Religious Convergences and Conversations

Though religion often provided the lexicon with which to discuss anti-Communist efforts, the problem of the Soviet Union was also undoubtedly a military and political one, and the American military prepared itself to confront the Soviet threat. But this fact did not result in an easy marriage between religious and military agendas; even though religious leaders and groups spoke with an anti-Communist tenor, they were often antimilitarist as well. Religious leaders from many denominations and groups criticized the use of atomic weapons in World War II, and nearly all religious groups opposed efforts to mandate UMT for young men. The military responded to these concerns in part by implementing policy changes in the structure of the chaplaincy and in the nature of the chaplains' mission to the military as well as employing a distinctly religious language to explain the military's Cold War mission. This discourse played out during the Korean War, as military policies and religious ideas were put into practice.

In many ways, religious communities' specific critiques of the Vietnam War, its effects on service members, and the ethics of its conduct were foreshadowed by earlier debates about the relationship between religion and the military. Ultimately, a marked shift by evangelical and conservative bodies toward embracing martial and nationalistic values during the early years of the Cold War is significant because it changed the tenor of the debate and constituted a realignment of religious and political groups. This shift was also broadly representative of the postwar realignment of religious groups along political rather than denominational lines.[44]

At the same time, politicians responded to the concerns and priorities of national religious leaders. Though many secular leaders believed chaplains had performed admirably during and after World War II, some insinuated that chaplains were rarely the "top notch" ministers who might be found in civilian churches.[45] This sentiment was given voice by Major General Harry Vaughn, a military aide to President Truman, in a September 1945 address to the Women's Auxiliary of Alexandria (Virginia) Westminster Presbyterian Church, where he stated, "You have to give the Roman Church credit. When the War Department requests a bishop to supply 20 priests for chaplains, he looks over his diocese and picks out the 20 best men. Frequently a Protestant [minister] does not have a church at that moment or is willing to go on vacation for about three years."[46] Though the General Commission on Chaplains registered a complaint, Vaughn's observation was not uncommon. Because chaplains generally fell outside of traditional ecclesiastical structures and hierarchies, it was easy to view them as outcasts in the ministerial community.

In response to these criticisms, the Truman administration and many denominational organizations worked to increase the visibility and vitality of their chaplain services. The most significant change came in the area of chaplain training within the armed services. Though each service continued to operate its own chaplain school, the Army Chaplain School was a model for chaplain training during the early years of the Cold War. At the outset of World War II, chaplain training was accomplished somewhat haphazardly at a school designed to train chaplains quickly—most went through only a one-month course before they went overseas. The school moved four times during the course of the war, which only increased a feeling of instability and impermanence. In 1946, the chaplain school moved to Carlisle Barracks, Pennsylvania, where leaders began developing in earnest a curriculum for chaplains and initiated distance-learning courses for Reserve and National Guard chaplains. In 1947, high-ranking chaplains met to coordinate between the three chaplain branches and began working on plans to offer an advanced course for career chaplains in all three services.[47] Several decisions and events slowed progress toward this goal, including the Army War College's move to Carlisle and the Korean War, but eventually the changes were enacted.

In addition to more conventional religious and military topics, the new curriculum included training on Soviet religious development, philosophy, and literature.[48] And, as they had been in the past, chaplains would be the primary instructors for the training and education of service members on moral and ethical issues. Thus, the chaplain school curriculum focused on the chaplain's responsibility for inculcating moral behavior and decision making within military units and for providing pastoral care for soldiers. The chaplain was to add both religious authority and personal, spiritual, and moral maturity to the military outfit. In the late 1950s, the Department of the Army's Education and Training Review Board recommended that all service schools, including the chaplain school, establish a "career course." The first career-course-trained chaplains graduated in 1963, and the course eventually provided substantial training for many field-grade chaplains serving in the war.[49]

In addition to formalized and improved chaplain training, many American military leaders wished to see an improved and more stringent training regime for American youth in anticipation of heightened military requirements in the future. In the years between World War II and Korea, President Truman and high-ranking members of his administration like George Marshall and John J. McCloy campaigned to push legislation that would mandate UMT for all male citizens, thus increasing the number of men available for immediate military service in the event of a security crisis.[50] When he addressed Congress, Truman made his case primarily in terms of military security, but he assured the public that the training not only would prepare men for war but also would serve to "train citizens" and ensure the "moral and spiritual welfare of our young people."[51] For chaplains, the UMT proposal would significantly expand the realm of the chaplain's professional responsibilities, as chaplains would have significant responsibility for ensuring soldiers' moral and spiritual fitness within the new training regime. However, even with this significant push from the White House, UMT legislation failed repeatedly in Congress.[52]

Yet, despite the anti-Communist fervor and the near-constant rhetoric of readiness and despite President Truman's reassurances that military training would strengthen the morality and faith of the country's young men, religious groups, liberal and conservative alike, were vehemently opposed to the idea. Liberal and mainline groups and leaders feared UMT would lead to militarism and the militarization of American society, while more conservative groups were skeptical that the military could do anything but corrupt the morality of young American men.[53]

Responding especially to the morality-based critiques of evangelical groups, in October 1948, President Truman appointed the Committee on Religion and Welfare in the Armed Forces to "encourage and promote the religious, moral and recreational welfare and character guidance of persons in the Armed Forces," and to challenge the claim that the military encouraged vice and immorality among its members and was particularly harmful to young men. For the most part, chaplains received a rousing endorsement from the committee. The final report concluded, "The importance of the work of the chaplain is today recognized as never before in the history of the Armed Forces. . . . There is nothing fundamentally wrong with the chaplaincy" except for the acute shortage of candidates for chaplain positions. The chaplaincy had developed for itself a critical place in the civic and moral education of American troops.[54] In July 1949, the secretary of defense created an Armed Services Chaplains Board to advise him on religious and moral matters. Though the moral and spiritual development of servicemen was technically the domain of commanding officers, chaplains were called on to implement the new program of character guidance.[55] In response to religious communities' calls for a more concerted effort to promote morality in the military, chaplains became the natural conduits for this information.

The character guidance program combined religious, civil, and moral themes, and as a result, the chaplain became a spokesman not only for his religious faith but also for a generic "American" morality and civic responsibility. The basic program, presented by chaplains, was delivered to recruits in six parts during their initial training and included the following topics: religion, basic moral principles, marriage and family life, sex education, citizenship, and individual responsibility. Additionally enlisted men below the E-6 grade, were required to attend monthly presentations by the chaplain.[56] According to the character guidance manuals, the program was based on "moral" and "natural" laws, which were derived from God. Belief in one Supreme Being therefore provided the basis for moral action by military personnel. Even when materials were not explicitly religious, most evoked Protestant Christian themes and presumed a similar theistic worldview for soldiers and officers. The chaplains who presented these programs were from various denominations and faith groups who held different views on military service, the use of force, and the role of the chaplain, yet these men were united in their belief in the importance of morality and spirituality to responsible civic and military service.

In addition to intensified and refocused training programs for chaplains and plans to increase military training across all segments of American society, the military highlighted the importance of chaplains when, in the face of post–World War II restructuring, the ratio of chaplains to servicemen decreased from 1:2,500 to 1:800. Though postwar drawdowns in the total troop strength meant that the number of active-duty chaplains declined in absolute terms, should a war begin, the number of chaplains required would be significant as more Americans entered military service.[57] Reducing the ratio for chaplain care suggested a new emphasis on morality and spiritual well-being in a peacetime force. The idea that the military must be ready not only in terms of weapons and combat training but also spiritually and morally fit for battle against the Soviets was a common trope.

The Korean War provided a real-world test of many of these early Cold War ideological concepts and policy changes, and chaplains were thrust into the field from their the parishlike ministries of garrison duty stateside or in occupation zones. The invasion of South Korea by Communist North Korea in June 1950 seemed to confirm Americans' worst fears about the aggressive and monolithic nature of Communism. America's fighting ability, and its collective faith, was put to the test. As expected, the outbreak of hostilities in Korea prompted the chaplain branch to increase its numbers to meet the requirements of a growing force. The Army struggled to fill its billets with volunteers, so ultimately 240 company-grade chaplain reservists were subject to an involuntary recall. The number of chaplains on duty, however, was never sufficient to put the branch at full strength, as troop increases outpaced chaplain acquisitions.[58] Army chaplains were not particularly eager for service in Korea, especially as initial engagements there resulted in heavy casualties for allied troops. The Navy faced similar challenges, and in order to preserve the spirit of voluntarism, it presented naval reserve chaplains with three options: volunteer for immediate active duty status, be prepared for mobilization from reserve status, or resign.[59] By the end of 1951, 160 had volunteered for active duty and were accepted (another 140 were rejected) and 1,486 chose the second option. Between July 1951 and 1952, a total of 620 chaplains resigned their commissions.[60] The relatively low number of volunteers and a significant number of involuntary recalls suggest that some military chaplains may have been uneasy with developments in Korea, but they may also simply reveal a human tendency toward self-preservation when given an option. Certainly, trying to avoid deployment to a combat zone was not unique to chaplains. Chaplains' hesitancy to volunteer for service in Korea contrasts markedly with their responses to the Vietnam War, during which there were initially far more volunteers for service than available slots.[61]

The Korean War caught the Chaplain Corps somewhat off guard, especially after a period of drawdown following World War II. Several hundred reservists and National Guard chaplains were called to active duty, and only a handful of exemptions were granted. Within a year of the invasion, U.S. Army chaplain strength increased, in real terms, by 71 percent, from 706 to 1,208. By November 1951, 1,448 Army chaplains were on active duty.[62] Several hundred of those chaplains actually served in Korea, and thirteen of them were killed there.

In many respects, combat ministry in the Korean War looked much like it had in previous wars. Chaplains held field services, visited the wounded in hospitals, and said prayers and memorial services for the dead. Some of the chaplains' experiences and postwar reflections and, most significantly, their treatment by the North Koreans, however, reflected the ideological nature of the Korean War. Even long after the war was over, chaplains emphasized the Cold War foundations for the Korean War. Chaplain Carl Hudson, who was stationed with the men of Task Force Smith, an understrength battalion from the 24th Infantry Division,[63] for example, recalled, "I was always glad of the opportunity to explain the workings and effects of Communism as compared to the life and blessings of being an American. . . . We saw all the horrors of war and misery caused by Communism."[64] The Geneva Conventions, identifying the chaplain as a noncombatant and entitling him to certain protections, were frequently, if not routinely, violated.[65] As the war entered a period of stalemate after 1951 and as ceasefire terms were negotiated, chaplains struggled with the basic morality of the war and the hardships of continued service in a combat zone. On the whole, the Korean War chaplaincy was, ill-equipped to handle this new sort of conflict, even though the religious and moral implications of the war seemed clear. Chaplains, and commanders, were convinced of the importance of faith and religion to successful warfighting but were unsure how to translate them into combat effectiveness.

In the aftermath of the Korean War, the Chaplain Corps compartmentalized its combat experience and refocused its efforts on promoting morality and character in the military. Baptist chaplain Frank Tobey, who was the Army chief of chaplains in 1959, asserted, "An essential deterrent against our enemy must remain the courageous heart, the right conscience, the clear head, the strong body fortified with the truth and obedient to the dictates of moral good."[66] Nuclear weapons and conventional forces would not be the only means of deterrence.

For evangelicals and conservative Christians, the military became fertile ground for missionary efforts, and chaplains and extramilitary religious groups emphasized conversion, evangelical witness, and personal action within the armed services. They explicitly linked the Christian way of life to the American way of life, and they gained power and influence within the Chaplain Corps and the military structure as a whole.[67] Two examples in particular illustrate the character and extent of evangelical involvement in the military. Early in the Cold War, evangelical activists found a champion in Army lieutenant general William K. Harrison, who proclaimed himself a "Bible-believing Christian." Evangelical Christians promoted him as "something of a religious celebrity," inviting him to address youth rallies and participate in national religious campaigns and broadcasts.[68] The American Tract Society helped him publish his personal testimony, *The General Speaks*.[69] Harrison and other high-profile evangelical Christians within the military's upper echelon helped the evangelical movement gain credibility within wider circles and establish beachheads within the federal government and military. In addition, evangelical groups encouraged evangelical Protestant chaplains to view their military posts as prime locations for evangelism. Anyone reporting to a new duty station—officer and enlisted, new recruit, draftee, or lifer—was required to visit the chaplain shortly after arrival. Evangelical Protestant chaplains looked upon this circumstance favorably. One commented, "What if every Protestant in your community were asked to report to your pastor?" Though a few more liberal commentators recognized the potential problems with requiring a visit to the chaplain, given an individual's First Amendment rights, most chaplains still viewed the interviews as "golden opportunities for personal ministry."[70]

Throughout the 1950s and 1960s, conservative Christians continued to identify both external and internal Communist threats to American liberties and security. If the world were divided into "two distinct camps—the Communist dictatorships and the Christian democracies," they argued, there could be no questioning of which side someone was on. Any hint of liberalism or interfaith cooperation was met with fierce resistance and charges of Communist infiltration.[71] When the National Council Against Conscription urged American males to refuse to register for the draft and "called upon the churches and people of the United States to observe a day of 'mourning and repentance,'" a group of evangelical ministers denounced the dissenting clergy, calling their position "unbiblical, unpatriotic, un-American, [and] contrary to the historic Christian faith."[72]

Mainline and liberal leaders, on the other hand, used the language of civil religion to emphasize more internationalist positions, and in some cases used it as a way to warn against the interpretation of America as God's chosen nation. They voiced concerns about the use of atomic weapons, supported civil rights causes, and advocated dialogue with Christians in Communist-controlled countries.[73] Yet as they staked out positions to the left of their conservative coreligionists, they retained the language of civil religion to prove their anti-Communist outlook; though these leaders did not assess an internal or domestic Communist threat with the same urgency as the conservatives, they frequently demonized both the Soviet Union and the People's Republic of China as dangerous examples of Communist oppression and control.[74] Unlike their more conservative counterparts, however, they tended to value the possibility of thawed diplomatic relations with the Soviet Union, its satellite states, and China.

Religious Responses to Initial American Involvement in Vietnam

As the Cold War intensified, and memories of Korea and Joseph McCarthy faded, imperial, security, and religious interests directed the nation's attention toward Vietnam. Between the French defeat in 1954 and Lyndon Johnson's commitment of American combat troops in 1965, American policy-makers reexamined how Vietnam fit into American Cold War strategy. The 1954 Geneva Accords recognized the territorial sovereignty and integrity of Vietnam, Laos, and Cambodia and decreed the cessation of hostilities and foreign involvement in Indochinese affairs. Vietnam was to be reunited (having been separated into northern and southern zones) by internationally supervised free elections in July 1956. Neither the Republic of Vietnam nor the United States pledged to abide by the terms of the Accords, although several scholars dispute this fact.[75]

In South Vietnam, Ngo Dinh Diem's rise to power reflected the Cold War's strategic calculus, American values, and the American attempt to implement or stage democratic processes abroad. Although the extent to which American actions, as opposed to Diem's own agency, propelled him to the presidency of South Vietnam has been hotly debated, the significance of his education, religion, and political leanings to his gaining and maintaining power seems unmistakable.[76] Catholic religious leaders and organizations threw their support behind the Diem government, and the Christian minority in Vietnam gave incentive to Protestant groups as well.

Direct assistance to South Vietnam began under President Dwight Eisenhower in 1950, and in an advisory capacity, Americans worked to shore up the Saigon government against the National Liberation Front (NLF), which included political, guerrilla, and regular military components. Viet Cong operatives used campaigns of propaganda, assassinations, and political organization to undermine the government of South Vietnam, and by 1957 they had secured both Chinese and Soviet support. The creation of the Military Assistance Advisory Group–Vietnam (MAAG-V) in 1950 cemented the relationship between the United States and Vietnam. Violence increased throughout the South in the late 1950s, and the advisory mission again intensified with the inauguration of John F. Kennedy in 1961, when he ordered a range of assistance programs designed to strengthen the South Vietnamese government and the Army of the Republic of Vietnam (ARVN). Collectively, these programs marked the beginning of a counterinsurgency campaign in Vietnam as the number of advisers grew from about 900 to more than 3,000 in short order. The initial efforts, especially using Special Forces operatives, looked promising, even with higher casualties. In 1962, the U.S. military established the Military Assistance Command, Vietnam (MACV). American responses in these early years of the war would form a critical backdrop for Lyndon Johnson's later decision for escalation in 1965.

The religious divisions present but buried in the 1950s came to the foreground during the Vietnam War as the language of civil religion and religious anti-Communism proved insufficient to mask the important underlying differences among religious communities in their responses to military and national security issues. Conservative Christians tended to view Vietnam within the paradigm of containment and tottering dominoes. They assessed the violence in Vietnam as an integral part of the worldwide

Communist movement, and they were convinced that the United States—both out of Christian duty and because of its developmental superiority—had to defend South Vietnam from the northern aggressors. More liberal religious communities, however, contextualized Ho Chi Minh's revolution in the paradigm of national liberation and argued that it was largely separate from the worldwide Communist movement.

For the most part, throughout the 1950s and early 1960s, American religious communities' views about the French war in Vietnam and American involvement, particularly as represented in national religious periodicals such as *Christian Century*, *Christianity Today*, *America*, and *Commonweal*, reflected the general public's sentiments. In the 1950s, there were more articles about Ngo Dinh Diem in the two Catholic periodicals than in the Protestant ones, while *Christianity Today* and *America* generally espoused more conservative and hard-line positions on matters like the domino theory, international Communist aggression, and American responsibility in the face of it. Within more mainline publications, however, foreign policy topics were overshadowed by coverage of the civil rights movement and the religious community's participation in it, reflecting this perspective's more cautious engagement with the Vietnam question.

Even as Diem's and Nhu's abuses of Buddhists in Vietnam became widely apparent and gained mainstream press coverage, Christian periodicals continued to lend cautious support to the American effort in Vietnam, though they urged Diem's replacement.[77] Once Diem had been assassinated, liberal and conservative periodical editors disagreed, however, about the extent to which the United States should be involved in Vietnam. More liberal editors, such as those at *Christian Century* and *Christianity and Crisis*, argued that the United States should not involve itself in any sort of campaign against North Vietnam, fearing that it might provoke a rapprochement between the Soviet Union and China.[78] More conservative Christian groups, on the other hand, urged and demanded total victory over Communism in Vietnam.[79]

Though Kennedy and Johnson enjoyed the general support of religious leaders and writers for American action in Vietnam through 1965, levels and types of support varied widely. The language of anti-Communism dominated early discussions about Vietnam, again providing an element of civil religious expression that could accommodate diverse points of view. As American policy-makers struggled over decisions about Vietnamese politics, military training, strategy, and objectives, religious leaders responded according to their particular theologies and views on Christian engagement in politics, international relations, and military affairs. In religious periodicals, disagreement over American policies and strategic objectives intensified as policy-makers and officers questioned Diem's effectiveness and the level of American support for regime change in Saigon.

As religious communities began to debate American involvement in Vietnam, chaplains followed American military personnel to Vietnam. Chaplain deployment to Vietnam was slow in the early 1960s, occurring on an almost ad-hoc basis, with little sustained attention to issues of organization, supply, coverage, or assignment patterns. Official histories from both the Army and Navy emphasized the minimal planning that was involved in chaplain deployment to Vietnam: according to the Army, chaplains "glided into the fury" of Vietnam, and the Marines identified early chaplain missions as a "drift into turbulence."[80] The first Army chaplain, Lieutenant Colonel John Lindvall, arrived in February 1962, and within days, two others—William Staudt and Elmore Lester—joined him. They arrived with no support and no supplies; standard-issue field kits, communion supplies, and hymnals had to be requisitioned on an emergency basis. By the end of March, eight chaplains, including one Air Force chaplain, were stationed in Vietnam, but Lindvall lamented that coverage was scarce because the military had "people in scores of places scattered throughout the 600[-] mile length of this country."[81] Lieutenant Earnest S. Lemieux, a Methodist, the first Navy chaplain to serve with onshore Marine units, was already stationed in Japan, simply waiting for orders that would take his unit to Vietnam. Lemieux arrived in Vietnam in April 1962.[82]

As the MACV staff chaplain, Lindvall was tasked with coordinating increasingly complicated and numerous chaplains' activities between branches, and he also established the components of a longer-standing chaplain section, especially for those stationed at and near Tan Son Nhut Air Base, such as a religious education program, regular worship services, periodic retreats, and a chaplain's fund. Chaplain presence in Vietnam grew alongside the increasing military presence; by 1963, more than 11,000 American military personnel were stationed in Vietnam. The Army had deployed ten chaplains, and they, along with chaplains from the Navy and Air Force served any and all military personnel in a geographic region regardless of which branch they were in.[83]

The sentiments of the first chaplains deployed to Vietnam reflected the broad public support for democracy and deeply rooted anti-Communism, but they also reflected general ignorance of the international political situation and of the specific state of affairs in Vietnam. Joel Earl Andrews, who arrived in Saigon in 1962, recalled in a 1972 oral history interview: "I knew very little. As a matter of fact, Viet Nam was sort of a magical name to me . . . you know, the Pearl of the Orient type of thing. I thought of lush jungles and people who were very tranquil and peaceful and so forth. And I had not really been very serious in following the media as to what was going on in Viet Nam. I knew nothing of the internal political situation." Andrews reported that his gaps in knowledge tracked those of the men he served: "The men were in the same predicament," given that "they knew very little. . . . We didn't even know geographically where [Vietnam] was located. . . . And I didn't know who the [South Vietnamese] president was. We had a vacuum of knowledge concerning Viet Nam at that time.[84] He, like many others, went to Vietnam because he was ordered to do so; he was there because of the growing American military presence in Vietnam.

At the same time, chaplains' activities revealed support for anti-Communist programs and goals of the United States military. Responding to a question about the chaplain's primary purpose in the military being to boost morale, Andrews replied, "All of us in the command and staff echelon were sorta' caught up with this whole ideological factor. And you know, in my character guidance . . . lectures . . . I would hit very hard on the communist angle and on the attempt of the Vietnamese to maintain their freedom—sort of a general approach to [an] international type of a communism conspiracy." Andrews emphasized that the entire command was well-versed in these sorts of issues while many of the men serving in the field were unaware of the political aspects of the war. He admitted, "As I look back now . . . I was a part of the propaganda effort, I think, of the command to instill some motivation in the man [sic] as to why they were there, their presence and so forth."[85]

Andrews's observations underscored the extent to which American military personnel and politicians at the time believed American involvement in Vietnam would be limited and short-lived. These illusions were quickly shattered, though. Andrews reflected that upon his return to the United States, he "was convinced it was going to be a long and drawn-out struggle."[86] The vacuum of knowledge that accompanied the first American military personnel into Vietnam would continue to affect future service members. And their rapid turnover meant that accumulated knowledge was difficult to establish and maintain.

During the early years of the Cold War, American military and religious cultures intersected at important and diverse points. Though most religious leaders and adherents called themselves anti-Communist, important theological and practical issues lurked beneath the surface of these claims. Liberal and mainline groups advocated a policy that focused on domestic issues and social justice within the United States along with containment, while conservative groups called for the liberation of peoples under Communist rule and the annihilation of the Soviet Union. Yet most of these viewpoints were obscured by a shared reliance on the language of civil religion and the anti-Communist fervor in the United States. As religious groups criticized military policies in the late 1940s, the administration and military officials responded with a conscious attempt to integrate religious and moral concerns into the structure and character of the military. The Korean War tested the relationship between religion and the military, and the chaplaincy emphasized a common American moral and religious heritage as a weapon for the Cold War. In the second half of the 1950s, as American involvement in Vietnam increased slowly but steadily, imperial, security, and religious interests combined to convince Americans that the Vietnam was a vital point on the containment line, even though they disagreed on specific policies and strategies for dealing with the country. As the war progressed, however, religious divisions resurfaced as more and more religious communities found themselves unable to align patriotic and civic ideals, their religious beliefs, and American action in Vietnam. Vietnam, then, acted as a crucible in which military and religious interests variously commingled and collided. Those interactions would have a lasting effect on American religious culture, the military chaplaincy, and the place of religion in the U.S. military.

CHAPTER TWO

Duty and Relationships

Chaplains' duties in Vietnam included a wide variety of pastoral and administrative tasks. In addition to conducting public worship services, carrying out sacramental rites, counseling troops on moral and personal matters, and advising commanders on morale and morality, some chaplains were also responsible for tasks more suited to stateside service, for example giving character guidance lectures and maintaining a religious education program. In addition to these prescribed duties, chaplains also assisted in civic action programs, worked with Vietnamese religious congregations and leaders, and coordinated delivery of holiday gifts and packages to troops and to Vietnamese civilians.

The composition of the Chaplain Corps in Vietnam reflected some of the demographic characteristics of the chaplaincy, and the number of chaplains in Vietnam highlighted the difficulties of ministering to diverse American troops in a spread out area of operations (AO). Chaplains worked together across denominational lines, across service lines, and with commanders to create a network of religious support for American military personnel in Vietnam, and throughout the war, their primary focus remained in the realm of pastoral care for soldiers and officers.

Chaplains' day-to-day experiences affected how they understood the Vietnam War and their participation in it. Their duties made them full members of both military and religious institutions, mandated ecumenical cooperation, and cast them in a variety of peer, pastoral, subordinate, and authoritative roles. Their duties and roles served to inform their sense of identity, especially as they negotiated a position for themselves within military communities. Religious and military aspects of chaplains' identity consistently placed them in the middle—in practice, not fully part of either the military organization or the clergy.

The course of the war had a pronounced effect on how chaplains experienced Vietnam. Chaplains in 1962 and 1963 faced a fundamentally different sort of war than those who served at the height of American combat in 1967–69, and the experiences of this latter group were substantially different from those of chaplains who were present during the American drawdown in the early 1970s. Thus, a brief review of the progression of the war is instructive here.

The advisory mission that began in the 1950s became more formal in the early 1960s, as turmoil in Saigon and increased Vietnamese and international protest against the excesses and abuses of the Diem regime forced the hand of American policy-makers to make critical decisions about the political future of Vietnam. Military chaplains' arrival in Saigon (now Ho Chi Minh City) in February 1962 coincided with the formation of Military Assistance Command, Vietnam (MACV).[1] By April, as the American military became increasingly embroiled in the armed conflict in Vietnam, eight chaplains—seven from the Army and one from the Air Force—had arrived at MACV Headquarters.[2] By September 1962, one Navy chaplain was stationed in Saigon as the support activity chaplain, falling under administrative command of Naval Forces Philippines and under MACV operational command.[3] Chaplains' duties and numbers remained limited until the introduction of American ground forces to Vietnam in March 1965.

The political turmoil in Saigon did not die down, and the military situation in Vietnam continued to deteriorate in the early 1960s. In November 1963 Kennedy and Diem were both assassinated, Diem with the tacit permission of American policy-makers, which increased uncertainty and instability in Vietnam for both South Vietnamese and American political and military leaders. The new American president, Lyndon Johnson, used Kennedy's legacy to push for increased involvement in Vietnam.[4] The upheaval prompted Hanoi to push maximum effort toward achieving victory in 1964 and led North Vietnamese general Vo Nguyen Giap to commit two North Vietnamese Army (NVA) divisions to the South.[5]

Between November 1963 and February 1965, Lyndon Johnson and his advisers worked through the decision to escalate and Americanize the war.[6] General William C. Westmoreland succeeded General Paul Harkins as the MACV commander in June 1964, and soon after, the incident in the Gulf of Tonkin on 2 August gave Johnson the political pretext he needed to escalate the war.[7] A resolution authorizing military force passed less than a week later and essentially gave Johnson carte blanche to prosecute the war in the manner of his choosing.

Johnson's opening salvo would be a limited strategic bombing campaign called ROLLING THUNDER, launched in February 1965. Fearful of Soviet or Chinese intervention if a full-scale assault were launched, Johnson severely limited the targets in ROLLING THUNDER, setting both the Red River delta rice paddies and major population centers off-limits. For their part, the Viet Cong (VC) responded by increasing attacks on American bases and airfields. Most of Johnson's advisers thought waging war in Vietnam would be a lengthy and costly endeavor, but it was politically and militarily unfeasible to leave American airfields and bases undefended.[8] The first American ground troops, Marines who landed at Da Nang in 1965, were charged with just this mission, and naval chaplains followed them there. Then, in mid-1965, Westmoreland requested 200,000 troops and Johnson approved forty-four maneuver battalions, the equivalent of five divisions, for deployment to Vietnam, though their movement was restricted and Viet Cong sanctuaries in Cambodia and Laos were off-limits. By August 1966, the Army had stationed 219 chaplains in Vietnam: 47 Roman Catholic, 170 Protestant, and 2 Jewish, and the number of chaplain billets rose steadily between 1966 and 1968.[9]

The period of Westmoreland's tenure as the MACV commander is sometimes referred to as the "Big Unit War," and Westmoreland is said to have employed a "search-and-destroy" strategy against the regular NVA units that patrolled and controlled the Vietnamese countryside, the goal of which was to bring American and North Vietnamese units to battle. Strategists and planners thought the American advantage in firepower and mobility would prove decisive.[10] American soldiers and Marines challenged the NVA across South Vietnam, and Westmoreland consistently pushed for more troops to do the job.[11] American troop strength peaked in South Vietnam in 1968, with just over 530,000 in-country. Chaplain strength also peaked in that year; in October 1968, 1,924 Army chaplains were on active duty, with almost 700 serving in Vietnam.[12] Chaplains who served with infantry, engineer, and artillery units during this period would have likely seen heavy combat and witnessed the loss of men to hostile fire, and they would have faced a higher risk of being wounded or killed in action. Chaplains stationed on big American bases in rear areas, though, would have had a vastly different experience, focusing their attention on standard religious services, counseling, and visiting the wounded in the hospital. Arthur Estes, a chaplain stationed with an Army aviation unit, reported that his soldiers lived in relative comfort and that, even though he logged many flight hours visiting troops in far-flung locations and conducted services regularly, all told, he "actually had more time that was more-or-less free of obligatory duty than at any other time in [his] professional life."[13]

In the late 1960s, what are thought of as typically "American" operations, that is, those involving heavy firepower, were certainly common, but they told only part of the story under Westmoreland. MACV, from 1965 to 1968, also conducted a counterinsurgency campaign in South Vietnam focused on winning the "hearts and minds" of the people, completing various development projects, strengthening the Saigon government, and rooting out VC and NLF opposition. The so-called rice-paddy war, which took place in populated areas, particularly in the Mekong Delta and around Saigon, was fundamentally different from the war being fought in the jungles and highlands of northern and central South Vietnam.[14] Ultimately, early pacification and nation-building efforts gained few successes, but the Americans understood well the complexity of the situation in South Vietnam. Chaplains would have likely accompanied units on many of these missions, though large-scale population-centric counterinsurgency efforts that included chaplains were more common after 1968.

Many historians view the Tet Offensive of January-February 1968 as the turning point of the war. As part of a "General Offensive–General Uprising," and during the celebration of the Vietnamese New Year, Viet Cong and NVA forces conducted simultaneous, coordinated attacks on more than 100 American and Army of the Republic of Vietnam (ARVN) installations, embassies, and cities. Though few of the attacks were ultimately conventionally successful, the audacity and tenacity of the attacks surprised Americans and began to sour them toward a war it appeared they might not win. In July 1968 General Creighton Abrams took command of MACV after Westmoreland was promoted to the position of chief of staff of the Army; it appeared to many that Westmoreland had lost the administration's confidence and had been promoted out of the MACV job into irrelevance in Washington.

Presidential candidate Richard Nixon campaigned on the promise that he would end the war in Vietnam "with honor," meaning that the United States would not agree to an unconditional withdrawal but actively seek to disengage from Vietnam. Ultimately, during Nixon's tenure, another 21,000 Americans died in Vietnam as he sought this negotiated peace, ending with few more concessions than likely could have been gained in negotiations years earlier. In terms of military strategy, as diplomats negotiated a settlement, "Vietnamization" became the centerpiece of Nixon's policy, a plan that called for the South Vietnamese to take more and more control of the war effort so that American forces might leave and South Vietnam might remain stable and intact. Eventually, Abrams and the MACV command pulled back on fighting NVA and VC units and focused instead on nation-building and pacification efforts.[15]

Then, in 1972, the North Vietnamese Army launched twelve divisions across the demilitarized zone in the Easter Offensive. The strategic initiative and momentum was clearly theirs, but the ARVN, with significant American assistance—particularly from close air support—defeated Hanoi's Army and destroyed its supply lines. Nixon then ratcheted up the bombing campaign in North Vietnam with LINEBACKER, lifting many of the targeting restrictions, which, according to some, had hampered ROLLING THUNDER, and hoping to bring the North Vietnamese to the negotiating table. In October 1972, negotiations looked close to completion but broke down when the South Vietnamese government was unhappy with some of its terms. Rather than continuing to negotiate, Nixon authorized LINEBACKER II, which concentrated American firepower on the Hanoi-Haiphong area. The devastation wrought by LINEBACKER II brought parties back to the table, and in January 1973, the combatants signed a series of peace agreements that ensured American withdrawal. Other details were to be settled internally by the Vietnamese. The last military chaplain left Vietnam on 28 March 1973. The last Americans left South Vietnam in April 1973.

Providing a Network of Religious Support

Like others who served in the war, chaplains experienced life in combat, at surgical hospitals and aid stations, on ships and river vessels, with engineer battalions, on air bases, and at various headquarters. And though, like other officers, a chaplain's experience of Vietnam was very much determined by chronology, geography, and unit assignment, their day-to-day lives featured some peculiar characteristics and general patterns based on their function and purpose within the military. The differences between the average soldier's experiences and those of the chaplain were sometimes exaggerated because, as a group, chaplains differed demographically from both the soldiers they served and their civilian counterparts.

Even at the height of the war, chaplains were required to serve at least a year in a stateside post before deploying to Vietnam, and many reported that this experience was critical to successful Vietnam service.[16] William Goldie, United States Army Vietnam (USARV) command chaplain in 1967, explained that this policy was designed to increase chaplains' effectiveness and safety while they were in Vietnam. He argued that chaplains who were assigned to troops in the United States would "be much more effective as counselors and as pastors to the soldiers in Vietnam" because they would be familiar with soldiers' training and circumstances. But he also recognized the problem of sending unarmed, untrained men into combat situations. He reasoned that if chaplains spent "a good amount of time in the field . . . learning how to stay alive we will have much less likelihood of running up the high score on Purple Hearts."[17]

Once chaplains were in-country, however, their experiences varied widely. Those who were assigned to combat units had to make important decisions about whether they would accompany troops into combat, visit troops in the field, or stay primarily in the rear and wait for men to return from patrols or the wounded to return to camp. Chaplains assigned to Combat Support or Combat Service Support units had quite different responsibilities, and their experiences were more akin to those that came with stateside garrison duty than to those of a combat tour. Navy chaplains' experiences varied widely as well. Chaplains assigned to Marine units faced many of the same challenges as Army infantry chaplains, while chaplains stationed on aircraft carriers dealt alternately with intense boredom and the frequent loss of pilots' lives. Those serving on hospital ships were well-acquainted with the destructive effects of war. Toward the end of the war, the offices of the chiefs of chaplains began rotating chaplains so they would spend no more than six months with a combat unit. But at least until 1970, many chaplains spent a full year in their original assignment, even with infantry or artillery brigades.

As the American commitment in Vietnam expanded, so did the number of chaplains. The Army operated with a large number of Reserve and National Guard chaplains who could be activated by necessity or, occasionally, by request. Often chaplains who wished to obtain a Regular Army position first fulfilled chaplain duties within Reserve or National Guard units. When they were called to active duty, some obtained the necessary Regular Army commissions and made the chaplaincy a career. Anticipating the buildup in Vietnam and the requisite increase in the need for chaplains, the Department of the Army implemented the "Program for Appointment and Ordering to Active Duty of Chaplains of Reserve Components of the Army" in December 1963 for implementation in fiscal year 1964.[18]

Designed to meet the active duty requirements of the Army, the Army Office of the Chief of Chaplains (OCCH) designed a procurement program for company-grade officers whereby "qualified individuals may apply for appointment as Reserve commissioned officers, Chaplains Branch, with concurrent active duty, and chaplains of Reserve components of the Army not on active duty who meet the requirements outlined herein may volunteer for active duty." Applicants for the program had to be younger than thirty-three and eligible for retirement under Department of Defense guidelines. Alternately, if they were under forty at the time of their appointment and gave up their retirement benefits, they could get a waiver from the Department of the Army. These waivers were generally only given to chaplains from underrepresented denominations.[19] Together, these policies meant that, when they deployed to Vietnam, chaplains were generally older than other service members, many with established professional identities in the civilian world.

Yet before the commitment of ground units to Vietnam in 1965, the chaplain branch, specifically in the Army, but in the other services as well, experienced shortages in several critical denominational categories. In fiscal year 1964–65, ten Protestant denominations had "failed notably" to meet their quotas for Army chaplains, according to the *Office of the Chief of Chaplains Historical Review*. The ten denominations in question had a collective quota of 214 but had filled only 42 of the billets, leaving 172 vacancies. And new chaplains did not appear to be forthcoming; seven of the ten denominations had not provided any new chaplains to the Army during that year, and the other three had provided only four chaplains total.[20] Additionally, the Roman Catholic Church, with a quota for nearly one-third of all available chaplain positions, consistently fell short of its mark, reflecting the chronic shortage of Catholic priests in the United States generally and the consequent reluctance of bishops to release priests for chaplain service even when they desired to do so, rather than priests' unwillingness to serve in the chaplaincy. In 1965, the Roman Catholic Church had filled only 308 of a total of 450 available Army chaplain positions, just 68.4 percent of its quota. The chief of chaplains regularly corresponded with Cardinal Francis Spellman, the bishop of the Military Ordinate, and other Roman Catholic archbishops to encourage the appointment of more Roman Catholic chaplains to Regular Army, Reserve, and National Guard posts.

Other denominations also experienced severe chaplain shortages, including the National Baptist Convention, which filled just 12 of 96 appointments, the Eastern Orthodox Church (2 of 26 appointments), the

Church of Jesus Christ of Latter-day Saints (4 of 20 appointments), and African Methodist Episcopal Zion (2 of 10 appointments). Especially notable here is the underrepresentation of minority churches, particularly historically black churches. On the other hand, several denominations, including all seven of the traditionally identified "mainline" denominations, which tended toward moderate politics and theologies, contributed more than their quota of chaplains.[21] Among more politically and theologically conservative denominations, the Lutheran Church–Missouri Synod and two evangelical bodies, the National Association of Evangelicals and the Southern Baptist Convention were also overrepresented. In all, these denominations filled nearly 159 percent of their collective quotas. Throughout the war, obtaining a chaplain's commission remained easier in the underrepresented denominations, but most qualified men eventually gained appointment as chaplains in the overrepresented ones as well, even if it took several rounds of applications.

Also important, especially to the experience of military men in Vietnam, were the very small denominations—those with quotas of fewer than five chaplains—that consistently supplied more than their allotment. Recognizing the disparities in the number of chaplains the various denominations were supplying, the OCCH reported, "A considerable number of the numerically smaller denominations have shown a great willingness to make their clergymen available for the Army chaplaincy, while some of the larger denominations have not always shown themselves capable of doing so." As the chaplaincy expanded, the services relied on smaller denominations—often those more theologically and politically conservative—to fill vacant chaplain commissions. The goal for the OCCH's office was to maintain the quotas of "small and miscellaneous denominations at current strength as far as this is possible without depriving another denomination that it is able to fill with suitable candidates."[22]

Ultimately, shortages in some categories would come to bear on service members in Vietnam, some of whom likely never saw a minister of their own denomination or faith group during their tour. The difficulties of filling chaplain vacancies according to the quota system and the assessment that having any chaplain available, regardless of denomination, was better than having none at all guided some postwar reforms. The pattern of demographic overrepresentation and denominational imbalance grew over the course of the war and was plainly evident by 1975, but the seeds of the problem were present early on.

Throughout 1965 and 1966, the same patterns continued. The increased demand placed pressure on the OCCH and denominational endorsing agencies to quickly identify and process potential qualified applicants. In September 1965, the OCCH issued new denominational quotas based on the overall membership numbers reported in the most recent *Yearbook of American Churches* and aimed to provide one chaplain for every 66,165 church members. The new quotas also took into account a particular denomination's history of supplying adequate numbers of qualified chaplains. In addition to appealing to the denominational endorsing agencies, the chief of chaplains also appealed directly to divinity schools and seminaries, "soliciting their cooperation in recruiting seminarians."[23] Even with these appeals and calling up Reserve personnel, however, the chaplain branch faced severe shortages.

At the other end of the spectrum, the OCCH also worked with a number of willing but technically ineligible chaplains who volunteered for service. During this period of rapid buildup, clergymen from around the world wrote to the OCCH to request a commission. However, many of these volunteers had to be rejected because of "age, lack of sufficient formal education, or past history in the military service." Another group consisted of former chaplains "who had twice failed to be selected for promotion to the next higher commissioned grade" or who were "nationals of foreign countries, and members of the retired reserve." When necessary, the chaplain branch sometimes waived the age requirement: for some, this qualification could be dismissed based on previous service as a commissioned officer in the military, and others waived their right to retirement eligibility in order to gain a commission. Later, in 1966, this policy was formalized so that commissions would be granted to certain denominations' volunteer candidates between the ages of forty and forty-five for five-year tours "without renewals and without retirement benefits."[24] In isolated cases, generally for Roman Catholic chaplains, the OCCH also waived weight and disability requirements.[25] In the end, by maintaining fairly strict, if looser requirements (by peacetime standards), the chaplain branch assured it could achieve its mission of providing professional, ecumenical, and well-qualified religious support to military personnel.

In addition to the influx of interested but technically unqualified personnel, the OCCH had to deal with changing expectations and procedures for chaplain assignment. In the months immediately following American troop commitment to Vietnam, according to the chief of chaplains, "so many chaplains continued to volunteer for service in Vietnam that this Office disapproved some volunteer applications on the ground that a sufficient number of more suitable chaplains were available."[26] The OCCH also announced that chaplains serving in long-tour areas should be prepared for possible transfer to Vietnam. The abundance of volunteers for Vietnam assignment suggests that early in the conflict, Vietnam was a respectable, even desirable, assignment that would appear favorably before promotion and review boards. As the war went on, many chaplains viewed assignment to Vietnam as inevitable, so they volunteered in order to exert as much control over the situation as possible.[27]

To complicate the quota system, the Army's rapid growth obligated the OCCH to constantly revise its working quotas to reflect the need for chaplains and to account for denominational history and reliability in providing qualified chaplains. Throughout the period of escalation and rapid chaplain procurement, old problems remained—Roman Catholic and Jewish chaplains were in critically short supply, as were chaplains from traditionally black denominations, while (white) Baptists, (white) Methodists, and the Disciples of Christ consistently supplied more than their working quotas required. Ultimately, filling vacant chaplain positions took precedence over a chaplain's denomination. As a result of policy, circumstance, and historical precedent, great disparities in number existed between the chaplain population, authorized chaplain quotas, a denomination's membership in the United States, and a denomination's representation in the armed services.[28]

Though reliable data to track trends in chaplains' denominational affiliation or theological orientation is not available, long-term trends within in chaplain demographics suggest that by the end of the war, as more liberal religious communities balked at sending chaplains to a war they did not support, the number of conservative religious adherents in the Chaplain Corps increased considerably. For example, some national Jewish endorsing agencies and seminary boards scrutinized their internal practices for assigning military chaplains and selective conscientious objection as opposition to the war mounted.[29] In its 1969 *Historical Review*, the OCCH reported that only small, conservative denominations had grown numerically.[30] And, according to historian Anne Loveland, in 1963, active duty Assemblies of God chaplains numbered 25, while by 1970, they numbered 42. In 1965, there were 489 Southern Baptist Convention chaplains in the armed forces, and by 1978, there were 735, a 44 percent increase.[31] The size of the Chaplain Corps did not grow at the same rate.

The denominational affiliation of chaplains who actually served in Vietnam is more elusive. Concrete numbers are difficult to compile because there was no standard system for noting a chaplain's denomination on the duty roster and the duty rosters are incomplete for the period under discussion.[32] The greatest difficulty, however, is in determining the theological orientation of chaplains belonging to the largest denominations. While the Baptist, Methodist, and Presbyterian denominations had all been identified as part of the Protestant "mainline" or "mainstream" in the United States, they also have significant evangelical roots, and by the Vietnam War, this designation as "mainline" meant little in terms of a common theological outlook. Especially given the frequent fracturing of these denominations into smaller and smaller groups, it is nearly impossible to argue with any certainty that a chaplain espoused a certain worldview based on the broadest designation of his religious affiliation. Occasionally, a duty roster would list a chaplain as "Southern Baptist" or "Cumberland Presbyterian," or the like, and in these cases, it is possible to draw conclusions about a theological orientation, but categorizing a "Baptist" or "Methodist" chaplain as either theologically liberal, moderate, or conservative is impossible without making a number of biased assumptions.

For most of the war, MACV and USARV chaplains operated under a system of area coverage, designed to ensure that they visited and ministered to most, if not all, American troops in Vietnam, particularly within a brigade AO. Chaplains were assigned to units upon arrival in Vietnam, and though they were not formally attached to units below the brigade level, they often informally claimed a smaller unit as their own by splitting primary responsibilities for coverage among all of the brigade's chaplains. In addition to performing their duties within their service and unit, as time allowed, they also ministered to other units and even other services. Especially early and late in the war, when small units were scattered across the country, chaplains had to travel frequently to visit units, and when they did, most visited all the units in their area.

Earl Kettler, a field chaplain, recalled that in early 1964, when there were about ten chaplains in Vietnam, his AO covered nearly a fifth of Vietnam, from Bien Hoa to Di Linh. He estimated there were just 250 Americans in his area, which was well below the required troop-to-chaplain ratio, but visiting them in such spread out locations required most of a month.[33] When chaplains did form close relationships with men in their units, they often felt responsible for visiting and ministering to those men, regardless of a unit's location in or out of the chaplain's technical zone. Samuel

Hopkins likened himself to his "circuit riding forefathers who evangelized the . . . American frontier" as he visited his unit in forty-two different locations around the corps area. He recalled that it took six weeks or more to visit them all. When he visited, he filled several roles. In the field, chaplains conducted worship services and devotions and provided personal counseling. In addition to fulfilling these ministerial duties, they may have brought the latest gossip or comfort items from the rear or home.[34]

The fact that chaplains could not be formally assigned to battalions, platoons, or company-sized units made it easier for them to minister to far-flung units. Chaplains who later attended the Army War College explained that in Vietnam, the "chaplain did not work directly for the battalion commander, was not part of the unit, and only showed up in the unit area to conduct services, perform counseling or conduct classes. The battalion commander did not 'own' the chaplain," and as a result the relationship between commander and chaplain remained undefined. They concluded that "in many cases, commanders and chaplains did not communicate as commander to staff officer."[35] But while the area coverage policy effectively addressed the problem of reaching units spread out over a large geographical area—it created others: chaplains below the brigade level often felt like outsiders within the staff structure, and commanders were occasionally reluctant to allow their chaplains to operate outside of their brigade's AO.

Although area coverage, in theory, provided for regular, if infrequent, chaplain visits to all units in Vietnam, some units appeared to be chronically undercovered. For example, commentary and analysis of the My Lai incident frequently cite the paucity of chaplain presence as a possible underlying cause for the American atrocity. Martin Gershen, the author of *Destroy or Die: The True Story of Mylai*, maintained that Charlie Company, the perpetrators of the massacre, had never seen a chaplain until the day before the incident.[36] Chaplain Harry Kissinger, who served with the 1st Battalion, 20th Infantry Division, 11th Brigade, of which Charlie Company was a part, interpreted the situation differently. In an oral history interview, he recalled that Task Force Barker was stationed north of his technical zone of area coverage, so his commander discouraged him from visiting, even occasionally. He exclaimed, "I'm sure he [Gershen] doesn't understand about the area coverage concept. . . . And I was following my orders from the brigade chaplain." Kissinger's actual zone of coverage was perhaps sixty miles south of Quang Ngai (the province in which Son My hamlet was located). Kissinger claimed that Task Force Barker was the only unit from the 1st of the 20th to be stationed that far north.[37] Though Kissinger's statements did little to address the problem of *infrequent* chaplain coverage, they illustrated the problem of chaplains not having consistent and predictable relationships with unit commanders.

The scarcity of chaplains also presented problems for faith groups with small quotas and small numbers of personnel. Because of their small numbers, area coverage was particularly important for Jewish chaplains, as they coordinated and provided for all Jewish military personnel and civilians in Vietnam. Jewish service members frequently expressed displeasure, to both the chiefs of chaplains and their congressional representatives about the scarcity of Jewish chaplains in Vietnam; until late 1968, only three Jewish chaplains, two Army and one Air Force, covered the entire country.[38] In terms of the quota system, Jewish chaplains were numerically over-represented, but the diffuse locations of American units in Vietnam made chaplain coverage for Jewish soldiers (and others of minority religious groups) difficult. Given these constraints, the chaplain branches worked to maximize their utility. Jewish chaplains were usually posted in central locations, such as Saigon, Tan Son Nhut, or Long Binh. They covered even larger geographical areas than their Protestant or Catholic counterparts and relied more heavily on lay leadership to provide religious support for personnel in the field. For example, Maj. Albert Hornblass, a surgeon, took on the lay leadership responsibilities around Pleiku in 1969 and 1970, holding services and arranging transportation to major military installations for High Holy Day services for more than ninety Jewish personnel.[39]

Rather than conducting many field services, Jewish chaplains concentrated on organizing services for the High Holy Days (Rosh Hashana and Yom Kippur) and other important religious observances (for example, Passover, Sukkoth, Chanukah, and Purim) in central locations and then encouraging and arranging for soldiers to attend. The limited coverage for Jewish service members and civilians in Vietnam was evident early on. In September 1965, the plea for more "religious aids" had made its way stateside, as Jewish service members requested prayer books and religious education materials from the Jewish Welfare Board.[40] In February 1970, to further assist Jewish and Christian chaplains in serving Jewish military personnel and civilians, the Commission on Jewish Chaplains created a set of "procedure guides" or suggestion sheets to outline some of the activities expected of Jewish chaplains and to educate Christian chaplains on how they could help. Their materials included pamphlets titled "Organizing Groups to Support the Chapel Program," "Maintaining a Roster of

Jewish Personnel," "Chapel Bulletins," "Kosher Food Supplies," "The Oneg Shabbat," "Passover Observances," "Counseling," "Conversions," "Torah Convocations," "Adventure with Jewish Books," "Field Visiting Programs," and "Overseas Tours of Duty."[41] These titles suggest that lay leaders were, in fact, assuming many of the duties that would typically be the purview of chaplains and were responsible for an extensive religious program for Jewish personnel. As troop levels declined, the Jewish chaplain's dilemma became more acute. Albert Dimont, a chaplain in 1972, recalled that his area of coverage was so large that he was able to visit only the major installations, and each only once a month.[42]

The area coverage policy remained chaplain doctrine throughout the Vietnam War. By the time of major troop withdrawals, the decline in the number of chaplains decreased the level of religious support available to troops. Although the Chaplain Corps remained at or above its authorized strength, the number of small detachments across the country meant that chaplain coverage was infrequent, and it was unlikely that a soldier would ever see or speak with a chaplain of his own denomination. In order to cover the widest area possible, and to keep personnel safe, chaplains were heavily consolidated in the Saigon–Tan Son Nhut–Long Binh area. They could travel to detached units only as transportation and free time allowed. In response to the reduced level of religious support, the MACV staff chaplain office began sponsoring other kinds of religious support that did not always require a chaplain to be present, for example, *Religion in the News*, a radio show offering daily devotionals, Component Meetings, training conferences, newsletters, and luncheons. At headquarters and other major installations, the MACV office used the current character guidance curriculum, titled "Human Self-Development," as the subject for monthly briefings and required Continental Army Command (CONARC) training.[43]

As drawdown commenced, the number of chaplains decreased from 400 chaplains to 150 in a short amount of time, meaning that some chaplains had to be transferred several times because their original units would leave Vietnam for the United States. USARV supervisory chaplain Leonard Stegman recalled that as coverage decreased, morale problems for chaplains increased. Already, chaplains faced serious challenges in bonding with military units, separated as they were from most of "their" men—so the high rate of turnover during the drawdown only exacerbated the problem. He also recalled running out of "volunteer" chaplains, and by the end of the war, many chaplains had been returned involuntarily to active duty and Vietnam. Especially as American public dissent grew louder and more impatient, chaplains naturally began responding to the difficult questions of faith and war. Stegman was a supervisory chaplain, and would thus counsel other chaplains as they arrived in Vietnam. He recalled that he "made it very clear that whenever [chaplains] came to Vietnam they had to close their minds to that [doubt and protest] because they were not here because of individual beliefs or convictions. They were here because of the men. If they could not serve under those conditions, I did not want them, and I made that clear in the Chief's office also."[44]

Though the Navy assigned its chaplains differently from the Army and Air Force in Vietnam, it also practiced a form of area coverage with many of its chaplains. Most naval chaplains who served on shore worked within the MACV chaplain system; this group comprised about 44 percent of naval billets in Vietnam, while the other 56 percent of chaplains were ship-based, percentages that reversed the usual apportionment of ship and shore chaplains. The ship-based chaplains who were assigned to the Military Sea Transport Service (MSTS) ministered to military personnel in all of the armed forces. On the long sea passage to Vietnam, these chaplains established counseling programs and formal character guidance and religious education curriculums.[45] Nearly 20 percent of naval chaplains in Vietnam served on aircraft carriers. Chaplains with the fleet could be responsible for covering as many as forty or fifty ships in the battle group. One of their primary functions, however, was conducting memorial services for pilots and servicemen killed in action.[46]

Other ship-based naval chaplains had less formal assignments that required them to cover between fifteen and twenty ships but that also allowed for short-term assignments to naval groups with pressing need. One of these "circuit riders," John Senieur, recalled that he and others "were frequently called upon to do additional duty where chaplains were not available or where tragedy had left a void." Senieur then went through a laundry list of his various Vietnam assignments: "I spent six weeks with the swiftboats and the Coast Guard cutters along the southern coast of Vietnam. I spent almost eight weeks in the USS *Repose* (AH-16) when the Catholic chaplain took ill, I was assigned to the USS *Oriskany* (CVA-34) following the tragic fires, I was in a battle with the *Carronade* and spent some time in destroyers during coastal bombardments."[47] These chaplains, dispatched in times of need, rarely would have had the time or sustained contact with specific units required to form lasting personal relationships, but their ministry highlighted the importance that commanders and chaplain leaders placed on a chaplain's presence in the face of danger or tragedy.

One facet of chaplain service that was markedly different from the world of civilian clergy was the *expectation* of ecumenical cooperation and interfaith work. Though ecumenism experienced a groundswell of support among liberal religious communities in the United States, it was never as programmatic and culturally entrenched as it was in the chaplaincy.[48] Because they served military personnel of many faiths and those with no religious affiliation, chaplains placed a high value on the ecumenical nature of their work and ministry. This focus was especially strong after World War II, as Americans chose to emphasize their common religious beliefs rather than their theological, doctrinal, or ritual differences.

Whereas the ecumenical movement in the United States had generally liberal political, organizational, and theological underpinnings, the ecumenical nature of chaplains' work in Vietnam was simply pragmatic. Catholic chaplains said Mass for units assigned to Protestant chaplains' care; Protestant chaplains helped locate Vietnamese priests to say Mass; and Evangelicals performed general Protestant services so that Mormon chaplains might conduct denominationally specific ones. In one case, Catholic chaplains and a Hebrew-speaking Christian helped conduct a Seder meal for Jewish men aboard the USS *Midway*.[49] "Cooperation without compromise," a Chaplain Corps motto, emphasized the chaplain's position in the middle of various faith groups and denominations.

As the diversity within American religious groups expanded, so too did the Chaplain Corps' understanding of ecumenism. From the chaplaincy's earliest inception in the late eighteenth century, American chaplains had come from an increasing variety of denominational and faith backgrounds. Early legislation about chaplains mandated they be ordained Christian ministers, but Abraham Lincoln successfully lobbied for that distinction to be removed in 1862, requiring instead that they be ordained clergy of a "religious denomination."[50] Still, in the nineteenth century, the Army Chaplain Corps was dominated by Episcopalians, who filled between 40 and 60 percent of chaplain posts, even though the "combined total of Episcopalians, Unitarians, Presbyterians, and Congregationalists amounted to only 14 percent of America's population."[51] During World War II, the military recognized Roman Catholic priests, Jewish rabbis, and ministers of six major Protestant denominational families as chaplains. By 1964, the Army recognized fifty-four denominations and faith groups eligible to supply chaplains to the armed services, and the number of qualified denominations and endorsing agencies grew throughout the 1960s and 1970s. By the end of the Vietnam War, the military recognized over 100 religious denominations and faith groups as chaplain endorsers, and by the early 1990s, that number had grown to over 150.[52]

In policy terms, the offices of the chief of chaplains and other military leaders had a stake in promoting ecumenism, equality, and respect for the growing diversity of chaplains and military personnel. Army Regulation 210-115, for example, prohibited "the engraving or permanent installation inside or outside of chapels, or the display on chapel grounds, of religious symbols and statues," including crosses, crucifixes, or Stars of David. In the United States, where chapel construction was ongoing and generally well-regulated, this posed few problems. In Vietnam, however, military chapels had a more ad-hoc feel. Engineer companies, with the assistance of other soldiers and officers, erected chapels quickly and with whatever materials were available, either locally or through channels; regulations rarely seemed to come into play. As a result, the Christian majority thought little of placing a cross on the steeple of a newly constructed chapel. When, in 1968, one such chapel was photographed, the director of field operations of the National Jewish Welfare Board (NJWB) contacted the Army chief of chaplains. The staff chaplain at USARV headquarters investigated, and the chaplains there solved the problem with a minimum of conflict. The various interactions demonstrated the chaplains' principle of "cooperation without compromise."[53]

One way that the chaplaincy formalized ecumenism as policy was by mandating that chaplains "be addressed as 'Chaplain'" and that they "identify themselves by this title in all official communications pertaining to their status as military officers or relating to their performance of duty as staff officers." The title obscured differences in faith group, denomination, and rank and highlighted the chaplains' religious and staff officer responsibilities. In more informal settings (both personal and pastoral), chaplains could use ecclesiastical or academic titles as appropriate.[54] In a study of the constitutionality of the Chaplain Corps, military lawyers explained that "the term 'chaplain' is here used to describe those clergy who engage in specialized military ministries which often take them outside and beyond their own particular denominational faith groups."[55]

Even as ecumenism remained a primary goal of the Chaplain Corps, some situations presented definite organizational and personal challenges to the model. Many Protestant groups were unhappy with the fact that Mormon chaplains were assigned as general Protestant chaplains because a good number of Protestant churches did not consider the Church of Jesus Christ of Latter-day Saints (LDS Church or Mormon Church) to be Christian.

Given the ecumenical tenor of religious conversation in the 1960s, how-ever, critics usually couched their objections in terms of qualifications and education. In 1962, President Johnson ordered the chiefs of chaplains to waive the requisite educational requirements for Mormons and accept "a limited number" of Mormon clergy as chaplains, in part because the LDS Church did not have officially ordained clergy or require seminary edu-cation for would-be chaplains.[56] The assignment of Mormon chaplains caused significant rifts within the Chaplain Corps and among civilian sup-porters of the chaplaincy. Critics accused the Department of Defense of unnecessarily watering down requirements to the detriment of the chap-laincy. The Christian Century, which by the 1960s was a key public voice for mainline Protestant progressivism, protested that "whatever the caliber and quality of the military chaplaincy may now be, a recent presidential order threatens to lower them."[57] The unsigned editorial insinuated that Mormon chaplains, by receiving a waiver, would not be held to the same educational standards as other denominations that did not require semi-nary training for clergy, such as the Christian Science Church. The General Commission on Chaplains and Armed Forces Personnel took up the issue in a January 1967 meeting. It concluded that the Department of Defense had not offered a "satisfactory" response to the commission's complaints and had done nothing to quell rumors that the commission and the National Association of Evangelicals (another major endorsing body) might refuse to endorse chaplains unless they were satisfied with the solution.[58]

In the field, Mormon chaplains had to negotiate the type of ministry that was possible given strict constraints—officially on the minister and unoffi-cially on Christians of many other denominations. Claude Newby, an LDS chaplain who served two tours in Vietnam, wrote two long and detailed memoirs about his experience as a chaplain. His memoirs illuminate some of the difficulties that Mormon chaplains faced, even as they present New-by's responses to these difficulties in a near universally flattering light. According to Newby, the greatest challenge was for LDS chaplains to pro-vide for the religious needs of all men in a given unit because they usually could not provide such services themselves; the corollary challenge was to provide acceptable chaplain coverage to Mormon soldiers, who would be spread throughout the country. Division chaplains also recognized that Newby, and other LDS chaplains, would be assets above the brigade level if they were used to provide denominationally- specific services to other LDS personnel.[59] When, for example, the Church of Jesus Christ of Latter-day Saints organized a religious retreat for all LDS personnel in Vietnam,

Newby reports that it fell on him to coordinate transportation and leave for all the Mormon soldiers in the division AO.[60] This sort of coordination and tasking outside of the battalion level would have been common for chaplains of minority religious denominations.

This level of negotiation and interdenominational cooperation, especially between Mormons and other Protestants, did not take place without tension. Newby reported that when he was stationed at Fort Bragg between tours of duty in Vietnam a chaplain named "Chaplain Blanke" (an alias in Newby's memoir) was particularly hostile toward him. According to Newby, Blanke was skeptical of Mormon chaplains' credentials and abilities after a bad experience with Newby's LDS predecessor. Blanke said it was "nothing personal" but he couldn't "understand how your church has the audacity to place you men in the chaplaincy to compete with professional clergy."[61] Later, Newby accused Blanke of filing a report of grievances in order to get Newby removed from his post for cause.[62] Newby does not record the outcome of this conflict (though he was selected for promotion), and we do not know Blanke's version of events, but such an interaction seems to represent the general sentiments of Protestant denominations toward Mormons in the 1960s.

In Newby's second tour of duty, he faced a situation where his responsibility to minister to all troops was apparently in conflict with his duty to minister specifically to Mormon soldiers. When Newby's weekly report occasionally showed more LDS services than general Protestant ones, chaplains at the division level worried. Newby explained that this was because "another chaplain came into my battalion and provided communion services, while I went about the division AO conducting sacrament services for as many LDS troopers as I could reach." Newby's division chaplain was considering moving him out of the division and into a headquarters slot, so he could minister to LDS personnel over a wider area and would have more Protestant chaplains with whom to coordinate. Newby, however, protested. He explained that "LDS members were well organized and empowered to care for one another" but also that he took his orders to provide spiritual support to men of all faiths seriously, and that his church required no less of him. Eventually, the division chaplain relented, and Newby remained with his battalion.[63] Mormon chaplains especially had to walk a fine line between ecumenism and specific denominational support, and they relied on other chaplains and official channels to facilitate the balancing act.

Within the military, chaplains answered to two primary authorities— the chief of chaplains for their respective services and their commanding

TABLE 2.I.

USARV Religious Activities Reports (Consolidated):
Services and Attendance

	Protestant Services	Protestant Attendance	Roman Catholic Services	Roman Catholic Attendance
July–Sept. 1968	17,605	464,111	12,777	344,363
Oct.–Dec. 1968	17,531	483,800	14,164	365,928
Jan.–Mar. 1969	18,351	460,530	14,162	351,234
Apr.–June 1969	21,836	504,232	15,333	392,612
Oct.–Dec. 1969	20,786	473,379	14,820	319,233
Jan.–Mar. 1970	18,694	425,514	13,724	290,622
Apr.–June 1970	17,131	395,256	12,163	249,000
July–Sept. 1970	14,859	316,890	12,027	201,661

SOURCE: Religious Activities Reports, RG 472, Records of the United States Army Vietnam, HQ USARV, Chaplain Section, Religious Plans, Training, and Operations Div., Box 1, "USARV Religious Activities Reports (Consolidated)," National Archives of the United States, Archives II, College Park, Md.
NOTE: No data available for July–September 1969.

officers. Both issued policy directives and professional guidelines designed to help chaplains minister effectively. As the Chaplain Corps placed itself on a wartime footing, some of these policy directives were either onerous or irrelevant. For example, in January 1964, the secretary of the army, via the adjutant general's office, issued a new set of "Professional Guidelines for Chaplains." The new directives recognized that in an Army at war, "the field is the normal environment for Army worship both in training and in combat." Chaplains, regardless of their assignment, were to prepare soldiers for war. The secretary of the army directed all chaplains serving troops to conduct a "minimum of one Sunday/Sabbath service and one weekday service" and to spend at least 50 percent of their duty time with troops. The OCCH directives also required the chaplain to avail himself for personal or pastoral counseling in his office or "other suitable place" at least one evening a week. Of course, this requirement would have been easy in a stateside post, where offices and "suitable places" abounded and where soldiers had easy access to such spaces. In Vietnam, however, suitable places were few and far between—chaplains often shared a tent with another officer, or their tents doubled as offices, so privacy and confidentiality were concerns, and not all soldiers would be available for a chaplain visit on a designated evening, especially if they were rotating in the field.[64]

Jewish Services	Jewish Attendance	Total Chaplains	Total Services	Total Attendance
396	9,455	484	30,778	817,929
401	9,452	450	32,096	859,180
605	11,042	446	33,118	822,806
443	10,278	476	37,612	907,122
435	5,048	452	36,041	797,660
523	6,493	416	32,941	736,893
552	8,827	369	29,846	653,083
499	5,899	417	27,385	524,450

Even so, most chaplains serving in Vietnam exceeded these mandated standards, especially regarding holding worship services. USARV records indicate that between July 1968 and September 1970 chaplains in Vietnam conducted, on average, between 4.89 and 6.22 services per week, the lowest average from July to September 1968 and the highest from April to June 1970. In the same period, chaplains conducted a significant number of pastoral visits: an average of 64.85 visits per week between January and March 1969 and an average of 39.72 visits per week between July and September 1970. Community relations activities slowed in 1970, down from about one every two weeks in 1968–69 to one every three weeks.[65]

Records for Air Force chaplains in Vietnam are more difficult to find, though individual reports suggest a similar commitment, with somewhat fewer services due to the consolidation of Air Force personnel at big bases rather than isolated outposts. Richard Miller, who was stationed at Da Nang Air Base in Vietnam, reported that between July and September 1967, his daily schedule could be broken down thus: visitation (40 percent), counseling and instruction (25 percent), chapel groups (10 percent), administration (10 percent), study and preparation (10 percent), and worship and sacramental rites (5 percent). Other chaplains reported the importance of making themselves available to airmen well after the duty day was over

TABLE 2.2.

USARV Religious Activities Reports (Consolidated):
Sacraments and Pastoral Care

	Pastoral visits	Sacraments	Communion	Community Relations	Offering Received
July–Sept. 1968	336,516	43,743	26,110	2,770	$175,419.92
Oct.–Dec. 1968	322,319	43,499	24,210	3,455	162,595.33
Jan.–Mar. 1969	375,984	51,214	29,394	3,380	none received
Apr.–June 1969	350,108	46,889	26,401	3,187	none received
Oct.–Dec. 1969	334,424	393,333	23,189	3,133	no data
Jan.–Mar. 1970	253,364	36,039	18,553	2,387	87,214.35
Apr.–June 1970	250,432	35,659	21,343	1,808	120,129.46
July–Sept. 1970	215,300	28,619	17,353	1,863	101,458.62

SOURCE: See Table 2.1.

NOTE: No data available for July–September 1969. No explanation is given for the anomalous value for sacraments between October and December 1969 or the lack of offering funds received between January and June 1969.

and into the early hours of the morning.[66] Throughout the war, chaplains maintained that their presence with the troops was the most important aspect of their mission.

Although records are incomplete, it is apparent that these general patterns continued even as American units began to stand down. For example, in fiscal year 1972, the chaplains of XXIV Corps provided a detailed accounting of their activities to the commanding general who then relayed the information to Creighton Abrams, the commanding general of USARV. In the first quarter of the year, the seven chaplains assigned to the corps (though there were never more than two at any one time) reported conducting 869 services, with a total attendance of more than 8,700, for an average of more than eleven services per chaplain per week. These numbers decreased over the course of the year, as both chaplains and other personnel rotated home. Even still, by the end of the year, each chaplain was conducting nearly seven services each week and continued to provide a substantial number of sacramental celebrations—mostly Confession and Communion—to American military personnel.[67]

Even though space and privacy and accessibility was a concern, Chaplains also managed to conduct pastoral visits regularly (see Table 2.2). Chaplain Berge Hoogasian, an Air Force chaplain stationed at Tuy Hoa Air Base, reported on the topics of some of his counseling sessions, most of which revolved around personal and social issues, many of which were not about the Vietnam War directly. Of the 297 sessions he held between April and June 1968, almost half were about "premarital," "marital," or "family" issues (48 percent), followed by "religious" (23 percent), "humanitarian assignments" (10 percent), "moral" (9 percent), "disciplinary" (4 percent), and "alcoholism" and "financial" issues (3 percent each). Although systematic records do not exist, other Air Force chaplains and Army chaplains reported counseling soldiers on similar issues.[68] This reporting also suggests that chaplains counseled service members on many of the same issues that they would have faced in stateside posts.

Commanders and the chiefs of chaplains recognized the unique spiritual, mental, and physical pressures on chaplains and as such authorized chaplains, both in the field and in garrison, to take one half-day per month for "spiritual exercises such as retreats and days of recollection" with an additional retreat period of up to ten days each year. This remained policy throughout the war, and chaplains in Vietnam sometimes attended religious retreats for chaplains of their faith group or even their specific denomination. The unpredictability of combat occasionally meant that scheduled retreats were cancelled or relocated, which often complicated chaplains' abilities to attend them.[69] Frequently, chaplains assigned to combat units—ostensibly the ones who might benefit most from such leave—were unable to get away for even short periods of time.[70] In 1971, a Religious Retreat Center opened at Cam Ranh Bay, the first of its kind in a combat area, demonstrating the United States' significant commitment to the religious and spiritual well-being of men in combat, chaplains and laypersons alike. The center housed an extensive library of more than 20,000 volumes of religious and spiritual books and print materials and provided meeting and living space for retreat attendees. Chaplains could also use the facility on an individual basis for personal days of recollection or longer periods of spiritual retreat, as allowed by military regulations.[71]

The chiefs of chaplains, through their respective departments, also issued directives intended to define the chaplain's role as both staff officer and clergyman. They recognized that chaplains needed to maintain their religious identities, but their function as staff officers had to be considered as well. In order to balance these two roles, chaplains were permitted to wear "appropriate vestments to conduct religious services," but they were also reminded that "civilian suits, etc. are not vestments" and that all chaplains "should wear their appropriate uniform going to and from the place of religious services."[72] These guidelines suggest the chaplain's identity, as expressed through his appearance, was at least as important as the official duty he was performing.

Pastoral and Military Relationships

Chaplains, as staff officers responsible to a commanding officer, often dealt more generally with troop morale and effectiveness. Most chaplains argued that their status as officers gave them access to commanders and officers, and their status as clergy kept them accessible to enlisted personnel. Others believed that a chaplain's advice—especially if it came from a chaplain who had previously served in the military or who demonstrated traditional military virtues—may have held special moral weight. Chaplains performed a variety of duties, including giving character guidance lectures and counseling conscientious objectors, and also performed several unofficial functions as well.

One of the roles that many chaplains found themselves in was that of mediator between enlisted personnel and their commanding officers. In a speech to history students at Regents University in Denver, Colorado, James McClements gave an extended example of this role. McClements served as an infantryman before becoming a chaplain, and he understood that the "chaplain's job was to be with his men in combat—the Private in the trench as well as the Commander in the lead."[73] He resolved to be a spiritual and moral adviser to both his enlisted personnel and his officers. With soldiers, he often cast his concern in a paternal or spiritual terms. He recalled encountering one soldier who "looked awfully tired when I stood by him in the chow line. I asked him what was happening. He said he was just doing his duty. Upon my prying, he told me he [had been] assigned to night guard duty every night for the [previous] two weeks." McClements then switched modes and approached the private's commander, who told him that the soldier was a "goof-off" and a "cry-baby," at which point McClements returned to the soldier.

The soldier supplied additional information—namely that he had a vision problem that prevented him from seeing well in the dark, but there was nothing in his medical records. The soldier reported that he had tried to alert his commander of the issue but encountered serious resistance. McClements kept talking and discovered that this soldier had worked as a medic on an emergency response team at home and wished to eventually become a doctor. The chaplain then went to the squadron surgeon to discuss the possibility of getting the private transferred to the medics, who were always in high demand. When McClements returned to the commander to offer this solution, he was careful to frame his argument for transferring the soldier in terms of military effectiveness. McClements insinuated that if the commander did not approve a transfer, he could be found guilty of negligence if the soldier were to fail during guard duty and an investigation were to prove that the soldier had, in fact, reported his condition. The commander quickly assented to the transfer. Later, McClements reported, the soldier earned the Distinguished Service Cross, the Army's second highest medal for valor in combat, for pulling a soldier from a burning vehicle.[74] Verification of the story is, of course, difficult, but it is at least a plausible series of interactions, if likely somewhat exaggerated to enhance the chaplain's image and his message. Here, the chaplain's military experience, his view of the soldier's and the commander's perspective, his understanding of military channels, and his advisory function enabled him to act as an effective intermediary for an unhappy soldier and commander.

Chaplains' flexible schedules and ability to travel away from a command post enabled them to observed firsthand and report about a unit's personnel after an engagement. James Johnson recalled that after any unit suffered casualties, he took the first available opportunity to visit evacuation and surgical hospitals to see the men. He acted not only as a chaplain—offering comfort and spiritual counsel to wounded soldiers whom he knew—but also as the commander's eyes and ears, gathering information about the severity of soldiers' wounds and the prospects of their return to duty. Upon his return to headquarters, Johnson would brief the commander about the physical and mental status of each soldier who had been wounded.[75] Though Johnson's official role did not require him to act as a liaison between wounded soldiers and his commander, his being chaplain gave him access to both groups that other officers or enlisted personnel might not have enjoyed.

At its most effective, the chaplain's relationship with a commander was one of mutual respect and support, and effectiveness was enhanced if the commander's staff shared a common sense of mission within and for the unit. One chaplain, who wished to remain anonymous, wrote in his survey response regarding the influence of his first commander: "I was blessed— my commander held chaplains in high esteem—every one [sic] knew it— not because he preached by word but by action—consequently we were very much a part of the team—had all the support one could expect."[76]

Generally, as long as provisions for chaplains' safety were in place, officers appreciated their presence, in their units believing that it increased troop morale and occasionally brought luck in battle.

But not all commanders felt this way about their chaplains. Commanders could frustrate a chaplain's efforts by impeding or limiting his ability to visit troops, conduct services, or perform other religious tasks. Conflicts between a chaplain and his commanding officer over moral issues, performance evaluations, the nature of religious services, or expectations about a chaplain's primary duty played out in a variety of ways. In some cases, a contentious relationship resulted in a neutral to negative Officer Efficiency Report for a chaplain. But more often, a commander simply complicated the chaplain's day-to-day routines and limited the chaplains' roles within the unit. In cases like these, chaplains identified themselves as right and perhaps even righteous, and thus supported by a "higher" authority.

In their personal accounts of the war, chaplains had a vested interest in presenting themselves as competent and capable ministers and mediators. They reported being nearly always successful in convincing their commanders of the positive effects of their presence and persuading nonbelievers to embrace faith—a common trope in spiritual autobiography. In one particular version, Claude Newby, the LDS chaplain who reported significant conflict with other Protestant chaplains and the division chaplain, also described the tension between him and one of his first combat commanders. According to Newby, the captain disliked the chaplain's presence (though it is unclear whether the commander disliked all chaplains or Newby in particular) and went out of his way to hamper his activities, for example, giving Newby false flight schedules and otherwise making his life difficult. In a brief confrontation, the commander told Newby, "I've been an atheist all my life. As far as I am concerned, you are a bad influence on the troops, and I am duty-bound to protect them from you. I'll do everything I can to make you miss flights and otherwise hamper your activities." Newby responded with a threat of his own: that if the officer gave him any more trouble, he and Newby would "be standing before the battalion commander."[77] But then, in a remarkable turn of events, Newby reports that after a communication breakdown between three platoons where the commander's unit could have suffered heavy friendly-fire casualties, the captain declared his atheism shaken, and thereafter requested that chaplains accompany his men as often as possible.[78] Even if the interactions between Newby and this officer did not occur as Newby reported, and it seems highly implausible, his construction of the events emphasized the value he placed on his relationships with military commanders and how he envisioned himself bringing the reality and assurance of religious faith to war.

Other commanders, while not openly hostile to the chaplains' activities, doubted that religious faith was an asset in battle. Curt Bowers recalled a unit commander who refused to attend field worship services but who "faithfully put the word out when divine worship was conducted for his troops." On one occasion, Bowers noticed the officer standing nearby during a service; he asked him, "Harry, what's going on? I thought you said you didn't want to go to church because you are not in sympathy with what I am preaching—the love of Christ and love of your neighbor." The officer responded, "Naw, Chaplain, I don't want my men to get too loving. They have to be fighters, and I don't want them to get too much of this Christianity stuff." The commander assured Bowers that he believed "a little bit won't hurt them," but he did not "want the guys to think I am getting soft."[79] Bowers, unlike Newby, did not record a miraculous change of heart, but the account still depends on readers accepting the existence of a fundamental tension between the realm of faith and the realm of war. Certainly for some soldiers, combat required them to harden their hearts and minds while for others, religion was an unnecessary and even dangerous distraction from the business of making war.

For many chaplains, however, their relationships with their supervisory chaplains were more problematic than those with their commanders. Supervisory chaplains were to provide spiritual support and guidance for chaplains under them, but this role was largely an unspoken one, and some handled this part of their jobs better than others. Albert Hanson, a Roman Catholic chaplain, reported that his supervisory chaplain was "useless—he was caught up in his own need to please the commander. In an 8 month period [he] never visited my AO, nor asked how I was doing."[80] Other chaplains were more charitable in their assessments. Douglas Sowards reported that "in Combat situations, each Chaplain was [so] busy taking care of his own units that he didn't have much time for socializing or giving much support to other chaplains, other than rare occasions. Most of the ones I knew were busy 'doing their own thing,' and trying to stay alive."[81] Joseph Beasley, who was posted at USARV headquarters and saw little if any combat action, remembered a similar situation: the goal was to finish the year and get out alive. Aside from this, Beasley also emphasized that there were rarely large concentrations of chaplains in any one area—even at Long Binh, one of the largest military installations in South Vietnam, only three chaplains were stationed permanently.[82] Many chaplains reported receiving little spiritual or professional support from chaplaincy channels.

Regardless of their official functions, however, chaplains, especially those serving in combat units and in nonadministrative positions, viewed their primary role as pastoral. They were in Vietnam to "bring God to men, and men to God." Donald Shea wrote simply, "Ministry is people where they are." Though clergy and laypeople in the United States frequently chastised chaplains for not taking a more prophetic stance on the Vietnam War, chaplains themselves insisted this was not their primary responsibility and some argued that to take a prophetic role would undermine their pastoral effectiveness.[83]

In addition to advising commanders on moral and spiritual matters that affected the unit, the chaplain also offered counsel to officers on personal matters. In the survey administered by Henry Ackermann to provide data for his official history of Army chaplains in the Vietnam War, most chaplains recalled that officers came to them regarding a variety of issues, including both personal and family situations and command and leadership matters. According to chaplains, officers' top concerns included "home and family problems," "leadership problems; stress of command," "homesickness, separation, and loneliness," "marital/romantic problems," and "the morality and ethics of war, particularly Vietnam." Enlisted personnel's top concerns were largely the same: "homesickness, separation, and loneliness," "home and family problems," "Fear (not getting home again, danger, death, etc.)," "marital/romantic problems," "personal problems (stress, anxiety, anger, depression, etc.," and "drug and alcohol problems."[84] Apparently, enlisted personnel spoke less frequently about the morality of war and the reasons for American involvement in Vietnam.

As the war went on, many chaplains became disillusioned by soldiers' apathy toward religion and with their behavior in general. Whereas early in the war, chaplains viewed positively the potential for ministry and their own effectiveness, during the drawdown phase, they were generally despondent. One wrote in an unofficial "After Action Report," filed in 1973, "As the total number of men diminishes, the relative paucity of those attending religious services becomes even more apparent. A spirit of killing time of simply waiting out one's DEROS [Date of Earliest Return from Overseas], a sense of boredom, etc. all contribute to make men apathetic and lackadaisical." Many of the men, he continued, were "religiously immature and grossly uninstructed" and therefore "fail[ed] to see any relevance or applicability of religious practices."

On top of spotty attendance at religious services and inattention to spiritual concerns, chaplains increasingly complained about the "sinful" and hedonistic lifestyles of many soldiers and officers in Vietnam. Chaplain John Kenney wrote that "the overwhelming majority of men are either actively engaged in excessive drinking habits, cohabitation, or recourse to prostitutes, drugs, etc. or, at least they are immersed in a milieu of continual and inescapable blasphemy, profanity, obscenity which pervades their consciousness and renders them feeling 'unfit' and 'unworthy' to come into contact with the sacred or whatever represents it and so they stay away in droves."[85] He estimated that "less than one per cent of enlisted men . . . participated in formal religion" and lamented the fact that a "chaplain may spend an entire day in getting to an isolated area (at considerable expense to the government and possible danger to himself), advertise time and place for services to be held, personally contact the majority of those present and then have no one show up."[86] This was a sense of defeat and frustration was rare early in the war. Chaplains, like other observers of U.S. action in Vietnam, frequently came to believe the war was a colossal mistake and a terrible waste of lives, even when they could salvage a redemptive narrative from the rubble.

Kenney in particular provided a clear voice of opposition and frustration in the late stages of the war. Chaplains, in his estimation, were frustrated by the war and the behaviors it engendered, but the angst was deeper. Chaplains, many of whom he believed had concluded that "a sincere approach to God could possibly help any man to solve his problems and live a better life," were feeling useless and helpless because the soldiers' and officers' "indifference prevent[ed] and preclude[d] that" possibility.[87] "This experience, repeated continuously," Kenney continued, "can make him feel that he himself and what he has to offer are about as useful and appreciated as another wart on the proverbial toad, and the disappointment in proportion[,] as he himself takes the role of clergyman seriously, bears all the more heavily on his own morale." The chaplain's morale, according to Kenney's interpretation, was critical not only for the chaplain personally but also for the unit: a demoralized and ineffective chaplain could only damage the military mission.[88] In a war in which small-group cohesion was important for both effectiveness and emotional and psychological support, chaplains' feelings of uselessness and isolation were likely exacerbated by the practice of area coverage, which isolated chaplains physically and inhibited the formation of close relationships between them and men in the field.

The tenor of the war and Americans' view of it had changed dramatically by the early 1970s not only because of increased drug use by American service members, fragging incidents, racial tensions, and protests but also because the very nature of the war had changed. Individual chaplains recalled the profound effect these changes had on their ministries. To most military personnel, including chaplains, President Richard Nixon's Vietnamization policy announcement signaled the eventual American withdrawal and an admission that the war could not be won. Claude Newby, who did not want to leave his troops in 1967, recalled having quite a different attitude at the end of his second tour in 1970. "In 1967 I had returned to an America where patriotism was still somewhat in vogue," wrote Newby. "Now, in 1970, I returned to an America where both patriotism and America's heroic young soldiers were increasingly held in disdain." This analysis of the trajectory of the home front's support for the war aligns well with other veterans' recollections—most veterans reported extreme disillusionment with home front protesters, often crediting them with more influence and vitriol than evidence suggests.[89]

Newby also commented on changing race relations among troops: "Where in 1966–67 and early 1969 infantrymen were infantrymen without regard to race or color, by 1970 even they showed evidence of succumbing to civilian and rear-area trends, of dividing into us and them." Other chaplains who served toward the end of the war also acknowledged the changes. Chaplain Thomas Confroy identified the change in the civilian attitude toward the war and soldiers as one from "respectful support" in the mid-1960s to "outright hostility" in the early 1970s, when "drugs, antiwar sentiment, and racial conflict . . . affected the troops." Confroy determined that his "work as a chaplain was greatly affected by these changes," as it went "from positive ministry during the first tour to a sometimes defensive ministry in the second." During his second tour, Confroy recalled that he had to approach his ministry as one of restricting immoral or improper acts rather than of encouraging religious faith and positive action.[90]

Chaplains' roles were complicated in part because they were at once part of and outside life within their units. In spite of this, some did bond with their units and formed lasting attachments to the men and their families. One group of Marines dubbed their chaplain, Vincent Capodanno, the "Grunt Padre." "Grunt" was a term generally reserved for enlisted infantry and was at once a symbol of pride and recognition of the toughest, most dangerous duties they faced. Chaplains, as officers and volunteers, would not typically qualify for this label. "What set Father Vincent apart," according to his biographer, "was the way he lived his ministry with the Marines. He was not a religious leader who did his job and then returned to the comfort of his own circle." Capodanno "lived as a Grunt Marine. Wherever they went, he went. Whatever burdens they had to carry, he shared the load. No problem was too large or small to take to Father Vincent—he was available to them day and night. . . . The Grunt Marines recognized Father Vincent's determination to be with them and one of them."[91] Capodanno was certainly not unique in these qualities. Some troops could identify closely with chaplains who accompanied them into combat situations, and thus could accord them the status of a buddy or fellow "grunt." But chaplains also commanded deference and respect as evidenced in the second part of the nickname. "Padre" acknowledged the chaplain's position as a clergyman, but it also reflected the chaplain's paternal role.[92] Though separated from enlisted men by rank, status, and often age, chaplains (even those of Protestant and Jewish faiths) became "padres," and soldiers sought them out for counsel, wisdom, comfort, and reassurance.

Indeed, just as bonds formed between soldiers during combat, they also formed between soldiers and chaplains. Chaplains held and comforted friends as they died and suffered through many of the same hardships as their men. Raymond Johnson identified the relationships he formed with his unit as one of the most important aspects of his Vietnam experience: "I have attended to their needs both physically and spiritually when the walls were crumbling and their 'cool' was beginning to shatter under the wake of genuine fear. . . . These were some of the same men I would pray a final benediction over. I suppose I can say with all honesty that I have never felt closer to a group of men before."[93]

Within their units, many chaplains found comfort, emotional release, and a renewed sense of faith. Richard Heim recalled a particularly cathartic moment: After troops had "carried many wounded back to the LZ," he recalled. "I stayed with [one soldier], prayed the Lord's Prayer, and quoted the 23rd Psalm until the dust off chopper arrived." Afterward, he continued, "when I got back, I remember seeing some body bags outside the aid station. . . . I went over and opened one, and there was the body of one of my trooper buddies. . . . We made many a jump together, and when I saw his body, I literally fell apart and cried."[94] In war, chaplains witnessed nearly every conceivable kind of physical and emotional trauma, and they had to find their own releases as well.

Both commanders and chaplains worried that chaplains' effectiveness over a long tour might deteriorate, which was, in part, the reason they were rotated to the rear. If a chaplains' presence was good for morale, what might a demoralized chaplain, the removal of a chaplain from a post, or even the death of a chaplain do to a unit? After seeing a chaplain's interaction with a wounded soldier and witnessing the chaplain's subsequent breakdown, a medic recalled, "I observed [their] . . . compassion for the sick and dying a dozen times a day. . . . I now understand how their hearts must have been broken again and again as they served God in that terrible conflict."[95] The soldier attributed his later turn to religion in part to this chaplain, but for others, recognizing chaplains' humanity, that their divine calling and military purpose did not shield them from the full range of emotions associated with combat, may have been detrimental. Chaplains had to find a balance between knowing and socializing with their troops, maintaining themselves as spiritual examples, and supporting the military institutions of which they were a part, all without lowering personal or religious-institutional standards.

Chaplains confronted a host of conflicts that revolved around their place in the military community, and their activities, though vital to the life of a unit, left many of them without a definite place either in the military hierarchy or in the civilian world. Again, we can return to Claude Newby's memoir as instructive. He wrote that he felt "alienated" from various groups in Vietnam, unable to perform fully any one of his roles. He disagreed (vocally) with Army policies, even when they clearly fell outside of his purview, "like six-month commands in combat, that all too often deprived soldiers of experienced officers." He felt separated from other clergy and civilian communities because he could not understand how they could send men "off to war with [their] hands tied and later welcome home the draft dodgers before expressing thanks to the faithful who served." Nor did he understand how "the American people . . . participated in or tolerated public abuse of its faithful sons and daughters."

Because his postwar reflections revealed alienation from civilian communities, we might expect that Newby fully embraced his identity as a soldier. However, convinced that he had served both units to the best of his ability, he concluded, "The soldier in me had been expressed. I realized that I was a soldier by virtue of wearing the uniform, holding rank, and experiencing hostile fire . . . [but] in reality . . . I was an observer and not a true warrior. Above all, I was not a hero."[96] In this self-deprecating assessment, Newby differentiated himself from other soldiers and enlisted men.

He could not comfortably fit in with any group; his functions and duties placed him firmly, and sometimes uncomfortably, in the middle.

By immersing themselves in the life of their new military communities, chaplains created identities for themselves that incorporated both military and religious characteristics. Ultimately, this process began as they carried out their day-to-day duties and culminated with their consciously invoking both military and religious language and ritual to find the meaning in and purpose of the war.

CHAPTER THREE

Conflict and Identity

As he rode with the convoy back to the base after a civic action mission to provide humanitarian assistance to a South Vietnamese village in June 1967, chaplain Paul Mitchell, who was scheduled to return to the United States the following day, reflected on his time in Vietnam. He had conducted three general Protestant services that morning, which was typical of his routine during his year in Vietnam, where he "had traveled many miles by land and air, led men in many worship services, visited, prayed, and counseled with them." Through this priestly ministry of presence, counseling, and conducting worship services, he helped soldiers deal "with their fears, hurts, and sorrows, trying to help them find answers to whatever questions and problems they had." But "there was another side to my life in Vietnam," he reported. Civic action projects had "consumed a goodly portion of [his] time and energy." Mitchell's unit worked with local orphanages, a leprosarium, and a local normal school. They collected and distributed monetary and material donations from the unit's members and from congregations, organizations, and relatives in the United States. These activities crossed geographical, cultural, and religious divides and represented an important facet of the American effort in Vietnam.[1] For Mitchell, his clerical identity was integral to both his ministry and civic action projects, but so too was his military identity as he participated fully in the unit's broader military and political mission.

Chaplains in Vietnam confronted a variety of situations that had the potential to induce conflict between their constituent communities or between the various roles they played and identities they assumed. This chapter explores the idea of role conflict as the primary paradigm for understanding the chaplains' experience. The literature on role conflict suggests chaplains were faced with irreconcilable conflict between their various identities and roles and thus dealt with the problem by compartmentalizing the roles, that is, separating them intellectually, or by privileging one role over the other, essentially minimizing one identity for another. This chapter, then, complicates the accepted narrative by examining chaplains' responses to a variety of specific situations that likely would have produced such role conflict. Chaplains' responses to the issues of conscientious objection, drug use, their noncombatant status, participation in civic action programs (CAPs), personal morality, and war crimes and atrocities all demonstrated specific sites where chaplains had to actively manage both their religious and military identities.

Chaplains' identity management in the face of potential conflict was far more complicated than the role conflict narrative allows. Moral, theological, and pastoral tensions tested chaplains' beliefs and worldviews and demanded that chaplains work out ways to reconcile potential conflict. In response to these tensions, chaplains managed their dual identities as clergymen and officers by developing crisis-based theologies and practical solutions to moral questions that helped them find and define meaning in war. This process was a fundamentally creative one, requiring chaplains to rethink their own work and ministry in light of their wartime experiences. Chaplains did not forsake either their military or their religious identity as they worked out solutions to conflict in Vietnam.

In published memoirs, autobiographical essays, letters, diaries, periodicals, and denominational publications, as well as in oral histories and in response to official history surveys, chaplains reported on their wartime experiences.[2] Although these narratives were clearly written in specific contexts, with specific audiences in mind, and for particular purposes, which may have been political, religious, or therapeutic, among others, they offer a valuable record of chaplains' activities and attitudes during the war. In this regard, chaplains' writings serve many of the same functions as the ubiquitous combat memoir or narrative, even though chaplains were noncombatants and only some witnessed combat with line units.[3]

Most of the accounts discussed here are from chaplains who served with Army and Marine ground combat units, a not unexpected imbalance given the public appetite for combat-driven war stories over those told by rear-area personnel and the relative distance from the battlefield from which Air Force personnel operated. Although Army chaplains substantially outnumbered ship-based Navy or Air Force chaplains, hundreds from those branches served as well, but fewer have published memoirs, and the Navy and Air Force have not compiled statistically significant surveys of these personnel. Furthermore, readers will notice few places where analysis is tied directly to a chaplain's race or denomination. The reason is pragmatic: The sources themselves only rarely reveal a chaplain's race, and not all even identify a chaplain's denomination. None of these are unimportant categories, but the relatively small number of chaplains' accounts would make any generalizations based on race or denomination problematic.

Of utmost importance is recognizing that chaplains themselves were the primary storytellers about their experiences. On a few occasions, this analysis relies on third-hand accounts of chaplains' activities, but these, too, are subject to the problems of memory and self-presentation. There are no unbiased sources. Due to the specific personal motivations of chaplains who chose to record and make public their wartime experiences, the religious practices and events discussed in this chapter are not comprehensive or necessarily representative—the record is simply too fragmentary. Yet even this highly selective and unrepresentative sample reveals chaplains' broad range of responses to liturgical, theological, and pastoral issues. A more representative or unbiased sample would likely reveal an even more complicated picture.

Theorizing on the Chaplain Experience: Role Conflict

Chaplains' position in the middle of religious and military worlds was institutionally mandated. Men who wished to serve as military chaplains in Vietnam had to meet two sets of requirements, military and ecclesial, before they could be appointed. The military required that they meet the age and physical standards for military service, though at the height of the war the different services occasionally waived some of these limits, especially for Jewish and Catholic chaplains who were in chronically short supply. On the ecclesial side, chaplains had to have completed three years of graduate study in theology or a related program and to have served at least two years in a parish or congregation. For chaplains from denominations without seminary training, equivalent education in another field sufficed. Seminarians who wished to enter the chaplaincy were generally commissioned as staff specialists as they completed their educational and pastoral requirements. Additionally, the military required that a chaplain be endorsed by an ecclesiastical agency, which could set its own standards. For most of the twentieth century, the military chaplaincy operated on a loose quota system to ensure denominational diversity. It tried to maintain a balance of one-third Catholic chaplains; one-third Liturgical Protestant (Episcopal, Lutheran, Presbyterian, etc.); and one-third evangelical Protestant, "other" Protestant, and Jewish. The categorization was, to be sure, problematic in some ways—the third category, especially, lumped together a large number of faith groups, representing a huge variety of religious practices, theologies, and doctrines, simply by the virtue of their not being Catholic or not having a formal liturgy. But it did reflect a desire to ensure some diversity and balance within the chaplaincy in order to meet the diverse needs of American service members. During the Vietnam era, the armed services occasionally relaxed these ratios as some denominations were unable to fill their assignments and others consistently offered more than their allotment, and by the end of the Vietnam War, the quotas, as a matter of practice and eventually policy, were revoked.

The in-the-middle position of chaplains—operating on one hand as ministers and on the other hand as cogs in a great war machine—has prompted many scholars and observers, particularly critics of the chaplaincy, to argue that the chaplain's role is defined by role conflict. As a sociological construct, role conflict, or role tension, is an important concept for understanding how human beings negotiate and balance competing demands on their time, attention, resources, and decision-making. The conflicts can be simple or complex, and humans make these decisions all the time—some without thinking at all, and others only after anguished considerations. Consequently, scholars have argued, an individual must resolve this conflict by compartmentalizing the roles, rationalizing away the roles' incompatibility (that is, cognitive dissonance), or abandoning one of the roles. Many observers argue that the American military chaplaincy system is rife with contradictions, ironies, and conflicts and have concluded that military chaplains tend to privilege their military identity and role over their religious one. When forced to choose between competing norms and values, they argue, chaplains are more military officer than clergy.

Shortly after World War II, sociologist Waldo Burchard suggested there were five basic tenets of Christianity that unequivocally prohibited violence and so would provoke role conflict for military chaplains. He argued the Christian doctrines "of love, of universal brotherhood, of peace, and of non-resistance to evil, and the commandment 'You shall not kill'" were "manifestly incompatible with the aims of a nation at war. Therefore it is impossible for the Christian in military service to put them into practice."[4] He concluded that chaplains compartmentalized their roles when such conflict occurred and subordinated their role as minister of religion to their role as military officer. Burchard's basic assertion that chaplains experienced and were unable to adequately resolve role conflict has remained a persistent one in the literature dealing with chaplains in the late twentieth century. Yet the realities of military ministry revealed that chaplains' duties and identities were determined more by conditions on the ground than by deep philosophical introspection, and this held true for both individual chaplains and for the institution as a whole.

Burchard's assessment is too simplistic, however. Because of strict entry requirements for chaplains, the group was self-selecting. Any chaplain who wished to quit could ask his endorsing agency to lift his endorsement, thereby making him ineligible for continued service, and clergymen were exempt from the draft, so they could not be compelled to serve as enlisted personnel. Seminarians were also exempt from the draft, even when other school deferments ended, so they had other options as well.[5] When from 1968 through 1970 chaplains were called up for a second tour of duty in Vietnam, only a few chose this way of avoiding service; Army chief of chaplains Francis Sampson reported the total was fewer than twelve. Most chaplains who served in Vietnam, therefore, likely had already determined the fundamental morality of faithful people serving in war. At the very least, they made a personal and conscious decision—one that most men subject to draft did not have the option to make—that their military service would not invalidate or threaten their faith or religious vocation.

As a group, chaplains would be expected to have the attributes of both clergy and military officers. As clergy, they would be expected to hold faith and religion in high regard, to display strong interpersonal communication skills, and to exhibit moral and spiritual leadership. As military men, they would be expected to achieve certain physical and mental standards, to accept and function within an intensely hierarchical system, and to value discipline and mission. By their assent to the philosophical, legal, and moral basis of the chaplaincy, chaplains demonstrated their willingness to operate in the middle ground, to go between military and civilian, secular and religious cultures. These attributes meant that, at least in theory, chaplains were well-suited to an environment that required both spiritual and military bearing.

Chaplains' specialized training prepared them for navigating both military and religious worlds. For example, chaplains who served during and after the Vietnam War all had graduate degrees in ministry, theology, or other similar fields. Their religious education provided chaplains with credibility in both religious and military communities. Graduate training for chaplains would have included historical, theological, and ecumenical studies, as well as training in counseling, religious education, and liturgical or worship leadership. Military training or prior service initiated chaplains into the workings of the chain of command, basic maneuvers, and military customs and courtesies, while their religious training and networks allowed them to create programs and coordinate supplies and services to serve military personnel.

Chaplains occupied ambiguous spaces in the structure of both their religious and military communities. While chaplains assigned to a Reserve or National Guard unit often served a parish or congregation in addition to their military constituency, those who served with regular units did so infrequently. When chaplains were deployed, they invariably left their local ministries, which placed them outside the normal rhythms and expectations of organized religious bodies. In the Roman Catholic Church, for example, chaplains served under the Archdiocese for the Military Services—an organization fundamentally different from the territorial organization of civilian Catholic parishes. In the Episcopal Church of the United States of America, chaplains served under the Suffragan Bishop for Chaplaincies. In the Presbyterian Church (including the Presbyterian Church United States of America), chaplains could retain their affiliation with their "home" presbytery or transfer to a presbytery closer to their military assignment. Church bodies with purely congregational structures created loose organizations to serve the specific needs of chaplains.

This model of cultural mediation or liminality is scarce within scholarship on military chaplains. The closest argument in this vein is Clarence Abercrombie's *The Military Chaplain,* a social science study of Vietnam chaplains, which focused on identifying and quantifying the existence of role or identity conflict. Based on survey responses from civilian clergy, chaplains, and military commanders, Abercrombie's study concluded that the traditional version of role conflict, whereby chaplains forsook their religious identities and roles in favor of their military ones, was not generally evident. Chaplains, he determined, fell squarely in the middle of civilian clergy and military commanders on theological, moral, and pastoral issues and did not display levels of militarism suggested by critics of the chaplaincy.[6] Abercrombie's study suggests that chaplains did not tend toward the extremes of either of their roles. Rather, they were astoundingly "average," their views indicating that conflict was minimal. Since his book was based on quantitative survey data rather than a qualitative study of chaplain behaviors and experiences, it does not account for the ways in which chaplains mediated between multiple communities or dealt with the conflict that did exist.

I argue, though, that conflict was an important feature of the chaplain's experience but that the conflict was not necessarily caused by irreconcilable roles and was not generally resolved by forsaking one role or identity for another. Instead, conflict framed chaplains' experiences and prompted them to work out practical solutions to problems that demanded flexibility, requiring them to move between the language, expectations, and rituals of more than one community.

Navigating Military and Religious Challenges

One of chaplains' major duties, both when stationed stateside and overseas, was to counsel men who believed they were conscientious objectors (CO) and thus might be eligible for separation from the military or reassignment to a noncombat unit. The Department of Defense Directive (DoDI) 1300.6, issued in August 1962, established uniform rules for all service members, both inductees and enlistees, in all services. The services were then to implement the regulation as appropriate. Army Regulation 635-20 directed that individuals "applying for discharge receive a counseling interview by a chaplain and that the chaplain submit a report of the interview to include the sincerity of the individual in his belief and an expression of his opinion as to whether the individual's objection to military duty is based on religious beliefs."[7] Other services had similar regulations.[8] Whereas earlier CO policies required membership in a historic peace church, during the Vietnam War one could declare CO status on the basis of any "deeply held" religious belief that precluded military service, though the requirements, regulations, and procedures for securing such status were still onerous and likely deterred service members, especially those who had already been inducted, from filing the claim. The chaplain's dual roles meant that either recommendation could potentially damage the chaplain's credibility—an assessment favorable to granting CO status could damage his unit's military readiness or effectiveness, but recommending against it would open the chaplain to charges of militarism and even doubts about his own religious commitment.

In 1965, in *United States v. Seeger*, the United States Supreme Court defined "religious belief" to include "a sincere and meaningful belief which occupies in the life of its possessor a place parallel to that filled by the God of those admittedly qualifying for the exemption." This expanded definition potentially could be used to allow atheist or agnostic soldiers to claim secular philosophical beliefs as the foundation for their objection, yet such arguments still faced significant cultural barriers as the *Seeger* decision retained the usage of "Supreme Being" and was often interpreted as still having a theistic component. The Office of the Chief of Chaplains (OCCH) directed that the *Seeger* decision and its implications for chaplains be incorporated into the curriculum at the chaplain school.[9] Yet the Army chief of chaplains also insisted that "mature ordained clergymen do not need detailed instructions on how to perform their pastoral functions in every conceivable situation; [and] that each chaplain is free to counsel each individual as he deems appropriate," giving chaplains significant leeway in the interpretation and application of this guidance.[10]

Chaplains in the field used their respective chief of chaplains offices as a source of information about new or unfamiliar denominations when a soldier claimed CO status. For example, one Army chaplain wrote to the OCCH to inquire about the legitimacy and views of the Radio Church of God (Worldwide Church of God). "We are interested," he wrote, "because a young 2LT MSC [Medical Service Corps], and ROTC graduate, and a member of the 70th Medical Battalion here, became involved with the church when he heard a radio broadcast in San Antonio while attending an Army school. Since his arrival here, he has applied for a discharge under the provisions of AR 635-20. This was refused. Now he may apply for a discharge as a conscientious objector. He refuses to do any detail which involves carrying a weapon." Ever vigilant in the struggle against Communism, the chaplain also wondered if the church might even be subversive "because of the nature of some of the teachings the Lieutenant's Commander says the young man has expressed."[11] The OCCH replied that the church was recognized and that its members did, in fact, "conscientiously refuse to bear arms or to come under the military authority."[12] This single example reveals some of the conflicts chaplains faced: a desire to make a correct decision; imperfect knowledge about religious denominations and practices in the United States; anti-Communist sentiment; and the duty to fulfill a military obligation. At the same time, it suggests that chaplains were aware of these potential conflicts and did not simply ignore their pastoral responsibilities. Rather than making a call on intuition or assumptions, the chaplain in this scenario sought additional counsel before advising the commander.

As dissent against the Vietnam War escalated, the American Friends Service Committee (AFSC), a subsidiary organization of the Religious Society of Friends (Quakers), issued advice for service members who wished to claim CO status and for the chaplains who interviewed them. In a pamphlet titled "Are You a Conscientious Objector to War?" the AFSC defined in simple, accessible language, the Supreme Court's definition of "religious belief" and "religious training," which made it clear that attendance at or membership in a formal church or religious organization was not required by law. It also explained the "Supreme Being clause" of the stated policy, which required a belief "in a relation to a Supreme Being involving duties superior to those arising from any human relation." The AFSC pamphlet made it clear that military personnel did "not have to believe in a Supreme Being in some anthropomorphic sense of a personality having a corporeal existence, because the 1965 *Seeger* case allowed for a 'parallel belief' for those who hold a 'sincere and meaningful' belief that 'occupies a place in the life of its possessor parallel to that filled by the orthodox belief in God of one who clearly qualifies for the exemption." Finally, it offered practical advice for those who were considering applying for CO classification: "If you hold liberal, questioning, or more unorthodox views on religion, you should apply for a CO classification. If you cannot conscientiously answer *yes* to the Supreme Being clause, answer with an *I don't know* or *Depends on what you mean*, or leave it blank. Then follow with a clear, simple statement of what you do believe. If you answer *no* to the Supreme Being question, you will probably be denied the special appeal procedure available to CO claimants."[13] By addressing both service members and chaplains, the AFSC recognized the critical position chaplains held in the process and the fact that chaplains' position within the military hierarchy might compel them to be less sympathetic than either their individual conscience or the applicable guidance might allow.

Dissent against the Vietnam War by many liberal and mainline religious groups that had not historically objected to war further complicated the issue. Whereas the *Seeger* decision allowed, in theory, for CO status to be granted based on something other than specifically-religious belief, in practice, it was a difficult argument to make. As the issue of conscientious objection came to the forefront of discussions for chaplains and others, the Department of Defense and the Department of the Army worked to set out criteria for establishing "religious belief," providing more guidance than the nebulous *Seeger* decision offered. They further rejected claims to selective conscientious objection, that is objection to a war in particular rather than to war in general. Top military officials determined that "objection to a particular war or to a particular armed conflict is not sufficient" and that an "applicant's objection must be founded on religious training and belief." Furthermore, and consistent with *Seeger*, the policy determined that "a mere personal moral code" was an insufficient basis for objection, as was objection based on "essentially political, sociological, or philosophical considerations." The applicant's belief must be "sincere" but its "reasonableness or orthodoxy" was irrelevant.[14]

Following the policy's nebulous and meandering specifications was difficult enough without the added ambiguity of a subjective judgment as to the origin, content, and sincerity of an applicant's objection. So in order to assist chaplains in interviewing soldiers, the OCCH issued a guide with "seven factors that would help them to determine the apparent sincerity of the applicant's belief" as well as a series of "questions that they might use as a guide."[15] When the application was brought before a full review panel, many of the panel's questions again hinged on an applicant's religious belief and commitment. Such questions ranged from the concrete, "Did the applicant attend a church school?," to more abstract assessments, for example, "What outward actions verify the sincerity of the applicant's religious belief," including "public expression of his belief," "sacrifices [made] in pursuit of his belief," or "patterns of conduct" that would signify his belief? The chaplain's evaluation was considered in two further questions: "What was the chaplain's evaluation of applicant's sincerity?" and "Did the chaplain determine conscientious objection to be based on the applicant's religious belief?"[16] Several people had to evaluate a CO's religious convictions in order for him to be released from service or reassigned, but the difficulty of assessing the sincerity of another's belief was quite evident.

Even though the suggested questions—for both chaplains and review boards—were long and complicated, the guidelines issued concerning the chaplain's interview of a CO applicant advised above all, "Keep the report simple!" According to the OCCH, previous reports "submitted by chaplains in accordance with references 1a and 1b show a tendency to include a great deal of verbage [sic] in support of the final opinion of the chaplain," which had led to some applicants using the chaplain's assessment as a basis for an appeal. "To this end," the guidelines indicated, the chaplain's report "should be limited to a simple statement relating to the sincerity of the applicant's belief and an opinion as to whether the objection is based on a religious and/or a philosophical belief/conviction. Reasons for the opinion of the chaplain need not be stated."[17] Chaplains' position between military and religious authorities placed them in an unenviable situation indeed: they were asked to evaluate and comment on another's sincerity of religious belief based on nebulous guidelines in the midst of an increasingly unpopular war within certain religious communities, but at the same time, they were voluntarily participating and had clear interests in preserving and advancing military efficiency.

While the issue of conscientious objection was a persistent one for chaplains at home and in the field, perhaps the issue that most clearly demonstrated tension between the chaplain's multiple roles and identities in combat was his status as a noncombatant, which prohibited him from carrying a weapon. According to the Geneva Conventions, as noncombatants, chaplains were not permitted to carry weapons.[18] American military regulations also stipulated that a chaplain "should not bear arms; he will not be required to bear arms." Shortly thereafter, however, the Army field manual added, "This nation, has, nevertheless, expected that chaplains accompany their troops into combat."[19] The danger for chaplains, especially against a Communist enemy, was that international law would simply be ignored. Chaplains pointed to the American experience in Korea as evidence that Communists did not respect chaplains' noncombatant status. They argued that in Korea, since the closest Communist equivalent to a chaplain was a party political officer, chaplains were executed or died with other soldiers in prisoner of war (POW) camps.[20] The accuracy of this particular interpretation is questionable, but the rumors certainly influenced chaplains' behavior in Vietnam. The Army chief of chaplains also set out to establish firm rules for chaplains' behavior in combat zones, particularly as it related to carrying weapons. The official policy of the chaplains' branches was clear: chaplains could not carry weapons under any circumstances; however, in practice chaplains had to determine for themselves on personal and practical levels whether they would comply with the prohibition. In one instance in 1964, a photograph of a chaplain armed with a .45 caliber pistol and a fragmentation grenade ran in U.S. newspapers.[21] After Curt[is] Bowers appeared in a January 1966 picture carrying a weapon, the OCCH grew increasingly frustrated by inquiries from Congress and civilians who were concerned with the actions of chaplains as portrayed in the media. Chief of chaplains Charles Brown told Theodore Koepke, the staff chaplain for the Military Assistance Command, Vietnam (MACV), "Some of these letters, and the time-consuming replies, could be avoided if our chaplains used a little discretion in their statements to representatives of the various news media." Brown reiterated the Geneva Convention protocol: "Chaplains are noncombatants. . . . They will not be required to bear arms. . . . Weapons will not be provided for female personnel or chaplains." At the same time, Brown acknowledged the significant pressures facing chaplains serving in combat situations: "It is understandable that a chaplain in the stress of the kind of war being waged in Viet Nam faces an individual dilemma and I hesitate to judge him from my position of apparent security. However, I can and do pass judgment on the unwarranted publicity that reflects immaturity and indiscretion, and necessitates explanation after explanation to the effect that we have not given up our traditional role of noncombatants and protected personnel."[22]

In response to these issues, the OCCH directed that chaplains would "under no circumstances let themselves be led into a discussion of the pros and cons of the noncombatant status of chaplains or permit themselves to be interviewed for a personal opinion or general discussion of the subject." If a chaplain could not avoid such an interview, the chief of chaplains expected him to "uphold the traditional position set forth in the Geneva Convention, Army Regulations nos. 165-15 and 310-34, and Field Manual No. 16-5." After the uproar over the photographs, the chief declared, "Under no circumstances will a chaplain admit that arms have been issued to him, or that he has arms in his possession, or be photographed carrying arms." The policy, as stated officially, went even further, addressing the common argument that unarmed chaplains placed an undue burden on their enlisted assistants and military companions in combat, stating, "The chaplain will not argue that without arms he is not carrying his proper load and is a burden to others; the wielding of weapons is the responsibility of his enlisted assistant."[23] Though the language seemed direct, it is easy enough to interpret these instructions as being more concerned with the perception and publicity of chaplains' carrying weapons than with the morality or wisdom of them actually doing so. Accordingly, chaplains frequently ignored these directions or altered them to fit their purposes.

Not all chaplains and commanders reached the same conclusion about the place of the chaplain in combat. Chaplain Al Arvay, for example, concluded that "even our own military people . . . didn't know exactly where we were to belong." He recalled a particular incident where his commanding officer asked him to carry a weapon: "When I was leaving[,] there was a rifle, an M-16 that was placed there and the sergeant [told] me the colonel wanted me to carry it because nobody else was going to defend me. I had to defend myself." When he refused, the officer got "very angry" with him.[24] Some chaplains refused to go into hostile combat situations because they would not carry a weapon and did not feel it fair or safe to rely on others for their defense. Others tried to ensure they remained with company-sized units at all times, but they occasionally found themselves with platoon-sized units when a company split up for tactical missions. Some chaplains carried weapons openly, though most chaplains frowned on this practice. Some decided they would pick up the weapon of a wounded man if they had to. Others relied on their enlisted assistants for defense, though many questioned "school-trained" assistants' abilities to protect them or the fairness of asking for such a sacrifice. Many commanders, on the other hand, appeared not to worry about potential conflicts with the Geneva Conventions. LDS chaplain Claude Newby concluded that "most field commanders . . . smiled on the chaplain carrying a weapon for his own protection, and some of them on occasion allowed or forbade a chaplain to go into a hot situation, depending on whether the chaplain was prepared to 'take care of himself.'"[25] A chaplain's usefulness in combat could have been immediately reversed if his presence endangered the unit. Clearly, though, chaplains came to a variety of conclusions on most of these issues.

Another issue that demanded significant attention by individual chaplains and by the chaplaincy as an institution was drug use among American military personnel, especially in the rear areas of Vietnam. The issue had perplexed American military leaders long before the engagement in Vietnam. Soldiers in the Philippines at the beginning of the twentieth century found abundant and cheap sources for opium, and alcohol use and abuse among service members had long concerned the top brass.[26] Lax Vietnamese drug laws, and the prevalence of marijuana, which was illegal in the United States but legal in Vietnam, and the difficulties of enforcement presented special challenges to commanders.[27] Soldiers reported that boredom, peer pressure, institutional culture, curiosity, and a desire to escape reality were among the top reasons for their drug use.[28] Chaplains could not fix the problem alone (nor were they expected to), but they were instrumental in alleviating the conditions, especially boredom, that prompted drug use and in providing counseling during rehabilitation. Dealing with drug use among American military personnel provided a clear example of the chaplain's role in his unit's moral and military life; the situation called for staff-officer support from a moral and spiritual perspective, which was the chaplain's primary job.

While the use of marijuana was illegal and caused significant worry in the armed forces, heroin caused much greater concern. One report claimed that "in 1970 there were 1,146 arrests for hard drugs. The following year arrests in this category increased to 7,026."[29] However, heroin users in Vietnam differed from those in the United States: they were likely to be from small towns (rather than urban areas), and the racial composition of heroin users was similar to that of the military service as a whole.[30] Most used the drug casually but were probably addicted: the purer form of Vietnamese heroin allowed it to be ingested directly or smoked, which reduced the risk of overdosing and infection from injections.[31]

The armed services determined it was both a military problem and a moral issue, and chaplains again found themselves in the middle. In 1970, AR 600-32 established that commanders were responsible for carrying out an aggressive prevention program, including orientations, refresher courses, and special briefings for service members "before [their] departure to and on return from overseas areas" and insuring that "limited rehabilitation of restorable drug abusers [was] initiated at the lowest unit level." Chaplains were involved because they, along with a medical officers, could reasonably be expected to assist soldiers and officers in finding and participating in appropriate individual and group therapy or counseling. In addition, the regulation stated that a "soldier seeking rehabilitation" who presented himself voluntarily to a commanding officer, chaplain, surgeon, or other designated person would "not be punished merely for admitting the use of drugs." For many commanders, however, the most immediate and expedient response often appeared to be separation from the military. Thus, chaplains (and other officers) walked a fine line between military policies, legal responsibilities, and their duty to counsel drug users.

A limited amnesty program instituted in 1970 aimed to curtail drug use among casual or experimental users. Frank Bartomo, assistant general counsel of Manpower and Reserve Affairs in the Department of Defense, spoke before a congressional subcommittee on Marijuana and Dangerous Drugs of the Committee on Armed Services in September of 1970. He noted that the amnesty program, which allowed soldiers to turn in any drugs or paraphernalia without fear of recrimination and then to receive counseling, moral, and medical support, had been especially successful in Vietnam. The amnesty program used a four-step process that included peer-mentoring and evaluation in addition to professional help from chaplains and surgeons.[32]

By the end of the war, however, the drug problem—especially heroin use—was so acute that the Army decided to treat soldiers before they ever left the field by setting up detoxification, rehabilitation, and treatment centers across South Vietnam, including at Cam Ranh Bay, Long Binh, and Binh Tuy. Chaplains were integral members of these treatment teams and were assigned as counselors in these facilities. Beginning in 1971, all service members had to pass a urinalysis drug test before they could rotate home. Command detained those who failed for treatment at a detoxification center. After a briefing and intake interview, the addicted (or using) soldiers were placed into a residential detoxification and treatment program. Enlisted intake technicians referred those with severe mental problems to psychiatrists for further care and others to chaplains. Doctors and nurses conducted physical exams and monitored the soldiers as they went through withdrawal, and chaplains helped facilitate individual counseling, group therapy, and education programs. After the soldiers were sufficiently detoxed, they were medically evacuated to Japan and then to the United States for further treatment.[33] .

Recognizing that drug use was becoming an increasing concern in the military, especially in Vietnam, the Army Chaplain School began to address the issue more directly. Though by 1972, it was too late in the war to have a real effect on the problem in Vietnam, the chaplain school began to offer chaplains and their enlisted assistants a supplemental course on drug counseling and working with drug users. The introductory materials focused primarily on alcohol and marijuana as the most pressing substance-dependence problems for the military. In addition to supplying statistics about alcohol and drug use, the course emphasized the role of "youth culture," particularly for understanding marijuana use and young male soldiers' rationalization for its use. The course took care to differentiate between the legal status of alcohol and the illicit status of marijuana and other drugs, but it treated the two as part of a wider problem.

The drug scene in Vietnam received significant attention in the new course, as did the consequences of addicted soldiers returning home. The drug problem, the instructor pamphlet asserted, resulted from "loneliness, boredom, fear, peer group loyalty, ease of access, and the low cost of purchase." Soldiers often expressed a desire to get off drugs as well, if for no other reason than the cost of continuing a habit in the United States. A $3-a-day habit in Vietnam would easily translate to a $150-a-day habit "back in the world."[34] The drug problem in Vietnam was pervasive and insidious, involving not only American soldiers but also Vietnamese children who sold the narcotics every day. Once soldiers returned home, of course, the problems continued: kicking the drug habit was difficult, especially given the emotional stress of returning home; drugs were prohibitively expensive in the United States; and doctors worried that malaria and other blood-borne illnesses would rise due to needle-sharing and blood donations.

Within the paradigm of rehabilitating soldiers and reducing drug use and dependence, the chaplain school course offered specific suggestions and techniques for chaplains to use in dealing with drug users. The first step for the chaplain, according to the course pamphlet, was to understand himself and "his own ability to handle conflict and transference of the drug abuser." Second, the chaplain could help provide an essential part of a "value system" for an addicted soldier, helping him to identify and deal with his "religious strivings, a fear of death, loneliness, and a sense of meaninglessness." Alcohol (or drugs), the course suggested, "provides something to fill the value-vacuum in the abuser's inner world," thus the chaplain could help a soldier reestablish quality relationships and boost his self-image in order to fill that void. Third, the chaplain should seek to "provide a relationship in which trust can be built, acceptance offered, and the grace of God made evident." Finally, the course emphasized that the chaplain's response to drug and alcohol abuse must be person-centered: the chaplain's focus is the "personal problem" rather than the "chemical problem," emphasizing the connection between the spiritual and the psychiatric. The course material concluded with the charge that chaplains should "provide an open, warm, responsible atmosphere in which the person in need of help can take a new look at himself and try out a new life style in the safety and encouragement of one who brings [the] spiritual dimension into focus."[35] Whereas servicewide regulations placed the chaplain within the larger military solution to the drug problem, Chaplain Corps curricular materials emphasized the moral, and often explicitly religious, underpinnings for drug rehabilitation and counseling. The chaplains in these circumstances seem to have valued the religious priority of pastoral care and counseling over the military value of moral and physical fitness for service.

Unfortunately, the historical record is thin on the issue of chaplains' effectiveness in addressing the drug problem. Some anecdotes suggest the overall program was of limited effectiveness. Chaplain Llewellyn Murdock, for example, commented in Ackermann's official history survey that "people on drugs need[ed] much more than we could provide." On the other hand, others assert that it was the advent of a fast and reliable urinalysis test that helped end this particular crisis.[36] Ultimately, though, regardless of effectiveness, how military chaplains involved themselves in the program highlights their liminal position and provides a clear example of some chaplains working to reconcile their religious and military identities and roles—and in many cases appearing to privilege their religious identity over their military one.

A fourth area in which chaplains' official and nonreligious duties overlapped with unofficial and religious ones was CAPs, which constituted a major part of the American effort in Vietnam.[37] As the chaplains' orientation guide explained, CAP activities were designed "to use military resources for the benefit of civilian communities, such as assisting in health, welfare, and public works project, improving living conditions, alleviating suffering, and improving the economic base of the country." "Such programs," according to the guide, "seek to gain the support, loyalty, and respect of the people for the Armed Forces and to emphasize the concept of freedom and worth of the individual." They were part of the U.S. campaign to win the "hearts and minds" of the Vietnamese people.[38] Chaplains would play a critical, though often unofficial, role in these programs.

American Army divisions had three basic civic action/civil affairs requirements within their area of operations (AO): "to establish a civic action program in the vicinity of the division base; to provide support for tactical operations; and to assist the government of Vietnam in winning the support of the Vietnamese people and in being more responsive in meeting the needs of the people."[39] CAP initiatives included both "short-range, high impact" projects designed to gain rapid acceptance in an area and long-range projects undertaken by units permanently stationed in a particular area. Short-range projects included "providing sick-call in hamlets and villages; distributing relief supplies; repairing bridges, roads, and culverts; constructing shower facilities, latrines, wells, and bulletin boards; and distributing candy to children." Long-range projects included "the improvement of district dispensaries; the construction of schools, libraries, village dispensaries, and playgrounds; the training of midwives and medical technicians; conducting classes in hygiene, sanitation, first aid, and the English language; and the sponsoring of orphanages, refugee camps, communities, leprosariums, and Boy Scout troops."[40]

The most significant way in which chaplains contributed to CAPs was through the collection and apportionment of donations—officially, nonappropriated funds—usually collected at worship services and other venues.[41] Chaplains in Vietnam, the United States, and other overseas posts made concerted efforts to raise money for various causes in Vietnam. A campaign to raise money for the Go Vap Orphanage, for example, yielded $32,736.48 in donations by mid-1965.[42] In the second quarter of 1967, military service members at Tuy Hoa Air Base donated more than $59,000 in materials and more than 2,600 man hours to civic action projects.[43] On some posts, chaplains conducted informal collection drives, and at others (mainly stateside posts), friendly fund-raising competitions between Protestants and Catholics emerged.

The Army chief of chaplains was quick to point out, and many commanders agreed, however, that participating in CAPs was not technically within the realm of chaplains' duties and suggested that chaplains should not become too entangled in them. In response to a MACV chaplain who wished to begin a program of sponsorship of Army of the Republic of Vietnam (ARVN) units in order to meet the "immediately urgent demands of dependents of Vietnamese servicemen for clothing, shoes, certain kinds of food, personal hygiene items, and so on," the chief replied that there was considerable merit in such assistance but that the chaplain should contact the United States Army, Vietnam (USARV) staff chaplain and the MACV chaplain to arrange for such assistance through recognized and supported channels. The chief was apparently wary of engaging in long-standing commitments, such as those made in Korea, from which chaplains had found it difficult to extricate themselves and their units.[44]

Chaplains frequently reported that their interactions with local Vietnamese civilians were among the most meaningful of their tours. Their efforts in this regard also increased goodwill in the United States among religious congregations and organizations. In 1971, for example, a United Methodist chaplain newsletter ran a picture of chaplain Ralph VanLandingham, installation chaplain at Bien Hoa Air Base, giving chickens to the sisters of Ke Sat Orphanage in Ho Nai. The picture was titled "So Children Could Have Eggs for Breakfast," and the caption told readers that the Protestant congregation at Bien Hoa had donated the $239 gift.[45] Navy chaplain Francis Burchell reported that his unit was involved in various civic action projects: "Benches were built and placed in the Cat Lo town library; repair three class rooms and dig a well for a school at Vung Tau; rebuilt playground equipment and built desks and chairs for a school at Cat Lo."[46] Chaplains also accompanied doctors, nurses, and medics on Medical Civil Action Programs, where they distributed treats to children and established contacts with local leaders.[47] The reports were not, however, free of paternalist attitudes. A chaplain at the Third Surgical Hospital reported to his colleagues at home that he was always "pleased to see the dedication and enterprise demonstrated by the educated and committed folk" at the "Catholic school and orphanage in Can Tho."[48]

Other congregations focused their efforts on supporting local religious communities. Donald Concklin's battalion donated their chapel to "Go Gong Village when [the] unit was relocated. The building was reassembled on its new location by personnel of the unit." The unit newspaper reported that the "donation of the chapel intact, is believed to be the first of its kind in Vietnam."[49] Donald Rich reported that he had considerable and sustained contacts with American missionaries and Vietnamese churches. Because he was a Protestant chaplain assigned to a remote area, he often relied on Vietnamese Catholic priests, most of whom spoke English, to provide coverage for his Catholic unit members.[50] James Johnson forged a long-lasting relationship with a local protestant Vietnamese clergyman, "Pastor Ha," while he was in Vietnam. Ha was killed in the aftermath of American withdrawal, and thirty years after the war, Johnson was able to contact and reconnect with Pastor Ha's daughter, who still lived in Vietnam.[51] Many chaplains understood that these liaisons with local religious communities and people were critical not only to the military mission but also to their work as ministers and pastors. Working with local people allowed them to develop a broad understanding of their purpose in Vietnam.

Morality in War

When chaplains arrived in Vietnam, issues of morality and religious practices present in the United States did not disappear, and they once again found themselves in the middle. As on stateside assignments, chaplains deployed to Vietnam walked a fine line between their two worlds. If they could not be held up as moral examples, they risked losing credibility as clergy. But if they could not relate to soldiers—in mess halls or clubs, in the field, or around base—they risked losing credibility as soldiers. In practice, chaplains had to make decisions about which issues were worth fighting over, set moral and ethical standards for themselves, and adapt to different situations. Chaplains frequently faced moral dilemmas when confronted with practices that were common to military life, including alcohol use, profanity, and sex. Chaplains responded to these situations differently, usually based on a combination of their own religious views, their understanding of the military situation, and their perceived relationship to the soldiers and officers with whom they worked.

For many evangelical and conservative chaplains, alcohol use proved to be a serious testing ground. In response to a query about the position of the Southern Baptist Convention (SBC) on chaplains imbibing alcohol, the SBC Chaplains Commission stated in a newsletter, in all capital letters: "THE SOUTHERN BAPTIST CONVENTION CHAPLAINS COMMISSION WILL NOT ISSUE DENOMINATIONAL ENDORSEMENT FOR A CHAPLAINCY POSITION TO A DRINKING MINISTER, OR ONE WHO IS REPORTED TO BE A DRINKER. FURTHER, THE COMMISSION WILL NOT CONTINUE DENOMINATIONAL ENDORSEMENT OF A KNOWN DRINKING SOUTHERN BAPTIST CHAPLAIN."[52] The position was unequivocal. For some chaplains, especially for those in conservative denominations that declared drinking alcohol to be sinful, the choice to abstain seemed easy enough. On the ground, however, the choice was more complicated. Chaplains made decisions about their own use of or abstention from alcohol, but they still had to relate to the troops, and to do so without compromising their personal beliefs or their ministry. In one apparently unsuccessful case, Joseph Dulany heard that his replacement was ill-received by the troops when he allegedly refused to enter the Officer Club "because the men were drinking beer."[53] Dulany does not, however, report whether or not he had gained the admiration or trust of his fellow officers by socializing with them. On the other hand, James Hutchens, who was uncomfortable with the heavy drinking that accompanied a ritual in which new unit members were inducted, decided to participate in the ceremonies, but he replaced the potent drink with lukewarm water.[54] He understood the significance of the initiation but chose not to abandon a central tenet of his religious belief. Curt Bowers, who was also a teetotaler, reported that upon returning from an extended period in the field, he found nothing but beer at the base camp when sodas had been promised as well but concluded after some contemplation, "I knew they [the troops] were looking, and I had made my stand in terms of alcohol, so I thought to myself, You haven't drunk up to this time, so don't start it now."[55] Though the situation as reported stretches the bounds of credibility, Bowers framed this dilemma in his memoir, written primarily for a domestic religious audience, as one of setting and meeting expectations rather than as one about the absolute immorality of a chaplain drinking.

Alcohol use was most likely less of an issue for Catholics, Jews, and mainline Protestants since their respective denominations tended not to forbid or frown upon drinking alcohol (although drunkenness was another matter) Their decisions, then, may have been less stressful and probably went unnoticed by the majority of men they served. Nevertheless, for chaplains for whom drinking was a serious moral issue, their decisions generally reflected compliance with their personal or institutional moral and religious codes.

Other moral issues such as profanity and prostitution likewise tested chaplains. Soldiers and officers frequently apologized for using expletives in a chaplain's presence, and again, chaplains responded in different ways. Some defused the situation with humor, others confronted the issue as a problem, and still others ignored it or dismissed it as an insignificant offense given the circumstances.[56] There were similarly diverse, though generally negative, responses to prostitution and to officers' tacit or explicit approval of it. Some protested loudly, others accepted it as an unavoidable if regrettable fact. Still others reflected on the strength of their own relationships with their wives at home, implying that though separation from their wives was difficult, their faith and marriage enabled them to resist temptation, or perhaps not even be tempted by the offer of easy sexual release.[57] Chaplains who served in combat and close to troops had to handle these issues in a much more delicate way than their colleagues who served in the civilian community or in rear areas of the military. Chaplains consistently recognized the moral ambiguities and stress brought about by combat. Issues that may have been black and white in "the world" became gray in Vietnam.

In many wartime situations, the pattern of chaplain responses to moral, ethical, and religious dilemmas was remarkably diverse. Chaplains serving with combat units made different decisions from those with support units. Chaplains' responses changed depending on the command climate in a given unit. Chaplains relied on their personal beliefs to make decisions. They prioritized needs differently. What chaplains *should* do in these circumstances was up for debate, and what chaplains actually did confirmed that there were a variety of reasonable responses to different situations.

But, then, some situations do not seem at all ambiguous. The moral and ethical lines seem to be very clearly drawn, and what chaplains *should* do is plainly evident. How should chaplains respond when faced with the killing of enemy civilians or Prisoners of War (POWs), the mutilation of corpses, rape and assault, and torture? By the standards of international law, general orders, human decency, and religious mandates, these acts are wrong. Surely in these instances, the chaplain should act. He should say something, do something, make noise, preach about it, alert authorities, alert the media, alert someone. But the evidence is unsettling. In the face of atrocities and war crimes—particularly those committed by Americans in the Vietnam War—chaplains appeared to do little in response.

While it seems a reasonable goal for chaplains to work to influence the morality and ethics of a military unit, however, expecting that a chaplains' presence and ministry would eliminate immoral and unethical behavior—even at its most extreme —is unreasonable. The problems with this expectation are easy enough to discern: First, Chaplain Corps doctrine and field manuals consistently stressed that the chaplain's primary function within the military was to provide for the free exercise of religion among soldiers and to provide spiritual and pastoral care to servicemen and servicewomen. Their mission, in the language of the Chaplain Corps, was to "bring God to men and men to God." Chaplains' functions in this area would therefore serve to increase troop morale and combat effectiveness. Having chaplains integrated into units was a matter of *military*, not religious, necessity.

Second, the chaplain's role as a staff officer sometimes restricted the range of responses available to him. Suffusing the command with positive moral and ethical virtues was, ultimately, the responsibility of the commander. The commander, not the chaplain, held the power in the relationship, and expectations as to what the chaplain would or would not do varied widely. Some commanders worried that giving the chaplain a prominent role in the unit would make the men "soft" and diminish the combat effectiveness of a unit. Other commanders saw the chaplains' only role as being to counsel and provide spiritual support for individual soldiers. Still other commanders used their chaplains to articulate specific values, including some related to the issue of atrocities.

In his memoir, chaplain James Burnham relates an incident that occurred in 1967 when he was assigned to a battalion attached to the Americal Division, based at Chu Lai. The battalion commander told Burnham of rumors about a company that was reportedly "shooting anything that moves" and asked the chaplain to talk to the men when they returned to rest and refit. Chaplain Burnham, after wrestling with what to say for a few days, finally decided on an approach using "mild biblical injunctions"—namely "do unto others as you would have them do unto you" and "whatever a man sows, so also will he reap." Burnham specifically shied away from the more obvious "thou shalt not murder." He warned against taking revenge and "doing things to make the peasants hate" American troops.[58] Burnham reports that things soon returned to "normal" and that the rumors stopped—but he is also very frank about the fact that he may not have had anything to do with it.

Other commanders took their chaplains' advisement and confronted the issue themselves: In 1967, recalled Parker Thompson, a supervisory chaplain, that one of his chaplains with the 1st Cavalry reported that soldiers had been cutting off the ears of North Vietnam Army soldiers for souvenirs. Thompson reported it to the division chief of staff, who reported it to the division commander. The chaplain recalled that "two days later our Commander had an officers' call. It was the only one of its type I ever experienced in the 1st Cavalry. He directed that *every* officer be present, down to platoon leaders, at one of several sessions. There were *no exceptions*." At the meeting, the commander warned: "What constitutes a crime in the United States of America, constitutes a crime in the 1st Cavalry. And I will prosecute anyone violating proper conduct to enemy personnel, living or dead. It's a short step from mutilating a corpse to mutilating a person."[59] In this instance, the chaplain's report to the commander resulted in a swift and strong command response.

Both of these apparently successful interventions relied on the close co-operation between chaplains and commanders. Creating a climate where atrocities would not happen—and would be punished if they came to light—could not be the chaplains' job alone. Further, logistical challenges and simple manpower issues worked against chaplains' abilities to ensure comprehensive, consistent, and continuous coverage and support to all units in Vietnam. The practice of area coverage ensured moderately con-sistent support, but most troops saw a chaplain only once every four to six weeks. Understanding the institutional culture and constraints in which a chaplain operated provides a starting point for understanding how chap-lains reacted to war crimes and atrocities, but it fails to take into consider-ation two of the most basic functions of chaplains, providing pastoral care and religious services and education. Chaplains occasionally used these opportunities to raise moral questions—clear evidence that chaplains worked to set a climate in which moral and ethical discussions were part of the daily rhythms of life. But this sort of quiet modeling and example may have had limited effects. As in many other cases, the massacre at My Lai is instructive.

At My Lai, the practice of area coverage and a general shortage of chap-lains meant that the company responsible for the massacre saw a chaplain only occasionally. In this case, the division artillery chaplain, Carl Cre-swell, had dropped by a Task Force Barker planning meeting the day before the mission. Creswell later recalled, "They were going to do insertion or combat assault or whatever it took in Pinkville," a location he described as "quite frankly, . . . the home of the 48th VC Battalion. And I went in there . . . it was just a courtesy call. I had no business there, chaplains do this, just stopped in to say 'hello' and meet the new commander." And while he was there, they "had the maps laid out on the board" and a major on the staff said, "We're going in there and if we get one round out of there, we're going to level it." And I looked at him and I said, "You know, I didn't really think we made war that way." And he looked at me and he said, "It's a tough war, Chaplain."[60]

Even away from the front lines, the chaplain held an informal position as a spokesperson for military moral decision-making. In his book, *On Kill-ing*, Dave Grossman, a retired army lieutenant colonel, recounts a story of a battalion chaplain at Fort Lewis, Washington, talking to a group of soldiers after a POW exercise. The soldiers suggest that enemy POWs be used to test nerve gas or claymore mines or be used to reconnoiter for nuclear and chemical weapons. In response, according to Grossman, "the chaplain cited the Geneva conventions and discussed our nation as a force of righteousness and the support of God for our cause." Grossman goes on to say, "To pragmatic soldiers this moral approach didn't go far. The Geneva Convention was dismissed, and our forward observer said that in school they had told him that 'the Geneva convention says you can't fire white phosphorus at troops; so you call it in on their equipment.' The young artilleryman's logic was 'if we're gonna find ways around the Geneva convention, what do you think the enemy is gonna do?"[61] Chaplains *saying* something or even modeling moral and ethical behavior could not necessarily prevent atrocities. In this case, the chaplain's position in the middle seems to have limited his effectiveness.

But more difficult to explain are numerous charges that chaplains, once made aware of atrocities, did little to make them known or to stop them. In the case of My Lai, though no chaplains were present at the massacre, division chaplains quickly became embroiled in the deeply flawed investigation and subsequent cover-up. In its report, the Peers Commission, charged with the formal investigation, placed significant blame on division personnel for not following through with their obligations to report potential violations of military law and conduct. It also advised that the two chaplains most directly involved, Captain Carl Creswell and Lieutenant Colonel Francis Lewis, be court-martialed. According to the commission, Hugh Thompson reported what he had seen at My Lai to Creswell, the division artillery chaplain. Chaplain Creswell, in turn, without reporting the matter to his commander, went to Lewis, the division chaplain, with the story. Lewis's efforts at investigation were futile, and he allowed the matter to pass without substantive effort to bring it to the attention of his superiors. Though neither had witnessed the action, and Creswell did inform Lewis, his superior, the commission concluded that neither chaplain performed his duty.[62]

In his defense, Creswell contended that he "should have done more" but that he had—albeit to a minimal extent—followed the chain of command and reported it to his supervising chaplain. A 1972 *New York Times* article claimed, "Such incidents, along with general frustration about the conduct of the war, have served to revive the old "two masters" problem concerning chaplains in the armed forces."[63] The edited volume, *Military Chaplains*, published by Clergy and Laymen Concerned about Vietnam (CALCAV) and edited by Harvard theologian and historian Harvey Cox, used this example to make the same point. According to many of the volume's authors, chaplains could not be expected to adequately fulfill their religious duties if they were saddled with military ones.

Other atrocities that never received the media attention or postwar scrutiny of My Lai most certainly occurred, though their extent and frequency are still hotly debated. Even in the limited number of reports of atrocities, however, chaplains are often portrayed as doing nothing, or perhaps going through a military chain of command but nothing more.

Chaplain Claude Newby writes that once he "saw two confirmed VC, a seventeen-year-old female and a VC Master Sergeant (or equivalent rank)," taken as POWs. He also recounted that he saw "two [ARVN] soldiers . . . interrogating a VC or native suspected of being VC. Wires ran from a hand-cranked generator to the suspect's bare genitals." He continued, "The Vietnamese interrogators seemed unconcerned about me watching them, which led me to conclude this type of interrogation might be a common practice." Newby did not, however, report the incident, inaction that he later regretted. He justified his response, however, saying that he "didn't know what to do as it involved natives on a native compound," implying that he might have done something had the incident involved an American soldier.[64] Army chaplain Joseph Dulany recorded several instances where he witnessed or heard about questionable behavior but did not report them or confront the men involved. Among other incidents, Dulany recalled seeing soldiers dragging women behind huts followed by screaming and crying; a truck driver intentionally running over someone on the side of the road; and violent interrogation techniques.

Chaplains' responses (or, perhaps more accurately, nonresponses) to atrocities and war crimes have provided rich fodder for those who identify role conflict as the primary framework for analyzing and evaluating military chaplains' actions. Gordon Zahn's extensive sociological study of a group of Royal Air Force Chaplains is a key example. Zahn, a pacifist, completed the study during the Vietnam War—it was published in 1969—and the reverberations of contemporary events are evident. When reporting that a significant number of chaplains responded that they could not comment on the "average" chaplain's response to hypothetical atrocities committed in a time of war, for example, Zahn wrote, "It is unthinkable that any Christian clergyman would be unable to express some judgment concerning such things as the killing of enemy prisoners or civilian hostages, the use of torture. . . . If there is a more plausible explanation it probably lies in . . . the mechanism of 'compartmentalization,'" leading—in his mind—to the chaplains' wholly unsatisfactory responses to the questions he posed. He continued, "The revolting record of alleged Viet Cong captives being slashed, keel-hauled, and otherwise maltreated by their captors had . . . brought what might have been another 'hypothetical question' to actuality." He expressed shock and outrage that "only 23 (62.2 per cent of the chaplains interviewed) took the position that the use of torture is intrinsically wrong and may never be permitted. This is somewhat surprising, of course. . . . One would have been justified in expecting unanimous condemnation of the practice from any sample group consisting entirely of Christian clergyman."[65]

More recent studies would suggest Zahn was perhaps overstating the extent to which Christians, even clergy, would object to torture or the commission of atrocity in war. In 2006, Stephen Louden repeated a similar critique, that chaplains were too beholden to their military masters to do anything of substance in the face of atrocities.[66] A poll released in 2009 by the Pew Forum on Religion and Public Life concluded that white, evangelical Christians were more likely to support the use of torture in limited cases (more than 60 percent responded affirmatively) than were their unchurched counterparts, only 40 percent of whom would sometimes support such measures.[67] Interpretations such as those put forward by Zahn and Louden are persistent in the limited academic literature about military chaplains, but they are too simplistic and are based on a too-narrow conception of the "Christian" worldview. Neither torture, nor war crimes, nor chaplains' problematic responses to them had disappeared in the intervening years between the Vietnam War and American intervention in Iraq and Afghanistan. Thus, rather than this apparent contradiction between chaplains' upholding given tenets of faith and their not doing enough to stop atrocities proving that they subordinated their religious identity or role to their military one, a more careful reading suggests that the primary source of tension for chaplains was *internal* to their religious worldviews and their understanding of their various roles within the military community.

During the Vietnam War, as mainline and liberal religious communities coalesced more and more strongly against the war, critics of the military chaplaincy frequently called for military chaplains to serve a prophetic function within the military—in the tradition of Jeremiah and the Old Testament prophets—and highlighted the chaplains' responsibility to advise commanders on matters concerning religion, morality, and ethics.[68]

Chaplains, however, usually understood their role differently. Consistently, during and after the war, chaplains claimed that their primary role was a priestly, or pastoral, one. They were present as ministers, not prophets. Their allegiance was to service members, not to the nation or even moral ideals. In one postwar survey of Vietnam-era chaplains, most said that their most important role was to be present—simply being near and with soldiers in the war zone. They also named counseling and visitation of the wounded as their other top priorities. Chaplains also identified these as their most important duties based on the relative allocation of time given to each.[69] Soldiers and officers likewise ranked the chaplain's ministry of "presence" as his most important duty in Vietnam, and the one that occupied most of his time. Officers ranked "counseling" second in terms of importance and time spent, while enlisted personnel ranked "visitation of sick and wounded" as second in importance (third in terms of time spent) and "worship services" as third in importance and third in terms of time spent. Granted, "prophetic witness" was not one of the choices listed in the survey, yet the surveys indicate no "other" responses that would have placed this activity higher on the list.[70] Not even the choice of providing moral and ethical guidance ranked higher. Indeed, one could conclude that the very idea of a chaplain serving as a prophetic voice within the military would have been far from most chaplains', commanders', or soldiers' minds. It is certainly possible to question and criticize their failure to act as a prophetic witness, but it is intellectually dishonest to dismiss it as irreligious or a perversion of Judeo-Christian scripture, doctrine, or practice.

This conclusion about chaplains' fundamental purpose in the war did not mean, however, that chaplains had a simplistic or even simply utilitarian view of atrocities or of the appropriate responses to them. Reflecting on his nonresponsiveness to war crimes in his memoir, for example, Chaplain Claude Newby wrote, "One of my great regrets is that I didn't interfere with [the] interrogation" he witnessed, but even if regret after the fact is appropriate, the decision at the time would also seem to demand an explanation.[71] And Chaplain Joseph Dulany—who also admitted to doing nothing in the face of possible atrocities—plainly interpreted his inaction as a failure to fulfill his duties as a clergyman and an officer. He wrote, "[Were they] atrocities? I'm not confident that any I witnessed or knew about achieved this level, but morally questionable? Probably." He asked himself, "What should my response have been? How could I have responded and maintained my stature and effectiveness as a unit chaplain? What can be learned from these instances that might be helpful to a chaplain in future combat settings?" Ultimately, Dulany had no answers to these questions, and he remained conflicted. Reflecting on his inaction, Dulany expressed his doubt that he had had the rank, training, or authority to question effectively such practices (some of which were de facto policies), so must have concluded, if unconsciously, at the time that he would be most effective as a chaplain if he did not report the atrocities. In these cases, he defined his role not by moral or religious absolutes, but by his devotion to ministering to the men serving in Vietnam. For Dulany, the problem arose from conflicting *religious* expectations, that is, in Vietnam he was expected both to set a moral standard and to provide a ministry of presence and comfort to men in war, which he felt sometimes meant holding back on moral judgment. The question was how to fulfill effectively all of his religious roles, not how to fulfill his role as both pastor and officer.[72]

Chaplain Joseph O'Donnell, in laying out what he determined were the essential characteristics of a successful chaplain, identified a significant potential source for internal conflict. The "chaplain," he wrote, "[must] understand the nature of confidentiality, or Rule of Privilege, as it is called in the Manual for Courts Martial, the operative, judicial portion of the Uniform Code of Military Justice. . . . It is quite restrictive, with a presumption of privilege for almost any one-on-one conversation. As a chaplain, I have to know when to keep my mouth shut. *Nothing could be worse for a chaplain than to be labeled someone who cannot keep a secret. If that occurs, his or her ministry is finished.* . . .There have been a number of federal court cases involving the Rule of Privilege. In my almost thirty years as a naval chaplain, I never heard of any chaplain deliberately violating this rule."[73] O'Donnell pointed out one area in which the chaplain's religious requirements and military duties interacted but might require him to privilege his religious obligation over his military one or even a moral appeal to reveal information about a war crime.

Sometimes, the quasi-religious nature of war and combat contributed to the chaplain's inaction in the face of atrocities. Not infrequently, soldiers' responses to the horrors of combat could resemble religious rituals, and in these cases, chaplains, too, could be swept up in the moment. Chaplain James Johnson recalled that, after a particularly intense firefight, there were "two dead VC . . . sprawled on their backs. Each one must have at least twenty holes in his face and other exposed body parts. Someone in the column takes his white plastic spoon from his C-rations and sticks the handle into a wound made by the fragments. The next soldier in line does likewise. By the time I pass the position, each dead VC has a dozen or more plastic spoons protruding from his body." Though the scene was gruesome, the quasi-religious ritual and solemnity struck Johnson: "There's no shouting or cheering as we pass the bodies. The defiant symbolism of 'sticking it to them' may be desecration of the dead, but this is a way of emotionally coping with what's happening each day of this god-awful war."[74] Johnson remained ambivalent, recognizing the action for what it was in a legal sense, but understanding and even sympathizing with the motive.

Chaplains' reflections on their own responses to atrocities are also telling. Chaplains' writing about war crimes and atrocities often reveals deep anguish about what they did or did not do. Some chaplains were surprised and disturbed by their capacity to hate the enemy, their little remorse for Viet Cong deaths, and their ability to stomach the horrors of combat. In his wartime journal, after going with a platoon on a patrol in which several suspected Viet Cong fighters were killed, James Johnson wrote, "I admit I'm glad to see these dead VC[,] but as a Christian, I'm not proud of my feelings. . . . These guys all have mothers and wives and girlfriends, but after what they did to the civilians I don't have positive feelings for any of them."[75] Chaplains, like other participants in the war, questioned their own moral responses to the horrors of combat. In Johnson's case, as in others, however, the conflict remained internal. If Johnson was unsure about his own responses in war, what actions might we reasonably expect him to take in terms of the entire unit's behavior?

Chaplains also identified a host of scriptures, doctrines, and practices that could be used to support a more restrained response to atrocities committed in wartime. Chaplain Jerry Autry, in his memoir about his service as a combat chaplain in Vietnam, wrote,

> You can think what you want about My Lai—it's awful and tragic any way you look at it because of bad decisions, poor judgment, and a thousand and one other things. But, in a situation like war, where your men are being killed daily, you're in a constant state of anxiety; you don't know who the enemy is, and bad things happen. Judgment can become impaired. Some days, it's pretty clear what's right and wrong, but about a guy like Calley [the commander of the unit responsible for the My Lai massacre], who maybe didn't have much emotional sophistication and was not overly smart, I would never be too judgmental. . . . At some time during his sojourn in Vietnam, an officer would be thrown into

a chaotic, confusing situation. Maybe this is not what happened with Lieutenant Calley, but he certainly was ill-prepared and ill-equipped. Understanding, tempered with mercy, is not a bad thing."[76]

This response requires careful analysis: it can easily be interpreted as making an excuse for criminal behavior—to suggest, even slightly, that an appropriate response to war crimes is compassion or mercy for the perpetrator, rather than condemnation and the renunciation of evil seems to violate many basic codes of morality, religious faith, and humanity. And it certainly seems to validate the critique that chaplains were more beholden to their military masters than to their religious calling. Autry's explanation falls well short of condemning even the act itself, but it does still exhibit a religiously-oriented response to the problem of atrocities. Autry's reading of Calley may be uncomfortable, problematic, and deeply flawed, but ultimately, "understanding tempered with mercy" is a religious response to the fact of atrocities. What it does not seem to be is a fully reconciled religious response that accounts for both perpetrator and victim.

But sometimes, if only occasionally, chaplains did do something. Their responsibilities in cases where they heard about atrocities after the fact were manifold: they were to act as spiritual advisers to soldiers who may have been involved in the crime, to seek justice on behalf of the victim, and to uphold military and legal regulations. To illustrate this sort of chaplain response, one narrative is instructive. Chaplain Claude Newby—the same chaplain who reported that he did not intervene during a questionable interrogation—learned of a truly horrific war crime several days after it took place. Unlike some of Newby's other stories, this one is fairly well corroborated by an extensive piece of investigative journalism, which culminated in the essay "Casualties of War" and a film of the same name.[77] Newby was a trusted spiritual adviser to a man to whom another soldier had confided that he had witnessed a war crime while on patrol with a pony team. The team had kidnapped a Vietnamese teenager, Mao, forced her to come on a patrol with them, then repeatedly raped and beat her. Eventually, members of the team brutally murdered her before they returned from the patrol. A soldier on the patrol team who refused to participate in the beatings, rape, or murder came to Newby at the urging of his friend, seeking spiritual counsel and guidance. Newby had to negotiate the issue of clerical privilege—in this case, it meant informing the soldier that if he talked to Newby in the presence of his buddy (as he wished to do), that privilege would not attach. He counseled the witness through the emotional process of taking the allegations to the commander, he worked with the commander to counsel other members of the unit who had heard about the atrocity, and he was a witness in the courts-martial hearings.[78]

On the whole, though, cases such as this one were relatively rare. Chaplains' responses—many of them deeply problematic and certainly flawed—to American war crimes and atrocities varied. Interpreting the variety of responses as specifically religious ones also requires careful attention to the silences in the sources. In both archival and published accounts, chaplains rarely, if ever, appealed to military necessity or military effectiveness to explain or excuse the commission of war crimes or the failure to report them. If they recognized moral ambiguity, they recognized the pressure of combat and the muddying of moral clarity in war. They were generally firm in upholding the importance of the chain of command, but they did not suggest that military commanders always (or even usually) made the right decision. When they considered their role within the military, the chaplain's focus was more likely to be on the significance of pastoral care in a war zone than on working through thorny theological, moral, and ethical dilemmas.

Even in cases that appeared to be morally black and white, chaplains' responses suggest a more complicated, ambiguous situation. Combat, emotion, duty, and perhaps even psychological necessity shaped chaplains' responses, just as it shaped the responses of other soldiers and officers. On the surface, it may seem that chaplains responded to these problems by compartmentalizing or simply rationalizing their inactivity, but this analysis suggests a more complicated scenario, namely, that chaplains dealt with these issues by making choices—sometimes conscious, sometimes not—that reflected the tensions and conflict *internal* to their religious worldviews and personal beliefs. More often than not, they privileged the role of pastor over the role of prophet or adviser. The choices were complex and certainly not immune from critique, but both priest and prophet are fundamentally religious roles.

If we return to the popular images of military chaplains, it is easy to see how the traditional interpretation of chaplains' responses to wartime atrocities supports both the first and third archetypes—the militarist and the incompetent. If we believe that the chaplain, facing intense role conflict, compartmentalized his roles and did nothing in the face of moral outrage, it becomes very easy to paint him either as complicit in the atrocities, that he was simply a cog in the military machine, or alternatively, as a bumbling, ineffective fool whose inaction and missteps had dire and deadly consequences. But as we might expect, the archetypes and popular images are too simple and misleading. Both analyzing chaplains' responses to war by taking into account their own interpretations and understandings and taking a more expansive view of what it might mean to be religious and act "religiously" in the midst of war leads to different conclusions. Collectively, chaplains were neither militant legitimizers of atrocity and violence nor paragons of religious and moral virtue, but neither were they entirely ineffective, paralyzed by the constraints and tensions inherent in mixing the realms of religion and war. Chaplains' position in the middle of military and religious roles and identities led to significant variations in their responses to morally complex situations. Chaplains' responses were determined by context as well as personal moral beliefs and religious training.

In all of these areas—from apparently mundane issues such as profanity, to complex ones like carrying weapons, to critically important ones such as responding to atrocities or war crimes—the chaplain discharged both military and religious duties. On one hand, military efficiency and necessity obligated the chaplain to act in the best interest of the unit and the military service to ensure his own safety, to make objective assessments about a service member's religious beliefs, advise commanders on matters of discharging or reassigning a soldier over CO status, to address drug use and addiction, and to assist with CAPs. On the other hand, the chaplain's commitment to the pastoral care of soldiers and officers and even to local Vietnamese communities compelled him to act in ways sometimes at odds with his military duties and potentially in conflict with deeply held religious tenets.

From this perspective, a chaplain's decisions may be interpreted differently. The decision to arm himself or not, for example, did not necessarily reflect a desire for self-preservation but rather reflected where the chaplain himself thought he might be most needed or most helpful. In drug counseling, the goal was probably not simply to return men to fighting condition but to mitigate both the need for and the effects of drug use on the whole person. In some cases, especially in humanitarian projects, chaplains' military and religious goals seemed to dovetail nicely, while in others, their military obligations and religious values and directives appeared to come into direct conflict. As chaplains confronted difficult religious and moral questions, they acted in ways to retain both religious and military authority and credibility. Chaplains frequently used religious language and beliefs to define their entry and assimilation into a new culture, though their status and identities remained ambiguous. In the midst of war, chaplains focused on practical solutions to the problems. When they were confronted with issues that demanded a religious response, for example, war crimes or atrocities, chaplains tended to privilege their duty to provide pastoral care and spiritual support to soldiers over their duty to ensure or enforce moral behaviors. In all cases, this flexibility allowed the chaplain to retain his status as a person in the middle and offered him a broad range of responses rather than narrowly prescribed ones.

Conflict was often central to chaplains' experiences, but centering this conflict in chaplains' dual roles as clergy and officer, assumes a fundamental incompatibility between religion (specifically Christianity) and war (and specifically the Vietnam War). Far earlier than widespread secular dissent, nonpacifist religious dissent emerged when Lyndon Johnson escalated the war by inserting American combat troops into Vietnam in 1965, and it intensified until the eventual withdrawal of American troops in 1972. Historian Mark Toulouse has argued convincingly that even major Evangelical and conservative Christian periodicals had turned against the war, or at least softened their support for it, by the early 1970s.[79] Given the cultural forces that aligned against the war, it was indeed difficult to imagine significant Christian responses to the Vietnam War that fell outside of general opposition to the war.

But the vision of Christianity that would make role conflict most likely or acute was generally not the vision of chaplains. Understanding how chaplains responded to various kinds of conflict in the Vietnam War reveals a different picture. At the most basic level, their writings demand a reinterpretation of the meaning and sources of conflict for chaplains. If the conflict arose from contradictions and inconsistencies *within* a chaplain's religious beliefs rather than from inherent role conflict, then how the chaplain resolved that conflict in both military and religious terms becomes more readily apparent. Rather than compartmentalizing or subordinating certain identities, the process of conflict resolution became an exercise in identity management that involved both religious and military concerns.

CHAPTER FOUR

Liturgy and Interpretation

Somewhere in Vietnam, in a bomb crater filled with water, Joseph Dulany baptized soldiers, and in those moments, remnants of death and destruction became founts for the symbolic waters of life. On another military base, James Johnson grieved as he held the lifeless body of a friend who was killed on a mission Johnson would have been on had he not stayed behind to baptize another soldier, and was left pondering the significance of trading a new spiritual birth for a death. Later, Johnson recorded in great detail the mutilation of a Viet Cong corpse by American servicemen with C-ration plastic spoons, and agonized over his inability to respond according to his moral beliefs. On a ship, Joseph O'Donnell anointed the mangled remains of eighteen Marines with the Catholic Sacrament of the Sick, a blessing performed as much for those left alive as for the dead. Curt Bowers baptized soldiers of different races, ethnicities, and backgrounds as others armed with automatic weapons stood watch to ensure their safety. Orris Kelly offered Communion to soldiers returning home, regardless of their religious preference, as a symbol of community and reconciliation. James Hutchens participated in every aspect of his unit's initiation ritual, though he substituted lukewarm water for liquor. Chaplain Tumkin went AWOL (absent without leave) when conditions at camp got too rough.

In the midst of day-to-day work—holding services, filling out paperwork, traveling to units, counseling soldiers, and visiting troops—and occasionally as a result of it, chaplains confronted a variety of problems in Vietnam. As chaplains worked through complex moral, theological, and pastoral dilemmas, they also adapted traditional religious practices and interpretations for the context of war and reframed the experience of war within religious paradigms. Doing so brought together two sets of cultural norms and values that at times appeared opposed to one another. Most often, chaplains—like those to whom they ministered—made decisions based on the exigencies of particular moments. As chaplains addressed the moral and theological problems described in Chapter 3, they also thought broadly about the morality of the Vietnam War, responded to changed liturgical and worship settings, and engaged in a creative process to lead the creation of diverse and dynamic liturgies of war, which were particularly suited to the war zone and further allowed participants to interpret their wartime experiences through a religious lens.

The Morality of the Vietnam War

Just as chaplains used a variety of religious lenses and interpretations to respond to questions of morality in war, so too did they use religious ideas, especially as perceived through the lens of the Cold War, to consider the morality of the Vietnam War as a whole. Their interpretations of the war's morality were especially important as they led soldiers, sailors, Marines, and airmen in worship and provided religious counseling. If chaplains could not credibly discuss the morality of serving in war, and of this war in particular, they risked losing the trust of those they were there to serve. Even so, chaplains were wary of engaging in this sort of theological exercise. Soldiers in combat needed reassurance of their moral goodness, perhaps of their salvation, because they also needed to remain militarily effective. Unsurprisingly, chaplains turned to proof texts and simple exegesis to accomplish these goals.

James Hutchens recalled that the sermons he gave before his unit deployed centered on the "responsibility to our government (Romans 13), the sixth commandment ('Thou shalt not kill'), and the problem of the Christian serving in the Army."[1] Hutchens crafted his sermons to reassure soldiers going into combat that what they were doing was not only morally defensible but also their duty. In the cramped quarters of troop ships, isolated at sea for three or four weeks at a time, soldiers, sailors, and airmen had ample time to question the morality of war and to participate in worship and Bible study. Curt Bowers recalled that the most common question asked was, "Can I be a Christian and still kill?" He answered using various examples from the Old and New Testaments to reassure soldiers of their duty and morality.[2] Yet he cautioned readers of his memoir not to frame this question solely in philosophical or theological terms. In combat, soldiers did not enjoy the "luxury" or safety of classrooms; they "were wrestling to find the real flesh-and-blood answers," for their battles would soon deal in flesh and blood rather than pen and paper.[3]

As in other wars, soldiers faced acute questions about morality, killing, and faith. In the heat of combat, few chaplains or soldiers were given to asking moral questions, and chaplains did not expect moral ambiguities to cloud or color the judgment of soldiers in the field. "In the midst of battle, everything seems impersonal," wrote Raymond Johnson. "Survival is a man's primary concern. Therefore, it's not fair to really pose the question of whether or not you can love your enemy under such conditions. You can't really require a black and white answer in the gray of conflict."[4] But once soldiers were out of immediate danger, Johnson concluded, morality and theology must necessarily reenter a soldier's (or chaplain's) conscience. Johnson suggested that while "Love your enemy" could not be a fair directive in the field, it became immediately relevant as soon as that enemy was captured. In such a case, a soldier was "responsible for rendering an answer to the question, 'How do I treat my enemy?' He becomes a real person. You must treat him as one who deserves to be called a creature of God."[5] This careful parsing of scripture and context suggests that chaplains did occasionally grapple with theological questions during the war. Johnson's language implied that combat, even for chaplains, dehumanized the enemy; if the enemy was not fully human, killing was simply a means for survival and could sometimes suspend ethical thinking.

In rear areas, however, after combat subsided, there were hints of moral questioning. Philip Caputo, a Marine officer and author of the memoir *A Rumor of War*, recalled a conversation with a chaplain that, at the time, angered him but later caused him to question the morality of the war. Caputo served as a platoon leader in 1965, and his unit suffered eighty-four casualties in two months, with twelve killed in action (KIA). In the mess hall one day, the chaplain said to him, "Maybe you could explain what we're doing over here. You've been a platoon commander. When we got here, we were just supposed to defend the airfield for a while and then go back to Okinawa. Now we're in the war to stay and nobody has been able to explain to me what we're doing. I'm no tactician, but the way it looks to me, we send men out on an operation, they kill a few VC, or the VC kill them, and then pull out and the VC come right back in. So we're back where we started. . . . I think these boys are getting killed for nothing."[6]

Caputo was put off by the chaplain's statement and responded that, all things considered, this war (Vietnam) was "not that bad a war" and that twelve KIAs were a minimal cost. The chaplain pushed back, emphasizing that twelve lives were lost and twelve families destroyed—and for what gain in the end? Caputo concluded, "The chaplain's morally superior attitude had rankled me, but his sermon had managed to plant doubt in my mind, doubt about the war. Much of what he had said made sense: our tactical operations did seem futile and directed toward no apparent end." The chaplain's words, along with "the events of that day, which had made a mockery of all the Catholic theology the Dominican and Jesuit priests had preached to me in high school and college" made Caputo question not only the execution of the war but also its meaning. He had been taught that "man's body is the Temple of the Holy Spirit; man is created in the image and likeness of God; have respect for the dead," but combat challenged these lessons, and he concluded, "Well, the four temples . . . had undergone considerable demolition, and it was hard to believe a Holy Spirit had ever resided in them."[7] This was the sort of prophetic ministry that home front dissenters wished chaplains would provide, but this example is nearly alone in published accounts.

After the 1968 Tet Offensive, chaplains were increasingly aware of religious dissent at home, demoralized troops, and the apparently waning chances for military success. Thomas Des Champs recalled thinking, "During that spring of 1970, I knew what the national news back home could not tell; we were not winning this war." Des Champs chose to reassure soldiers, even though he considered the situation hopeless: "As God's emissary to the troops, I found myself telling them everything would be 'all right.' But in my heart, I knew that everything wasn't or couldn't be 'all right.' No words can describe the horrors of war or the effects that it can have upon men's souls." In deciding to reassure soldiers, one might argue that Des Champs had abdicated his religious responsibilities in favor of military ones. Yet Des Champs viewed it differently. Rather than ignoring a religious conviction, Des Champs reinterpreted it to accommodate new circumstances: "To combat the impact of the horrors of war, I adopted a philosophy of divine confidence that even while the world appeared to be going to hell, God was still in control." Critics might dismiss this as simple rationalization, though the process of adaptation deserves more consideration than that argument affords.[8]

Other chaplains confronted the morality of warfare and their role in it when they were called upon to minister to Vietnamese civilians, often the victims of American military action. Richard Kemp, a Christian Scientist chaplain, wrote that ministering to Vietnamese civilians "[has] been quite challenging to my metaphysical position." After holding the head of a wounded Vietnamese man, and later learning that he was a North Vietnamese Army regular, Kemp was reminded of the scriptural injunction

"Love your enemies . . . pray for them which despitefully use you and perse-
cute you," which had been highlighted in that week's lesson-sermon.[9] When
Kemp ultimately concluded that "truly our enemy is that which defiles man,
and not a person," he was expressing his new theological understanding of
scripture in light of war.[10] Kemp's understanding of the enemy also affected
his relationship to the war. His interpretations of the morality of war and of
his relationship to the Vietnamese enemy show a case in which a chaplain
might be seen as undermining a national or military goal and upholding
his religious convictions. Competing roles or identities did not cause Kemp
to abandon or even question his faith or ministerial duties; rather, moral
conflict and religious reflection allowed Kemp to reach a different conclusion about the nature of the war.

Of all the first-person accounts considered in this study that tackle the
morality of the war, Corbin Cherry's collection of poetry, *From Thunder to
Sunrise*, is the most explicitly critical and anguished about the morality of
the war and his participation in it. In an early poem Cherry laments, "There
is no way that I can justify this war / these lives that are snuffed out each
day" and "The greatest crisis that we will have to face, / as we remember
those that died here, / is to recall all of the things/that we have done in
this place."[11] For most chaplains, however, the morality of the war figured
little in their recollections of their tours in Vietnam. The war, and their
presence in it, was a fact, an unavoidable culmination of choices, circumstance, and luck. Even Cherry, who was deeply ambivalent about the war
and unconvinced of its goodness, resigned himself to the duty that called
him to Vietnam. In anticipation of his arrival in Vietnam, he wrote, "All of
this seems so simple right now. / I fly there, / I get off the plane and do my
job." He knew he would do the job set before him, though his inexperience
terrified him—he had seen war movies, not war; had hiked, not humped
through jungles; had seen people die, "but not killed or being killed."[12]
These were the differences that would matter in the combat zone. The big
picture could not be seen without intense focus on the particulars of the
war on the ground, as it was actually experienced. Chaplains' first-person
accounts focus on the acts of ministry and worship in the midst of war.
While it may appear that this microlevel focus on the particularities of religious practice in Vietnam distracts from larger historiographical, theoretical, or analytical questions, in actuality, such a focus allows us to shift the
frame on these questions. How chaplains understood and reinterpreted
religious rituals, scripture, songs, and sacred meaning reveal how they
understood the larger war and their place in it.

The context of combat, where the threat of death or injury was ever-present, compelled many chaplains to perform their religious duties outside of the strict confines of their denominational practices or personal beliefs. Throughout Vietnam, conducting worship services and administering sacraments occupied a significant portion of chaplains' time. Religious practices in the field allowed chaplains and other service members to actively redefine what it meant to be religious in the military.[13]

Chaplains' lived experiences of religion in war are best understood by examining "liturgies of war," public acts of worship and community ritual that served to assign meaning to the combat experience.[14] Chaplains, as the primary liturgists—official leaders of these public acts—played a key role in this process. Chaplains and soldiers together reinterpreted familiar traditions and created new liturgical forms in part to make religious ideas compatible with combat and with the circumstance of war, but they also provided a direct link to religious traditions "back in the world." These wartime liturgical practices involved reassessing and reconfiguring the practice, as well as the meaning, of sacrament, scripture, song, and space. These creative, improvised liturgies were uniform in neither content nor meaning, but they allowed chaplains to interpret their combat experiences in religious ways to resolve potential conflicts between faith and war.[15]

Examining liturgies of war as both militarily and religiously significant also clarifies the ways in which the two realms interacted. It would be easy to write off confluences as simply one's borrowing language and meaning from the other sphere of experience—to conclude that the language of blood sacrifice in war, for example, had no religious significance, or to say that the song "Onward Christian Soldiers" had no military meaning. Yet taking into account both sets of cultural norms and values reveals more about each of these cultures than a single analytical perspective would. What conclusions can be drawn when "God" and "Country" appeared interchangeable in some liturgies of war, or when a Jewish soldier participated in a Christian celebration of Communion? Considering these examples simply as corruptions of "true" religion by asserting that only traditional religious interpretations deserve analysis would disregard any sort of religious meaning that may have existed. On the other end of the spectrum, dismissing the potential military significance of such events would downplay the intimate connections between religious and military experiences.

Studying wartime worship or liturgical practices only from the chaplain's point of view does pose certain analytical problems. Most notably, such an approach ignores enlisted personnel and officers' participation in and responses to these liturgies. This chapter focuses on chaplains' creation of, participation in, and interpretations of religious practice in war and emphatically does not claim that officers or enlisted personnel came to the same understandings, even as they participated in the liturgies of war alongside chaplains. In fact, given the treatment of religion, faith, and religious practices in nonchaplain memoirs, one cannot make this claim. Journalist Michael Herr wrote poignantly of the difference between organized and personal religion: "The Soldier's Prayer came in two versions: Standard, printed on a plastic-coated card by the Defense Department, and Standard Revised, impossible to convey because it got translated outside of language, into chaos—screams, begging, promises, threats, sobs, repetitions of holy names until their throats were cracked and dry, some men had bitten through their collar points and rifle straps and even their dog-tag chains."[16] While some chaplains may have agreed with Herr's assessment, soldiers' religious practices and interpretations probably differed widely from traditional, organized religious views.

Furthermore, chaplains' interpretations of the liturgies of war were not uniform. Based on their own theological ideas, education, background, and military experience, chaplains interpreted religious practices in diverse ways. Therefore, the individual interpretations presented here are not necessarily representative or typical accounts of wartime liturgy but instead are offered as proof of the dynamism and diversity in interpretation and practice available to chaplains. Finally, it is important to bear in mind that the small number of accounts and limited demographic data limit the ability to make generalizations. It is likely that with a broader range of chaplain accounts, an even wider range of practices and interpretations would emerge.

Liturgical practices varied widely among the religious groups represented in the military, but perhaps none more than sacramental practice and interpretation. Though only Catholics and mainline Protestants would claim the centrality of formal sacraments to their worship, "sacrament" defined more broadly may mean any act of ritual or ceremony that served as an outward sign or manifestation of inward grace. Thus, evangelical and low-church Protestants took part in sacramental practices, even if they would not label them as such. For the most part, liturgies of war did not create new sacraments—though soldiers and chaplains occasionally spoke of "baptism by fire" as the "sacrament of war"—but instead reinterpreted more traditional ones.[17]

The issue of sacramental ministry and denominational or faith-group specificity as opposed to ecumenicalism elicited strong opinions on the part of chaplains and their denominational organizations. Some denominations insisted their chaplains maintain strict standards in their sacramental ministries, practicing, as much as possible, the discretion expected of ministers in the United States. Chaplains from the Church of Latter-day Saints (Mormons) usually followed their denominational rules exactly, while other chaplains adopted more liberal policies in the war zone. Addressing some of these challenges, the Lutheran Church–Missouri Synod, a very conservative confessional group in the United States, issued a statement to its chaplains regarding the sacrament of Communion. It began, "In all circumstances the Lutheran chaplain shall administer Holy Communion in accordance with the scriptures and the Lutheran Confessions." Yet, at the same time, the chaplains' manual acknowledged that "exceptional cases arise in ministering to the men and women in the armed forces" and that "in such situations, a Lutheran chaplain may administer the Sacrament of Holy Communion to such personnel as have been baptized; are able to examine themselves; are conscious of the need of repentance; hold the essence of faith, including the doctrines of the Real Presence and of the Lord's Supper as a means of grace; and profess acceptance thereof." On first reading even this policy seems exceptionally rigid, but it can be understood as a doctrinally closed denomination's attempt to balance competing interests—desiring on one hand to uphold the sanctity of Communion by "withholding participation in the Sacrament from those who reject scriptural teaching regarding it" and on the other hand to welcome one who "devoutly believe[d] his Lord's Word of promise as conveyed through and in this Sacrament."[18]

Yet despite the occasional injunction against an ecumenical practice of certain sacraments, traditional religious rituals took on different meanings in combat, especially because chaplain coverage was often infrequent and irregular.[19] The system of area coverage meant that most men saw a chaplain only once every four to six weeks. A slim majority of soldiers and officers reported some sort of contact with a chaplain about once a week, but many of them would have been stationed in the rear, at large bases.[20] In the field it is little surprise, then, that men of many different faiths attended field services when they were offered. Commenting on the attendees at one of his services, James Johnson wrote, "Soldiers of all faiths attend the service, as usual, including several Catholics and one Jew. They all take communion. War and the daily threat of death is a great equalizer."[21] For Johnson, it appeared that confessional particularities mattered little. Ecumenism that would have been nearly inconceivable "back in the world" was accepted and even celebrated in battle. Though it is impossible to say how the participants might have interpreted the same event, the chaplain felt that worship and the sacrament of Communion represented not a particular faith tradition but instead simply a divine presence in war.

Most chaplains always took Eucharistic elements (wine and communion wafers) with them into the field. However, many Protestant denominations, whose worship emphasized scripture and proclamation through preaching, served Communion only once a month or once a quarter in stateside churches. Commenting on this practice, John Schumacher wrote that in Vietnam, "I simply felt that I could not follow the tradition of a once a month Communion, which is the practice of many denominations. I knew that this could possibly be the last time a soldier would take communion. Things are different in a combat zone and this was one of those differences."[22] Chaplain Gary Baxter remembered celebrating Communion with soldiers after the battle on Nui Ba Den: "Twelve people out of that company had been killed. The battle was still raging within eyesight of where we were. It was an intense battle yet these young soldiers were able to shut out the death and dying for a few moments in the communion event as they turned from death to life in the elements of the Eucharist. They were able to grasp hope in the midst of despair, life in the midst of death, resurrection in the midst of dying."[23] Here, the Eucharist did not simply represent a divine presence in war; the chaplain had interpreted it in a combat-specific way, emphasizing the significance of life and resurrection—not only of Christ, but of humans—as experienced through Communion. The presence of death and destruction, rather than separating soldiers from their faith, made religious beliefs more meaningful. And the chaplain, as the conduit of such meaning, took on a great deal of responsibility as both a symbol himself and the interpreter of religious symbols.

At other times, chaplains interpreted their sacramental ministries as possibly influencing soldiers' well-being and sense of safety. Chaplain Thomas Des Champs recalled one occasion when he, his driver, and gunner fell under a rocket attack while waiting for their jeep to be pulled from mud. The men were pinned down in a bunker as the enemy zeroed in their fire. In that moment, Des Champs recalled, one of the soldiers called out,

"Can we have communion, Chaplain?" Des Champs had some Communion wafers and a flask of wine in his pockets, so he agreed. He reminded the men that he was a Protestant chaplain, but he told them that all were welcome to Communion. "At that moment," he continued, "another rocket exploded overhead. More dust and dirt fell. After removing the wine and wafers from my leg pockets, I stood up and blessed them. I passed the bag of wafers around to the men and then the flask of wine. Some men made the sign of the cross before taking communion, others did not. But there was not a man who did not take communion that afternoon." Up to this point, Des Champs's story is similar to those of other chaplains who served Communion to men of different faith groups, but Des Champs took his one step further: "By the end of the short service," he asserted, "the rocket attack ended. God must have been watching over us that afternoon, because no one in the entire firebase had been hurt or killed by the attack."[24] Des Champ's story may well be exaggerated—there is no way to tell if the unit he traveled with that day (as he does not identify it exactly) was actually pinned down by fire as he offered Communion—but his reinterpretation of stateside Communion practices and his analysis of the event as a spiritually significant moment in the midst of chaos are salient regardless.

The armed services strove to ensure that soldiers had religious support from their time in basic training to their reentry into civilian life, so the chaplain's role as an interpreter of religious meaning continued as soldiers left the field and prepared to return to the United States. Orris Kelly, a chaplain with the 4th Infantry Division, reflected on his role in the soldiers' spiritual, physical, and emotional journey that took them from combat in Vietnam back to civilian life in the United States, where by the late 1960s, protest against the war had strengthened in terms of numbers, rhetoric, and action. When soldiers left Vietnam, the base chaplains met with them. He recalled that one of the chaplains who was responsible for meeting with soldiers as they left Vietnam would tell the men, "We don't know how you feel about Vietnam or what happened to you personally. We don't know what your sense of the church is, or what your sense of your relationship to God is. We don't know what you are going to face when you go home. We can't explain all those things. But one thing we came to do before you [leave is] to offer our faith through Holy Communion and the Eucharist."[25] Most of the soldiers took the chaplains' offer. Kelly believed that at this moment, the chaplain's interpretation of the sacrament of Communion was more significant than its traditional religious meaning. The chaplains offered Communion to the soldiers as a symbol of the Christian faith as well as a symbol of reconciliation and transition back home. The second interpretation could stand regardless of a soldier's individual religious beliefs.[26] Here, Communion represented something potentially different from what it had on the battlefield. In the midst of combat, Communion was a reminder of Christ's resurrection, of the victory of life over death, and of God's presence in all circumstances. In preparation for return to "the world," however, it represented reconciliation, connection to the divine and to humanity, and healing. And when chaplains were unsure of a soldier's faith, they offered their own faith in its place.

Combat also amplified baptismal rituals—a stark symbol of new life amidst death. Chaplain Joseph Dulany recalled baptizing men wherever possible, even in bomb craters filled with water.[27] In his reinterpretation, the bomb crater was not a remnant of death but a fount for the water of life. For chaplain Curt Bowers, the baptism of several soldiers of different ethnicities, backgrounds, and denominations represented "a time of great rejoicing and blessing as we who were brothers in warfare became brothers in Christ."[28] Christian baptismal rites represented entry into a religious family akin to the family that war's sacrament—baptism by fire—had formed, and, at the same time, provided soldiers with a familiar ritual through which they could establish a link to the "real" world that waited at home.

Occasionally baptism and death were closely linked as chaplains baptized many men just before they died. At other times the two stood in marked contrast to one another. James Johnson recalled the moment just after he had baptized a soldier and held services when he learned that a close friend had been killed on a Medical Civilian Assistance Program mission that he too would have been on if he had not been holding services. He wrote, "I'm alone with Stiver's body. I feel a sense of rage boiling up in me. I can't take his death! He seems so alone here in the open air. His body is waiting for transportation to Saigon for graves registration and then back to his grieving family. It is all too final, too quick. He chose to live a good life. He didn't get a chance to choose how to die." Thinking about his own mortality and about Stiver's death, he simply stood there. Relieved that he had been spared but angry that Stiver had died when he had not been there, Johnson ultimately resolved to move on: "I sat with Stiver for perhaps five minutes, mesmerized. Butch's baptism and Stiver's death are such a stark contrast. It's not fair. I hate it. But I must go on."[29]

Chaplains also used religious rituals and sacraments to bless the dead and to heal the living. Joseph O'Donnell, a Catholic chaplain, recorded administering the Sacrament of the Sick to eighteen dead Marines who arrived on a helicopter. "About thirty Marines and sailors stood around the body bags on the elevator, waiting for me," he wrote. "These eighteen men had been dead for two days; I knew that. The Catholic Sacrament of the Sick is for the living; I knew that too. But I knew what I had to do." As men watched and waited, O'Donnell remembered, "one by one, I unzipped each body bag, and anointed whatever I found there. It was not pleasant. But it was the most solemn and powerful prayer service I have ever experienced. In the midst of all the action, there was absolute silence and lots of tears."[30] Blessing the dead with a sacrament for the living provided a sense of finality to death but also served as a healing service and a prayer for those who were still alive.

Corbin Cherry, in a poem titled "The Memorial Service," which details a memorial service for three soldiers who had just died, acknowledges that the service was really about the "hundred or more" who had gathered to say goodbye. He reinterprets the bowing of heads, normally the posture of prayer, as a sign of "pain and the emotional ache of not understanding." He continues, "My understanding is that war has given to me / a basic realization of the value of unity." And though the three dead "all came from different religious backgrounds, . . . Our prayers are for them, / to one God, Who created us all." The poem invokes the deep pain of loss and grief but also offers an interpretation of salvation and religious meaning that emphasizes similarity over difference and substitutes a universal deity for a specific one.

The uncertainties of combat also seemed to amplify the significance of a chaplain's presence to administer sacraments. Chaplain Andrew Shimek recalled an incident where a soldier was killed within minutes of saying confession to and receiving the Eucharist from him. Shimek was also able to administer the Sacrament of the Sick before the soldier died.[31] And though, like other accounts, this one may be hyperbolic in its claims of such a rapid chain of events, for chaplains, the immediacy of their work and presence in the face of danger and death was a critical justification for their military commission. Chaplains and soldiers believed that chaplains embodied a religious presence on the battlefield. Some troops interpreted a chaplain's presence on a mission as a literal manifestation of "going with God," while others were certain that the chaplain brought heavy fire and danger—one unit apparently nicknamed its chaplain "the right reverend magnet ass"—an obvious, if crude, expression of the intersections of the sacred and profane.[32]

Usually field services combined sacramental, scriptural, and musical elements. Curt Bowers wrote about a typical field service: "Communion was a very worshipful, meaningful time to all of us. I remember dirty, grubby, battle-scarred hands reaching up toward heaven as I would gently place a wafer in their hand. They would take it with tears in their eyes, thanking God for keeping them safe thus far." Afterward, they often sang "Amazing Grace," a hymn historically connected to the abolition movement in England. Of particular importance in its new context was the second verse:, "Through many dangers, toils, and snares / I have already come / 'Tis grace hath brought me safe thus far / And grace will lead me home." Curtis Bowers reflected, "Some of them did go home—to their eternal home." The hymn and communion together "took on special significance for the combat soldier and for this chaplain who celebrated it with heaviness in his own heart, yet with gratitude to Jesus who drew near to us on the battlefield."[34] As chaplains led soldiers in worship on the battlefield, they interpreted their experiences in religious ways. Soldiers who died went to their "eternal home"; chaplains appropriated an abolitionist hymn to fit wartime circumstances; in the midst of combat, soldiers reached toward heaven to receive Communion. Perhaps, though, it was just as likely that soldiers simply died, that the hymns they chose were simply familiar, or that soldiers reached up to another human to receive a ritualistic symbol of faith. But unsurprisingly, chaplains chose not to interpret these experiences in secular ways; their analysis remained religious. Their education, vocation, and experience gave them an explicitly religious worldview and idiom through which to describe combat.

Other hymns relied on more militaristic themes to provide the soundtrack for battle. For Claude Newby, "The Battle Hymn of the Republic" took on different meanings depending on the situation. While filling a stateside post, his commanding officer ordered the song sung at every service prior to a live-fire infiltration course.[34] In this case, the song, which blended militaristic and Christian themes, served to instill a sense of courage and duty in often reluctant trainees. On the battlefield in Vietnam, though, Newby recalled Easter services in which he and his men changed the line "as He died to make men holy, let us die to make men free" to "as He died to make men holy, let us *live* to make men free."[35] The song, given new lyrics and thus imbued with new meaning, offered hope and reassurance to soldiers that their efforts were worthwhile and good. Combat soldiers used the song to reinforce their commitment to life rather than the nobility of death, though one suspects the original lyrics were never far from their minds.

Chaplain David Knight also used lyrics from "The Battle Hymn of the Republic" to give meaning to his role in the war. Before the war, he wrote, he was "caught up with the same naive idealism" regarding combat as many others were, considering himself not only an officer and minister in the United States Army but also "an officer and minister in the Army of God, with a mandate to carry that 'terrible swift sword.'"[36] Knight had conflated God and Country, and had used a line from the "Battle Hymn of the Republic" to make the connection. The "terrible swift sword" encompassed literal and physical meanings in Vietnam.

Other patriotic songs also worked themselves into the repertoire of chaplains conducting field services. Wendell Danielson recalled that for many of his troops "God Bless America" became the benediction for many field services attended by personnel of diverse faiths. He acknowledged that the song "for us, is difficult to sing"; for example, he "knew the Doc wouldn't make it past the fourth line. He never finished, 'From the mountains, to the prairies,'" he explained, because "tears come to his eyes and he stops singing. Nobody, however, notices." Danielson wished for each man to express his feelings and faith, and if the song allowed him to do that, so be it. "God help us if the words become simply words and the love is reduced to sentiment," he concluded. "For my men this song becomes a prayer." In combat, he asserted, a secular song was offered as a prayer in part because "it is difficult to find a prayer that will be accepted by everyone. One is too long, another too short. Also there are Jewish and Roman Catholic personnel present. This song bridges the gap. It says what we want to say."[37] Thus, a hymn generally reserved for Fourth of July celebrations in the United States took on new meaning in Vietnam as men thought about their homes and their purpose for fighting. In place of specific theological or doctrinal prayer, this hymn offered common ground on the basis of patriotism and civic duty. In the context of a religious service, it may have exemplified the intense connections between faith in one's god and faith in one's country, or it may have conflated the two.

Civilian religious groups also published materials for use in the field. In addition to the ubiquitous Testaments and pocket Bibles that religious groups of all sorts distributed, some took a more creative approach. Relying on the popularity of folk music and guitar masses, especially among young people in the late 1960s and early 1970s, one denominational press published and distributed a "Vietnam Songbook" that took tunes from folk songs and rock music and revised them with Christian lyrics.[38] Other chaplains wanted to capitalize on the popularity of gospel music and recorded and broadcast gospel and "country church"–style programs to service members at Da Nang Air Base.[39] Chaplains and churches alike recognized that the potential congregation in Vietnam was quite unlike that in the United States—it was overwhelmingly young and male, whereas the churchgoing population back in the world would have been more heavily female and older. Though the stress of combat often meant that anyone available in the field was likely to attend a service, on large American bases, chaplains still had to work to attract service members to their activities, and they often employed methods not fundamentally different from efforts in the United States.

Supply shortages—especially of chaplain kits, field organs, and portable tape players—were fairly constant, so chaplains often had to be creative with the materiel they had on hand or provided their own supplies for conducting worship services. One chaplain wrote in his denomination's chaplain newsletter that "things were a bit hectic," because he had been preparing for a second tour since he had received his orders. He wrote, "I missed organ accompaniment for worship during my last tour in Vietnam, and determined not to be without it again. I had our organist record some hymns and spliced those together to form tapes that includes [sic] a prelude, hymn, Gloria Patri, Doxology, hymn, and postlude. I then recorded those on cartridges, and brought a portable cartridge player to use in the field. I then found a company that sells pipe organ music commercially, and proceeded to put it in the same format."[40] Chaplains could not always rely on formal channels to provide the materials they thought necessary to carry out their pastoral mission. Because they recognized the comfort that familiar music might bring to soldiers in the field, chaplains worked to provide it.

The use of music in the field was clearly significant to shaping the religious practices and experiences of service members, but it played a different but similarly significant role in rear areas. On big American bases, relatively distant from combat, some chaplains arranged for choral groups and a more traditional music program. In 1966, the group The Tan Son Notes performed at Trinity Baptist Church in Saigon, and in 1968, men from the Protestant Chapel Choir in Pleiku performed an Easter Cantata. Chapel choirs also performed with Vietnamese performers, emphasizing the interfaith and ecumenical interactions that could take place between religious groups, especially in Saigon. As in the field, the intent of the musical programs was to offer a sense of constancy and normalcy in the midst of a situation that provided anything but.

In addition to using songs and religious music to make war-zone worship more meaningful, chaplains also interpreted combat experiences through scriptural references. Chaplain David Knight recounts one instance when he was caught alone with a platoon whose lieutenant had been wounded and evacuated. According to Knight, the platoon did not know where to go or what to do next, so the soldiers looked to him for both military and religious guidance. While the soldiers looked to him, Knight recalled, "I was looking to someone else for answers. In the blackness, I silently prayed for God to guide us. Without knowing where I was I said, 'Go that way!' Our backs were so up against the proverbial Red Sea that I had no recourse but to simply trust that He who makes a way where there seems to be no way would lead us safely out of the snare." While Knight only implicitly compared himself to Moses saving his people, the parallels were clear. "The whole experience," Knight recalled, "had been a walk through 'the valley of the shadow of death' under the guiding hand of the Great Shepherd."[41] Though it seems unlikely that Knight made these connections explicit in the heat of battle, his postwar reflections reveal how some chaplains interpreted combat situations. For Knight and others, biblical stories and scriptures were the most obvious way to make sense of their two worlds, allowing them to retain both a military and religious identity.[42]

When reflecting on combat situations, chaplains consistently invoked scripture. Chaplain Stanley Beach remembered that he and Chaplain Vincent Capodanno "spent Easter Sunday morning ministering to those men. It made a deep impression on both of us and those moments of looking into the eyes of Marines who were experienced with death, gave us a greater appreciation of the hope of the Resurrection in Jesus Christ."[43] Regardless of the soldiers' experience of Easter in combat, chaplains like Capodanno and Beach articulated their belief that war amplified religious meaning and could take on meaning beyond the immediate context of combat.

Near-death experiences and the juxtaposition of worship and battle highlighted philosophical and theological questions about life and death. Understanding these experiences required reexamining scripture and tradition in light of combat. The question of why certain men died in battle while others lived, for example, haunted soldiers and chaplains alike, and they came up with varied answers.[44] Some chaplains adopted the idea that combat was an uncontrolled experiment, where safety could not be guaranteed to the faithful and where weapons and ammunition served no other purpose than to kill anyone with whom they came into contact. Samuel Hopkins agreed with the old soldiers' adage, "Sometimes the bullets have our name on them and sometimes they are addressed to 'to whom it may concern.'"[45] Other chaplains, however, took exception to this theology. One response was to attribute everything in battle to God's will, and this conclusion allowed for easy, if not emotionally satisfactory, answers to the question of why some men died in combat and others did not. After a friendly fire incident in which an American soldier was killed, James Hutchens argued against the common belief that accidents like this were merely tragic, reassuring himself and others that "for the Christian, these 'accidents' have a different meaning." Referring to Psalm 91:5, "You will not fear the terror of the night, or the arrow that flies by day," he determined that "a sovereign God in absolute control directs not only the enemy's 'arrows that fly by day' but also the 'arrows' of his own company." Hutchens's time in Vietnam convinced him that there was "no such thing as a bullet inscribed 'To whom it may concern.' God alone determines the length of a man's days."[46]

Still other chaplains viewed both of these interpretations as fatalistic, believing instead more in human agency in wartime. James Johnson argued that such fatalism was "poor theology" which revealed a "kind of predestined attitude that people have begun to voice here in Vietnam." He contrasted it with his own theology in which "God helps those who help themselves," and in Vietnam, they helped themselves "by staying low and hopefully, out of harm's way." He reasoned that "if there's nothing you can do about your destiny, then one would never buckle a seat belt, have a fire alarm, or get a medical checkup." In rejecting a Calvinist theology and instead accepting the doctrine of free will, Johnson concluded, "It's not brave to needlessly expose oneself to the enemy . . . . It is better to err on the side of safety than to be killed because of faulty theology that gives no power to the God-given position of the right of self-determination."[47] Chaplains used scripture to explain, justify, or rationalize their experiences in war, but they also used their experiences in war to read scripture in new ways.

Liturgies of war provided opportunities to interpret scripture in ways that were immediately relevant to soldiers facing combat. Once again, David Knight provides an example of this type of interpretation. While rereading the Psalms before an important battle, he recalled, Psalm 91:3–8 "seemed to leap right off the page." The verses were "speaking directly to me, saying 'You will make contact with the enemy, but I will be with you and, as you trust in Me, not a single bullet will hurt you.'" Knight told the unit's captain, who then told the men of Echo Company, that "God had promised to shield them in the coming battle."[48] Whether by providence, fate, or luck, none were wounded in the battle, even under heavy enemy fire. Knight's faith was affirmed.[49] In this way, Knight followed a long tradition of political leaders invoking religious or spiritual protection for troops before combat, so in some ways, the particular circumstances were unremarkable. For Knight, however, the incident took on spiritual significance, and it is evidence of one way that chaplains dealt with the question of fate or providence in war.

For evangelical chaplains, services before and during combat emphasized the need for individual salvation through Jesus Christ. The official mission of the Chaplain Corps, however, was not to proselytize or promote religion or to ensure the good behavior of military personnel, but rather to provide religious support for those who wanted it. This distinction between ministry and mission was most significant away from the battlefield, and it led to some conflict between liberal and evangelical Protestants. One draftee who had served his tour with the 9th Infantry Division, for example, wrote to the chief of chaplains to volunteer to return to Vietnam in order to evangelize soldiers. He noted that "none of [the chaplains] that I heard ever gave the reason why and how to be saved."[50] Most chaplains, however, used field services as opportunities to reconcile faith and combat and to provide a connection between soldiers and their own religious traditions. Salvation it seems, even at a time when death may have weighed heavily on soldiers' minds, took a subordinate place to the succor of religious faith and comfort.

No scriptural reference, it seemed, was off limits for reinterpretation through the lens of the war. Wendell E. Danielson, in an article for *The Chaplain* magazine, offered an extended exegesis of Psalm 46 to address the common doubts of soldiers and chaplains, to reinforce the confidence of the psalmist, and to assign meaning to Vietnam. He began with the first line of the psalm: "'God is our refuge and strength, a very present help in trouble.' This, I thought, is what we need to hear. Tomorrow there would be trouble, perhaps more than anyone realized. In several hours these men would helilifted into the jungle. For some of them this would be a new experience; most of the men had done it many times. Some troops would not return to this sand again but no one talked about this. Each man knew it would be someone else."[51]

The next part of the psalm indicates that God remains changeless, so men should not fear the problems of this world. The psalmist then invokes imagery of earthquakes and violent storms, which Danielson equates to the barrage of demoralizing news from home: Letters that began, "'Dear

Jimmy . . . I don't want to cause you any worry but they've taken the phone away, cut our electricity off, and we're two months behind with the rent. We'll make out okay, don't worry about us.' . . . or 'Dearest . . . I've had it. When you return the children and I will be gone,'" quickly became the domain of the chaplain, who counseled men dealing with these kinds of personal problems. And Danielson expressed his frustration with the home front's apparent detachment from the war. "There is the common enemy, Charlie," he wrote. "But what about wives who can't wait? Or parents who won't write? Or friends who don't seem to care? How does a young man perform 24 hours a day when he has received two letters in the past seven months? Charlie should be our only concern yet it doesn't work that way." Danielson's interpretation of the first verses of the psalm reveal his deep frustrations with the things affecting soldiers' morale and his intimate understanding of the uncertainty of men facing combat.[52]

Danielson continued his exegesis, expressing a more general sense of the futility of war and the power of God. Addressing verse 9, "He makes wars to cease to the end of the earth; he breaks the bow, and shatters the spear, he burns the chariots with fire!," Danielson questioned his God's will for all of humankind: "The modern spear and bow are far more effective than the psalmist ever imagined." And he asked, "Why doesn't God do something? Soon? Like today?" Yet even in the face of such doubt, Danielson interpreted the psalmist's final lines, "I am exalted among the nations, I am exalted in the earth. The Lord of hosts is with us; The God of Jacob is our refuge," as a statement of God's sovereignty and as a sort of mission statement for chaplains and other ministers. He concluded, "There is much that must be done—instruction to give, an example to set. Who will do this? For my men this is my responsibility. They must be shown faith and love and courage. If my example in living these virtues is not louder than my words I become the tinkling [cymbal]." Danielson appropriated and accepted the language of 1 Corinthians 13 as central to his mission. The so-called Love Chapter in the Christian New Testament exhorts followers to exhibit love in all they do and declares that actions without love are meaningless. At the same time, Danielson called on his chaplain training and his understanding of the Chaplain Corps' mission to define his role. The chaplain's "responsibility," he wrote, "remains the same whether in Garmisch [Germany] or Vietnam or the United States. The opportunity is always here to bring men to God and God to men. This is and always will be the high calling. To do less is to do nothing."[53] Danielson reinterpreted scripture while still acknowledging God's power and sovereignty.

As they followed sacramental and worship traditions, chaplains carved out sacred space in the midst of war zones, so that the two were not wholly separated, but experienced together. One chaplain recalled baptizing a soldier in the Saigon River while his platoon guarded the area from hostile fire. These sorts of events where religious observances are guarded by armed soldiers are recorded in several photographs. The liturgical space was defined not only by the chaplain's actions and the worshippers' presence but also by the ostensibly inviolable perimeter formed by armed soldiers.[54]

Combat forced some chaplains and soldiers to reconsider the meaning of physical space as it related to religious experience. James Johnson compared a Christmas Eve service in Vietnam to the ones being held in the United States on the same occasion. "It's time for the service. We're muddy. No white shirts, ties, high heels or stained glass windows in church today. I hope there will be no blood stains either." But beyond noting the physical differences, Johnson experienced "a warm feeling reflecting on God's intervention in life through Jesus Christ," adding, "Sometimes, though[,] it's hard to see or evaluate how or when his intervention comes to this god forsaken place."[55] Johnson believed the meaning of the service could be the same no matter the circumstance. But whereas the inherent goodness of Christmas and of God perhaps went unquestioned in a church, the battlefield required men to find a deeper level of trust and faith in order to arrive at the same truth.

War also altered the spaces in which worship took place. Liturgical colors and ornate vestments were replaced with jungle fatigues, makeshift altars and chapels, and portable mass and Communion kits. While many chaplains and soldiers believed that God revealed himself in battle, the sacred space created by a simple alter, hymns and prayer books, sacramental elements, or a chaplain's combat vestments, was shielded—at least psychologically—from the war going on around it. Worship services and the chaplain's presence provided a connection to "the world" and the past, offering a brief, albeit incomplete, respite from battle. Earl Kettler wrote to his wife, "My goal each day is to live and teach the love of God, remembering that I'm not an extension of a machine gun. When a man comes to my Services I feel he has a right to have a few quiet moments to hear the love of God. There is still love."[56] In field services, chaplains created a space between war and civilization, as the nearness of combat gave their words, presence, and the acts of worship new meaning.

Occasionally combat left no time for worshipful reflection. The liturgical space was frequently invaded by artillery fire, by helicopters and airplanes, or by unexpected attacks. Chaplain Newby recounted an Easter service in which a resupply chopper interrupted his sermon, which was not unusual. The situation, however, changed when the helicopter crashed nearby, at which point, Newby recalled, the "worshipers abandoned the service and dashed to the crash site, fearing troopers were being cut to pieces by the spinning main rotor. Amazingly no one was hurt. Even more amazing, about the time we made that happy discovery, a 105mm artillery round exploded in the burning vegetation about a hundred feet behind where I'd stood to conduct the service. The falling chopper had drawn Easter worshipers from the 'kill zone' just in time!" In this story, even a crashing helicopter saving a group of worshippers from artillery fire became a sure sign of God's Providence. Of course such a story could be easily exaggerated, but by recounting this story, Newby stressed the potential dangers of serving in combat and his belief in the constant grace and mercy of God.

Soldiers and chaplains built makeshift and semipermanent chapels in rear areas all across Vietnam. Chaplains recalled some of these structures being raised in three or four days. Construction involved found materials, misdirected supplies, and the occasional budget allocation. Chaplain Robert Hess recalled the construction of a chapel outside of Ban Me Thuot from "'scrounged' material and a Bronze cross made from 'duster' shells, pews of ammo boxes and 'home made' chandeliers of tinted Plexiglas, and even a 'bell' in the steeple (with nobody supposed to ask where it came from)."[57] The Air Force chaplaincy's official history reports that chaplains took the time "to adorn their surroundings with works of art." In 1966, for example, "Chaplain Calvin W. McCarter purchased seven paintings with funds donated to the Protestant Chaplain Fund of Ton Sun Nhut to bring a touch of beauty to the 377th dispensary ward," including an eight-by-eight-foot mural titled "Christ at Cam Ranh Bay" by Airman Robert Ward. Another chaplain, John F. Albert, arranged for twenty "reproductions of religious art distributed to the sites on the northernmost outposts of the area."[58] More so than in combat areas, soldiers in rear areas used materials available to them to re-create recognizable worship spaces. The chapel represented a piece of the world they knew and understood.

Be it in the field or in the rear, the chaplain himself often represented sacred space. Joseph Dulany believed that his most important opportunities for ministry came when he let soldiers know he "struggled at times with my faith as they did." He wrote, "I invited them to join the journey as together we looked to God for faith and assurance. I shared from my heart and conviction with the men. I wept with them at memorial services. I prayed, as best I could, in the worst of situations at hospital bedsides and after enemy contacts. Sometimes, the only thing that I could do was sit with a person."[59] Dulany and other chaplains understood that the liturgies of war they created did not have to be formal, organized, or standard to be meaningful.

However and wherever they were carried out, liturgies of war returned power to God and some agency to humans, and these liturgies may have allowed those who participated to experience worship, healing, and reconciliation in the midst of combat. Chaplains led the service members and officers who joined them in worship in the effort to reconcile their faith with their experience in war. As they confronted moral questions about the war and the horrors of combat, soldiers and chaplains found that liturgical experiences centered on sacrament, scripture, songs, and space linked them to the world outside of Vietnam and at the same time created new spaces that transcended boundaries created by traditional religious interpretations and denominational or faith-group divisions.

In the midst of war, chaplains called upon their creative energies to interpret, invent, and revise religious practices. Collectively, these might be called crisis-based theologies or liturgies.[60] Formed by the exigencies of war and sometimes in the heat of battle—far away from the detached and objective classroom or the sanctified space of a church—these new religious practices emerged from the tension between the poles of dogmatic inflexibility and dangerously open relativism. If standard religious traditions could not be reinterpreted, they would lose their power to buoy the human spirit, yet if they became too flexible, too open, they would lose their meaning. The chaplain operated in this area of tension.

Reinterpretation and invention of religious traditions occurs in many traumatic situations. The hospital chaplain baptizes stillborn babies; a first responder anoints bodies at the scene of an accident; a minister tells a gathered congregation that God "called a child to heaven" because saying anything else would seem callous. To some, these responses to trauma reflect a turn away from difficult, complex theological questions and toward carefully administered pabulum to soothe and reassure. On the battlefield, however, this type of pastoral care is necessary and even welcome. And some critics would argue that well-considered, articulated theologies that do deal with these gritty, important questions should not be ignored. Theology and liturgical practices must be transferable to just such crisis-based situations for the pious's claims of universality to hold.

The origins and effects of liturgical and theological reinterpretation on the battlefield are important for two reasons: First, they are sure evidence of chaplains' internalizing the motto "cooperation without compromise." Originally intended to ensure the integrity of chaplains' personal beliefs and religious practice, the motto became a call for stretching the logical bounds of ecumenism. What would almost certainly be deemed compromise "back in the world" was instead sanctioned, even lauded, during war. Second, they suggest that chaplains did not always have the theological and philosophical resources at hand to deal adequately with some of the questions they faced. In essence, chaplains improvised because their kit bags were underdeveloped. Chaplains' deficiencies reflected both their seminary training, which was largely designed to prepare ministers or priests for parish and congregational work, and their chaplain training, which encouraged ecumenical cooperation without providing adequate skills for negotiating tense and trying situations.

In carrying out their pastoral mission, chaplains called on a variety of religious ideals to address questions of morality in war, and similarly, chaplains generally settled on liturgical flexibility as the appropriate response to interreligious and interdenominational differences. The context of combat, especially in areas where the threat of death or injury was ever-present, compelled many chaplains to perform their religious duties outside of the strict confines of their confessional, denominational, or personal beliefs and tenets. Chaplains found it was possible for Christians to serve in the Vietnam War, to believe fundamentally in its ostensible purpose, to find war morally abhorrent, and still to interpret it in religious ways so that their God emerged in control and their faith intact or strengthened. During the war, they addressed moral, military, religious, and liturgical issues pragmatically. Ultimately, chaplains had to resolve their experience in combat so that their faith and their religion did not give way to cynicism, despair, and nihilism, and this process of reconciliation began in Vietnam but continued as they returned home.

CHAPTER FIVE

Discourse and Debate

Chaplains' dual status as clergy and officers often situated them on the margins of two communities in which they were ostensibly full members. This simultaneous position as insider and outsider thrust chaplains into public discourse on the Vietnam War as both symbols and spokesmen in a conversation about a war that challenged American religious, cultural, moral, and military ideals. The military chaplaincy offered a safe topic for discussion because it was connected to military and civilian, religious and secular worlds, but not central to any of them. While chaplains' participation in the war demonstrated many ways in which tension between religion and warfare could be reconciled in practice, public discourse about chaplains and the chaplaincy more often revealed the tension developing between the military and American society, and usually prompted chaplains to defend their profession publicly. Though chaplains' writings on such issues were unlikely to affect either policy or practice and they usually wrote in support of the chaplaincy as an institution, their contributions often reflected their ambivalence about the war and the uncertainty of their position vis-à-vis their religious organizations. In national media coverage about the war, chaplains became symbolic subjects in a debate where one's position on the military chaplaincy roughly tracked one's overall assessment of the Vietnam War. Conversations about chaplains revealed important fissures within the home front religious community and demonstrate how the debate over chaplains stood in for larger debates over Vietnam and an American national destiny.

The narrative of religious dissent during the Vietnam War has been well told by historians, but an examination of media coverage of religion in relation to the Vietnam War reveals a wider range of religious responses and interpretations than has been popularly imagined. In addition to widespread dissent, religious beliefs also prompted many faithful people to support the Vietnam War and induced deep ambivalence and uncertainty in others. The diversity of responses—all religious—emphasized both the diversity of religious beliefs in the United States and underscored the extent to which American religion had been reconfigured along political rather than denominational lines.

Discourse by and about chaplains in newspapers and periodicals highlights the multiple ways in which chaplains related to such communities on the home front. Communities of readers and writers coalesced around the public discourse presented in newspapers, weekly periodicals, newsletters, and denominational periodicals, as these publications not only presented facts to and reported on events for their audiences but also offered a specific way of understanding those facts within a culturally determined context, thus shaping and reflecting the values and culture of the communities around them.[1] When chaplains, religious leaders, laypeople, and secular journalists wrote about chaplains, the chaplaincy, and Vietnam, they demonstrated the various sets of norms and values that held weight within each community. Chaplains themselves contributed important voices to the debate. They offered experientially grounded observations and attempted to establish connections with both military and civilian communities. Their position in the middle of multiple communities enabled them to communicate across these lines, employing the language and culture of each one to establish their credibility and to communicate one community's cultures and values to the other.

There were two kinds of discussions about chaplains: First, there was a philosophical discussion about the morality of war in general (and the Vietnam War in particular) and the chaplain's proper role in war—the driving question being whether the chaplain should be primarily priest or prophet. Second, there was a policy-oriented discussion about civilianizing the chaplaincy, which would remove (or significantly reduce) federal funding and military entanglement for chaplains. Chaplains, former chaplains, and civilian observers participated in both debates, though not always on the same terms. In any case, proponents of all positions argued forcefully, and the media coverage of the debates about the chaplain's role and whether or not the chaplaincy should be civilianized was indicative of broader cultural and political divides within the American public.

American Religion and the War in Vietnam

The nature of the American war in Vietnam intensified connections between the home front and the battlefront. In addition to short tours of duty that rotated veterans back to the United States rapidly and the intense social pressures of the late 1960s that deeply affected the U.S. military, the ubiquitous and striking images of Vietnam broadcast into American homes contributed to the mounting unease about the war. The first "televised war" brought the American public unprecedented access to images of the battlefront, even though much of the action occurred in dense jungle and mountainous terrain half a world away. Extensive press coverage of the war made wartime images real and iconic: Thich Quang Duc's self-immolation on the streets of Saigon in 1963; war protesters placing daisies in home-coming soldiers' guns at a 1967 antiwar demonstration at the Pentagon; the carnage at My Lai revealed in 1969; the publication of the Pentagon Papers in the *New York Times* in 1971. These words and images would become the weapons of the war at home, pitting policy-makers against students against family members against veterans.

As the war in Vietnam escalated, American public support for the war declined. The tipping point for public opinion—when more people opposed the conduct of the war than approved of it—coincided roughly with the Tet Offensive in January-February 1968.[2] On 27 February 1968, Walter Cronkite, the venerable and trusted evening news anchor for CBS, said, "It is increasingly clear that the only rational way out will be to negoti-ate, not as victors but as an honorable people who lived up to the pledge to defend democracy." It is often said that Lyndon Johnson cited this moment as the one where "middle America" was lost.[3] Westmoreland requested 206,000 more troops, but Johnson rejected the proposal. In March of that year, Johnson announced that he would not run for reelection in 1968 and would seek to negotiate a peace agreement with North Vietnam. Casualties continued to mount in Vietnam, and the antiwar movement gained trac-tion and attention at home.

When the mainstream national media portrayed religious people in relation to the war in Vietnam, especially after 1967, its coverage was over-whelmingly about religious protest. William Sloane Coffin, Yale's antiwar chaplain, and other prominent religious leaders formed the group Clergy and Laymen Concerned About Vietnam (CALCAV); the Berrigan brothers, Daniel and Phillip (both Catholic priests), burned draft cards and aided draft resisters; and mainline religious bodies such as the National Council of Churches released increasingly critical statements about the war in Viet-nam.[4] By the end of the 1960s, debates about Vietnam within religious com-munities had taken on a sharp edge and revealed deep divides. It is true that the historic peace churches had been consistently critical of war in general and of previous American military conflicts, but "Christian Pacifism" came under intense scrutiny during the Second World War. Theologian Dietrich

Bonhoeffer, for example, asserted that Christians could morally join the fight against evil regimes such as the one in Nazi Germany, and Reinhold Niebuhr proclaimed a message of Christian Realism, which plainly stated there were times when war was morally necessary. For the most part, American Christians and Jews supported the basic premises of the Cold War—to contain and eventually defeat atheistic Communism—but on the specific issue of Vietnam, religious communities split over the execution of Cold War policies.[5] Religious communities across the political spectrum debated the Vietnam War—they discussed its origins and its conduct, as well as American national security, religious obligation, and the nature of the enemy. And although these internal conversations were approached from many different angles, changed over time, and could be contentious, coverage of the war in mainstream national publications frequently focused on growing religious opposition to the war, glossing over the theological and moral debates that took place *within* religious communities.[6]

Especially for conservative and evangelical denominations, these internal conversations revealed important theological and doctrinal shifts over the course of the war, in some cases fundamentally changing a denomination's official stance on military service and the war in Vietnam vis-à-vis the Cold War, and paved the way for even more dramatic shifts in the post-Vietnam era. Perhaps the most dramatic example is the position shift of the Assemblies of God (AOG), the largest Pentecostal denomination in the United States. Although the AOG had long established itself as a pacifist church, institutionally committing its members to noncombatant service or conscientious objection, in 1967 it "dropped the entire argument for pacifism" and changed its formal statement on war to the following: "As a movement we affirm our loyalty to the government of the United States in war or peace. We shall continue to insist, as we have historically, on the right of each member to choose for himself whether to declare his position as a combatant, a noncombatant, or a conscientious objector."[7] Throughout the Cold War and the Vietnam War, the AOG became progressively more politically conservative and supportive of American military efforts. In 1967, AOG chaplain David Plank published *Called to Serve*, which exalted military service and the military chaplaincy and equated patriotism with godliness.[8] And within the pages of the *Pentecostal Evangel*, AOG ministers and lay readers explored ideas about the relationship between the American military mission in Vietnam and God's will. Such discussions, however, rarely included the role military chaplains played in the war.

The Southern Baptist Convention (SBC), one of the largest conservative evangelical religious bodies in the United States is another example. Between 1966 and 1972, the SBC consistently passed peace resolutions, which denounced the horror of war as being contrary to God's plan for the world and called for an end to hostilities in Vietnam, but remained supportive of troops serving there. The 1966 resolution read, in part, "Therefore, be it RESOLVED, That this Convention reassert that the great Christians [sic] goal of history is the reign of peace, both in the hearts of men and in world affairs. . . . Let us here call Baptists and fellow Christians throughout our land to renewed prayer for our American troops, for their loved ones, for our enemies, and for world leaders, that they may somehow be led of God together to find the high and honorable road to peace and gain together the wisdom and courage to walk it." As the war went on, the peace resolutions continued to extol the Christian virtue of peace but also offered explicit support to the American national government in carrying out its policies and efforts to end the war, indicative of the intellectual tightrope that conservative evangelicals had to walk between denouncing the evil of war and their support for anti-Communist U.S. government policies and military efforts. During the period 1966–72, only one of the SBC resolutions explicitly mentioned military chaplains; the 1968 resolution simply acknowledged that many Southern Baptist ministers were currently in service in Vietnam.[9] Other statements by SBC leaders pointed to a more militaristic stance on the war. C. R. Daley, editor of the *Western Recorder*, the periodical of the Kentucky Baptist Convention, wrote that there was "no just and honorable alternative" in Vietnam except to pursue "a successful end," which ostensibly meant an American victory. Noting that the war violated God's plan for peace, he nevertheless held that the war was as "holy a war as a war can be" and "the lesser of evils."[10]

Was there conservative and evangelical anguish over the Vietnam War? Yes, but as George Bogaski has suggested, the anguish was fundamentally different from the moderate and liberal variety; for conservatives and evangelicals, the primary concern was why America was not winning rather than whether the war was morally right, which was the focus for liberal religious communities.[11] Within conservative denominations, especially those that were broadly supportive of the war effort, the chaplaincy was rarely a subject for debate or consideration. Though military chaplains sometimes contributed to denominational publications and the like, usually writing in support of the war effort and their ministry, they were assumed to be carrying out a righteous task in a righteous war. For conservatives, there was little need to question the chaplain's place or purpose in the Vietnam War. Most of the critical and analytical conversations and debates about military chaplains appeared in the national press—which was trying to cover the whole of the war, including the antiwar movement—and in moderate and liberal religious publications.

When chaplains received attention in the national press, it was usually in the context of broader discussions of the Vietnam War, and more often than not, chaplains were quoted in support of the war effort and in defense of their role in it.[12] In 1966, the *New York Times* gave substantial column space to remarks by a Reform rabbi who had recently returned from a tour in Vietnam as a chaplain. The unnamed chaplain, according to the *Times*, "asserted that those seeking peace in Vietnam by attacking the Johnson administration are helping to prolong the war." The chaplain acknowledged that although Vietnam War "doves"—including those in "the Congress, among the clergy, or among the people in general"—may be "well-meaning and patriotic," they are "doing what the 'hawks' in Hanoi most desire" by portraying the United States "as the aggressor and the Vietcong and the North Vietnamese as the 'innocent victims'" of a "sinister" American plan.[13] Chaplains were often consulted in reports about how war protests affected troops in Vietnam, and their responses varied. A 1968 article in the *Baltimore Sun* reported that the Navy's chief of chaplains, Rear Admiral James Kelly, said that "war dissent is a detriment to American fighting men in Vietnam striking at the very heart of their strength, their conviction that what they do is both necessary and right," adding that protests were both "unjust and immoral."[14] In 1970, though, Kelly offered a somewhat more optimistic assessment, saying that the "American serviceman has refused to be dehumanized by the war" and that "the detractors have not succeeded in dissipating . . . morale" because the serviceman "is less concerned about public opinion than the job at hand." Kelly still believed the antiwar protests "were injurious" from a strategic perspective because "they aid the enemy" and give troops "room for doubt."[15]

While some outspoken chaplains defended the American role in Vietnam and criticized the antiwar movement for its deleterious effects on the war effort, others worked to sidestep the political origins and motives for the war, shifting the focus to the religious needs of the troops or offering brief theological explications about the problem of war and evil in the world. These chaplains used their position as clergy to gain credibility with a secular audience, but one that might be inclined to trust clerical authority on moral issues. In an article about how GIs understood religion in relation to the war, one chaplain said that only time would tell whether the war in Vietnam was positive, and that he hoped it was. He essentially hedged his answer, allowing for the possibility that the war was a mistake, but emphasizing the positive motives and minimizing the traumatic effects of American military intervention.[16]

Likewise, Richard Dryer, a Jewish chaplain, implored readers of the *American Israelite* not to make up their minds about the war too quickly: "Being truly liberal means to approach a subject with an open mind, to examine impartially both sides of a matter. War is evil. There is no doubt about that. But the issues in Vietnam are not simple." Dryer went on to offer a staunch defense of the American effort in Vietnam, explaining that he had initially been opposed to the war as well but that the plight of the South Vietnamese and the needs of the soldiers in Vietnam changed his mind. He implored other American Jews to consider those issues as well.[17]

Finally, Army chief of chaplains Gerhardt W. Hyatt gave an extended interview to the *Washington Post* in which he attempted to explain the chaplain's role in the war and offered his observations on the problems facing Americans in Vietnam and in society more broadly. Though he insisted that "religion" and "life" could not be separated, he said that his job in Vietnam was "to bring the comfort of God to man . . . when he is having what must certainly be the most terrifying experience of his life" and not "to dissuade [or] lead men into conscientious objection." Hyatt concluded that the situation in Vietnam was fundamentally a problem of failed human relationships. Repairing broken relationships, in Hyatt's view, had the potential to address both international and domestic political turmoil.[18] Chaplains like Dryer and Hyatt used their clerical and military experience to address audiences in language they could relate to. Their nuanced positions offered in the midst of heated debate are easy to overlook for all the bluster, but they illuminate a significant type of religious response to the Vietnam War. All of these examples revealed a deep divide among religious communities, yet religious dissent and protest received far more attention in the mainstream media than did competing conservative viewpoints.

When newspaper editors moved away from simple reporting and toward editorializing on religion and the war, the tenor of articles was notably more critical of military chaplains. A 1966 article on the general religious atmosphere of the day summed up the *New York Times*'s editorial position well: "The compliance with Governmental policy that was widely expected from the religiously affiliated in the 1950s has been almost reversed. Church protests against the war in Vietnam are now massive and substantial, for example."[19] Thus religious communities' opposition to the war predated—and perhaps foretold—widespread public opposition to the war. As this secular opposition grew, religiously oriented critiques also became more pointed. By 1968, most national press coverage of the religious response to the war centered on war protests and religious dissent, such as that of Yale University chaplain William Sloane Coffin and Philip and Daniel Berrigan.[20] Military chaplains were rarely mentioned in such articles; when they were, it was in the context of liberal groups offering a critique of the chaplaincy. For example, the Episcopal Peace Fellowship gave military chaplains significant attention at their 1972 annual meeting, but the program focused primarily on ways to reform the chaplaincy along less objectionable lines than the current arrangement where they assumed chaplains were limited by their involvement in the military and beholden to secular norms and regulations. The pastoral efforts of chaplains received no attention in the meeting report.[21] Such coverage left little room for alternate viewpoints.

But even outspoken critics of the war recognized that many religious Americans supported it and the U.S. government. Richard John Neuhaus, the pastor of St. John the Evangelist Lutheran Church in Brooklyn, New York, and Protestant cofounder of CALCAV or Clergy Concerned, wrote an extended analysis of the church's role in the Vietnam War for the *Annals of the American Academy of Political and Social Science*, a secular, academic journal.[22] Neuhaus envisioned this article, which appeared in the October 1969 issue of the journal, as a response to the broad question: "What effect has Vietnam had on organized religion, and what are some of the possible implications for civil religion in America?" With few exceptions, he noted, "no publication in the mainstream of the American religious conversation has supported the war. The war policies of the Johnson and Nixon administrations have, on the other hand, received almost consistent support from the self-consciously conservative (fundamentalist or 'evangelical') Protestant publications," including "a host of avowedly rightist publications of the Christian Anti-Communist Crusade [*sic*] genre."[23]

Neuhaus clearly recognized that the war prompted a variety of responses from religious people, but he charged that the "mass media" had helped form an image of "relentless religious opposition to the war." He wrote that in the national media, "religion's attitude toward the war comes across in terms of clergy leading protest marches, granting sanctuary to draft-resisters, abetting military deserters, and burning draft cards collected in raids on Selective Service offices." He acknowledged that the Protestant base of the National Council of Churches had been "officially, if often mildly, critical of war policy at least since late 1966." On the other hand, he noted, church bodies, like the Southern Baptist Convention "pursue[d] an avoidance course, assuming that unless there is an indication to the contrary, the churches will do what comes naturally, which is to profess neutrality, but, in effect, to support government policy."[24] For Neuhaus, official neutrality was just as problematic as outright support.

While Neuhaus was deeply critical of such support, his underlying assumption was nevertheless correct: many Americans continued to support the military effort in Vietnam by invoking the language of civil religion and by encouraging chaplains' ministries within the military. And they did so in public venues—consistently gaining political ground that liberal and moderate Christians had conceded. In a speech to the SBC in 1966, convention president William Dehoney proclaimed that "our nation's purpose in Vietnam is right, our motives are righteous, and our cause is just." In addition to fighting "Communist aggression," he claimed, "we are working to win a peace." But he saved his highest praise for the work of chaplains and Christian soldiers in Vietnam who contributed to the "untold story of Vietnam—what we are doing for the people." Dehoney praised them for their extensive "humanitarian activities," including "building schools and churches, and establishing village hospitals, and opening market places, and planting gardens, and financing pig projects." Concluding his speech, he quoted Southern Baptist chaplain Francis Garetts, who said, "We have such a good feeling about what we are doing for these people, like rescuing someone from a burning building."[25] For Dehoney and Garetts, the war in Vietnam was simultaneously an ideological, geopolitical battle and a salvific mission.

Fundamentalist preachers also cast the war in religious and anti-Communist terms: Carl McIntire, the founder of the Bible Presbyterian Church and vocal supporter of the Vietnam War, declared the effort in Southeast Asia a "righteous and holy cause," and Billy James Hargis, a prominent evangelist, argued that Americans were fighting "for freedom . . . security and protection of the United States" against a serious and able "aggressor."[26] Even more moderate evangelicals endorsed military action and weighed in on strategic decisions. Editors at *Christianity Today*, an interdenominational evangelical weekly, advocated the continued bombing of North Vietnam in order to stop its aggression.[27]

In the face of growing arguments from liberal and mainline camps that compulsory service in Vietnam violated Christians' right to make moral decisions against the orders of their government, the National Association of Evangelicals (NAE) adopted a "Law and Order" resolution in 1966. It derided the "unamerican [*sic*] mood which has invaded our society" as "godless, revolutionary, and disloyal to government." Invoking Romans 13, the resolution then committed evangelicals to obey scriptural injunction "to respect the authorities over us."[28] Not until after My Lai and the Cambodian incursion did *Christianity Today* soften its editorial position. In 1971, an editorial called for "honesty in government," and in May the magazine conceded that "perhaps we should never have gotten into Viet Nam in the first place."[29] Yet many conservatives continued to call on Americans to support the government and the war through the end.

In his book *A Chaplain Looks at Vietnam*, published in 1968, chaplain John O'Connor made the case, from a Catholic, prowar standpoint, for the inherent morality of the United States effort in Vietnam and urged support for military efforts there. O'Connor consciously used his position as a chaplain who had served in Vietnam to gain credibility with an increasingly skeptical American audience. Though O'Connor later admitted that he regretted publishing the book and that it had been a "mistake," at the time, he was responding to biases that he saw within the American media. He went on a lecture circuit to promote his book and to talk about what he considered the side of the war that had gone uncovered.[30]

Regardless of official denominational statements, though, individual chaplains who served in Vietnam—even those who belonged to mainline and liberal churches, defended at least some parts of the American effort in Vietnam. Overwhelmingly, chaplains who wrote for denominationally specific audiences, in newsletters or other publications, focused on organizational and pastoral rather than prophetic issues that they faced and requested support from their home congregations and religious groups. Chaplain James Thompson, nearing the end of his tour in Vietnam, for example, summed up his thoughts on his experience: "I have a great respect for the men I have served. I believe them to be the unsung heroes of this war—the advisors, who in groups of two and three live with the ARVNS and depend almost totally on them for everything. It is a frustrating job at best, and lonesome. They were always glad to see the chaplain. I am only sorry that it was so hard to get around to see them."[31] Few, if any, chaplains writing for denominationally specific audiences ever mentioned the morality of the Vietnam War as a major consideration in the field. They commented on the loneliness of deployment or on the destructive nature of the war, but their assessments of the war were ambivalent at best.

For Neuhaus and other religious leaders, the two sides of the issue seemed clear. The theologically mainline and liberal churches and leaders generally lined up in opposition to the war, while conservative and evangelical churches and leaders lined up in support. Both positions, and many in between, were supported by scripture, religious tradition, and reason. Yet, adding chaplains' voices to this mix revealed a more complicated picture. Despite a growing number of conservative Christian chaplains in the military, there were a significant number of chaplains from denominations that criticized the war harshly. Whether or not they agreed politically or theologically with the American war effort in Vietnam, the fact of their continued service demands reconsidering traditional narratives of religious responses to the Vietnam War. Faced with questions about the potential tensions and contradictions between faith and war, between religiosity and Communism, chaplains serving in South Vietnam, as did religious people in general, responded in a variety of ways. Some denounced war and the U.S. government, and others supported them without question. Most chaplains however, fell somewhere in between. Some tried to balance dissent against the Vietnam War with allegiance to the United States. Others questioned the strategy and tactics of Vietnam without doubting the righteousness of its fundamental aims

Priest versus Prophet: Defining the Chaplain's Role in War

Though chaplains had served with American military personnel from the country's founding, the professional duties and expectations of chaplains were not constant. George Washington and other Revolutionary era commanders valued chaplains for their morale-boosting function among troops; in the Civil War, chaplains on both sides assured men of the fundamental righteousness of their cause; on the Western frontier, chaplains also doubled as library officers, post teachers, bakery and commissary managers, and even medics; and in the early Cold War, chaplains played a central role in character guidance instruction in the military.[32] As the chaplaincy increased professionalization and education levels within its ranks, chaplains' duties became more focused on specifically religious endeavors, and because chaplains were usually drawn from a pool of civilian clergy, developments within American religious communities necessarily affected the military chaplaincy.

In the 1960s, as the wave of religious revival and adherence peaked and began to decline, politically and theologically liberal Americans began to reconsider the role of religion in public life. They took cues from World War II theologian and anti-Nazi dissident Dietrich Bonhoeffer, who advocated a "religionless Christianity," one in which God's people on earth undertook earthly tasks without looking to the supernatural for guidance or support. Liberal religious adherents and secular activists took one of Bonhoeffer's most quoted statements to heart: "God would have us know that we must live as men who manage our lives without him."[33] In his book *The Secular City*, published in 1965, Harvard sociologist and theologian Harvey Cox argued passionately that secularization and urbanization were not the enemies of Christianity but rather its product. Cox's book became a handbook of sorts for liberal activists and seminarians; Protestant Christians could better the world by working in it, by engaging with American culture.[34] Thus, as there had been in previous periods of revival, there were significant calls to move away from the "institutional" church, grounded in ornate and well-established buildings and steeped in tradition, and into communities, where liturgical innovation and inclusion would be the norm.

Conservative and evangelical Christians engaged in American culture and politics as well, finding particular success in the period after World War II in gaining large audiences and increasing their number of adherents. Evangelical preachers were among the first to use radio to reach mass audiences, and Billy Graham's revivals harkened to evangelical camp meetings of the nineteenth century. By 1940, Charles Fuller's *Old-Fashioned Revival Hour* was broadcast on 450 radio stations each week, and by 1943 boasted a weekly audience of more than twenty million.[35] Between 1952 and 1971, Southern Baptist Convention churches gained more than 6,300,000 adherents, a 78 percent increase, and the Presbyterian Church in the United States, the conservative wing of American Presbyterianism, experienced a 54 percent increase.[36] Though old mainline denominations gained numerically more adherents and were generally larger than their conservative counterparts, evangelical and conservative denominations clearly had greater momentum; the total increase in the number of religious adherents reported was 46 percent, and of the sixteen denominations (of thirty-five total) that reported higher than 46 percent growth, only the Catholic Church is not logically identified as "evangelical."[37]

Even as evangelical and conservative churches experienced rapid growth, it took place in the context of the Cold War culture that emphasized—at least on the surface—consensus on religious and moral issues and the ecumenical Judeo-Christian foundation of American society and culture. Within this context, chaplaincy leaders echoed the growing concern for ecumenical cooperation and respect for religious pluralism, emphasizing its historical roots, but conservative groups continued to influence the military's character guidance programs and to cast the Cold War in explicitly religious terms. Exactly how best to provide spiritual support for American military personnel became an important issue as the Cold War solidified and as disagreements over the Cold War emerged between conservative and liberal religious groups.

A distinction from Max Weber's sociology of religion framed the debate that ensued. Some writers referred to Weber's typology explicitly, but even those who did not engage Weber's theory directly described their positions in analogous ways. In *Economy and Society*, Weber identifies three ideal types of religious authority: the priest, the prophet, and the magician. (In the chaplaincy debate, only the first two were ever considered with any seriousness.) Each holds a particular place within a given society, and each fulfills a specific role and religious need. The priest is essentially a functionary of a "regularly organized and permanent enterprise concerned with influencing the gods." The priest receives his authority by virtue of tradition, ritual, and law, and he is bound by the same. His most important relationships on earth are social, and he is "actively associated with some type of social organization, of which they are employees or organs operating in the interests of the organization's members." A priest draws on systems of religious concepts, and he is usually educated within the confines of a particular religious system.[38] A prophet, on the other hand, is a process agent. He appears when a community is threatened, revealing divine truth, and intercedes on behalf of the community. Weber identifies two main kinds of prophetic witness: ethical, through proclamation, and exemplary, through modeling. Whereas a priest operates within formal structures and traditions, a prophet usually emerges from the outside or margins of formal religious authority. A prophet, by virtue of divine calling and personal charisma, is to speak truth to power and to attract followers.[39]

Generally, those who doubted that Christians should serve in war, or should do so only in the face of extreme evil, and questioned the morality of American intervention in Vietnam believed that chaplains should play a prophetic role and that their close ties to the military compromised their ability to reveal perhaps unpopular truths to military authorities. Those who found Christian service in war acceptable, valued submission to governmental authority and emphasized the spiritual needs of military service members thought that chaplains' primary role should be priestly or pastoral. Chaplains themselves almost always emphasized their priestly or pastoral role, unsurprising given chaplains' self-selection for service in the military.

In 1970, as American forces were beginning to withdraw, in response to growing concerns that a chaplain's conscience was unnecessarily and detrimentally fettered by his institutional position within the military, the General Commission on Chaplains and Armed Forces Personnel (GCCAFP) released "Guidelines for Free and Responsible Expression of Conscience in the Military." As might be expected, the GCCAFP did not find the chaplain's religious role and his military one to be mutually incompatible. Instead, the four guidelines were intended to resolve conflict when it did arise. Widely circulated, in both GCCAFP and denominational publications, the guidelines recognized the potential tension between a chaplain's role as a clergyman and his role as an officer and that his dual responsibilities to church and state would never be easily reconciled. The first guideline asserted that a "chaplain's presence among his men is a constant reminder of the fact that the church is identifying with all persons in all conditions." The second stated more emphatically that "Holy Scriptures require the church to minister to men wherever they may be found." The third outlined the expectations and demands on chaplains by both the church and the state. The fourth and longest guideline set out a recommended course of action if the other three seemed in conflict. It concluded, "If after exhausting all efforts the chaplain finds that reconciliation still is not possible, the dictates of his faith and denomination determine his course of action."[40] According to the GCCAFP, the chaplain's primary role was a priestly/pastoral one, but the chaplain's spiritual conscience demanded a role for the prophet as well—if faith and war conflicted irreconcilably, faith should prevail.

In November 1966, toward the beginning of a long buildup of American forces in Vietnam, and well before public opinion tilted against the war, the mainline Protestant periodical the *Christian Century* published a three-part series on the military chaplaincy, and the issue of the Vietnam War echoed throughout. Although the *Century*'s readership was never very large, its influence in academic circles was significant, and it was (and is) often taken to be the voice of mainline to liberal Protestantism in the United States, a conclusion that is now contested by some scholars.[41] However, even if the *Century* was not representative of mainline views, the series reveals some of the reasons that Vietnam would become so divisive in religious communities. It provides a framework for understanding the debate about chaplains and enables us to contextualize other, more isolated references to a chaplain's role in war found in other publications. In the initial foray into the subject, two of the three articles presented were clearly opposed to the military chaplaincy—either in principle or in its current form.

William R. Miller, a layperson in the United Church of Christ, calling upon the archetype of the incompetent chaplain, began his article by refer- ring to the Anabaptist chaplain in Joseph Heller's *Catch-22*: "The chaplain was sincerely a very helpful person who was never able to help anyone." The critique that followed was steeped in this sense of irony; the funda- mental problem with the chaplaincy, Miller went on, was the "sheer incon- gruity of a pious imitator of Christ trying to be relevant while acting as part of a system for which the Gospels made no provision whatever." The best the chaplain could do, according to Miller, was to punch a young enlistee's "T[ough] S[hit] Card," since the chaplain's "powers of exorcism are greatly diminished in our matter-of-fact secular age."[42] When it came to Vietnam, Miller concluded that the chaplain could not seriously preach about pac- ifism, but he could "ever so cautiously, *ask* whether indeed God is the co-pilot of our bomber pilots as they rain death on Hanoi and Haiphong." Miller was skeptical, though, that chaplains would even go this far, add- ing that they preferred instead to "wrap such questions in impenetrable abstractions and couch them in a letter to the *Link* or the *Chaplain* rather than risk demoralizing our Christian fighting men."[43] Chaplains, in Miller's estimation, were unlikely to purposefully cause discomfort or disruption within the military system in part because they were constrained by the system in which they operated, so their primary outlet for dissention or dis- agreement with policies was in discussions with other military chaplains.

Ultimately, Miller concluded that the military had far too great an influ- ence on religion, and specifically on the prophetic ministry of the church and its leaders. But Miller argued that he wished to take a broad view of the chaplaincy's mission, and to attempt to disentangle the chaplains' mission from the military mission, insisting there was, in fact, a critical place for a military chaplaincy, albeit in vastly different form from its contemporary constitution. But in order to figure out how chaplains should operate in a military environment, understanding the military mission was critical. "Quite emphatically," he wrote, somewhat ironically, "I do not wish to call attention to the fact that the principal function of the armed forces is to kill people." This critique was implicit throughout the rest of the article as Miller asserted that serving as a uniformed officer required the chaplain to "harmonize his beliefs and what they imply with the objectives of a secular enterprise," and that the resulting cognitive dissonance must be resolved because "an effective army cannot countenance sedition among its officers and men."[44] Conflicting allegiances could not help but produce problematic outcomes as the chaplain balanced his military and religious duties. Miller concluded that the impetus for change, to help chaplains disentangle themselves from the military mission, had to originate with churches more fully seeking to serve the Church in the world.

Norman MacFarlane, a former Navy chaplain, wrote the most scathingly critical article in the series, focusing on the political and military characteristics of the chaplaincy system. MacFarlane charged that chaplains who worked to uphold moral integrity within the military "have drunk the cup of hemlock," essentially sacrificing their moral bearings and integrity for their careers. He went so far as to claim that "no chaplain who challenged the command on a moral issue has survived the next selection board," citing that in December 1965 only 67 percent of chaplains who were up for promotion to lieutenant commander were selected, as opposed to 95.7 percent of other officers. MacFarlane's view, though a minority position for chaplains, was nevertheless evidence of the diversity of chaplain viewpoints and opinions. Chaplains, even with common cultural and social characteristics and a shared social position, did not respond unanimously to the challenges presented by war. This fact was not unique to Vietnam, but the public critique of the war by nonpacifist religious groups highlighted potential divisions within the Chaplain Corps.

MacFarlane's critique extended to the fact that chaplains were often expected to take on duties that other officers would not. He reported that at sea he had become the "library officer, tours officer, movie officer, public information assistant," as well as "publisher of the ship's newspaper [and] organizer of children's parties in foreign ports," in addition to performing other duties unrelated to the chaplain's specific work. But he lamented the fact that many Navy chaplains were "rotting professionally in the Navy when there are 60,000 empty pulpits in America."[45] He also critiqued what he believed to be the Navy's tendency to write off religion, complaining that commanders prohibited or impeded active chaplain activities and undermined the religious program that chaplains offered.[46] The "muzzled ministry" was a common expression among those who called for an overhaul of the military chaplaincy. Chaplains had to be able to speak their conscience, liberal critics cried, and this was difficult if they were under the thumb of military commanders.

In the third article in the first part of the *Century*'s series, Navy chaplain Albert F. Ledebuhr defended the chaplaincy to a generally liberal and skeptical audience. Ledebuhr used his personal experiences as a chaplain to establish credibility with *Century*'s readers, and his references to the social justice movements of the 1960s and the ecumenicalism and racial integration in the Chaplain Corps established his bona fides as a progressive thinker rather than a militant participant in the war. Social movements of the 1960s exhorted Christian leaders to take their faith and ministry outside of church walls—to take the church to the people, rather than forcing people into a church. Ledebuhr put himself and his fellow chaplains in the company of antipoverty and civil rights activists with his assertion that "the ministry of the church is at its best where the clergyman, armed with the gospel, comes face-to-face with people where they work, sleep, eat and play." He argued that war was part of human nature and that the military chaplain was needed to provide "spiritual ministry for people where they are and as they are." Ledebuhr dismissed what he determined were major objections to the military chaplaincy and took especially careful aim at those who he terms "idealists" who argued that chaplains should not associate themselves with men or organizations trained to kill. Ledebuhr challenged his fellow clergymen to similarly abandon congregation members who served as police officers, government workers, or industrialists as they were similarly implicated in the war effort. He acknowledged the spiritual dangers of the chaplaincy—including the competition for rank and prestige and the conflation of Christianity and "Americanism"—but concluded that the potential rewards far outweighed the risks. Chaplains, Ledebuhr argued, were no different from civilian clergy; they were imperfect, but their work was critical.[47]

As Ledebuhr continued, he confronted the Vietnam War in particular, and chaplains' participation in it. Concluding that their presence was most effective when soldiers were at the greatest risk, he opined, "Risk is especially present these days." Ultimately, though, Ledebuhr thought the rewards were more personal than institutional or military: "Such a personal ministry of total identification is one of the real joys of the military chaplaincy." He closed by recounting some of his experiences in Korea, and he reminded readers of recent chaplain activities in Vietnam, for example, Naval chaplains had logged more than 9,000 counseling sessions between April and June 1966 and more than 500,000 had attended worship services—proof, he wrote, that even "'professional killers' are also moved by the gospel."[48] Whereas Miller and MacFarlane emphasized the prophetic failings of the chaplaincy, and especially the chaplain's problematic relationship to the military, Ledebuhr focused on the success of priestly ministry and the needs of military personnel. Prophecy had its place in Vietnam, but so too did pastoral care.

The series prompted several letters to the editor, most of which came from chaplains, and most of whom defended their ministry in response to Miller's and MacFarlane's articles. Two chaplains wrote from Vietnam explaining that chaplains retained some of their connections to civilian religious communities even when they were overseas. Richard McPhee, stationed in Bein Hoa, Vietnam, wrote to defend the position that simply changing chaplains' uniforms or rank structure would do little to address the underlying difficulties that Miller and MacFarlane noted.[49] Expressing an alternate view, J. George Hilton, assigned to the 6th Battalion, 71st Artillery, wrote that as the church reexamined its mission in the military, the chaplaincy could be fundamentally changed. He envisioned a civilian Chaplain Corps whose members could "just as effectively plough through the mud and march in the dust and carry on his mission as do the journalist and technical representative and Red Cross director in the thick of things in their soiled jungle combat fatigues."[50] Such responses from chaplains in the field demonstrated an understanding that issues surrounding the chaplaincy could not be separated from current U.S. military actions. At the same time, their responses offer evidence that chaplains were not walking in lockstep in their views on the future of the chaplaincy.

Reserve and retired chaplains also chimed in, usually defending chaplains and the chaplaincy. They articulated the ambiguity in the chaplain's position and attempted to bridge the divide between communities. Donald Shaner, former line officer in the Navy and at the time a reserve chaplain, disagreed with MacFarlane's point of view but admitted that Ledebuhr "perhaps paints the picture a little too rosy." Shaner suggested examining the historical developments of the chaplaincy in the United States to emphasize the advantages of the modern chaplains' cultural skills and structural position.[51] Retired chaplain William Sodt argued that the problems that Miller and MacFarlane pointed out were due to chaplains' and the chaplaincy's unwillingness "to accept this lowly role as servants and mediators."[52] Sodt considered admirable the chaplain's ambiguous position and flexible cultural role within the military, modeled after Christ and Paul, in which chaplains could become all things to all men. Another retired chaplain declared that MacFarlane's article was a "sorry reflection on the state of the chaplaincy in the Navy or an unconscious commentary on his own inadequacy as a chaplain and a clergyman." Chaplain Alfred Klausler assured "those whose sons are in the armed services, whether in

Vietnam or some other theater, that by and large our chaplains are doing their tasks as servants of God." Then, addressing the theologically well-read readers of the *Century*, Klausler reminded them that Paul Tillich had served as a military chaplain in the First World War and that Karl Barth had served as a reservist in the Swiss Army.[53] Klausler's references to two renowned twentieth-century theologians helped to establish his credibility as a religious authority, especially with the generally liberal audience of the *Century*. These three responses framed the problems and potential solutions in familiar terms—suggesting that the chaplain's priestly role be reconceived and arguing that relationships within the military should be reformed—and avoided the particular moral complexities of the Vietnam War in particular.

None of the letters that were critical of the chaplaincy or supportive of Miller's and MacFarlane's observations were from chaplains. And while such letters responded to articles about the military chaplaincy, they also introduced new terms and problems to the debate. One letter addressed both the series of articles and the subsequent letters that had been published. John Sayre, who identified himself as writing from the Episcopal Peace Fellowship, argued that the primary difference between the military chaplaincy and the civilian pastorate was that the "essential business of the war machine is to kill, burn and destroy." This environment, Sayre concluded, made it impossible for military chaplains "to say a word of Christ against their army's share in the massacre of a people, or against escalation."[54] Sayre's letter changed the terms of debate from the theoretical responsibility of the church to minister in the world to the morality of the war in Vietnam. Though subtle, the difference in emphasis was significant. Many conversations about the war and the military chaplaincy between advocates and those opposed to it began from fundamentally different points of view as to the nature and purpose of the chaplaincy and foreshadowed the growing rift within the Protestant Christian community over the war in Vietnam and the aims of American foreign policy. Later, these same divides would grip secular society as well, but the split within the churches was earlier, and chaplains were caught in the middle.

Even civilian pastors who supported the church's ministry to the armed forces questioned the chaplain's total involvement in the war machine. In a letter to the *Century*, Carl Landes, who identified himself as pastor of the First United Church of Christ in Franklin, Ohio, wrote: "News accounts tell us that the first Protestant chaplain to lose his life in Vietnam was buried in Arlington cemetery 'with full military honors,'" and that, according to his supervisors, he "always reflected confidence and ability, which seemed to radiate religious graciousness." But Landes was unimpressed by and skeptical of the accolades. "Isn't it a rather sad commentary," he wrote, "on the sickness of our society, and of the church, that a representative of the Prince of Peace is buried 'with full military honors'?" Landes did not argue that chaplains had no place in the war, but he questioned whether giving a chaplain "full military honors" was appropriate. Landes invoked Jesus' teaching to love one's enemies to make his point: "If Jesus were speaking to his ministers today, would he not say: 'If you radiate graciousness only upon those who are your friends, what are you doing more than others? Even the communists do that.' . . . Whatever the church's responsibility to the men we conscript to kill our 'enemies,' isn't it time at least to separate the church of the Prince of Peace from the cult of the glorification of war?"Landes argued that if he could recognize the chaplain's priestly role in combat, then the church should demand it retain its prophetic one in peace.[55]

The debate in the *Century* continued well into 1967, highlighting its importance and salience. In January, MacFarlane—the author of one of the original articles—responded to the chaplains' letters. He claimed that there was a "remarkable disparity" between the letters he personally had received and the ones that the editors had published. "Certainly no active duty chaplain who despises the system is going to let you publish his feelings for all the world to see," he argued, essentially making his case based on the lack of self-criticism by active-duty chaplains and insinuating serious self-censorship among chaplains. MacFarlane reported that he had received five letters from chaplains, only one of which disagreed with his main points. The "many letters and phone calls [he received] from non-chaplain military people," he noted, suggested that he was correct on most, if not all, counts. "No one outside the chaplain community has come to the defense of the chaplains," he concluded, "and the chaplains have not done very well in defending themselves. If there was ever any doubt about the veracity of what I have written, I think the chaplains have pretty well dispelled it."[56] MacFarlane's analysis about chaplains' hesitancy to write in with critical perspectives is very likely correct; the tone of the discourse invited defensive responses from chaplains.

Between 1967 and 1970, the period of the most intense fighting in Vietnam, editorial content about chaplains in the *Christian Century* dwindled. As the *Century's* opposition to the Vietnam War increased significantly, the editorial board chose to publish concrete political criticism over largely symbolic debates. Toward the end of the war and immediately after American withdrawal from Vietnam, however, the debate began again. Recalling earlier critiques of the chaplaincy, Robert Klitgaard wrote an article that placed significant blame on chaplains for dehumanizing the modern American armed forces. Beyond simply suggesting it was impossible for chaplains to play a prophetic role in the military, Klitgaard, a former enlisted man in the Army, insisted that chaplains were actually deeply complicit in the problems inherent in military service. Far from being "muzzled" by command, he claimed, chaplains' self-assumed priestly role made them "all too happy to take part" in the military mission.[57]

Klitgaard's article had all the marks of a polemic of a disgruntled soldier. Titled "Onward Christian Soldiers: Dehumanization and the Military Chaplain," the article was deeply critical of the war in Vietnam and similarly critical of those who made such a war possible, including military chaplains. The article begins by addressing a hypothetical "you"—a soldier about to enlist in the military: "One of the first officers you meet at army basic training camp is the military chaplain." Then Klitgaard shifts to a more objective statement, using third-person pronouns: "Basic training is a pretty harrowing experience for most people. Its goal is to turn individuals into a homogeneous, obedient, malleable group." But he quickly lapses into the first-person perspective as he describes basic training, his own anguish standing in for rigorous analysis: "As our cattle trucks arrive, harassment begins. We are attacked by the training cadre." Klitgaard's direct engagement with the reader, primarily through the use of first-person pronouns, adds to the article's sense of urgency, in no uncertain terms reminding the reader of what is at stake. "The average trainee," Klitgaard writes, "knows that within four or five months he will be in Vietnam. [He] finds himself compelled to take the Vietnam situation seriously."[58] The article was utterly unlike the impassioned but well-considered, and in most respects fairly balanced, trio of articles from 1966. Klitgaard's essay reflected more clearly the editorial slant of the *Christian Century* in 1970.

In other arenas, critics of the chaplaincy were more blunt: in a Harvard lecture, Puerto Rican Roman Catholic bishop Antulio Parilla stated plainly, "I believe that [chaplains] are not doing their job adequately. . . . They are army men before they are churchmen and must submit to higher brass who are not religious."[59] Parilla's assessment of the chaplaincy was embedded in a much larger critique of American culture and imperialism, but the insinuation was clear: Military chaplains could not do the prophetic work of antiwar activism because they were beholden to the military.

Whereas the *Christian Century* was a nondenominational publication, unencumbered by the day-to-day implications of its pronouncements on actual chaplains and chaplain endorsement policies, denominational bodies largely understood that chaplains were a fixture in this war (and likely the next), so debate in these groups coalesced around questions of how chaplains could be effective pastoral ministers—as priests—rather than how chaplains could work to change the military system or affect the trajectory of action in Vietnam—as prophets. In order to explain how military chaplains, who were generally disconnected from institutional hierarchies, conventions, and cultural contact, could operate effectively in the field of denominational audiences, chaplains emphasized the mission-oriented nature of their work, and their writings drew parallels to civilian ministry, especially to the work of missionaries, who were charged with evangelizing unchurched populations.

The Baptist General Conference, an organization that brought independent Baptist and evangelical churches together, featured stories by chaplains in its newspaper emphasizing the mission work being carried out around the world. Chaplain Roger Bradley said he wrote his article, for example, to "inform our Conference family of the work of their military chaplains with a view toward arousing a sense of urgency in prayer in their behalf."[60] Bradley's statement of purpose highlighted his position in the middle of civilian and military communities as he relied on his position as a chaplain and as a pastor to urge a specific response to new information. Bradley emphasized the evangelical role of chaplains as a way to create a common vocabulary for thinking about chaplains; according to the Baptist General Conference, they were more like missionaries than simply pastors or military officers.

American Jews were especially attuned to the challenges that Jewish service members faced when they were deployed, given that they were away from the institutional fixtures of Jewish life and the limited coverage Jewish chaplains were able to provide. For much of the war, Jewish endorsing agencies required that all able-bodied male seminar graduates register for a sort of rabbinical draft, which would assign a number of newly minted clergy as chaplains in the armed services. As dissent against the Vietnam War increased among American Jews, the *Jewish Advocate* and other Jewish publications reported on these developments and at the same time continued to run many stories about Jewish service members in Vietnam and the chaplains who served them.[61] In 1968, the Executive Committee of the Association of Jewish Chaplains of the Armed Forces took a strong stand against rabbis claiming Conscientious Objector status in order to avoid service in Vietnam as a chaplain. Some more liberal denominations had encouraged this course of action because they believed rabbis who objected to American involvement in Vietnam should be able to exercise choice in the matter. Jewish chaplains and the majority of the Jewish religious institutions, however, disagreed. "Because many soldiers might be fighting in Vietnam for a cause which they did either not understand or opposed," Rabbi Bertram R. Korn, head of the association, explained, "the military chaplain was particularly needed," adding, "the greater the confusion in the mind of servicemen on duty and the more dangerous the situation he confronts, the greater is the needs of that soldier for the presence and comfort of a chaplain of his faith."[61] Rather than arguing that chaplains had a moral obligation *not* to serve, Korn maintained that the absence of moral clarity necessitated the chaplain's presence and ministry.

At other times, especially when chaplains were addressing their colleagues and thus did not feel as compelled to publicly defend their professional choices, the debates over whether their role should be priestly or prophetic was more complicated. Some chaplains believed they were called to both tasks. The *Chaplain*, published by the General Commission on Chaplains and Armed Services Personnel, was the most common site for these debates. The bimonthly periodical frequently included first-person accounts of the chaplain's work in Vietnam as well as preaching, counseling, or teaching advice, short book reviews, and stories of general interest to military chaplains. The *Chaplain*, as a publication concerned itself with the minutiae of a minister's life, focused almost exclusively on his or her priestly role as a functionary for a religious community. In his column "Preaching Clinic," for example, James Cleland, dean of Duke Chapel at Duke University in Durham, North Carolina, wrote on topics ranging from "The Twenty Minute Sermon," to using anecdotes effectively, to selecting scripture passages outside of the lectionary readings. These articles showcased the Protestant thrust to the publication and emphasized chaplains' preaching and pastoral roles. Another writer suggested that chaplains take up running or some other form of physical activity as a way not only to meet military requirements but also to invigorate their body and mind.[63]

In late 1970, Chaplain Wendell Wright wrote a reflective piece titled "The Problems and Challenges of a Ministry in Vietnam." While he did not claim that his experience was universal or even typical, Wright addressed his article to chaplains who had *not* served in Vietnam (and perhaps to the limited number of civilian readers who took an interest in the subject). Like chaplains who wrote for denominationally specific audiences, Wright concluded that "the problems and challenges of the ministry in Vietnam are not really so different from those experienced by a Christian minister or priest anywhere serving his people." Though he acknowledged the differences in the "situation," the "environment," and "the circumstances" in which a chaplain worked, Wright focused on the similarities. "There is much more intensity and tension because of the war, but the chaplain still brings to his people the basic message of the love of God through Jesus Christ and it is this redeeming, releasing, and freeing good news of the gospel that brings life to men in combat just as anywhere else in the world."[64] Wright's message stood squarely in the face of civilian critics' claim that the military chaplaincy was fundamentally different from civilian ministry because of its institutional setting. He also emphasized the chaplain's pastoral role to provide for the spiritual care of a specific group of people within a specific social context.

As the American drawdown in Vietnam occurred in the early 1970s, contributors to the *Chaplain* engaged more consciously in the wider religious debates about the ethics, practicality, and ultimate future of the chaplaincy in the U.S. military. The editors recognized the cultural impact of criticism of the chaplaincy and wanted chaplains to be aware of issues facing the wider community and to act accordingly. Yet the articles were not all one-sided defenses of the status quo. Jack Boozer, a professor of religion at Emory University in Atlanta, Georgia, wrote there was "considerable justification" for the criticism leveled against clergymen and chaplains for their being "either absent or indecisive in the high-risk struggles for human dignity and community since the early 1950s," and he exhorted the chaplaincy to change its course.[65] A later article specifically addressed the question of the chaplain's role in prophetic ministry. While the article concluded that attacks on the chaplaincy for not emphasizing this role were generally unfounded and represented a misunderstanding of the chaplain's primary function, the essay nonetheless demonstrated that chaplains—both individually and organizationally—were aware of and concerned with broader public debates.[66]

Civilianizing the Chaplaincy

Implicit in debates about chaplains' roles were questions about the chaplaincy itself. Not until the early twentieth century, concurrent with the wider Root reforms within the entire Army, were chaplains fully integrated within the military's systems of uniform and rank, and these two issues—the most visible signs of a chaplain's military status—drove discussions among chaplaincy critics and supporters during the Vietnam War era. From the Revolution to after the Spanish-American War, chaplains operated only within a loose hierarchy, reporting directly to the adjutant general rather than to a chief of chaplains or chaplain general. During the Mexican-American War of 1848, the first war in which American chaplains accompanied troops outside of the United States, the Army also experimented with a civilian Chaplain Corps but deemed it a logistical and tactical failure.[67]

Although chaplains had served alongside American soldiers since the Revolution, there were significant variations in the historical models that could be followed. Most notably, during the Vietnam War, the Wisconsin Evangelical Lutheran Synod (WELS) called upon its civilian pastors to serve one-year "tours of duty" in Vietnam as civilian chaplains. WELS leaders believed that the theological and doctrinal integrity of their church would be compromised if they asked their pastors to perform military or government functions in addition to religious ones. They also argued that the specific spiritual needs of WELS service members would go unmet by non-Christian, Catholic, or general Protestant chaplains.[68]

Even denominations that endorsed a significant number of chaplains worried about the chaplain's spiritual well-being in the midst of the military structure. Leaders of American religious groups were concerned that chaplains' detachment from institutional structures might weaken their theological or religious foundations and concluded that ongoing spiritual training and support was essential to their success. While chaplains in hierarchical or Episcopal churches basically operated within certain boundaries, churches and denominations with a looser ecclesiastical structure needed to exercise some supervision or control over their chaplains. Denominations such as the American Baptist Convention worked to find a balance between freedom and control for chaplains.

In an article for the *American Baptist Chaplain*, Reverend William Flood wrote that the convention recognized that chaplains (and others without congregational commitments) were participating in "a new form of mission" and deemed them "pioneers in new fields of service." But, he continued, the convention worried that "the permissive attitude" of the denomination toward chaplains' work, which was really "an expression of confidence and the freedom of ministry enjoyed by Baptists," would be "misunderstood by some." Yet this freedom, according to Flood, did not come without cost: "We can readily see how strong the structures are in which we work" and that a "pastor is generally called to a congregation because he seems to 'fit' or at best can meet their needs." Within the military, however, assignment was at the discretion of military officers and the "congregation" was not a denominationally specific one. Thus, Flood continued, chaplains were "equally influenced by the structure in which they serve . . . the atmosphere is charged with tensions for most individuals," including chaplains and nonchaplains. Civilian ministers' concern was "reflected in the suspicion" of military chaplains and other "unstructured ministers" and in the question "When are you coming back into the ministry?" Flood determined that the real question at hand was this: "If the shaping of a pastoral identity is the concern of a local congregation, who shapes the identity of the chaplain?" Civilian ministers could not help but conclude that the chaplain was left to his own devices because he was part of a military rather than a religious institution. But Flood, himself a chaplain, asked his colleagues to reconsider. He wrote that the structure of a chaplain's service would "indeed shape his ministry" but could not "create his spiritual image." The challenge for the chaplain, then, was maintaining a "ministerial image and identity."[69]

Other chaplains contested the idea that civilian ministers were freer than their military counterparts. In a *Washington Post* feature article about military chaplains (later reproduced in several other national newspapers), American Baptist chaplain Lyman Sale Jr. is quoted, "I'm not selling my soul to the Army any more than I sold it to the civilian church. . . . I'm not dependent on my parishioners for my salary any more and it's amazing how that will free a man. . . . If some little old lady doesn't like what I say I'm not going to be fired next week. I don't have to live with a telephone network of gossip about what I do." William Greider, the article's author, pointed out that chaplains did have to sometimes deal with demanding commanders, a military version of the "little-old-lady-syndrome," but reported that most chaplains saw these challenges as simply "part of the game of getting along in the military," little different from similar pressures in civilian churches.[70] In another summary report of chaplains' attitudes, Associated Press reporter George Cornell quoted an anonymous United Presbyterian Church chaplain. "In my experience as a chaplain," he said, "I feel a greater freedom in or out of the pulpit than 90 percent of my civilian colleagues. In California I found ministers afraid to speak their minds because the session was ruled by members of the John Birch Society. Civilian ministers are muzzled far more than military chaplains."[71] Making comparisons between their ministry and civilian ministry were important ways that military chaplains could defend their work, making the mysterious, unfamiliar environment of the military seem more like civilian ministry. Pointing out the ways in which civilian ministry could be limited by politics, money, and personality enabled military chaplains to reframe the debate as one not over the morality of the Vietnam War but over the need and efficacy of ministry in a variety of settings.

The idea of civilianizing the Chaplain Corps rarely entered public debate, but it came up more and more as moral and religious opposition to the Vietnam War increased. In the 1960s the opening volley over the correct place for chaplains in contemporary military service was fired by Rabbi Martin Siegel, who served as a Navy chaplain for two years. In a 1962 article in the *Christian Century*, he argued that with the "emergence of a permanent military establishment, the military aspects of the chaplaincy have begun to take precedence over the religious."[72] Siegel blamed this change in part on the fact that "in recent years a substantial number of line officers and enlisted men have left the service for a short time, taken the requisite religious training (often not too rigorous), and immediately returned to the military as chaplains." "Such chaplains," he continued, "are essentially 'military men'" who had "thoroughly internalized the professional military pattern." Siegel also lamented the fact that chaplains often lost "contact with their own religious tradition" due to frequent reassignments and deployments. He also criticized the chaplains' widely touted focus on ecumenism, arguing that the widespread cooperation among chaplains of different faith groups occurred not because they "have suddenly learned to get along but because most chaplains are out of touch with their particular religious tradition."[73]

Siegel, like others before him, suggested that the chaplaincy be civilianized, essentially advocating a return to an earlier American model when chaplains were "civilian clergymen who volunteered or were assigned to service with the military." He pointed to the success of the West German model for the chaplaincy, where civilian chaplains served for a maximum of five years. Chaplains could then operate without fear of "military reprisals" and would be better able to counsel young men and women who were new to the military. A civilian Chaplain Corps, Siegel further argued, would reduce the likelihood of professional concerns getting in the way of ministerial ones, allowing the chaplain the freedom "to use the weight of his moral and religious tradition rather than his rank to get things done." Though he did not mention American involvement in Vietnam explicitly, Siegel anticipated that chaplains would soon be serving "personnel who are for the most part 'short timers' used to 'civilian' religious traditions," and that a military Chaplain Corps would increase the divide between professionals and draftees in the modern military.

Siegel criticized the military chaplaincy at a time when there were few chaplains deployed with military personnel—the first chaplains had arrived with the Military Assistance Command, Vietnam (MACV) staff in late 1962, and chaplains did not serve in Vietnam in large numbers until 1965. He objected to the chaplaincy on a variety of grounds but charged that there was a fundamental problem with military service by "a basically civilian-oriented and often pacifistically inclined body of men."[74] Siegel's article foreshadowed debates premised on similar assumptions long before the majority of Americans turned against intervention in Vietnam.

Public response to Siegel's article was significant: The *Century* chose not to publish individual letters but rather offered a summary of the various responses in a later issue of the magazine. Titled "Whither the Military Chaplaincy," the article revealed the editors' generally negative view of the chaplaincy in its current form, though they attempted to give an unbiased overview of the letters to the editor on the topic. They began, "Volleys of protest were shot in this direction by military chaplains of high rank and low from almost every branch and subdivision of the armed forces. (The Marines have not yet landed, but we expect them any minute.)" Siegel's critics, the editors went on, believed that he had "used a blunderbuss on a delicate and complex problem and with his broadsides slew the innocent as well as the guilty."[75]

In the first section of the article was an analysis of the responses to the tone and content of Siegel's argument, most of which came from chaplains themselves. First, the letters in support of the chaplaincy did not seem to fall along denominational or sectarian lines, nor did the "one-sidedness of the chaplains' rebuttals suggest that they were expressing a military or official position." Rather, they were more personal; they resented the implication that the military "always has an adverse effect on the clergymen who serve within it." Second, chaplains emphasized their education and extensive training as evidence of their ability to navigate complex institutional positions. Ten chaplains stationed in Texas, for example, reminded readers that in the U.S. Air Force, chaplains could not "receive a commission without the ecclesiastical endorsement of his own church, or an agency designated to have this authority by his own church." And third, regarding Siegel's critique of professional ambition within the chaplaincy, the editors quoted several chaplains' responses. One chaplain wrote, "The 'professional ambitions' of career chaplains have their counterpart in the civilian ministry's competition for status. . . . One may still recall the civilian seekers of deanships, bishoprics, 'First Churches,' lucrative synagogues and denominational offices." Another wrote that "the man of God in the armed forces is no more in tension with his milieu than is the man of God in suburbia or the inner city." Ultimately, the *Century* reported, though none agreed with Siegel's central thesis, only one chaplain denounced it.[76]

The second section of the article dealt with the broader issue of the church's responsibility to men and women in the armed forces. Summarizing the viewpoints from various letter writers, the editors declared that "with an unpardonable indifference the churches have let the chaplaincy develop in its own untended way, leaving a vacuum which the military has had to fill. Many conscientious chaplains are aware of and saddened by the weakness and ambiguity of the churches' relation to their ministry." They exhorted American Protestants to pay close attention to the military and their chaplains who served there. The article encouraged continued discussion about the chaplaincy and the churches' relationship to the armed services.

As the war in Vietnam dragged on, the *Century* became increasingly critical of the military chaplaincy. In the 1966 series, discussed above, former Navy chaplain Norman MacFarlane suggested the most radical changes to the chaplaincy's structure. Whereas Albert Ledebuhr and William Miller recommended primarily religious-based initiatives to transform the chaplaincy, MacFarlane's emphasis was on the military. To address a problem that he determined stemmed from the chaplain's position as an officer, he advocated that the military abolish the system of rank and promotion for chaplains. He suggested that the number of active-duty chaplains be decreased—even as the level of American armed forces in Vietnam expanded—and that those who remained be consolidated under a single chaplains' service in order to increase efficiency and consistency across the various branches of service. While MacFarlane recognized the impact such changes might have on the relationship between the churches and the chaplaincy, his focus remained on eliminating the tension between chaplains' military and religious duties.

As the war wound down and opposition to it reached a fever pitch, liberal and moderate religious groups called for the civilianization of the military chaplaincy. The Presbyterian Church (U.S.A.) declared, "The Church and its Chaplains must be keenly sensitive to the erosion, exploitation, or softening of its witness."[77] The Episcopal Church acknowledged the "necessity for a ministry to the military community" but maintained that it must be "a ministry for which both priestly and prophetic roles are stressed." It conceded that the chaplain was responsible for ministry to military personnel in a variety of situations but also declared that "the Chaplain is also the public voice of conscience who introduces a self-critical dimension within all institutions. His responsibility therefore is to ask the difficult moral question, whether this particular kind of participation is allowable from a Christian moral perspective. The dilemma is whether the Military Chaplaincy can ask these questions, given its dependence on the military structure."[78] In 1968, the American Jewish Congress voted unanimously to terminate its participation in the military chaplaincy system in its current form, concluding that the military service was "fundamentally incompatible with faithful performance of [chaplains'] sacred mission."[79]

While there were some deep divisions within religious communities' ideas about the military chaplaincy, the national press reflected a bias toward civilianizing or significantly reforming the chaplaincy. In a 1968 *New York Times* article that presented diverse viewpoints on the chaplaincy, for example, the headline nevertheless highlighted the reform position, which urged civilianizing the chaplaincy, and led with a former chaplain who agreed with this position. In many ways, this rabbi's call reflected long-standing debates about the possibility of civilianizing the chaplaincy, whereby individual denominations or organizations would be responsible for the salary and material support of chaplains.[80] In the same article, Rabbi Arthur Hertzberg told the *Times* reporter that he was "terribly grateful" for his time as a chaplain "because it made it easier now to be an out-and-out dove on Vietnam." On the other hand, representatives of the Presbyterian Church, the Southern Baptist Convention, and the General Commission on Chaplains said that they were skeptical that American denominations would have the financial resources to fund a civilianized chaplaincy, and they doubted that such a move would actually alleviate the tensions that Hertzberg and others identified.[81]

Ensuring the chaplain's effectiveness, regardless of his formal position in or level of integration within institutional structures, would require close cooperation between the military and American religious organizations. Chaplains and their advocates frequently cited their position in both military and religious communities as being advantageous for their ministry to the military, yet this very structural position was the primary location for debate over the chaplaincy during the Vietnam War. Critics of the chaplaincy and of chaplains charged them with complicity in an immoral and unjust war, insisting that their positions as officers prevented them from performing prophetic functions within the military. Supporters of the chaplaincy, on the other hand, insisted that the chaplain's structural position was the very thing that allowed him to be an effective minister within the military hierarchy.

Two articles from *Time* magazine, published just three years apart, exemplify the broader cultural shifts taking place during the course of the Vietnam War, offering a longer-term view of the military chaplaincy and its members and revealing a trend that as opposition to the Vietnam War increased, so too did criticism of military chaplains. The first article appeared in 1966 and focused on the increasing number of chaplains and their relationship to the men serving overseas. After reminding readers that chaplains had served with U.S. military troops since the Revolutionary War, the unnamed authors asserted that "Viet Nam is a new kind of war," where "chaplains have become airborne circuit riders." The decentralized fighting meant that chaplains were holding far more services than in the past. According to Army chief of chaplains Charles Brown, they reported, "We used to hold three or four or maybe ten services a week. Now our chaplains are saying services in the combat area to at least ten and sometimes as many as 50 separate detachments of soldiers."

But while the number of services increased, according to the article, chaplains held few illusions that more men were attending their services—in fact, the Chaplain Corps estimated that only about 17 percent of troops attended services regularly on Sunday and about 60 percent never attended at all. Chaplain Frank Vavrin said he didn't "believe for one minute that old saw about there being no atheists in foxholes," while others attributed scarce service attendance to decreased mortality from combat wounds. Air Force chaplain Robert Cortez, for example, suggested that "the Viet Nam war is considerably less deadly than World War II," where, he recalled, "there was constant fear in so many cases—sitting all alone in a foxhole getting shelled, or on a rolling ship scanning the sky for kamikazes. The fear was there and it made you think of God. Here, relatively few guys are confronted with death every day."[82] The article ended with two stories of chaplains who had earned the respect and admiration of their troops. Both chaplains sustained wounds in their efforts to minister to soldiers on the front lines. One soldier even insisted, "I can't talk about him [the chaplain] . . . you just wouldn't understand. You haven't been with us." This view of combat religion avoided entirely the morality of the war at hand—for one thing, in 1966, Cold War sentiments still ran high and opposition to the Vietnam War low. Furthermore, it assumed that chaplains would serve with soldiers and that soldiers would come to respect their chaplains, and there was no question of whether chaplains could serve both God and men faithfully.[83]

Three years later, a second article assumed a far more critical tone. Like other stories in the mainstream press, it focused on increasing religious protest and calls for civilizing the chaplaincy. The article cited the San Francisco Conference on Religion and Peace and its co-chair, Rabbi Joseph Glaser, as primary advocates for abolishing the military chaplaincy. Glaser told *Time* that chaplains "do not have freedom of movement, and they do not even have freedom of conscience" within the military, given their official functions to support the military mission, as outlined in the Army Field Manual. Richard John Neuhaus, a longtime critic of the Vietnam War, told the magazine that chaplains "expose[d] themselves to 'spiritual prostitution.'" Neuhaus, *Time* concluded, believed there was an "unresolvable contradiction between Christianity's gospel of peace and a minister's participation in war. . . . In trying to resolve the contradiction . . . many chaplains simply arrange their values along military lines, like good soldiers." Though it did not cite specific names, the article suggested that some ex-chaplains who had become disenchanted by the war and military service were now protesting against it.[84]

The article countered this antiwar view by asserting that "the majority of chaplains serving in Viet Nam, however, are convinced of the justice of the American cause, and a few have gone out of their way to support it in a somewhat untraditional manner": the chaplain, for example, who liked "to take a turn firing M-60 machine guns from Huey helicopters," another who wore "a shoulder holster and a .45 even when in Saigon," and a third who said, "I could kill a man in a second. After you see how vicious the V.C. can be, it's hard to separate yourself from it." Rather than making all chaplains sound like gun-toting militarists, however, the article insisted that occasionally the "nature of the war" called on chaplains to perform otherwise forbidden acts in combat. In one instance, Jerry Autry, a chaplain with previous military experience, landed in a Viet Cong village with an inexperienced platoon "commanded by an equally green lieutenant," and "when [the men] froze, [he] rallied them and led the charge." The author of the article concluded: "Like many chaplains who go on patrols or fly on combat sorties with airborne troops, he has discovered that his unarmed presence can make the men jittery."[85] Clearly, many chaplains still deployed had self-interested reasons for justifying and rationalizing their participation in war.

Reporting on the two extremes of wholehearted endorsement of and participation in the war and activism against it, the *Time* piece recognized that military chaplains faced a difficult moral situation. The article quoted Navy chaplain John A. Rohr at length. He argued that "in a world where peace is still unattainable the fact of wars' existence 'must be borne even as we strive to abolish it.'" He said that Christianity "needs both kinds of ministers—the civilian picketing for peace and the chaplain serving 'those brave young men who bear so disproportionate a burden of the sins of the world.'" The authors also acknowledged that "most chaplains, of course, are far more appalled at the cruelties of the war than fascinated by its glory—yet few have asked for release from service." For example, chaplain Philip Seeker chose to return to his unit "convinced" that the war "was still 'unwise'—but not evil enough to keep him away from his men."[86] Ultimately, the quite critical article ended on an ambiguous note.

In a war that inflamed political, religious, and ideological passions, arguing about chaplains offered a safe battleground on which to hash out opposing views about the Vietnam War itself. Chaplains' actions were unlikely to affect the outcome of the war, but they represented one logical intersection between faith and war. Mainline, liberal, and conservative religious groups alike had to work out the role their ministers would play in ministering to the military. By the end of the war, evangelical and conservative Christians especially had embraced the pastoral/priestly role for chaplains, and they supported chaplain ministry with a significant number of chaplain endorsements and informal backing. Liberal groups especially clung to a prophetic ideal for their chaplains. When it appeared that this ideal was not being met, mainline and liberal communities chose to withdraw their chaplains rather than engaging the military directly.

CHAPTER SIX

Reflection and Reconciliation

Though chaplain David Knight went to Vietnam with romantic visions of war, wishing for a "baptism by fire," he returned with a more sober view of it: "I saw the horror, the brutality, and the sinfulness of a nation raped by [war]. I witnessed war as the ultimate breakdown of human morality." Nevertheless, Knight concluded that his wartime experiences allowed him to return "home with a greater understanding of the Lord than ever before. . . . I discovered that, regardless of man's sin and rebellion, we are not at the mercy of an impersonal God. We are not subject to chance or fate. Regardless of circumstances, despite the tragedy, He is very much in control."[1] Far from subordinating his religious identity to his military one or even compartmentalizing the two, Knight's reflection on the war fundamentally linked his religious beliefs with his military experience. Knight's interpretation of the war embodied both his religious self and his military self. He defined the war in hybrid terms because he worked and lived in the middle of a multitude of cultures and institutions with widely varied expectations. This in-the-middle position was significant not only during the war but after as well.

Other chaplains also chose to cast their wartime experiences in a religious light. When chaplains reflected upon their experiences as chaplains and as servicemen in Vietnam, in memoirs, published diaries or letters, on websites, or in interviews, they did so in a way that brought the religious and moral conflicts of the war to the forefront. In the midst of chaos and combat, chaplains generally turned to pragmatic solutions to conflict and used their ambiguous identities to mediate between diverse groups of people. As we saw in Chapters 3 and 4, especially, chaplains only infrequently wrestled with complex theologies in the midst of war, instead opting for casuistic analysis, mingling military and religious meaning. After the war, however, they became more reflective, and their published accounts of Vietnam can be read as acts of public reconciliation to explain their roles, identities, theologies, and behaviors in Vietnam. In their first-person accounts, chaplains provided—perhaps unconsciously—their audiences with a counternarrative of redemption and fulfillment to the dominant narrative of despair and defeat that emerged from much first-person post-war writing about the Vietnam War.

The pacifist critique of military chaplains dismisses these accounts as evidence of rationalization and cognitive dissonance—chaplains justifying otherwise inexplicable and inexcusable participation in war, but this analysis is simply dismissive and does not take chaplains' postwar reflections seriously, either as first-person accounts or as contributions to the vast memoirist literature of the Vietnam War. Their accounts are thus ignored by scholars of both the military and religion. But if we acknowledge the presence of bias and the tendency toward positive self-representation in these accounts, and look for broader patterns as well as unique contributions, we find a more compelling and complex narrative. Again, it is one that is deeply informed by chaplains' position in the middle of military, civilian, sacred, and secular communities. This small group of accounts actually offers an important and substantial revision to the traditional Vietnam first-person narrative. Analysis of these postwar writings helps explain how and why chaplains' wartime positions and actions sometimes seemed so disconnected from their faith traditions. The process of reflection and reconciliation outlined here clarifies how chaplains dealt, after the fact, with the conflicting demands of their military duty, religious calling, and personal moral codes.

The sort of theological interpretation, conflict resolution, and identity formation that began in Vietnam continued when chaplains returned home, as they began to make sense of the war and to share their experiences with others. While chaplains' responses to the war varied widely, some patterns emerged. Overwhelmingly, chaplains spiritualized combat and their participation in it, often adhering to the conventions of religious autobiographical writing but generally deviating from patterns more common to the combat memoir or trauma writing.[2] Furthermore, rather than revealing deep-seated role conflict leading to the militarization of the chaplaincy, chaplains' memoirs suggest that chaplains, at least in retrospect, may have actually privileged their religious identities over their military identities. As they returned home, chaplains, as did other returning veterans, addressed new audiences and new questions, and writing gave them a way to reconcile conflicts that emerged from their experiences in Vietnam.

When they told their stories publicly, chaplains related their experiences and interpreted combat using religious language, images, and ideas so that their faith was affirmed and their God remained in control, even when their faith in the military, fellow chaplains, or the government faltered. Back in the relative safety of the United States, chaplains viewed their experiences through religious filters. The conflict resolution that began on the battlefield continued in the process of healing and assigning religious meaning to the war after the fact.

"Bad" Chaplains and the Challenges of Genre

Chaplains' responses to and evaluations of the Vietnam War are articulated most clearly first in their own published accounts and, second, in their responses to an official survey sponsored by the historian's office at the U.S. Army Chaplain Center and School. Taken together, they reveal much about chaplains' interpretations of the Vietnam War.[3] They are not, however, representative of chaplains' views. Those chaplains considered in this study who published book-length works (either memoirs, diaries, or letters) were generally career chaplains who tended to hail from conservative, evangelical, and/or Pentecostal denominations, and they usually had significant experience with a combat unit in Vietnam. Of the 28 book-length memoirs considered here, there are 9 by Baptist chaplains; 4 by Methodists; 3 by evangelical Presbyterians; 3 by Lutherans; 2 by Catholics; and 1 each by LDS, Nazarene, Episcopal, Full Gospel, and Grace Brethren chaplains. The remaining two are by authors whose denominations are unidentified. Judging by the denominational affiliation of the authors of and the contents of 26 of the 28 books, 14 of them can be easily classified as "evangelical" or "conservative" in outlook, while only 4 fall unequivocally into "liberal" or "mainline" categories. The other 7 are, for one reason or another, more ambiguous, but the texts reveal a generally evangelical, but not always conservative, perspective. When denominational or theological orientation is significant to the analysis, it is noted. Most of the citations to published accounts in this chapter are from chaplains who would likely identify as conservative and evangelical. The race of the authors is, in most cases, unknown, and none of the memoirs appear to be written by chaplains from historically black churches, and no authors identified themselves as a member of a racial minority group.

There is a striking disparity in service affiliation of the memoirists: fully 24 of the memoirs in this study were written by Army chaplains and 4 were by Navy chaplains. To the best of my knowledge no Vietnam-era Air Force chaplains have written memoirs. Proportionally, there were always more

Army chaplains than there were Navy and Air Force chaplains combined, but the proportion was closer to 2:1 during the Vietnam War, rather than the nearly 5:1 ratio suggested by the published accounts. Of course, determining why Navy and Air Force chaplains *did not* write is significantly more difficult than understanding why Army chaplains *did*, although one can speculate that Army chaplains were likely more inclined to write because they had a greater chance of serving with combat units than did chaplains of other services; they were often witnesses to combat and close to combat troops. This does not, of course, explain why Navy chaplains serving with Marine units were less prolific, but it does offer a reasonable explanation for why ship-based Navy chaplains and Air Force chaplains have not contributed substantially to this literature. This is an important gap to consider in analyzing these sources; the inclusion of more first-person accounts from Air Force and Navy chaplains would have provided a wider range of interpretations and responses, and it may have tempered the prevalence of some of the overt spiritualization of combat found in the combat-focused Army narratives. Further, it is important to remember that some chaplains, including those in the Navy and Air Force, served under the operational command of Military Assistance Command, Vietnam, and all chaplains participated in the area coverage system described in Chapter 2. Ultimately, this meant that chaplains from across the services may have had similar experiences.

The official history survey data is also almost exclusively from the Army. Though the data represents the views of a wider group of Army chaplains than does the memoir literature, chaplains who were disillusioned by the war and by the chaplaincy would likely not have responded to an official request. Henry Ackermann, the study's author, did not code the data according to denominational affiliation, though most chaplains identified their denomination. A chaplain's race was also impossible to track unless a chaplain identified himself as a racial minority or was from a historically black church. Neither occurrence was common—most likely due to the small number of minority-race chaplains who served in Vietnam.[4]

To be sure, these biases and gaps are important—the full range of chaplains' voices is simply not in the historical record, and the conclusions here should not be taken as representative of all chaplains. Clearly, the small number of sources on the military chaplaincy limit the diversity of chaplain voices available to the public, particularly from chaplains who had negative feelings about their time in Vietnam. Nevertheless, they demonstrate a fairly broad range of responses to the war and to the military chaplaincy. A more representative sample would likely increase the range of responses—probably on the negative end of the spectrum. It is possible, though I believe unlikely, that there are a significant number of Vietnam-era chaplains who suffered a severe crisis of faith as a result of their service and left the chaplaincy, the ministry, or their faith altogether but whose stories do not appear in published or archival sources. It is more likely that chaplains who are not part of the historical record changed their views over the course of the war and joined the collective religious pacifist antiwar movement.

Unsurprisingly, the sources that are available portray chaplains in a near universally flattering light; chaplains writing about themselves—either for publication or in response to an official survey—rarely shared or admitted instances where they themselves performed poorly or acted contrary to their training as clergymen and officers. Yet, surely some chaplains failed in Vietnam—according to their own standards or those of their commanders or the men they served. A sampling of third-person accounts about chaplains helps to contextualize chaplains' first-person accounts. While some service members held their chaplains in high regard—more than eighty enlisted soldiers deployed to Vietnam later became Army chaplains, many because of the positive example they saw in their own chaplains—others presented more skeptical, even cynical portraits of chaplains. Both positive and negative assessments of chaplains by service members emphasize the diversity of their work and effect.

Chaplains who were awarded the Medal of Honor have been fairly consistently singled out for praise among the men they served. One of them, Vincent Capodanno, a Catholic Navy chaplain who served with Marines in Vietnam, was honored on 21 May 2006 with the title "Servant of God," a first step on the way to canonization in the Catholic Church. A reporter for the *National Catholic Register* interviewed some of the men in his unit. Ray Harton witnessed Capodanno's death in September 1967 during Operation Swift, an engagement in the Que Son Valley, along the border of Quang Nam and Quang Tri provinces in the I Corps region, which pitted about 300 Marines against 2,000 North Vietnamese regulars. Harton, who was seriously wounded during the battle, recalled that Father Capodanno found his way to his side, comforting him by saying, "Stay calm, Marine, someone will be here to help soon. God is with us all here today." Harton credited Capodanno with giving him a sense of peace like he "never witnessed before and never witnessed since" and believed Capodanno's touch "really had something to do with me still being here." Harton continued,

"I do believe the second Father Capodanno leaned over and touched me, that was God touching me through him." According to Harton, when Capodanno, who was also wounded on his face and hands, left him to attend to another wounded man, "a machine gun opened up and killed both of them."[5] Harton's recollections about Capodanno were not unusual. Daniel Mode, a Catholic seminarian (and later a priest), wrote a biography of Vincent Capodanno titled *The Grunt Padre*. Mode's biography relied heavily on the testimony of Capodanno's fellow service members and presented a very positive picture of the chaplain.

Other enlisted personnel spoke highly of their chaplains as well. As part of the official history research, Henry Ackermann placed advertisements in the *American Legion Magazine* and others requesting information from and about chaplains who served in Vietnam. Amos Shumway, who identified himself as an "Administrative NCO," wrote Ackermann to praise one chaplain in particular, though he did not hold chaplains in universally high regard "Most Chaplains with whom I came in contact," he wrote, "were field grade, either in staff offices or at the Chaplain's School. Many of them were content to play the part of a staff officer—attending social activities and functions, making TDY [temporary duty] trips of questionable validity, and generally enjoying the benefits of their rank." The exception was Chaplain Gene Little, whom Shumway praised for his work: "Chaplain Little served in Viet Nam with distinction—going into Cambodia with his troops."[6] As was the case with Capodanno, the chaplain's consistent *presence* with his men, rather than any specific religious rite or counseling, was singled out for praise.

Not all servicemen described chaplains as saints and battlefield heroes. Though tasked with supporting service members of all faiths as well as atheists and agnostics, chaplains did not always provide such help. Philip Paulson, an atheist soldier, expressed disappointment with the chaplains with whom he came into contact. His unit's chaplain, for example, was a "fundamentalist Christian who saw the devil in virtually everything he didn't believe in." Paulson felt he could not express his nonbelief because he felt that being atheist was "perceived as tantamount to being a communist." Paulson, perhaps crediting the chaplain with more military authority than he traditionally or officially had, believed that "Army chaplains wielded a lot of power; their opinions could make the difference between whether or not you got promoted. So, I was quiet about my nonbelief in God."[7] Paulson's experience with chaplains led him to question the institution and to clarify his self-identification as a "humanist" rather than an adherent to any organized religious group.

In the *Veteran*, the newsletter of Vietnam Veterans Against the War, James May wrote a scathing critique of some of the chaplains he knew in Vietnam, associating them firmly with the militaristic, racist, and hyper-patriotic views that he also attributed to the U.S. government and military hierarchy. May homed in especially on one "large, fat, loudmouthed Every-thing-else," who "prated about being on a crusade against the 'Chicoms' while chomping a cigar," adding that "most of the troops hated him." In a "vain appeal to the troops" the chaplain's "prayer was often obscene," May wrote. One that stood out was "Please, God, let the bombs fall straight on the little yellow motherfuckers." May's overall assessment was that the chaplain "must have had a fun war, slept when he wanted, plenty of chow and no danger ever, except when four black troops beat the stuffings outta him once."[8] The chaplain came to represent what was wrong with the mil-itary's mission in Vietnam—for May (and likely for others) the chaplain could not be separated from the military.

Jerry Lembke, the author of *The Spitting Image*, which refuted the perva-sive story of veterans being spat on in American airports upon their return from Vietnam, responded to May's piece in a later issue of the *Veteran*.[9] Lembke, whose well-known critique of Vietnam's legacy adds credibility to the debate about chaplains, agreed with May and began, "May's portrayal of chaplains was not too flattering, but I wouldn't quarrel with it." Then he went on to describe three chaplains he worked with, only one of whom gained Lembke's respect. One chaplain, assigned to Headquarters of the 41st Artillery Group, was Chaplain Elsie, who Lembke described as a "char-acter out of Joseph Heller's *Catch 22*." For Elsie, "ministering to troops was only a day job for this career man," who also became the "unit's self-desig-nated procurer." On one occasion he "did an enlisted man a 'favor' by tak-ing a contraband AK-47 off the soldier's hands before he got caught with it," later explaining to Lembke that the weapon "would become a war trophy" for another officer. Lembke reported that a second chaplain went AWOL when he couldn't take the conditions in Vietnam.[10]

Lembke's interactions with a third chaplain were more positive, though not because the chaplain cultivated positive feelings about a specific reli-gion or for the United States. This chaplain, a Catholic and former mission-ary, toured firebases around LZ Betty, near Phan Thiet, each week. Lembke reported that during his visits, the chaplain "really deepened my own understanding of what the war was about." The chaplain believed that the "United States would not win the war because the Vietnamese people did not want us there" and that the war was "as an act of American imperialism." In the end, Lembke wrote, the chaplain "gave me a deeper respect for the beliefs of other people and even 'relativized' for me the very notion of religion."[11] This unnamed chaplain and the chaplain from Philip Caputo's *A Rumor of War* come closest to the prophetic ideal encouraged by the chaplaincy's critics—both retained a critical edge in their dealings with soldiers but remained focused on pastoral care and personal relationships rather than on speaking out about the horror of Vietnam.

Lembke was further troubled by the fact that chaplains frequently interpreted Romans 13, which directed Christians to "Render unto Caesar the things that are Caesar's," to justify Christian service in war and to separate moral from military considerations, because the interpretation discounted the soldiers who were troubled by the war. Lembke "left Vietnam pretty disgusted with the chaplaincy as an institution." When he wrote the Office of the Chief of Chaplains to report his experience with chaplains, he recalled, the reply was a "classic upbraiding of dissident behavior, and a chastising of my bad attitude and lack of commitment to the mission."[12]

Chaplains did not have to be purposefully bombastic or offensive to soldiers in their care to be ineffective. Sometimes they said or did the wrong things, not out of malice, but out of ignorance or fear. In his book *Dispatches*, journalist Michael Herr writes of a chaplain who told a badly wounded soldier that his legs were fine, when, in fact, both had been amputated. When the soldier found out he insisted that the chaplain take the cross off of his uniform, then looked at the chaplain and said, "You lied to me, Father. . . . You cocksucker. You lied to me."[13] The chaplain's credibility, not to mention any opportunity for ministry or even pastoral care, was gone. For Herr, chaplains were not separated from or elevated above the everyday traumas of combat, but alongside the other very fallible human beings who populated the war. From these accounts from nonchaplain writers, the contours of the three chaplain archetypes—the saint, the militant, and the incompetent—begin to emerge. But, even if they temper the positive view of chaplain activities in Vietnam presented in the chaplains' own accounts, these, too, are incomplete. Few chaplain narratives include incidents that cast them in a negative light, but if they do address failures, they are still cast within the redemptive narrative, contextualized so there is a lesson learned or a religious belief affirmed. Chaplains needed to justify their ministry and actions in Vietnam, and they needed to successfully navigate between the worlds of Vietnam veterans and their religious communities.

Chaplains Write the Vietnam War

Chaplains' narratives are in no way free from the issues of memory and selectivity that haunt other first-person narratives. Some chaplains, however, were themselves aware of these issues as they wrote, addressing the issue of memory explicitly in their retellings. They did not, however, assess the situation uniformly. In the official survey, Henry Ackermann posed an open-ended question near the end of the survey, asking chaplains to recall "two brief narratives of what you consider the most significant events of your Vietnam ministry." The responses varied from blank pages to a few scribbled sentences to pages of dense, typeset prose. A few chaplains, however, commented on the question itself: Donald Shea responded, "These 'war stories' cannot help but be enhanced by age and apocryphal valor. Ten years is too long to expect credibility to last in these 'story' narratives. Sorry."[14] Shea, who answered all of the other questions on the survey, assessed the purpose and accuracy of the stories he could tell and chose *not* to share them, a choice that was surely as important as the choice made by chaplains who published books or wrote at length about their time in Vietnam.

On the other end of the spectrum were chaplains who attested to the accuracy of their memory, and their memoirs. Claude Newby explicitly addresses his sources for *It Took Heroes*: his memory, interviews, and "personal and official journals," among others. He then assesses the issue of memory. "Not to brag," he writes, "but my memory is verifiably exceptional, especially for directions, lay-of-the-land and chronology. This ability I've validated through research and revisits to places of long ago. Almost always, my recollections of sites and events are accurate as to geographic orientation. And usually sites and layouts are the way I remembered them—schools, houses, farms, streams, roads, and dates and sequences."[15] Newby offered this assessment as proof of his credibility, but actually verifying Newby's superior memory is significantly more difficult. The official record on chaplain activities in Vietnam is thin, indeed. This direct statement notwithstanding, we do not know which events, people, or reflections he left out; though the book is long—more than 500 pages—Newby, as did others, certainly made choices about what to include and what to expunge, and on this issue he is less forthright.

Most authors, however, fell somewhere between the two extremes. They recognized the fallibility and selectivity of memory yet chose to record personal narratives and reflections in spite of those limitations. After several aborted attempts at recording his Vietnam experience, Joseph Dulany eventually wrote his memoirs while recovering from hip replacement surgery. Though he "utilized records, notes, letters and journals" to "verify time-lines and experiences," he writes in his book, *Once a Soldier*, he was "confident that there are many errors in this document," and "apologize[d] in advance for the most obvious" errors, for which he blamed his "memory or lack thereof."[16] He continued that he was unsure that he had much to add to the vast, and ever-expanding, literature on the Vietnam War, but he claimed authority and credibility nonetheless: "I have written as I experienced it." But he also acknowledged that the reader would be "experiencing this glimpse of my reality through [an] admittedly marred, imperfect, scratched, and chipped lens."[17] Even with the caveats, however, Dulany essentially asserted that his memoir was "true"—that is, it accurately reflected his experiences and observations during his military service.

For many authors writing about their time in Vietnam, the authority of personal experience was crucial to the credibility of their memoirs. Few made claims to be historians or to represent a larger group with their writing, but many claimed the essential truth of their personal experience. Jerry Autry, a memoirist who has also been active on Internet sites and who has given at least one public interview, also asserted his desire to "share the truth" in his memoir. He recognized, however, the problem of identifying what is true: "Sometimes I have to ask, 'What is the truth?' My recollection and the recollection of my Vietnam buddies do not always mesh. Who is right? Or is there a right?" He concluded that more often than not "the stories and facts are the same, but details are often different." He recalled one instance where he met a veteran "who was with another unit who said he was attached to our unit for a bit." Autry did not remember the man, but several others from his unit did, and the veteran had "constructed an entire scenario" around being attached to Autry's unit. Autry asked, "Is this untrue; true? I simply don't know and don't know whether it matters." For Autry, and most other chaplains (unlike the historians who write about them), "Truth is not relative." He defended the basic reliability and veracity of his account, even though memory, in the words of his buddies, may be "like a vinyl record that is worn and may skip a bit." With his concluding sentence, Autry reached the heart of these intense methodological and philosophical questions: : "This is my story and how it was."[18]

In his memoir, James Burnham lamented that he "did not keep a daily diary during [his] year in Vietnam" because "so much has faded or been lost in the decades since—people's names forgotten, locations uncertain or confused." Although he had contacted several of his old acquaintances and used the advantage of collective memory to reconstruct the past, Burnham recognized that most memories are "irretrievably gone," in part because of the vagaries of memory, but also because he could not access the collective memories of his native Vietnamese acquaintances. Crucial witnesses to Burnham's ministry and to the war as a whole were simply unavailable. Nevertheless, Burnham also claimed the authority of personal experience: Some of the memories may be inaccurate, he wrote, but "they are as I remember them."[19] For religious leaders, especially, the question of truth, authority, and personal experience is deeply tied to their own beliefs about the nature of religious truth, reconciliation, textual creation, and divine authority.

Chaplains, like other servicemen, were susceptible to war trauma and the romanticizing of war. Both during the war and after, for many veterans, chaplain and nonchaplain alike, writing provided an avenue for communicating their wartime experiences to a wider public and for personal reflection and healing—what Samuel Hynes, author of an insightful book examining British and American combat memoirs from the twentieth century, called the simultaneous need to report and to remember.[20] Occasionally the two needs merged, particularly when the writing was therapeutic and revelatory in nature.

Chaplains' firsthand accounts are situated within three traditions of autobiographical writing. First, they wrote within the tradition of combat memoirs because, although chaplains were noncombatants, most who published firsthand accounts were assigned to combat units and experienced the Vietnam War close to the fighting.[21] Whether or not chaplains were aware of these conventions as they wrote is, to some degree, immaterial—isolation from a literary tradition is, in fact, one marker of the combat memoir. Samuel Hynes writes that for most combat memoirs, "there is nothing to suggest that the author is aware of any previous example: no quotations or allusions or imitations of earlier models. . . . War writing, it seems, is a genre without a tradition to the men who write it."[22] However, whereas narratives of this sort focus almost exclusively on combat—"drums-and-bugles" or "blood-and-guts"—chaplain narratives contained relatively little discussion of *combat*, even for those who served with forward units.[23] With some exceptions, chaplains tended to focus on their religious duties of worship, sacrament, and counseling as the primary markers of their time in Vietnam.

The literary antecedents, merits, tropes, and recurring images and themes of Vietnam combat narratives have been widely discussed in scholarly literature, particularly within the fields of Comparative Literature and American Studies.[24] For the most part, however, these works, like Hynes's, focus on the combat soldier as the primary narrator of Vietnam war stories. The Vietnam narrative, as it has been re-created within this scholarship, however, remains an unfinished one. The first-person accounts, rather than following traditional narrative norms and structures, often devolved into chaotic, messy, and undisciplined descriptions of war, indicating not a sense of closure but rather a profound loss of innocence and meaning. These narratives are profane and often explicitly concerned with sexual metaphors of war. They are frequently dystopian and play off simultaneous and contradictory images of the soldier as victim and perpetrator.

Throughout the 1990s and 2000s, scholars worked to contextualize Vietnam War literature within a broader American cultural context. Not surprisingly, chaplains' first-person accounts have been almost entirely absent from these scholarly discussions. Chaplains have been ignored in such studies probably because they rarely participated in combat; they have not produced much writing about the war; their publications do not bear the same critical weight or display the literary panache of Tim O'Brien's or Michael Herr's work; and, perhaps most importantly, they do not conform to many of the popular narratives of the war.[25] Professor of English and American Studies Alex Vernon argues that "personal narratives by male noncombatant military persons—white males especially— are easily the most neglected of all military life writing in Anglo American criticism, because they are ignored both by scholars who concentrate on the combat memoir and by those who focus on historically marginalized voices (women and minorities)."[26] Thus, if we consider chaplains narratives within a broader context of first-person Vietnam War accounts and thus as part of a whole literary tradition, the differences between the traditional combat narrative and the chaplain's narrative are immediately apparent. Chaplains, even those who saw significant action when they were attached to forward operating units, did not discuss combat in great detail. Here, it would appear that traditional views of authority hold true—those who participated in combat may write about it; those who did not, may not do so. The issue is not proximity but involvement, and thus legitimacy and credibility.[27]

Combat memoirs were also meant to memorialize, and sometimes sacralize, those who had been lost in war, and chaplains' writings fulfill this role expertly. Claude Newby, for example, was troubled by the sentiment some others expressed that the Vietnam War was perhaps not worthy of the memoirist's treatment, and he cited a letter he received from a "military man" who expressed his view that the "Vietnam War is over, and it's time to forget it. Please quit telling war stories and leave the war behind us." Newby, however, asked, *"Can we forget the event and still remember those who served and sacrificed so much?"* He recalled the feeling he had when he wrote down his "chronicle" of his experiences in Vietnam: "Suddenly, a great weight lifted from me—a mental, emotional, spiritual burden of near tangible proportions. . . . Thus, with my war memories on paper and in the computer . . . the gnawing almost ceased for the first time in more than a quarter of a century, and I felt free of a vague melancholy. . . . *I don't have to remember anymore. Now, whatever happens to me, the story is preserved, lest we forget.*"[28]

In his own memoir, Jack Brown claimed, "In a real sense, this book is also a memorial tribute to the tens of thousands of American men and women who served their country and who lost their lives in Vietnam during that unpopular war." The war memoir, published for all time, would attest to the sacrifice Brown witnessed others make; by virtue of his memories, written down, Brown would make sure that others were not forgotten. The memorial would also be for "the family members and friends of those who served there, of those who died there, of those who were wounded there, of those who were imprisoned there, and of those who are still listed as missing in action." The devotional written word would become, in the words of Jay Winter, who was writing about World War I, "sites of memory" and "sites of mourning."[29]

The second tradition of autobiographical writing within which chaplains' memoirs fall is that of spiritual or religious autobiography, which has been a significant part of religious practice, from Augustine of Hippo to the Puritans of colonial New England and beyond. Augustine of Hippo's *Confessions* modeled confessional writing as a way to experience God's grace, and public accounts of conversion were required for membership in the Puritan church community. Puritan autobiographies therefore related to broader social, political, and cultural concerns within their communities; they signified that an individual "had come into alignment with certain linguistic, behavioral and cultural expectations."[30] Some chaplain memoirs and publicized diaries assumed the conventions of the conversion narrative or spiritual autobiography, wherein they not only reported on daily experiences but also provided theological and religious reflection on those experiences. Chaplains also wrote for clearly religious audiences; they frequently employed religious vocabulary, images, and references, which might seem alien to a secular reader. Furthermore, their books were often published by small denominational or religious presses. A chaplain's ties to the civilian religious community may have weakened, so many of these publications were part of a his reentry, written to reassure readers that he retained, understood, and remained committed—as the Puritan authors of conversion narratives did before him—to the "linguistic, behavioral and cultural expectations" of their respective religious communities.[31]

Even among the chaplain memoirs within this literary tradition, the focus varied. Thomas Des Champs, who emphasized his Vietnam service in his memoir's title—"The True Story of a Highly Decorated Vietnam-era Chaplain"—nevertheless began by writing: "I believe that where you come from and how you were raised has a great influence on whom and what you become. For this reason, I would like to tell you about my hometown, my parents, the people I knew, and the culture in which I was raised." Des Champs wrote of his family and his early religious experiences before moving on to his military experiences.[32] Jim Ammerman, on the other hand, buried his Vietnam experience deep within the middle of his book, *Supernatural Events in the Life of an Ordinary Man*. Ammerman also began with his childhood, focusing on his belief that God called him to minister to "Army officers," a call Ammerman believed he answered when he was assigned to the Command and General Staff College at Fort Leavenworth, Kansas.[33] Other memoirs, such as Connell J. Maguire's *Follies of a Navy Chaplain*, Arthur Estes's *Paratrooper Chaplain*, and Kiyo Itokazu's *A Chaplain's Pilgrimage*, clearly focus on the chaplain's military service, but the authors' respective tours in Southeast Asia appear as only one of many subjects.[34] Each of these authors contextualized his pastoral and military lives differently, but the spiritual components of each narrative are quite clear.

Chaplain Jack Brown viewed his personal writing (in journals) and his public writing (in the form of his book, *Another Side of Combat*) in religious terms. He began writing as a spiritual discipline when one of his "college or seminary professors encouraged [him] to keep a daily journal," which he began doing just before deploying to Vietnam as a chaplain with the 101st Airborne Division.[35] Brown calls his memoir a "devotional book of memories" where "each devotional chapter is based on my day-to-day journal that was kept faithfully during that memorable year. I also share my philosophy about war, the American serviceman or woman, and the Christian faith as it relates to military service."[36] Brown hoped his spiritual journey might be of help to others in a similar situation.

Chaplains hope their stories would be significant not only to others who served in the war but also to religious audiences who were unsure of what to make of the war and of the chaplaincy. Often Christian chaplains left readers with religious messages that emphasized the importance of faith in times of struggle and the significance of the Christian evangelical mission. "While it was my privilege to serve on a very real battlefield at the front, many who read this book have battlefields and front lines of a different nature," Curt Bowers wrote. "Those of us who follow Christ are all called to immerse ourselves in the battle of life. None of us are called to stand on the sideline or retreat to some quiet, secure place while life-and-death struggles are taking place all around us."[37] Bowers clearly associated actual warfare with spiritual warfare: the same skills he needed as a military chaplain, Christians would need as they encountered resistance and conflict in their own lives.

Chaplains also wrote in this tradition to leave a tangible legacy to their families and religious communities. And others wrote down their experiences because friends and family members suggested it.[38] In most cases, chaplains believed they had important, legitimate stories to tell. Claude Newby wrote that he began writing his Vietnam memoirs "as part of my autobiography. . . . I listed several good reasons for writing my life story. These reasons included a desire to leave a chronicle of my life that my posterity may 'know' me, gain some advantage from the lessons life taught me, and cherish their heritage."[39]

Finally, the third tradition of autobiographical writing within which chaplains wrote is trauma writing or therapeutic writing, even when they did not consciously do so. Writing, both fiction and nonfiction, has been explored extensively in the context of the therapeutic treatment of post-traumatic stress disorder (PTSD).[40] James W. Pennebaker, a research psychologist, conducted experiments in the area of post-trauma writing in order to assess the idea that if a "trauma is cognitively prolonged and, because the person cannot talk to friends and relatives about the distressing subject, they can become socially isolated" and that writing may provide a way to "organize and assimilate" the traumatic memories. In his study, Pennebaker worked with students and found that those who wrote about traumatic events and the emotions and feelings associated with them sought medical attention for illness less often than their control-group counterparts, which suggested they had improved immune function and ability to withstand infection. Over 75 percent of them described the long-term benefits of the writing in personal terms—for example, it "made me think things out" or "helped me look at myself from the outside/sort out my thoughts."[41] Pennebaker concluded that "narrative expression, whether written or spoken, has a naturally organising (controlling and structuring) effect," but that "writing permits subjects to engage their traumas to a degree and at a rate at which they feel comfortable."[42]

Clinical understandings of PTSD, its diagnosis, and its treatment also highlight the extent to which chaplains, especially those who joined combat infantry units on patrols or served in hospitals, could experience deep psychological trauma as the result of the war. Until recently, scholars and clinicians considered "war trauma" as roughly equivalent to "combat trauma." Now, however, it is believed that the rates of PTSD and the responses to treatment may differ between those who were exposed to combat and those exposed to "abusive violence," which might include rape, the killing of civilians, or constant exposure to the wounded and dying. The primary concern for those in combat is survival, whereas the primary concern for those exposed to persistent violence against human beings is the threat to their moral sensibilities and psychological well-being.[43] In Vietnam, which was in large part an unconventional war, these boundaries were occasionally murky: the threat of death was pervasive, and abusive violence was prevalent in many sectors of the war. Chaplains, regardless of their assignments, were unlikely to be immune to the abusive violence of the Vietnam War.

However, many experts agree that "normal developmental factors are also relevant: the soldier who is a few years older than the average combatant and possesses a more integrated sense of self and purpose has greater insulation against serious trauma than does a late adolescent who is still in the process of more active maturation."[44] Thus, chaplains might be expected to suffer from lower rates of PTSD than enlisted personnel and other officers. Again, this is not to suggest that some chaplains, especially those who served with combat units and went into the field, did not experience extreme trauma. At the same time, the area coverage system likely meant that chaplains did not always form close relationships with their chaplain peers or with members of a particular unit who could, after the war's end, help them cope with wartime traumas. Still, though, in comparison to other service members, chaplains likely had more intrapersonal and emotional skills with which to deal with trauma.

James Johnson began writing his memoirs as a therapeutic exercise to help him deal with PTSD and his memories from combat. "A friend who knows about some of my combat experiences suggests I write a book about them," he wrote. "I immediately discount his suggestion. I am not certain why, but soon, I do begin writing. I had kept very detailed diaries and journals in Vietnam and now I begin a process of what I later will refer to as a therapeutic journal. And when feelings resurface due to dreams, or in my waking moments, I record these feelings. I simply record what I'm experiencing." Johnson continued writing over the next year, and in so doing, he wrote, "my pen becomes my therapist." "Eventually," he continued, "the vividness of my dreams begins to diminish. My feelings aren't gone, but do begin to heal. The longer I am away from Vietnam, the less preoccupied I am with the trauma that I experienced there."[45] Of the chaplains whose accounts focus specifically on Vietnam, Johnson's was the most self-aware and self-reflective about his purpose for writing a memoir. Johnson was keenly aware of the therapeutic nature of autobiographical writing after trauma—the benefits for him were be both spiritual and psychological. In the introduction, Johnson acknowledged, however, that his memoir was "about more than just trauma. . . . It's also about coping, feeling, growing up, bonding, being cynical, loving, being loved, being vulnerable, placing values in perspective, and even humor."[46] While Johnson wrote mostly about his tour in Vietnam, the title reveals the wider significance of the book for Johnson. His war did not end on the flight home—it was, for him, a "Thirty-Year Vietnam Battle," and the story of the war was fundamentally wrapped up in the story of his life, and the lives of his friends and family.

Other chaplains also wrote frankly about PTSD and trauma, and some also addressed the spiritual nature of their healing. Curt Bowers's conclusion combines the trope of spiritualized combat with healing from PTSD. At the very end of his book, after he describes his flashbacks to Hill 65, where he experienced combat firsthand and saw his friends die, Bowers addressed Vietnam veterans explicitly: "In summary, let me say to those who read this book—to those who identify with its story—the men, the places, the emotions, and to those who have, to some degree, suffered from PTSD: There is help and there is hope." He encouraged them to seek help from the Veterans Administration hospitals, where they would find clinicians "well versed in the syndrome," but he also emphasized the spiritual dimension of healing after trauma. He wrote, "In addition, and I believe of greater importance, is the recognition that Jesus Christ our Lord is the ultimate healer and the Great Physician."[47] Bowers believed that his Christian faith, his understanding of PTSD, and his retelling his story all played a significant part in healing the lingering wounds of Vietnam.

Like Bowers, other chaplains used their personal stories to help other veterans deal with their experiences in Vietnam. William Mahedy, an Episcopal chaplain, helped pioneer counseling and therapy efforts at veterans' centers after the Vietnam War. He believed that Vietnam represented for many veterans a "dark night of the soul" from which many of them had not returned.[48] Though Mahedy's work was not about his experiences as a chaplain per se, his commitment to the spiritual lives of Vietnam veterans was significant. Having witnessed war, he was able to relate to them, and he could appreciate more fully the trauma brought on by combat. He understood their needs in part because he understood his own. Mahedy believed he wrote so that others could experience the journey out of the dark night of Vietnam.[49] At the end of his book, Mahedy printed a liturgy of reconciliation that he compiled for a healing service that was part of a veterans' retreat. Mahedy noticed that many soldiers had not dealt with the grief, loss, anger, or guilt that remained from Vietnam. As a veteran and clergyman, he was able to aid others in this process of resolution and closure. "The three Scripture readings used were relevant to the issues of war and peacemaking," he wrote. "The prayers, including the prayer of consecration, were written around this theme. We confessed our sins, especially those of 'violence and hatred,' receiving for these sins the forgiveness of God. . . . Hymns were selected according to the theme. The unity and deep yearning for the peace of mind that only reconciliation can achieve was more evident at the service."[50] Mahedy had evaluated his Vietnam experience in religious ways and used his experience as a veteran, a counselor, and a clergyman to help others do the same.

Beyond distinct literary contexts, chaplains wrote within historical contexts as well. Memoirs often tell readers about the social, political, and cultural worlds of the time period in which they were published as much as they do about those of the past. Chaplains, like other memoirists of the Vietnam era, grappled with the broad geopolitical issues of the Cold War, the domestic politics of Vietnam, and the ongoing questions of American involvement in the world. In the 1980s, for example, as Americans began to recover from the trauma of Vietnam, they sought to exorcize the demons of Vietnam through literature and film and to commemorate the American experience in a national monument. Vietnam became a symbol of the political and cultural battles of the 1960s and 1970s. The coauthor of Curtis Bowers's memoir reflected that during those decades, "there were many battlefronts, not all in Southeast Asia. Some were on college campuses. Others intruded on the sanctity of our homes. Sharp differences of opinion divided us. We found that a nation divided against itself could not stand against the enemy. Like it or not, those of us who lived during those years found ourselves thrust into the fray."[51] The veteran, chaplain included, was a victim of these battles, traumatized by the experience of war, demonized by antiwar demonstrators, marginalized by the veterans of World War II.

Others, also in the 1980s, placed the narrative of the Vietnam War's trauma into the context of heightened Cold War tensions of the Reagan years. Bowers wrote, for example, "It has been over twenty years since I flew out of Tan Son Nhut Airfield on my way home from Vietnam to the United States. That country has now been swallowed up by the forces we had fought against." Then he moved to wider global concerns: "There are still wars and rumors of wars in that region and all over the globe. Central America is a focus of our efforts against the Marxists. The Strategic Defense Initiative (SDI) is the hotly debated defense against the Soviet missile threat. Star Wars is a household word. The Soviets are bogged down in Afghanistan and no doubt will be for the foreseeable future. The Middle East is a tinder box waiting to be lit. Mothers everywhere still pray that *their* sons will not go to war. Things have not changed much—certainly human nature has not changed at all."[52]

After a lull in the 1990s, and since renewed military activity after the terrorist attacks of September 11, 2001, several chaplains have published memoirs or devotional collections.[53] Indeed, chaplains have received renewed attention in the wars in Afghanistan and Iraq; as it had during the Vietnam War, the chaplaincy has emerged as a site for examining the functions and compatibility of religious belief and practice during war. Vietnam-era chaplains have responded to this increased attention by speaking out about the chaplains' role in war, about the Iraq war, and about the nature of religious practice during war. Jerry Autry addressed the issue explicitly in his memoir: "Writing about Vietnam while the Iraq War is going on has been excruciating. Day by day, as I sat, watched, read—it was Vietnam revisited."[54] Autry used his experiences in Vietnam to become a "constructive critic of the war," emphasizing the distinction between supporting the soldiers participating in it and championing the political objectives of the war. He concluded, "We learned our lessons, and this fact alone may be the lasting legacy of Vietnam if there is one—the soldier is just doing his job."[55] As he wrote, Autry revealed, "I decided to intersperse my own thoughts and writings . . . about Iraq in the middle of my Vietnam story." For Autry, the two stories could not be separated.[56]

Jack Brown's book also took a long historical view of the Vietnam War; he only obliquely referred to Iraq—insisting that a nation's leaders, serving "their citizens and soldiers well," should "do their utmost to avoid war"—and instead reminded readers of the origins of the Vietnam War itself. "Now since this book is about mortality and the Vietnam conflict," he wrote, "a bit of history should not be forgotten. In 1945, Ho Chi Minh spoke in Hanoi to an estimated half million Vietnamese. American military personnel stood on the stage with him as he declared Vietnam's independence from French and Japanese rule. He began his speech by quoting the first few sentences of America's Declaration of Independence. He sought friendship with America." For Brown, the tragedy of Vietnam occurred in the time between the hopeful declaration of Vietnamese independence and the 1995 opening of the American embassy in Vietnam. The lessons of Vietnam, which would be debated "endlessly" by historians, according to Brown, must be learned in order to avoid a too-costly war or a too-costly peace.[57]

Searching for a Postwar Identity and Meaning

In their narratives, chaplains saw themselves change in ways that reflected their identity and their faith. For many, their tours in Vietnam represented a time of physical, emotional, and spiritual challenge and change. "I was forty pounds lighter. My hair was sprinkled generously with gray. I had long scars to remind me always where I had been," James Hutchens reflected. But he recognized that these were merely physical changes and that deeper changes occurred because "for nearly a year I had lived and worked beside many fine men, some magnificent men. Together we had seen good men suffer and die. Together we came out to find life very precious and more purposeful and meaningful that we had ever known before. Because of the living and dying, I would never be quite the same again."[58] But even though these were important, Hutchens believed that "above all this there was another difference. Now I *knew* by what I had witnessed that the living God still reveals Himself to men who truly seek Him. Before, I had been taught it and had read it. Now I had experienced it." In the end, he concluded, "God still makes Himself known. He still makes His presence felt just as surely as He did to Moses and Abraham, to Paul and to John. Now as a minister of the gospel of Jesus Christ I could stand to declare what

I had seen and heard."[59] Many chaplains changed physically, and some carried battle scars and wounds. They remembered the men and officers with whom they served. They reacted to institutional problems and situations. But through their experiences, they continued to find strength in their religion and faith. Surely some chaplains lost their faith or were unable to reconcile their faith with their Vietnam experience, but they have not recorded this displacement publicly. Chaplains who chose to write about Vietnam did so for personal and public reasons and were willing to expose their experiences and selves in ways that others could not or would not.

For some chaplains, Vietnam renewed their sense of calling and purpose. In the midst of carnage, they found a real place in which the things of "this world" fell away, and only God could remain. Raymond Johnson wrote, "My batteries are re-charged, 'My youth is renewed like the eagle's.'" He found his "soul is filled with a new surge of inner strength. I must return to that real arena where the living paradox of life's humor and tragedy, love and hate, is lived out before the eyes of men. This is where I belong!"[60] At the end of his tour of duty Johnson recognized paradox, not irresolvable conflict. What he saw changed him, but his faith was not shaken. Toward the end of his time in Vietnam, he was not deflated or defeated but hopeful and even uplifted. In the midst of war, Johnson believed his God had revealed himself.

Even those who struggled to find meaning in the Vietnam War did so on religious terms. After the war, Jackson Day struggled to reconcile his Vietnam experience with the idea of an all-knowing, all-powerful, and all-loving God. His experiences taught him that in war God could not be all three. He wrote that God could encompass "any two out of the three, perhaps, but not all three, it's just too contradictory. If God was all powerful and all knowing, he couldn't be all loving or else he would do something to stop what was going on. If he were all powerful and all loving, then he couldn't know what was going on, or he would do something." To resolve the conflict, Day reasoned "that God was all loving and all knowing, but had given up the power, as God gave up the power on the cross. We weren't helped because God couldn't stop what was going on, but God suffered with us, and perhaps that was enough." The resolution came full circle thirty-five years later when he returned to Vietnam: After "looking at the regeneration of the country of Vietnam," he wrote, "perhaps God has some power after all, and we simply had too short a horizon."[61]

Day was also challenged to rethink some of his recollections about the nature of life and death and his mission in Vietnam. During an educational tour in Vietnam in 2004, Day was showing the tour guide, Dr. Ed Tick, a specialist on PTSD and Vietnam, pictures from his combat tour. Tick noted that Day was the only living thing in one picture. Day recalled this scene and others like it, when "soldiers welcomed a break from the work of preparing a firebase. The denuded trees were part of the package—an explosive charge would be set off which would at once clear an area in the center where helicopters could land, and farther from the explosion, clear the trees of leaves, improving the line of sight." Day was reminded that for soldiers in combat "all of these things meant life, or a better chance of life, for those [in Vietnam]." He "saw no death in the picture. Ed Tick, who wasn't there, saw no living things but the chaplain, and to view the picture fresh through his eyes was a revelation into a new truth."[62] Even seeing himself surrounded by death, Day resolved to find redemption.

This process, however, took years. When Day returned to the United States after his tour of duty, he joined Vietnam Veterans Against the War and eventually resigned his commission with the National Guard. Rather than continuing his ministry, Day returned to graduate school for a degree in Public Health and worked in the private health care sector for several years before eventually returning to the pastorate in Maryland and becoming involved with Vietnam Veteran Ministers, a group of veterans and clergy who work together to minister to Vietnam War veterans. From this vantage point, Day said it was possible to see his experience in Vietnam as a rich source for personal growth, renewed faith, and strengthened personal relationships.[63]

Others interpreted their Vietnam experiences with a different theology, in which God was neither responsible for, nor necessarily revealed in, the horrors of war. Instead they found a source of hope for the future in the war. For James Hutchens, Julia Ward Howe's "The Battle Hymn of the Republic" served as a symbol of his beliefs. The hymn was written during the Civil War, and it has served as a religious justification for a call to arms for American military men ever since: "Mine eyes have seen the glory of the coming of the Lord; / He is trampling out the vintage, where the grapes of wrath are stored; / He has loosed the fateful lightning of His terrible swift sword; / His truth is marching on." The song called soldiers to join the Army of God as he wiped out his enemies. "What did Mrs. Howe see?" Hutchens asked. "She saw . . . what every soldier ought to see. I saw it, as did many others. . . . Coming events have a way of casting their shadows before them. The wars of the ages have all pointed to it. The insatiable cry for peace demands it: *The glory of the coming of the Lord*, the Prince of peace, who alone can establish peace." He concluded that Vietnam was a "vivid foreshadowing of the unprecedented glory and wrath of God that shall be unleashed upon a 'crooked and perverse generation' at the coming of the Lord."[64] But the hymn also demanded response: "Oh, be swift, my soul, to answer Him! / Be jubilant, my feet. / Our God is marching on. / Glory, Glory, Hallelujah!" And Hutchens replied, "Even so, come Lord Jesus."[65] Hutchens evaluated Vietnam and his particular combat experience from a premillennial eschatological point of view, wherein the horror of war was a precursor to the return of Christ on Earth, a sign of the coming triumph of the Christian God and the imposition of a millennial peace. He and others endured not because God had already been revealed but because he would be revealed.

Others still were more pessimistic about the war and the potential lessons that could be gained from the war. Chaplains were some of the first individuals to criticize the war as pointless and wasteful, even if they supported its purported anti-Communist goals. As Robert Falabella left Vietnam, he was "filled with mixed emotions." He felt "a certain joy . . . that the nightmare was over" for him. But he agonized over this response: "It may have been over for me but it was not over for so many others still there. How could I be happy, when my friends were still there?" His connection to the soldiers ran deep, and as he looked at his watch, he saw that it was "about two thirty in the morning, a dangerous time for those boys in the field; a lonely, fearful time for the boys on ambush; an agonizing time for those seriously wounded and in the intensive care ward at the 12th Evac Hospital, and hospitals like it all over the corps area." In a matter of hours, Falabella would be home, but in Vietnam, a few more hours would bring daylight, and "the boys, still shivering from the chilly rains will then have another day to be scorched by the sun, bitten by insects, and revolted by the leeches that will be drawing their blood when they ford the canals. They will be wondering who will get the job of point man this day, and whether there will be many booby traps in the areas they must enter." Falabella repeated his question, "How can I be happy when some of those young men who are now alive will be dead before this day is out, others perhaps without their limbs, their arms or their sight?" Like Dulany's questions about his responses to atrocity in combat, Falabella had no answers. He left in agony. He determined, "I had come to Vietnam in apprehension, but with hope. I find I left it in disappointment and with sorrow."[66] Falabella saw no redemption or salvation in war, but he believed he saw the essence of humanity in it. The relationships he had formed with soldiers sustained him, and prompted him to be an outspoken critic of the war. Falabella's experiences underscored the conflict between the positive and negative aspects of war, for what he believed war could accomplish—the ability to equalize men and venerate humanity in the image of God—it also threatened to take away by its equal application of death and destruction.

While many of the men who served in Vietnam may have found solace, comfort, or reassurance in their faith, chaplains were in a unique position because they were the ones who actually represented that faith physically. Chaplains were intimately connected to ministry, mission, morale, morality, and faith. The title of Henry Ackermann's book on chaplains in Vietnam, *He Was Always There*, expressed the sentiment of many officers and soldiers about the chaplains who served them, demonstrating that on some level, chaplains had fulfilled their primary mission of presence and pastoral care. For chaplains, however, the phrase "He was always there" applied not to other clergy or humans, but to God. James Hutchens wrote, for example, "When I sought Him on the ship to Southeast Asia, He was there. . . . When I cried out to Him for men who were suffering pain and death, He was there. And one day when I lay on the ground with nothing to offer but blood and pain and desperate pleas, He was there. . . . He was always there."[67] However, what chaplains may have given to others by their presence and their ministry, they could not provide for themselves.

In the end, chaplains clearly were not uniformly satisfied with their experience in Vietnam; many faced severe trauma and doubt about their faith, the chaplaincy, the U.S. government, and the American people. Billy Whiteside, a Methodist chaplain, recalled personal hurt and professional hindrance when the United Methodist Church publicly announced its support for draft resisters going to Canada. He recalled one young soldier who, upon hearing this news, lamented it was "terrible when your own church turns against you," and Whiteside had little to say in response to reassure the soldier that he still had a place in the church. When he returned from Vietnam, Whiteside told a newspaper reporter, he was "screwed up." "I was filled with rage and doubted God's love—God's love was the last thing I felt," he continued, but another chaplain eventually helped him find his faith again by listening and understanding. After the war, Whiteside continued in the chaplaincy for seven years at the disciplinary barrack at Fort Leavenworth, where he developed a holistic pastoral care program.[68] Whiteside's Vietnam experience tested his faith and his ministry, and while he eventually found his faith again and renewed his ministry, he did not believe the war or his participation in it were themselves redemptive.

Other chaplains left Vietnam with serious doubts about the Chaplain Corps and the chaplains with whom they served, particularly their supervisory chaplains. Kiyo Itokazu, a Southern Baptist chaplain who served with an engineering battalion, wrote in his official survey response that the Vietnam experience "made me realize the diversity of chaplains' ministry. Some really cared and ministered, some cared only for self-aggrandizement, and some seemed to enjoy the war, i.e. priest carrying a grease gun from place to place."[69] Jan Friend reported an "Alcoholic Catholic chaplain" who hindered unit coverage.[70] David Kent concluded that by the end of his tour in Vietnam, "some of the idealism wore off. I saw chaplains as more human, fallible, and self-seeking."[71]

The "self-aggrandizing," "promotion-seeking," and "self-serving" supervisory chaplain emerged as a consistent counterpoint to the image of the combat chaplain accompanying his troops into battle. Jan Friend wrote that a major hindrance to his ministry was the "unusually self-serving supervisory chaplain who nevertheless had the [brigade commander] convinced he walked on water."[72] Friend continued, "Precious little was provided by senior chaplain, prior to, during, and subsequent [to] my ministry in Vietnam that aided preparation for that ministry or processing it, meaning afterwards, leaving the distinct impression that everyone was equally ignorant of what to expect, how to deal with it or debrief from the experience." But Friend also echoed Itokazu's sentiment, commenting that "some chaplain colleagues were impressive in their ministry and creativity under the circumstances while others broke under the pressure and were sent home and were clearly more interested in how the tour would serve their 'careers' than in facilitating ministry to soldiers or encouraging supervisees."[73]

Even more than lost faith in their fellow chaplain clergy, chaplains who responded to the official history surveys reported significant doubts and anger about their civilian counterparts. For some, it was a question of practice. Robert Hess wrote, "I tend to be 'angry' with the church in the civilian community for not being as ecumenical as I witnessed the church worshipping together in the mud of an artillery hill in 3-tiered Jungle."[74] Said an anonymous respondent, "I was hurt by the hostility I encountered from ministers in my home presbytery. . . . I felt, and I still do, that they judged me and 98 percent of others who served without appreciating our position."[75]

Others expressed deep resentment toward the media and the public for undermining what they saw as a justified—if operationally flawed—mission in Vietnam. "I was proud to be a part of a totally moral and courageous effort by my country to preserve liberty for a weaker nation," wrote Charles LeClair. "It should have been done. It should be done again if needed anywhere in the world. The agenda of the media to demean America's involvement in VN had the reverse effect with me."[76] An anonymous chaplain expressed concern with media distortions of actions in Vietnam: "I became convinced . . . that the public is unthinking, uncaring, and all too easy to fool. The news reporting what people believed was distorted beyond belief. In my hometown newspaper, I read about several actions in which I had participated. The accounts were so distorted that except for dates, names of people and places I would have never recognized them as being the actions in which I was present."[77]

Still others expressed a profound crisis of faith in the U.S. government and the civil religious principles that seemed to guide the country before the war. Some chaplains blamed the government for losing the war, for not committing adequate resources to defeating Communist forces in Southeast Asia. Marvin Trott, for example, wrote, "My faith remained unchanged toward God. However, my faith in our government and our leaders dramatically changed for the negative." He expressed his distrust in religious terms, "I believe God gave the US the best nation on earth to follow after righteousness and peace and we failed to use our power to annihilate Hanoi and bring it to its knees." Ultimately, Trott concluded, "We had a right to be there and help the South Vietnamese to win the war against the North Vietnamese invaders."[78]

Only a few chaplains reported seriously diminished faith in the American government and in their own system of beliefs as a result of their experiences in Vietnam. In the 600-plus surveys and published accounts, only a handful reveal the sort of anguish one might expect given the tenor of other writing about religion and the Vietnam War. Conversion, rather than apostasy, was the norm. James Juhan, a Southern Baptist minister who at the time of the survey was in the process of converting to Roman Catholicism, wrote an anguished reflection of the effects of Vietnam on his intellectual, spiritual, and ministerial life. Juhan had served two tours in Vietnam—in 1967–68 with the infantry and then in 1970–71 with a signal battalion. In Vietnam, he wrote, "[I] became very realistic. I did not think the world was full of hope any more – I became a humanist—I left my church, my belief system, and my God." He concluded that he could no longer "feel all is right with the world." Whereas Trott believed that we lost the war by refusing to annihilate the North Vietnamese, Juhan believed the primary mistake was being there in the first place. His despair was both corporate ("We should not have been there") and individual ("I should not have been there.") Juhan thought that in the context of the turbulent 1960s, Juhan thought his service in Vietnam put him on the wrong side, literally and figuratively: "Martin Luther King and [Robert] Kennedy were killed while I was in Vietnam, and I was on the wrong side of the ocean." Juhan's refrain "We should not have been there" peppered his entire response. By the end, he concluded, "I died a thousand deaths for each memorial service I held."[79]

Occasionally, chaplains wrote in direct opposition to the traditional narrative of the war. Other nonchaplain accounts of the Vietnam War suggest a loss of personal innocence, are often adamant that the military could have won the war without political and civilian interference, and paint Vietnam as a horrific episode of the memoirists' life, resulting in demons to be exorcised, not memories to be cherished and celebrated. Although Samuel Hopkins called Vietnam "a futile war in an exotic land," for example, he also described his tour as "the most exciting year of my life" and said he often remembered these "stories and pictures in my head" with "blissful revere [sic]," a phrase unlikely to appear in soldiers' and officers' accounts of the same war. He concluded the introduction with a sort of historiographical plea: "May the opening and recording of these mental files broaden and balance the perspective about serving in Viet Nam."[80] Charles LeClair concluded that his service as a chaplain in Vietnam was "the most significant role of [his] life," which made him feel "satisfied," "adequate," and "properly utilized."[81] Lloyd Kincade concluded that his Vietnam ministry was "the greatest thing I have ever [done] or will ever do. I would do it again 100 times if necessary."[82]

Even when they were disillusioned by "Vietnam," many chaplains concluded that the experience had been a spiritual testing ground, a crisis out of which they had emerged with a stronger faith. When he was in Vietnam, Douglas Sowards felt "patriotic and willing to serve" his country but later concluded he "had wasted two years" of his life "along with thousands of other Americans" and that "those who died did it in vain." Even in the face of this damning conclusion, however, Sowards wrote that Vietnam helped him learn "about important priorities," that "living close to death or a crippling injury" changed his life, that he "learned to share [his] faith in Christ in a better way."[83] "Vietnam" became a site in which Sowards, upon reflection, could eventually find his spiritual resolve renewed. Similarly, Jack Moyar became convinced that the longer he "was in Vietnam the less [he] believed about the 'rightness' of the war" but concluded that his purpose there was "to be a pastor to the military." And like Sowards, Moyar reflected upon the effect that proximity to death had on his faith. "Had my faith not grown," he asserted, "it would have died."[84] Donald Shea remembered that by the end of his tour in 1972, he "felt good about the ministry but bad about the inane war."[85]

Others also recounted broken and rebuilt faith. Lloyd Kincade, a Disciples of Christ chaplain, placed three heavy Xs by the survey option that indicated "strengthened faith" as a result of Vietnam. Yet he also observed that "the old WASP American religion was shot down. My faith had to be rebuilt to the real world we live in and not the TV world of today."[86] Larry Wedel determined that the stresses of Vietnam made his "prayer life . . . more meaningful" and revealed the "reality of God's mercy, love, and presence."[87] Jack Brown wrote that Vietnam forced him "to go to the grass roots of [his] faith time and time again and concentrate on life and death issues on a one-to-one basis." Many chaplains could not accept easy answers that traditional views of faith might provide.

Still other chaplains concluded that Vietnam clarified their religious beliefs and what they considered "important." "My dependence on God as a direct source of strength was increased," wrote David Kent, whereas "'organized' religion became less significant." The experience of Vietnam liberated his spirituality from the "traditional" type he had "learned in seminary."[88] Floyd Lacy, a National Baptist Convention chaplain who deployed from December 1968 to December 1969, reported that "in combat, I quickly sorted out what was real, what was important, what was vital as opposed to some of the seemingly unimportant things we argue about in our private little theological corners." He added that he "would not trade [his experience in Vietnam] for anything" but also that he "would not care to repeat [it] any time soon."[89] Jack Brown wrote, "I believe that my religion was stripped of the nonessentials. The love of God, the abiding presence of God, the care of God and the promise of abundant and eternal life through His Son Jesus Christ were emphasized over and over again in my own life and in my ministry to my men."[90] Ambivalence about both the war itself and the place of organized, official religion within it was a persistent characteristic of chaplains' reflections.

Chaplains' basic faith in God's redemptive powers extended beyond the war. Samuel Hopkins attributed the potential for lasting peace to humanity's faith in God and in the restorative power of that faith. "Vietnam has changed since we were there, and so have we," he concluded in his book. "The story once lived has not ended, but continues onward. And that is how it should be. Life goes on, and we can too if we place our faith in God and promise to love each other more dearly in the days still allotted to us. Shalom."[91] Even when they lost faith in their government, their church, or the American people, chaplains usually retained faith in God. Even with his grim assessment of a senior chaplain and of certain aspects of his ministry, Kiyo Itokazu reflected that "Vietnam was a critical event in my life. Crisis is a turning point. It either strengthens or weakens. For me it strengthened my faith by relying more on God and myself."[92] Survey respondent Donald Robinson observed, "In moments of crises, religion—theology especially, breaks down; that is, denominational differences, whether it is form of worship or what actually constitutes the sacrament, goes by the wayside. Catholic, Protestants, and others come together with one common goal, to gain strength and courage from one another and from God—no matter what their beliefs about him may be."[93] William Trotsauch echoed these reflections: "Dealing with the crisis of a hot combat situation, seeing your friends killed or maimed forced me into either abandoning faith or finding consolation in my faith. Fortunately, it was the latter."[94]

Fully 82 percent of the chaplains who responded to Ackermann's survey reported that their faith had been strengthened by their Vietnam experiences; only 2 percent responded that their faith had been weakened.[95] When we compare these numbers to the results for the same question asked on the soldier survey, the difference is striking. Among nonchaplain officers and enlisted men, only 33 percent said their faith was strengthened, while 61 percent reported it unchanged.[96] Further analysis of nonchaplain memoirs reveals a similarly ambivalent attitude toward religion (both of the organized and personal varieties). In his study of the American soldier, historian Peter Kindsvatter suggests—as does the Chaplain Center survey—that soldiers' memoirs reveal that while many soldiers were "skeptical about organized religion's support of war," they "still retained their personal religious beliefs."[97] Kindsvatter is careful to point out, however, that some men were not religious, that there were, in fact, atheists in foxholes, and that "religion" did not always provide solace to those in harm's way. Jesse Glenn Gray, in his historical-philosophical work *The Warriors*, suggests that a soldier's interpretation of religion in combat was primarily determined by whether his faith was "otherworldly" or "this-worldly." The soldiers with "otherworldly" faith—based first and foremost on the supernatural and the divine—had a generally positive interpretation of religion, as combat did not fundamentally require them to reassess their religious beliefs, but those with "this-worldly" faith—based primarily on social and ethical beliefs—often struggled to reconcile war's destructive nature with their belief systems.[98]

Chaplains confronted conflicts surrounding morality and war and their own place in the military community and ultimately resolved them in specifically religious ways. Operating in the middle ground demanded that chaplains—isolated from both their religious communities and the military family they served—reconcile their personal faith with their actions in and the meaning of the Vietnam War. In his final analysis of the war and its lessons, Samuel Hopkins emphasized that his "perspective as a faithful believer in God is that with humility and hopefulness we can endure the vagaries of warfare, without minimizing the horrific waste of lives or savage destruction of property that infernal fighting inflicts upon us. The world is full of conflict and tragedy, yet we must find a way to live confidently and joyfully amidst personal and collective suffering." In his work as a hospital chaplain, Hopkins used his experiences in Vietnam to form a connection with suffering patients. "I frequently assure the afflicted that the day of the Lord will surely come," he wrote, "and that justice will ultimately prevail; a certainty in the next life, if not in this world. . . . I have learned to celebrate the positive aspects of my tour in Vietnam, while being respectful about the many sacrifices suffered there."[99]

Chaplains' postwar reflections formed the final part of a complex personal conflict resolution process that began in combat, and their reflections signified their role as people in the middle by taking ideas, roles, and beliefs that could be in tension and reconciling them to one another. These first-person accounts played a significant role in a chaplain's reentry into a civilian religious community and exemplified one method of postwar reconciliation that lay outside the traditional Vietnam narrative of defeat and despair that is presented in much of the first-person writing about the war. In this way, their memoirs mediate between popular images and perceptions of the Vietnam War and the lived experience of it for many American servicemen and servicewomen. Eventually, many chaplains assigned a positive religious meaning to their wartime experiences and reaffirmed their faith in God and, in many cases, in humans as well. Certainly there must have been chaplains for whom war did not affirm their faith, but generally, they have not made their accounts public. Writing about and reflecting upon the religious meanings of Vietnam were vital for many chaplains' healing process. The process of writing and reflection itself became religious rituals that chaplains used to spread their beliefs and to make sense of their experiences of religion and war, especially for conservative Christian chaplains. Chaplains' conflict resolution process involved both personal and communal healing since, by sharing their accounts with others, chaplains also provided soldiers and other religious people with alternative ways of interpreting the war.

In the Vietnam era, faith—in God, in the United States, and in other humans—had often faltered, and in many chaplains' accounts, what is perhaps most striking is the clear and pointed divergence from the traditional Vietnam-era personal narrative. The collective narrative formed by chaplains' first-person accounts and responses to the official history survey stand as a pointed counternarrative to the traditional interpretation of Vietnam. Within American collective memory, "Vietnam" was the source of confusion, sorrow, failure, disillusionment, and betrayal; it is code for all that went, according to the myth, horribly wrong in the 1960s and 1970s. The United States lost its way; it lost credibility on the world stage; it lost its innocence; it lost an air of invincibility—either by virtue of its own moral failings or because the military was betrayed by its civilian master. This mythical portrait of Vietnam has been perpetuated in memoirs, histories, art, cinema, and journalistic accounts.[100] Whereas soldiers' and officers' narratives tend toward the hopeless and grim, chaplains' recollections generally end with reports of spiritual renewal and restored, even strengthened, faith. Chaplains, writing against the traditional first-person narratives of Vietnam, chose to interpret the war in specifically religious ways that altered the end of the narrative. Even if the Vietnam War itself was not positive, for them, God could—and did—redeem even the horror and trauma of war.

CHAPTER SEVEN

Dissent and Mission

"To hell with Jehovah." One line in one song included in the Armed Forces Hymnal sparked the controversy. In 1974, a tense congressional election year, the inclusion of Sydney Carter's song "It Was on a Friday Morning" provoked accusations of blasphemy not only from religious groups but also from American politicians and policy-makers, including Senator Strom Thurmond and Secretary of Defense James Schlesinger. The incident was a flash in the pan of the larger "culture wars" that increasingly engulfed the United States, but it indicated a growing divide between the ecumenical ideals of the traditional chaplaincy and the increasingly sectarian and conservative nature of the changing Chaplain Corps. These debates fit well within the narrative of the rise of the Religious Right, the withdrawal of mainline religion from the public sphere, and the military's post-Vietnam search for a mission and function.

Institutionally, the chaplaincy faced serious questions about its utility, organization, and mission after the Vietnam War. Liberal and mainline religious groups felt betrayed by what they viewed as chaplains' prophetic failure and openly criticized the Chaplain Corps' effectiveness. Some went so far as to accuse them of complicity in the tragedy of Vietnam. Conservative groups, on the other hand, continued to promote an evangelical mission to the military. Liberal and secular observers launched a civil court case that sought to declare the military chaplaincy unconstitutional on the basis of the First Amendment, while conservative and evangelical Christians gained traction in political circles and in the military. The chaplaincy continued to face shortages of Catholic, Jewish, and liturgical Protestant chaplains. It admitted women to the Chaplain Corps for the first time in history in the 1970s, and worked to reconfigure the way chaplains were assigned to units—all partly in response to the Vietnam experience.

The process of theological interpretation, conflict resolution, and identity formation that took place in Vietnam continued when chaplains returned home, and the Chaplain Corps, deeply affected by the experience of Vietnam, similarly underwent a process of reflection and reorganization. This chapter examines three trends or episodes that illustrate the ways in which the chaplaincy responded to post-Vietnam concerns. First, in the 1970s, the military chaplaincy responded to ongoing attacks from liberal and mainline religious groups and from secular critics about the constitutionality and moral advisability of maintaining a military chaplaincy. The Chaplain Corps' response, along with the changing demographic of the Chaplain Corps, demonstrated the degree to which the military chaplaincy had become divorced from its mainline roots. Second, the chaplaincy undertook a major ecumenical project to produce an armed services worship book, and its inclusion of the song "It Was on a Friday Morning"—an ironic and meditative song about Jesus Christ's crucifixion—created an uproar among conservative Christian groups and secular politicians who deemed the song blasphemous. Though it is only a single episode whose significance to the macro-level issues is minimal, it is symbolic of larger fights, and it holds an outsized significance within the Chaplain Corps' historical archive. Both sides in this instance dug in and insisted on the fundamental rightness—and righteousness—of their position. This challenge exemplified the chaplaincy's attempts to retain independence and its historical commitment to ecumenicalism as well as the Religious Right's increasing cultural capital and political power. Finally, these cultural crosscurrents—declining liberal support for the chaplaincy and rising conservative power—affected the organizational culture and perceived mission of the chaplaincy, shifting it toward the political and Religious Right and expanding its operational role outside of its traditional mission to provide religious support for military service members.

Major changes were afoot between the 1970s and 2000s, and the Vietnam experience informed and influenced many of them. This process of reflection, resolution, and reorganization, both individually and institutionally, left important legacies for the expression of religious practice within the American military and for the role of chaplains. Postwar changes eventually endangered chaplains' ambiguous position within military and religious structures as changing demographics, doctrines, and interpretations threatened to undermine the chaplaincy's historical emphasis on religious and pastoral support for service members and ecumenism within the Chaplain Corps.

As the war wound down, liberal and mainline religious groups continued to call for the civilianization of the military chaplaincy. Furthermore, several books appeared in the late 1960s that set the tone for the debate. In his book *A Chaplain Looks at Vietnam*, John O'Connor argued for the inherent morality of the U.S. project in Vietnam and military support there. He used his position as a military chaplain to establish both military and religious authority for his conclusions, but the book received little attention, and it is seldom mentioned by scholars. Harvey Cox, on the other hand, a Harvard scholar of religion in the United States who edited a collection of essays titled *Military Chaplains: From a Religious Military to a Military Religion*, argued against the Vietnam-era chaplaincy system. In particular, an essay in the collection by Gordon Zahn, author of a critical examination of the Royal Air Force Chaplaincy during the First World War, examined the potential for role and identity conflict, particularly in combat, but did so on intellectual and philosophical grounds rather than experiential ones. A third book, published by the General Commission on Churches and the Chaplaincy, *Church, State, and Chaplaincy: Essays and Statements on the American Chaplaincy System*, presented a more balanced view of the military chaplaincy but still raised some fundamental doubts about the chaplain's ability to act as a moral compass during war.[1]

The chaplaincy did not welcome this attention. When someone recommended that the Army chief of chaplains buy a copy of Cox's book, he replied, "Forget it! We've had experts try to sabotage us! It's an effort to salve their own conscience for their own inadequate effectiveness in their ministry and divert attention from the utter bankruptcy of their philosophy."[2] The gulf between civilian critics and the military chaplaincy seemed to grow ever wider. "Due to the broad chasm between the chaplain and his civilian counterpart," a 1970 chaplain school document stated, "there exist numerous misconceptions of the chaplain's mission and role. This large gap is due not only to the Vietnam War and anti-militarism, but also to a lack of knowledge on the part of the civilian clergy as to the true role and mission of the military chaplain in uniform: ministering to the soldier in the environment in which he lives."[3] Chaplains and civilian clergy were speaking different languages when it came to assessing the chaplain's proper role within the military establishment or even whether the chaplain had a place in the military at all.

Later, two studies were published to refute or at least provide an alternative view to Cox's collection of essays. Clarence Abercrombie's *The Military Chaplain,* a social science study of Vietnam chaplains, focused on role or identity conflict. Based on survey responses from civilian clergy, chaplains, and military commanders, Abercrombie concluded that role conflict, as it was traditionally understood, whereby chaplains forsook their religious identities and roles in favor of their military ones, was not generally evident. Chaplains, he determined, fell squarely in the middle of civilian clergy and military commanders on theological, moral, and pastoral issues and did not display levels of militarism suggested by chaplain critics. In other words, they were more military-minded than their civilian counterparts and more religiously-minded than their officer counterparts.[4] A second book, Richard Hutcheson's *The Churches and the Chaplaincy*, offered a direct critique of Cox's collection. Hutcheson had served as a chaplain and his book unabashedly supported the military chaplaincy system in the United States.[5]

Far more than a simple historiographical blip, this quick profusion of books about military chaplains after the Vietnam War highlighted the extent to which that war had called into question very basic assumptions about the military chaplaincy and the rightful place of religion in relation to the military and American foreign policy. Ultimately, the First Amendment provided fertile ground for both supporters and critics of the chaplaincy. At issue was the delicate, and incredibly murky, line between the establishment clause of the First Amendment, which prohibited the government from establishing a national religion, and the free exercise clause, which guaranteed Americans the right to freely practice religion. The tension was obvious—preserving the right to free exercise of religion for some (including chaplains) would almost certainly run afoul of the establishment clause and vice versa: applying the same standards of non-establishment guiding the civilian world in a military context would almost certainly encroach upon individuals' right to the free exercise of religion.

Critique of the chaplaincy hailed from secular circles as well: In 1962 and 1973, the American Civil Liberties Union (ACLU) challenged the constitutionality of the military chaplaincy, and in 1979, two Harvard law students filed a civil suit requesting "declaratory and injunctive relief" from their tax burden to pay for the U.S. Army's "religious support program."[6] The ACLU had long been critical of many of the military chaplaincy's policies and programs. In 1962, Lawrence Speiser, director of the Washington office, protested to Secretary of the Army Cyrus Vance that the character guidance program amounted to "religious indoctrination." Vance referred the matter to the Army chief of chaplains, who defended the program's religious orientation by insisting that while it was "theistically oriented" and based on traditional American spiritual and moral principles, the program did not support any specific religious doctrine or institution.[7] Following the incident, the Army chaplaincy revised the curriculum to prevent future complaints. It prohibited chaplains from using the character guidance classes "to deliver a sermon, to announce religious services, to upbraid troops for nonparticipation in chapel programs, to show religious films, or to expound on their own theological views."[8] Later, it removed "One Nation Under God" as a topic to be discussed in basic training.[9] Despite these changes, in 1968 the ACLU revived its protest of the character guidance program, arguing again that it violated the First Amendment.

The ACLU's 1973 complaint was broader. The board of directors declared that "abolition of the present program [the chaplaincy] is required by the principle of the Establishment Clause of the First Amendment." It asserted that individuals possessed the "right to access to a minister of his denomination, and the ministry's right, derived therefrom, to be present in the military environment," and thus declared "it would continue to be incumbent on the military to provide those minimum support services necessary to insure that the right of mutual access is effectively implemented."[10] The complaint offered few suggestions for implementing such an acceptable program, essentially ignoring the logistical, budgetary, and practical issues that had long stymied chaplain civilization efforts and stalled debates. Randolph Jonakait, who, at the time of the report was a graduate research fellow at New York University, narrowed the scope of his report to the "abuses" of the U.S. Army chaplaincy, which he defined as any structural or practical measures that did not further the chaplaincy's constitutionally allowable goal of furthering religious freedom (free exercise) for members of the U.S. military. Jonakait concluded that abuses existed "in every major aspect of the chaplaincy's structure."[11] He reported abuses within the chaplaincy system from the selection and endorsement of chaplains, to chaplains' nonreligious functions, to the chaplaincy's commitment to ecumenicalism, to the inclusion of chaplains in the military officers' personnel system of promotion and evaluation. As with the earlier complaint, reviews were conducted and minor modifications were implemented.

More worrisome to the Army chaplaincy was the 1979 lawsuit brought by Joel Katcoff and Allen Weider, two third-year Harvard Law students.

Whereas the ACLU report necessitated a thorough response from the Army, the lawsuit demanded thousands of hours to fulfill discovery requests and to craft solid legal arguments.[12] Whereas Jonakait's report claimed abuse of the free exercise clause, Katcoff and Weider's suit alleged that the chaplaincy violated the establishment clause of the First Amendment. The final complaint included 123 interrogatories and "requests for production of documents," and, following liberal discovery procedures of federal courts, the plaintiffs requested information about the Army chaplaincy for a six-year period starting in January 1974. The plaintiffs requested information about the "organization, personnel, duties, policies, and funding of the Army chaplaincy and of all employees, military and civilian, who were involved in any way with its religious program" as well as information on "rank, promotions, performance evaluations, discharges, entrance educational requirements, denominational goals, chapel and other facilities, sacred items and religious literature paid for by the Army, missions, retreats and religious-emphasis weeks, religious education, the unified curriculum, devotional programs, fund-raising, religious libraries, and chaplain career-oriented professional education and training."[13] The plaintiffs claimed that in its current form, the military chaplaincy (specifically in the Army) violated the "three-pronged test" set down in *Lemon v. Kurtzman* (1971) to determine violations of the establishment clause.[14]

The Army and the chaplaincy responded by assembling a three-tiered defense team composed of personnel from the Office of the Chief of Chaplains, the Department of Justice, and the Army's Judge Advocate General. The government's first official move was to reply to the complaint with three technical arguments that were "unrelated to the substance of the chaplaincy program": First, the "plaintiffs lacked standing and the issues constituted political questions," second, the "complaint failed to state a claim upon which relief could be granted," and third, "the claims were barred for want of sovereign immunity." The defense team hoped the courts would resolve the case without having to wrangle over substantive issues regarding the structure and practice of the chaplaincy. Following the technical arguments, the government moved for a judgment on the pleadings or a dismissal, arguing that the *Lemon* test was particularly ill-suited to determine First Amendment violations in this case because military life differed so fundamentally from civilian society.[15] The battle lines seemed clear: Katcoff and Weider relied on modern tests of church-state entanglement and the clear fact that the government (and therefore taxpayers) were supporting religious programs within the military, and the chaplaincy and its lawyers defended the military chaplaincy based on historical precedent and military necessity.

Judge Jacob Mishler heard arguments in the case in March 1980 and in August denied the Army's motion for dismissal. He ruled that the plaintiffs did have standing as federal taxpayers, that the court had the authority to review the claim, and that "a ruling on the constitutionality of the Army chaplaincy program could not be handed down without a full factual record describing the chaplaincy and its programs."[16] Thus, both sides were sent back to formulate substantive arguments to make their cases. Because they felt it would open up all chaplaincy programs to continuing court inspection and regulation, the Army, over the objection of the Department of Justice, sought to appeal Mishler's decision on the technical merits of the case. Eventually, however, Army lawyers were dissuaded from this position and decided not to file the appeal.[17] Mishler was also not inclined to decide the case through a motion for summary judgment because he felt the case merited testimony on chaplains' activities and policies.[18] Then, unexpectedly, in November 1981, the chief judge of the Eastern District Court of New York removed Mishler from the case, replacing him with Joseph M. McLaughlin, who, anxious to expedite the suit, set a March 1982 date for a hearing.

During the course of discovery, chaplains and lawyers involved in the case uncovered several instances of the misuse of appropriated (i.e., government) funds by chaplains; for example, some had used such money to purchase library materials and sacred items (such as candlesticks and Bibles). Israel Drazin, a chaplain and lawyer on the case, concluded that the "misuse resulted from lack of sensitivity to the problems, ignorance of the law, overzealousness for religion, and the generally misguided and improvident view that whatever a chaplain considered to be good and righteous and needed must be an acceptable item of purchase." These problems threatened to undermine the Army's argument about the chaplaincy and bolster the plaintiffs' claims of "excessive entanglement" between the government and religion. Around the same time, the *Army Times* reported that the Air Force had issued a directive prohibiting its chaplains from performing religious services, including baptisms and weddings, for military retirees. The story cited the constitutional prohibition of "state-sponsored religious activity." This action, albeit by another branch of the armed services, threatened to undermine the Army's stance on the constitutionality of the chaplaincy. The *Army Times* story, however, was misleading; the directive was a long-standing one that concerned dependents of military personnel, but the potential for damage to the *Katcoff* suit was clear.[19]

Legal wrangling, over both technical and substantive matters continued for nearly three years. U.S. Attorneys working on the case preferred to argue technical matters of standing, while the chaplains wished to make substantive arguments about the unique nature of the military chaplaincy as compared both to other clergy and to other government employees. Eventually, both types of arguments were included in the government's motions.[20] McLaughlin heard oral arguments in October 1982 and rendered his decision in February 1984, concluding that the plaintiffs did have standing before the court.[21] He was generally not persuaded by the government's reliance on historical precedent for justifying the chaplaincy. In the end, however, McLaughlin concluded that Congress had undertaken to legislate and regulate the chaplaincy and that congressional decisions about the chaplaincy should be given great deference by the court. He wrote, "The balance struck by Congress cannot be rejected by this Court in favor of the untested possibility that a civilian chaplaincy might also meet the religious needs of the military community," concluding that the plaintiffs' "remedy, if there be any, lies with Congress."[22]

Katcoff and Weider filed an appeal on 11 June 1984, reiterating their arguments that the Army chaplaincy violated the establishment clause of the First Amendment and claiming that McLaughlin's dismissal of the three-pronged *Lemon* test to judge the chaplaincy was incorrect.[23] After another round of written arguments, the Second Circuit Court handed down its decision on 22 January 1985. The judges determined the chaplaincy was constitutional but remanded the case to the district court in order to determine whether certain chaplaincy programs exceeded "permissible constitutional limits."[24] The government decided to seek summary judgment on the issues left undecided by the circuit court. Then, in 1986, Katcoff and Weider contacted the U.S. Attorney's office offering to drop the case in return for not having to pay the government's expenses for the appeal.[25] The U.S. Attorneys and Army lawyers were inclined to agree to the settlement, while the chaplains were less sure; they felt that dropping the case at this stage left important questions unresolved and left them open to future litigation. Eventually, the arguments for dismissal won out; there were few benefits to be gained by further litigation, and the chaplaincy had much to lose.[26]

Whereas memoirs and first-person accounts had been the primary mode for chaplains as individuals to make sense of the Vietnam experience, external pressure from litigation, particularly the Katcoff case, prompted the chaplaincy as an institution to reconsider many of its programs, policies, and goals. Though the legal issues were only marginally settled, the result of the *Katcoff* case was that the chaplaincy's *existence* as part of the military appeared to be on firm constitutional footing, though because the case was dropped, a future challenge could yield different results (though cases since then have suggested that such an outcome is unlikely). Many viewed the chaplaincy's mission, however, as substantially limited by the court case, which seemed to suggest that the chaplaincy existed, in a legal sense, only to allow military personnel their right to the free exercise of religion. The unsettling conclusion for many chaplains and religious leaders was that the chaplaincy was not intended to, and should not be used to, promote religion, morality, or morale. If those things were natural consequences of the chaplains' work, so be it, but in the balance of First Amendment rights, whatever free exercise rights chaplains possessed were clearly secondary to prohibitions against establishment.

The years following Vietnam were critical ones for the chaplaincy as it responded to a host of critics from mainline and liberal religious and secular groups as well as to civilian litigation on the issue of constitutionality. These challenges prompted chaplains to take a defensive stand against their critics rather than encouraging open dialogue about the chaplaincy's role and challenges within the modern military. Furthermore, this narrowing of chaplains' perceived mission led them, especially in light of the rise of conservative influence, to seek out new areas to work in the post-Vietnam military.

Conservatives Gain Influence

At about the same time that the Chaplain Corps faced intense scrutiny from liberal secular and religious voices, conservative Christians saw themselves ascendant in the American political arena and public consciousness and thus in a position to defend the military chaplaincy. The rise of the so-called Religious Right in the United States has been well-documented and analyzed by scholars.[27] As the number of conservative and evangelical Christians in the United States grew, so too did their attachment to conservative political groups. One salient feature of the movement was its insistence that liberalism threatened the Christian foundations of the United States and that Christianity, or at least their brand of it, was under attack by the prophets of religious pluralism and tolerance.[28] Certainly the 1960s and 1970s witnessed a profusion of new religious movements, splinter groups, and non-Christian religions. Within the chaplaincy alone, the number of officially recognized religious endorsing agencies had grown from just 10 in the 1940s to well over 200 by 2000.

Parachurch organizations, such as the Full Gospel Men's Business Fellowship International, the Campus Crusade for Christ, the Navigators, and the Fellowship of Christian Athletes, intensified their efforts to minister to military personnel. Chaplains' reactions to these groups, which were clearly evangelical in their outlook and mission, varied. Some "theologically liberal" chaplains felt threatened by them, fearing that "too much evangelistic activity and involvement by outsiders may raise church-state questions."[29] At the Marine base in Camp Pendleton, California, senior chaplains banned them altogether.[30] For the most part, though, chaplains seemed to accept these organizations—their money, resources, and people—as significant aspects of ministry to military personnel, and the Chaplain Corps' leadership frequently encouraged cooperation with them.[31]

In 1974, the Army, Navy, and Air Force compiled a new worship book for use in the Armed services. The new hymnal represented years of work on behalf of the Chaplain Corps from all three military services as well as the input from civilian leaders. The book eliminated denominational and faith-group distinctions for the hymns, and included music from a variety of styles and religious traditions.[32] "It Was on a Friday Morning" was included as one of several folk songs in the new volume. British composer Sydney Carter wrote the song as an ironic meditation on the crucifixion of Christ. The song's inclusion created a near-immediate uproar from conservative Christians and the politicians who relied on their support. The publication of the *Book of Worship* and the subsequent furor over the song's inclusion in it illuminated quite clearly two competing and very divergent pressures on the post-Vietnam chaplaincy. On one hand, the book represented a deepening commitment to ecumenism, pluralism, and tolerance for religious and cultural diversity. On the other hand, such significant protest over the simple inclusion of a song in a hymnal highlighted the extent of conservative religious and political reach.

These competing values came to a head over the inclusion of Carter's song. Carter himself insisted the song was not a "hymn" in the traditional sense and that the context in which it was sung and the attitude of those singing it mattered a great deal.[33] Carter's song was written from the perspective of the thief who, according to Christian scriptures, was crucified next to Jesus Christ. The thief asks Jesus a series of questions, intent on discovering why God would allow an innocent man to die and ultimately blaming God for the sins of the world. The thief offers a litany of people and spirits one might blame for the crucifixion of the "carpenter, a-hanging on the tree" and for the depravity of humanity: Pilate, the Jews, the Devil, Adam, Eve, the crowd that freed Barabbas—none of them, according to the thief, would have existed in the absence of God's plan and creation. The thief blames the carpenter's God "up in Heaven" who "doesn't do a thing" to stop the execution. The most damning lines appeared at the end of the song when the thief says:

"To hell with Jehovah,"
To the carpenter I said.
"I wish that a carpenter had made the world instead.
Goodbye and good luck to you.
Our ways will soon divide.
Remember me tomorrow,
The man you hung beside."
"It's God they ought to crucify instead of you and me,"
I said to the carpenter, a-hanging on the tree.

Furor erupted over the "blasphemy" of the song probably in no small part due to upcoming national elections. Many conservative Christians expressed outrage at the song. In 1975, South Carolina Senator Strom Thurmond, a retired major general in the Army Reserves, complained to Secretary of Defense James Schlesinger. In 1976, nearly fifty members of Congress complained to the Department of Defense or one of the chaplain services. Almost universally, they called for the song to be removed from the hymnal, by razor blade if necessary.[34]

In the face of the controversy, chaplains insisted that any order to remove or replace the song should come from the "theological" or "church" side of the chaplaincy, rather than from the "military" or "governmental" side. For most of them, the issue was a fundamentally theological one and it would be inappropriate for the Department of Defense or other official branch of the U.S. military to decide the song's fate. According to the chaplain services, critics could not cite a single instance of a church organization requesting or demanding the song's removal. Furthermore, they argued, removing "hymns from the manuscript because they are objectionable to one or another of the involved religious denominations" would leave the military with a "thin hymnal indeed!"[35] One chaplain argued even more explicitly, "If we started objecting to a hymn because we don't like the theological content, then some of the more conservative Protestants could go after the ones about the 'bleeding heart' and 'the Mother of God,' and the Jews can certainly take off on the Trinitarian ones, and then many can take off on the Mormon hymns and the Christian Science hymns and where do you stop?"[36] Chaplains tended to approach the inclusion of the song pragmatically and based on the chaplaincy's long-standing commitment to ecumenical cooperation.

Chaplains, in fact, did not shy away from the controversy, and even engaged the issue directly when the hymnal was released. In an introductory pamphlet called "Hello Hymnal," issued by the Air Force Chaplain Board, chaplain James Chapman wrote specifically about the controversy and the inclusion of Carter's song: "Some have said that it is not even a hymn. Other critics have denounced it as blasphemous." Then Chapman offered three justifications for the song's inclusion. First, he appealed to the chaplain's duty to minister to all people, arguing that "the questions asked by the thief are the ones many of our people still ask when confronted with the Crucifixion" and that the song gave chaplains "a vehicle to deal with these mysteries." Second, he presented a theological interpretation of the song: when the thief says, "'It's God they ought to crucify instead of you and me,' . . . he stumbles on to the glorious solution," Chapman asserts, "God is being crucified instead of you and me! That is the Gospel!" Finally, Chapman argued from a devotional point of view: "This hymn *can not* be simply sung and dropped," he wrote. "You've got to deal with it. We recommend you use it as a basis for a Good Friday meditation. You'll be forever grateful to Sydney Carter."[37]

Even when chaplains admitted they should have foreseen the controversy the song's inclusion might cause, they defended the integrity of the process and of the final product. Air Force chief of chaplains Henry J. Meade said, "It was probably poor judgment that inserted that hymn, but it would be bad judgment to excise it."[38] Eventually, with prompting from Secretary of Defense Donald Rumsfeld and the eventual concurrence of the chiefs of chaplains, it was decided that the song would be eliminated from future printings of the *Book of Worship*.[39] Conservative Christians, calling upon what historian Anne Loveland has termed the "Sectarian Ideal," gathered political and public support to demand changing an official publication of the U.S. military. Conservative influence in the military continued to grow throughout the 1970s and 1980s and well into the 2000s, even as the institutional chaplaincy continued to insist on ecumenical cooperation and expanding pluralism.

Organizational Restructuring and
Changing the Chaplaincy's Mission

The effect of Vietnam on the structure of the American military was apparent even before the war ended. The proposal in 1971 for an all-volunteer force (AVF) provoked strong reactions in many circles. Terence P. Finnegan, a retired Catholic Air Force chief of chaplains, criticized the plan as resulting in "nothing but a mercenary army" and warned that it would be "the beginning of the end for the United States."[40] Of course, the AVF did come, and it did not begin a dangerous and precipitous decline in American military power. But it did fundamentally change the U.S. military and its relation to society.

Even before the last American troops left Vietnam in 1973, the U.S. Army Chaplain School held a workshop in anticipation of its eventual end, focusing on what the Army chaplaincy might face in 1975 and after. The goal of the workshop, titled "Army '75: The Chaplain and the Soldier in the Army of 1975," was to "establish conclusions and guidelines for the chaplain in planning and executing a local post-religious program for 1975 period and beyond." The Office of the Chief of Chaplains and the chaplain school produced and distributed materials for the workshop, which reflected their analysis and assumptions about the future. The Chaplain Corps envisioned a garrison model, rather than a combat model, for future chaplain ministry, which would focus as much on ministry to military families as anything else. The Chaplain Corps also recognized that chaplains' authority as religious leaders might decline as fewer Americans turned to organized religion to fulfill spiritual needs and provide moral guidance. They asserted that "through 1975 we will see a continuing loss of moral authority by the churches as institutions because of the lack of credibility and apparent hypocrisy."[41] Thus, chaplain school instructors suggested that chaplains "of the future will be more active in the community life of the military post. He will be less of a religious expert and more the participator in aspects of community life which offer meaning and service. His authority will depend on his own demonstrated value in the interpretive role, not on his ordained authority."[42]

However, many of the changes that would confront the U.S. military and the chaplaincy after Vietnam were unexpected, and sometimes even contrary to the conclusions set forth by the chaplains. Among other things, the Chaplain Corps asserted that "the Army of 1975 will not be an all-volunteer Army but will be organized and structured very much as it is today . . . no drastic changes will take place in the organization and structure of the US Army." And, as far as the chaplaincy was concerned, it stated, "There is no foreseen change in the mission of the chaplain. But changes will occur in the perspectives and ways and means to make the ministry more relevant." Another section concluded: "The US Army will continue at a level of between 850,000–1,000,000 men in the '70s. To maintain this force level a mixed volunteer/draft system will continue to function."[43]

Even though the demographic assumptions proved wrong in nearly every way, the chaplains who participated in the workshop recognized changed imperatives for spiritual guidance and worship styles. Eventually, the Chaplain Corps established revised guidelines for ministry, including the "need for new forms of worship: modern language liturgies, simpler liturgical forms, folk and modern music, etc." The guidelines reflected the liturgical creativity that chaplains and military personnel engaged in during the Vietnam War. Chaplains, in the final report for the workshop, recognized the need for more "dialogue in spiritual matters between the chaplain and the people he serves" and for increased skills for chaplains in the area of pastoral counseling, especially in the wake of the ongoing trauma of the Vietnam War. They predicted that the legacy of Vietnam would mean that "concepts surrounding drugs and sex will be matters of commonplace concern," which reflected a societal tendency to take a "free and frank attitude" toward them, prompting "old taboos" to be "shunted aside in an attempt to 'tell it like it is.'"[44]

Perhaps most importantly, the workshop participants—career Army chaplains who would continue to shape post-Vietnam chaplain ministry—concluded that "the chaplain will often have to serve as mediator between the military establishment and the young soldier. The chaplain will have to become more alert to the sociological and political trends of the times." Chaplains would be challenged to assert their significance due to "smaller military budgets" and ever more "severe questioning by the young soldier of the role of religion, clergy (chaplain) and church (chapel) in society." The chaplain would be increasingly involved in "domestic Peace Corps type projects" and "play an increasingly important role in community relations and liaison."[45] And while some of the chaplains' conclusions and predictions clearly did not come to pass, many chaplains demonstrated a sophisticated understanding of the chaplaincy's changing role within the U.S. military, the changing religious atmosphere within the United States, and the legacy of the Vietnam War.

One chaplain attending the advanced course at the Air Force Chaplain School in 1976 wrote that the "single most important development in the Air Force chaplaincy from 1970–1975" was the "withdrawal of U.S. forces from South Vietnam and the fall of South Vietnam." He reasoned that "foreign policy from 1965 [to] 1975 was strong on survival of democracy in South Vietnam," but that "great amounts of U.S. resources (men, money and materiel) were expended in South Vietnam and brought back a 'zero' return." He argued that "national involvement in South Vietnam divided our country (war protest, Kent State, refusal to pay taxes) and the problem of amnesty still faces us and divides us," which made the nation "doubt and question our institutions (governmental and military) and leadership." In his estimation, all of these factors led the United States "to a limited position of 'isolation' in foreign policy."[46] All in all, chaplains recognized what they believed to be a damaged and weakened civic faith, which had been exacerbated by the declining membership within American mainline and liberal faith communities.

As chaplains returned to the United States, the legacies of Vietnam for stateside ministry were apparent. Air Force chaplain historian John Groh wrote that American involvement in Southeast Asia with "Prisoner of War (POW) and personnel Missing in Action (MIA); Operation Homecoming and the 'other' homecoming; operations Babylift and Newlife; [and] . . . the resettlement of Indochinese refugees" deeply affected American military chapel installations as chaplains worked with stateside congregations and groups to provide assistance to those affected by the war and to bring closure to those who had fought in Vietnam.[47] In addition to direct legacies of Vietnam, the military chaplaincy also had to cope with the move to an all-volunteer force, which meant it was dealing with older service men and service women with more dependents. This demographic change moved the chaplaincy to emphasize "family life" at the same time that it dealt with ongoing problems of alcohol and drug use and contentious race relations. In response to high rates of injury and post-traumatic stress disorder (PTSD), more chaplains had to complete Clinical Pastoral Education training, which prepared them to work in hospital settings with trauma victims and their families. Additionally, chaplains continued to play an important, though changing role in character guidance training, which underwent a substantive revision and was renamed human self-development.[48]

In the immediate post-Vietnam years, these sorts of changes, based primarily in pastoral care, counseling, and ministry areas, dominated chaplains' thinking. Army Director of Combat Developments Gordon Schweitzer reiterated the extent to which chaplains reconceptualized their role after Vietnam, most strikingly by moving away from the focus on combat and front-line chaplaincy that dominated the war years: "Chaplains were pastors, counselors, and preachers. Clinical pastoral education and the emphasis on parish development contributed to the organization and delivery of religious support for the soldier and family members on installations." Chaplain activity specialists (chaplain assistants before 1977) were trained primarily in building maintenance and office administration, and by 1983, fewer than 50 percent of active-duty chaplains had combat experience.[49]

As the chaplaincy redefined its role, it also underwent organizational and doctrinal changes that affected how it carried out its mission.[50] The post-Vietnam drop in manpower resulted in a significantly older Chaplain Corps than had served in Vietnam. In the Air Force, nearly 50 percent of all chaplains were over forty-six years old, compared to just over 34 percent in 1971. Across the board, the numbers of Protestant, Catholic, and Jewish chaplains decreased, and only the number of Eastern Orthodox chaplains rose.[51] At the same time, the Chaplain Corps dropped its system of denomination-based quotas for filling chaplain slots. The reasons for this change were numerous: for example, the number of waivers and exceptions allowed during the Vietnam War had already weakened the quota system; some denominations were consistently providing more qualified chaplains while others rarely met their goal; and the number of denominations contributing to the chaplaincy proliferated at a rapid rate.[52]

In responding to the shortage of chaplains, changes in force structure, and developments within American religious communities, the armed services also explored commissioning women as chaplains within the integrated AVF structure. Several national denominational churches had ordained women into full-time ministry and wished to endorse them as chaplains, and the military was restructured to integrate women into previously all-male units. Shortages within the Chaplain Corps led to aggressive recruiting drives in seminaries, and some of the recruiting posters—like others of the early AVF era—appealed to women. Bonnie Koppell, the first Jewish woman to attend the Army Chaplain School, saw such a poster in 1976 when she was a student at Reconstructionist Rabbinical College in Philadelphia, Pennsylvania, and was inspired to apply to be a chaplain. When the Orthodox contingent of the Jewish Welfare Board did not veto her application, Koppell received endorsement in 1977. She attended chaplain school at Fort Hamilton in 1979, where she was one of three women in a class of 108.[53]

The issue of accepting women as chaplains was not entirely new, however. During the Civil War, Ella Gibson Hobart was elected chaplain by the First Wisconsin Regiment of Heavy Artillery, but her official appointment was denied by Secretary of War Edwin Stanton.[54] Then, with the creation of the Women's Army Auxiliary Corps (later Women's Army Corps) in 1942, some female ministers challenged the all-male limits on chaplains. However, since few servicewomen objected to the all-male chaplaincy—nationally, after all, clergy were almost all men—their applications were dropped. Women continued to serve alongside chaplains as directors of religious education, a post that was available to and often filled by female civilian leaders.[55]

In the late 1960s and 1970s, women had gained prominence as ordained ministers in several national denominations. For example, women qualified for ordination in the Methodist Church of America and in the Presbyterian Church (PCUSA) in 1956. By the 1970s, women were being ordained in the Episcopal Church, the Lutheran Church of America, Reform Jewish congregations, and a number of other smaller denominations. According to the 1970 U.S. census, 3 percent of all American clergy were women.[56] As might be expected, women faced challenges in this new environment. In 1987, fully thirteen years after the first women were commissioned chaplains, Navy chaplain Carolyn Wiggins wrote in the Navy Chaplains' professional journal, "We [female chaplains] leave an accepting seminary to enter a hostile chaplaincy working with male chaplains who have often never worked with clergywomen and have difficulty accepting us as professional colleagues. They often show disdain for our presence in the Navy Chaplain Corps."[57] Female Navy chaplains identified significant cultural barriers that challenged their work, including reticence of commanders to accept female chaplains; difficulty socializing in a male-dominated chaplain system; difficulty in obtaining desirable assignments, such as aboard aircraft carriers, which would facilitate promotion and professional advancement; and trouble finding role models and mentors among women who had deployed with the Navy. Women also faced the sexism of their military flock, who hewed more closely to traditional, gendered roles and expectations than did the mainline denominations that first endorsed female chaplains.

Chaplain leaders also examined their organizational structure for clues as to the causes of problems in Vietnam. The system of area coverage meant that brigades or the equivalent were the lowest level of assignment for chaplains—that is, a brigade chaplain and three or four assistants were responsible for providing religious support for all units assigned and attached to the brigade in addition to any other units that might be in the brigade's area of operations (AO). In theory, the system enabled chaplains to provide coverage at the battalion and company level, but in practice, it meant that chaplains could rarely form close connections with the units they served. It also strained chaplains' relationships to commanders. Area coverage later came under serious scrutiny by chaplains at the Army War College who wrote that "this doctrinal and manning concept presented difficulties for commanders and chaplains" because "the chaplain did not work directly for the battalion commander, was not part of the unit, and only showed up in the unit area to conduct services, perform counseling or conduct classes."[58] On duty rosters, only the brigade chaplain was listed as "staff chaplain," so few chaplains had direct access to commanders within the parameters of the chain of command and the guidelines set out in the chaplain's field manual about the chaplain's staff responsibilities.[59]

In 1978, in order to clarify command-chaplain relationships and to insert chaplains more directly into the life and workings of battalion-sized units, the Army Chaplain Corps instituted the "Forward Thrust" doctrine, based on the new Army operations manual FM 100-5 and the emerging Air-Land Battle Doctrine. Army chief of chaplains Orris Kelly, who had served in Vietnam, and Donn Starry, the Commander of Training and Doctrine Command, who was responsible for recruiting, training, and educating the Army's soldiers, worked to assign chaplains as far forward as possible in order to provide coverage to company-sized units.[60] In 1984, the Army took the concept even further by instituting Unit Ministry Teams (UMT) as the primary source of religious support for Army units. The UMT consisted of a single chaplain and a chaplain assistant who would be assigned to a single battalion or outfits of similar size. They would provide "direct religious support" to their units of assignment and "general religious support" to attached units during peacetime, during field training, and in wartime operations. Rather than chaplains being assigned to deployed units as the need arose, they would remain with specific units in both stateside and overseas posts whenever possible.[61]

The Navy also restructured its Chaplain Corps in the 1970s in response to post-Vietnam staffing and organizational concerns. Reflecting on the period, one Navy chaplain wrote in 2005 that immediately after Vietnam, "force shaping, or downsizing became a reality of life for all branches of the service. Throughout the 70s the naval services cut back on billets and ships, and the Chaplain Corps . . . explored new ministry delivery models."[62] The chief of naval operations authorized the establishment of "Fleet Religious Support Activities" (FRSA), in order " to meet the emergent needs" of the Navy. For the first time, modern chaplains were "assigned to an administrative command positions[,]" "ordered into an FRSA UIC[,] and . . . concurrently assigned to operational platforms when ordered to do so by their FRSA chaplain-commander."[63] The FRSA emphasized a team approach to ministry, the flexible assignment of chaplains, coordination between ship-based and shore-based ministries, and the development of a new lay-leader program. In the late 1970s the FRSA program was discontinued and replaced with a new "alternative ministry delivery platform," the Dependents Assistance Board (DAB). The DAB focused on providing a central location for chaplain support of deployed commanders and their families.[64]

These structural changes reflected the chaplaincy's concern with ministry to military families and to adjusting to new strategic and tactical military paradigms. Additionally, the chaplaincy became more dedicated to "institutional ministry" in the years following Vietnam.[65] Chaplains were involved in redesigning character education programs and in increasing commanders' and chaplains' knowledge about minority religious groups. In the 1980s, Chaplain Matthew Zimmerman was tasked to create "a handbook for commanders on less familiar religions, FM 16-1," which he deemed a "very interesting project." He recalled, "Back in those days we had a lot of new sects, cults, etcetera that were coming into existence every day and they were making themselves felt on installations. Commanders didn't know what to do. Somebody would show up and ask for permission to wear a simulation of a sword, and the commander wouldn't know if it was a legitimate request or a con job. It just went on and on." In response, the Chaplain Corps implemented a system in which such requests were authenticated by headquarters or leaders of the denominations involved. Then, the chaplain and commander could know what the "parameters were for any particular sect, cult, or any denomination that came up."[66] The creation of the new handbook exemplified chaplains' institutional responsibilities and justified, at least in part, the military's insistence that chaplains have broad religious and theological training in order to provide support to personnel of any faith.

The chaplaincy's focus on institutional ministry and response to increasing calls for pluralism and secularism were evident in the evolution of the Navy Chaplain Corps' official seal between 1962 and 2001. In 1962, the seal included the words "Chaplain Corps" at the top and "U.S. Navy" at the bottom. The emblems on it were a compass rose with an anchor in the middle, with a cross to its right and the Tablets of Stone, surmounted by the Star of David, to its left. The seal thus reflected the martial and religious traditions of the naval chaplain service. In 1981, Hebrew numerals replaced Roman numerals on the tablets—a sign of increasing cultural sensitivity to minority religious groups. And in 1996, the seal gained a Muslim crescent, for the first time including an emblem for a non Judeo-Christian faith group. By 2001, however, all religious imagery had been removed from the Chaplain Corps' seal and replaced with the image of a scroll with the words *Vocati ad Servitium* (Called to Serve) on it, as well as an eagle, holding an anchor and the compass and an open book. The eagle, according to the Navy's website, was "stationed as sentinel to guard the free exercise of religion for Sea Services personnel. The open book . . . suggests the doctrines, scriptures and guiding principles of religious tradition and wisdom."[67]

The official move toward pluralism was prompted, at least in part, by the growing diversity of military personnel. Yet the Chaplain Corps grew ever more theologically and politically conservative in the post-Vietnam years. A segment on National Public Radio's *All Things Considered*, aired on 27 July 2005, examined growing tensions within the military Chaplain Corps. Correspondent Jeff Brady reported that nearly 60 percent of the military's chaplains were "evangelical" (though he did not attempt to define the term more precisely), even though only 40 percent of military personnel identified as evangelical.[68] Other sources also cited the twin trends of growing religious diversity among military personnel and the ever more evangelical Chaplain Corps. A *New York Times* story cited Air Force statistics that showed there were about "3,500 [enlisted personnel] who say they are . . . Hindus, Buddhists, Muslims, pagans, druids or shamans, . . . 1,600 who say they are atheists and about 50,000 who say they have no religious preference, out of a total of 280,000."[69] The number of evangelical chaplains in the military and their positions therein did not always conform to the image of the military discriminating against evangelical chaplains. Brady surmised that in the current religious climate, Catholic, Presbyterian, or other chaplains were simply "hard to find," and Air Force chief of chaplains Charles Baldwin—himself a Baptist—concurred. He said, "In the Air Force, we're not saying let's go hire evangelicals today. We're looking at those who have presented their credentials and who want to serve the men and women in the Air Force." Those interviewed in Brady's report concluded that many of these difficulties in recruitment and retention stemmed from mainline and liberal opposition to the Vietnam War, which had long-lingering effects on those denominations' willingness to send new chaplains to the military.[70] In addition, clergy who were sympathetic to mainline and liberal religious groups' antiwar tendencies were unlikely to volunteer for chaplain service.

As the chaplain services made more and more concerted efforts to ensure pluralism and ecumenical cooperation, chaplains, especially conservative Christian ones, pushed back, both by bringing several lawsuits against the military services and the Department of Defense and by gaining support from prominent conservative Christian groups. Though the controversies about the chaplaincy's structure, mission, and policies emerged over a variety of issues, they all reflected the growing conservatism of military chaplains and highlighted the extent to which they came into conflict with long-standing historical traditions of ecumenicalism and cooperation that had marked the American chaplaincy since its inception. Chaplains became champions for sectarian and denominational causes and individual free exercise rights as opposed to furthering their roles as cultural mediators between diverse groups of people. At the same time, Congress emphasized the free exercise rights of non-Christian military personnel with a 1987 amendment to the military's uniform regulations, indicating a broader cultural shift.[71] To be sure, not all of the lawsuits and controversies stemmed, even indirectly, from chaplains' experiences in Vietnam, but the changed demography of the Chaplain Corps, coupled with a changing American religious landscape, thrust the debates into the public eye.

In 1996, the Department of Defense faced a lawsuit in response to Air Force, Army, and Navy directives that barred chaplains from participating in the Catholic Church's Project Life Postcard Campaign, which involved religious adherents sending postcards to members of Congress encouraging them to override President Bill Clinton's veto of a partial-birth abortion ban.[72] The chaplains' lawsuit alleged that the directive unfairly infringed on their right to the free exercise of religion and the right to political participation. The military chaplaincies sought to reinforce the wall of separation between church and state by ensuring its chaplains could not be construed as speaking on behalf of the military, which would violate antilobbying laws prohibiting active-duty personnel from attempting to influence political policies or elections. The military branches reasoned that chaplains could contact members of Congress but could not participate in an organized campaign. Chaplain Vincent Rigdon, who was named in the suit, however, said the directive created a "conflict between two chains of command I am under. . . . There is the military structure and then there's my calling in the church and what that requires."[73]

The Washington, D.C., Circuit Court ruled in favor of the plaintiffs. Judge Stanley Sporkin opined, "What we have here is the government's attempt to override the Constitution and the laws of the land by a directive that clearly interferes with military chaplains' free exercise and free speech rights, as well as those of their congregants. On its face, this is a drastic act and can be sanctioned only by compelling circumstances. . . . The 'speech' that the plaintiffs intend to employ to inform their congregants of their religious obligations has nothing to do with their role in the military." He concluded that "the chaplains in this case seek to preach only what they would tell their non-military congregants. There is no need for heavy-handed censorship, and any attempt to impinge on the plaintiffs' constitutional and legal rights is not acceptable."[74] The *Rigdon* decision, which the government declined to appeal, set a clear precedent for the free exercise rights of military chaplains.

In 2000, another suit, this time against the Navy, addressed the issue of denominational preferences and discrimination when chaplains were considered for appointment, assignment, retention, and promotion.[75] Even though denominational quotas were abandoned more than twenty years before, the plaintiffs alleged that the Navy favored Roman Catholics and liturgical Protestants (including Methodists, Episcopalians, Lutherans, and Presbyterians) at the expense of non-liturgical Protestants (including Baptists, Charismatics, and Pentecostals, among others), which, they argued constituted the establishment of religion, in violation of the First Amendment. In August 2008, the U.S. District Court for the District of Columbia ruled that the chaplains lacked standing because "mere personal offense to government action did not give rise to standing to sue."[76]

Also in the early 2000s, the Air Force Academy came under fire from both religious and secular critics who complained that cadets were being vigorously and unconstitutionally proselytized by Air Force Academy faculty (including chaplains) and other cadets. An investigation concluded: "Senior faculty and staff members, in efforts that may have been well-intentioned, have made public expressions of faith that some faculty, staff and cadets believed to be inappropriately influential or coercive. As a result of this, some military and civilian faculty expressed concern about the impact of religious affiliation on their personal career advancement."[77] Lutheran chaplain MeLinda Morton had been instrumental in bringing these accusations to light, an action that provoked conservative Christian outrage directed at both Morton and the U.S. Air Force Chaplain Corps.[78] Morton was removed from her post as executive officer of the chaplains' squadron, though the Air Force claimed it was for reasons of continuity rather than as reprisal for her outspokenness.[79] Morton eventually resigned her commission.[80] Morton's accusations appeared on several conservative news websites and blogs, which reported that Morton, a "chaplain"—the quotation marks were used mockingly in the comment—wanted "Christ out of the Air Force Academy." One blog post, at FreeRepublic.com, prompted nearly 400 comments, mostly derisive of Morton's position. Many questioned women's fitness and ability to be ministers; others suggested potential assignments for Morton—Greenland and Antarctica being popular destinations—and still others derided the Air Force Academy for cowing to liberal demands and training cadets on religious sensitivity.[81]

Partially in response to these claims and the investigative report, the Air Force issued a new directive to its chaplains, clarifying its position on proselytizing and public sectarian prayer. The interim guidelines, published in 2005, set out eight guiding principles for balancing concerns over establishment and free exercise throughout the Air Force. The first recalled that all members of the Air Force were sworn to uphold and protect the Constitution of the United States. The second stated that the Air Force would accommodate the free exercise of religion except as "limited by military necessity" but that it would not endorse programs or actions that privileged one religion over another or the idea of religion over irreligion. The third principle affirmed that "service before self demands respect for the Constitution, our Air Force and each other, and an understanding that in the military our service begins with a commitment to our responsibilities, not only our rights." The fourth reiterated that chaplain programs, in service of religious support for military personnel, fell under the purview and responsibility of commanders. The fifth reminded commanders, supervisors, and superiors that their position required special attention and care when they were dealing with religious issues because of the potential for confusion regarding an official endorsement of religious belief. The sixth principle declared discrimination or mistreatment of fellow Air Force personnel to be unacceptable. The seventh concluded that the Air Force would build a successful team "by stressing our common Air Force Heritage" and by recognizing and valuing "the many heritages, cultures, and beliefs represented among us." The final principle entreated Air Force chaplains to remember that in a "time when many nations are torn apart by religious strife . . . our ability to stand together as Americans and as airmen," representing many religions and no religions standing, "shoulder-to-shoulder" "[is] part of our heritage and our strength."[82]

The guidelines included policies regarding "Religious Accommodation; Public Prayer Outside of Voluntary Worship Settings; Individual Sharing of Religious Faith in the Military Context; The Chaplain Service; Email and Other Communications; and, Good Order and Discipline." The directive stated that "public prayer" was generally inappropriate in official settings such as "staff meetings, office meetings, classes, or officially sanctioned activities such as sports events or practice sessions," though it did allow for brief, *nonsectarian* public prayer in "non-routine military ceremonies or events of special importance, such as a change-of-command, promotion ceremonies or significant celebrations" provided that the "purpose of the prayer is to add a heightened sense of seriousness or solemnity, not to advance specific religious beliefs."[83] These guidelines did not apply to chaplains' general or denominational worship services. The Navy also issued similar guidelines that would regulate public prayer in official settings.

Responding to significant pressure from conservative religious groups and members of Congress, the Air Force issued revised guidelines in 2007. Most significantly, it added a provision that stated, that the Air Force "will respect the rights of chaplains to adhere to the tenets of their religious faiths and they will not be required to participate in religious activities, including public prayer, inconsistent with their faith." Additionally, it softened the language on prayer in public or official settings. The revised guidelines read, "Public prayer should not imply government endorsement of religion and should not usually be a part of routine official business. . . . Further, non-denominational, inclusive prayer or a moment of silence may be appropriate for military ceremonies or events of special importance when its primary purpose is not the advancement of religious beliefs."[84]

The revised guidelines sparked an immediate reaction. The Associated Press issued a release summarizing the changes: "The Air Force released new guidelines for religious expression, dropping a requirement for chaplains to respect others' rights to their own beliefs and no longer cautioning top officers about promoting their personal religious views." "The revisions," the AP reported, "were welcomed by conservative Christians. But critics called the revisions a step backward and said they did nothing to protect the rights of most airmen."[85] A *Stars and Stripes* article reported that Representative Walter Jones (R-NC) and Billy Baugham, executive director of the International Conference of Evangelical Chaplain Endorsers, both stated that the revised guidelines did not "go far enough" in protecting chaplains' rights to "pray in Jesus' name." Baugham was quoted as saying, "The Air Force has a mind-set that because my chaplains pray in the name of Christ that it constitutes recruiting. But that's nonsense. That is how we believe we must pray."[86]

Congress soon involved itself in the controversy. A provision in the National Defense Authorization Act of 2007 would have legislated chaplains' rights to offer sectarian prayers in public (official) settings.[87] Three U.S. representatives, Randy Forbes (R-VA), Todd Aiken (R-MO), and Walter Jones (R-NC), threatened to block passage of the entire bill unless the provision was included. The provision would "add language to each of the service sections (including the Academies) stating that chaplains 'shall have the prerogative to pray according to the dictates of the Chaplain's conscience, except as must be limited by military necessity, with any such limitation being imposed in the least restrictive manner feasible."[88] The Senate did not include a similar provision. The Conference Report, however, directed the secretaries of the Air Force and Navy to rescind their most recent policies and guidelines on religious exercise and to reinstate earlier policies (from 1999 and 2000), which did not include strict guidelines about sectarian prayer in official settings.[89] The congressional order marked a major moral victory for evangelical military chaplains, who held that their First Amendment right to free exercise guaranteed them the right to pray "in Jesus' Name" at any and all military functions or worship services. Similar provisions and directives have been included in Defense Department authorizations through 2013.

The war in Vietnam precipitated a significant number of organizational and cultural changes within the military chaplaincy. The immediate post-Vietnam years marked critical ones for the chaplaincy as it faced intense scrutiny and critique from mainline and liberal religious groups and confronted growing conservative Christian power within military and political circles. The combination led the chaplaincy to defend its mission and ministry in terms of protecting military personnel's right to the free exercise of religion, even as it moved culturally to the right. At the same time, official chaplain channels faced a changing military organization and mission and responded to increasing religious diversity within the military by reemphasizing the chaplaincy's historically ecumenical character and its commitment to military families. The values of conservative Christianity and religious pluralism collided in the 1990s and 2000s with a series of court cases and congressional actions that privileged the chaplain's individual free-exercise rights over his traditional role as the guardian of others' free-exercise rights. Chaplain activities became more obviously sectarian at the same time that religious adherence declined among enlisted personnel. Although the early post-Vietnam responses suggested the Chaplain Corps, wishing to insulate itself from liberal and mainline critiques, might limit some of its chaplains' more evangelical tendencies, chaplains—and eventually chaplain leaders—were emboldened by the rise of the Religious Right within American politics and culture. These shifts ultimately threatened not only the chaplain's traditional role within the military but also the Constitutional assurance against the establishment of religion.

CONCLUSION

In 2003, former chaplain and Vietnam War Medal of Honor recipient Charles Liteky, formerly known as Angelo, again found himself opposed to an American war. He addressed an open letter to American soldiers in Iraq on 7 May of that year. His letter proclaimed that he had renounced his Medal of Honor because "what the U.S. was supporting in El Salvador and Nicaragua, namely the savagery and domination of the poor, reminded me of what I was a part of in Vietnam 15 years earlier." He declared the war against Iraq unjust and unlawful, but he also conceded, "I'm sure you believe that what you are a part of is right and just. I once believed the same of my participation in the Vietnam War."[1] Liteky's post-Vietnam statements revealed deep regret over his own complicity in the Vietnam War, anger and disgust over American foreign policies in the Vietnam and post-Vietnam eras, and a yet-unfinished process of reconciliation and recovery from the war. Following one protest at the School of the Americas, Major General John LeMoyne, the post commander at Fort Benning, called Liteky and invited him to participate in a symposium on human rights. When later he was asked if he thought the Medal of Honor had anything to do with LeMoyne's invitation, Liteky responded, "Yes, I guess I did use the medal consciously. I didn't for a long time, but I see now that it provides me with a certain respectability even though I've renounced it."[2] The significance of Liteky's public actions, such as renouncing the Medal of Honor, relied heavily on his status as a Vietnam veteran, chaplain, and Medal of Honor recipient.

James Johnson, on the other hand, experienced a more typical post-Vietnam journey. After his service in Vietnam, he stayed in the Army as a chaplain, then after retiring from the Army and earning a doctoral degree in counseling, went into civilian pastoral counseling. He believed his experiences in Vietnam helped him in counseling others who experienced severe trauma, including psychological, physical, and sexual abuse and estranged familial relationships. Writing his memoir, *Combat Chaplain: A Thirty Year Vietnam Battle*, helped him to come to terms with some of his Vietnam experiences, and it provided him opportunities to speak with military chaplains who had deployed to Iraq and Afghanistan. He retired in 2005 after being declared permanently disabled from the effects of

PTSD and renal cancer, which he suspects was caused by Agent Orange. Into the twenty-first century, more than forty years after his tour of duty in Vietnam, Johnson maintained close contact with several Vietnam veterans through online e-mail lists and Internet sites.[3] For Johnson, "Vietnam" echoed constantly through his daily routines and activities; he could not leave it behind, and it would not leave him.

Jackson Day had yet a another kind of post-Vietnam experience. He had entered the military chaplaincy because he believed it was the only logical solution to his vocational calling to ministry and his renunciation of conscientious objection as a personal philosophy. "I never made a decision to be a chaplain," said Day. "I made a decision to . . . serve in the Army, and I made a decision to be a minister. Put those things together, and I'm a chaplain." The Vietnam War, however, brought about personal and political crises for Day, as he experienced firsthand the death and destruction wrought by war and the breakup of his first marriage. When he returned from Vietnam, he became active with Vietnam Veterans Against the War and resigned his military commission. For several decades, Day left the ministry altogether, earning a master's degree in Public Health from the University of North Carolina at Chapel Hill and working in the public health sector. Slowly, Day became reacquainted with his own Vietnam story and began building a website to document it. The website put Day in contact with others who served in Vietnam and their family members. He became involved with the group "Vietnam Veteran Ministers," and eventually decided to reestablish himself as a congregational pastor in Maryland.[4]

For Liteky, Johnson, and Day—and nearly 3,000 other chaplains—Vietnam carried an individual burden of experience and memory. Their official positions, unofficial duties, and personal conflict-solving mechanisms placed them firmly in the middle of sometimes converging and sometimes colliding worlds. They lived and worked at the intersection between religion and war, between church and state, between denominational and faith group communities, between Americans and Vietnamese, and between civilian and secular worlds. Chaplains relied on their theological and military training as well as personal moral codes and an understanding of their roles to carry out their work in Vietnam.

Though they performed similar duties and often interpreted their wartime experiences in an explicitly religious light, chaplains' actions in and responses to war in Vietnam were diverse. Some chaplains acted heroically and others avoided risk; some supported the war, and others protested it; most remained in ministry, but a few left it altogether. Chaplains, just as other groups of veterans, did not experience, understand, or remember Vietnam monolithically. The image of all military chaplains conforming to one of the three popular archetypal chaplains—the battlefield hero, the militant legitimizer of war, and the bumbling incompetent—simply does not stand up under scrutiny. At best, we can say there were some of each, though the more likely conclusion is that chaplains, individually and collectively, embodied characteristics of all three archetypes at various times—each of the chaplain types contains truthful observations.

But beyond diversity within the relatively small group of chaplains who wrote publicly about their experiences in Vietnam, certain patterns do emerge. First, and most significantly, I reject the argument that chaplains, as a group, when faced with conflict between military and religious values, were likely to forsake their religious beliefs in favor of military values. Such a view relies on a too easy distinction between "military" and "religious" worldviews and values. In fact, for many chaplains, military and religious values sometimes aligned rather neatly. In cases where the two did seem to conflict, chaplains emphasized different religious values in various situations and often worked to bring religious and military values into the same space. Sometimes, this meant invoking the language, symbols, and rituals of civil religion, which intertwined religious and martial themes. Frequently during the war, chaplains took civilian religious practices and reconstituted them to suit a wartime or combat atmosphere, for instance by altering lyrics to hymns or offering communion to soldiers of all faiths. These acts represented religious reinterpretations, grounded in the experiences of a particular community, place, and time, not perversions of "true" religion. After the war, especially as they reintegrated into civilian religious communities and shared particular presentations of their wartime selves to wider audiences, chaplains tended to interpret wartime experiences through a religious lens, by concluding, for example, that God's power was still evident in the destruction of war.

Second, chaplains broadly understood their primary role in Vietnam to be pastoral rather than prophetic. Most believed that their personal convictions about the morality of war in general or the Vietnam War in particular were irrelevant or at least unimportant to their ability to minister to military personnel serving there. For the most part, they did not find *inherent* contradictions between being faithful and serving in the military. When chaplains were faced with difficult and conflicting choices, the difficulties often stemmed from what appeared to be contradictions *within* a certain religious system rather than between military and religious values or cultures. In fact, examining how chaplains responded to these contradictions in this light helps elucidate the moments when "military" and "religious" worldviews appear to be similar, if not identical. Rather than forsaking religious values, chaplains instead emphasized certain religious outlooks and interpretations over others. Altogether, this emphasis manifested itself most clearly in the chaplains' pastoral focus. Perhaps the most obvious example is the overall pattern of how chaplains responded to witnessing or hearing about atrocities or war crimes in the Vietnam War. Even in the face of a clear moral wrong and the opportunity to voice prophetic claims, chaplains frequently privileged their role as pastor and comforter over that of prophet and adviser. The choices chaplains made were often morally and ethically problematic, to be sure, but they cannot be written off as irreligious or perversions of "true" religious faith.

Third, many chaplains, like other Vietnam veterans, experienced a sense of alienation from both religious and secular civilian communities as a result of their service in Vietnam, yet the overall narrative from chaplain veterans of Vietnam is remarkably positive. In terms of relating to civilian communities, many were angered by media portrayals of Vietnam soldiers and veterans, while others were dismayed by what they viewed as a shortage of institutional denominational support. A few chaplains' memoirs and postwar writings mirror the major historiographical interpretation that the military's ability to win in Vietnam was undermined by weak political decision making, but most focus on the more personal narrative of experience and faith. And it is in these narratives that the difference between chaplains' writing and that of other service members is most plainly evident. Chaplains had access to religious idioms and philosophies that eased their transition back to the world and allowed them to make sense of the war. Overwhelmingly, they wrote that the war strengthened their faith and ministry, that the Vietnam War was proof of God's sovereignty, that they found God even in the midst of hell. These observations were strikingly different in tone and conclusion from the vast corpus of Vietnam War first-person writing by nonchaplain participants.

Chaplains' individual experiences and reflections about the Vietnam War are also significant because they speak to broader unresolved debates within Vietnam War scholarship. First, and most important, chaplain accounts provide a more complex picture of religious responses to the Vietnam War, countering a dominant narrative of religious dissent and protest about the war. Chaplains' responses ranged widely, and discounting their religious language about the war as the product of co-option by the military is misleading. Second, chaplains' postwar reflections, namely memoirs and other first-person accounts, offer insights into noncombatant, nonminority men's experiences of war. In Vietnam in particular, where so few personnel were involved in direct combat, uncovering noncombatant voices helps to produce a fuller understanding of the war effort and its long-lasting psychological and cultural effects. Chaplains' recollections may also be useful for considering other dual-profession military officers such as doctors and lawyers. People in these professions who serve in the military have to deal with two sets of professional norms and values, which may not always be compatible.

Yet it is important to remember that individual chaplains' accounts are also part of larger institutional and cultural stories. The military chaplaincy—as an institution, as a bureaucracy, and as a group of people—also underwent significant changes in the wake of Vietnam. Demographically, the chaplaincy became more conservative and more evangelical after the Vietnam War. As more conservative Christians entered the chaplaincy, judicial challenges and the cultural prominence of conservative religious and political beliefs increased the sectarian nature of the chaplaincy. Some chaplains asserted their free-exercise rights to the detriment of the chaplaincy's historically ecumenical focus. At the same time, the military's religious diversity increased, as did the number of religious groups that supplied military chaplains. In the early 1970s, the Chaplain Corps commissioned female chaplains for the first time, indicating a more progressive stance on the issue of ordaining women than many of the chaplaincy's conservative supporters would have liked. The Chaplain Corps received strident criticism for its ineffectiveness in reporting and preventing war crimes and atrocities in Vietnam, and partly in response to that issue, the chaplaincy reorganized itself to be more responsive to small forward operating units. Chaplains who attended the Army War College determined that "Vietnam" represented a wide-scale failure for the chaplaincy, even if individual chaplains did succeed in ministry. And as was the case for individual chaplains, the specter of Vietnam haunted the military chaplaincy for the next several decades, especially as the United States found itself in other unpopular wars against insurgent forces in Iraq and Afghanistan and continued to face questions about diversity and inclusion.

Chaplains' experiences and public debate about their proper role within the military also revealed broader cultural uncertainty about America's religious and civic faith and foreign policy. At the beginning of the Cold War, many Americans coalesced around the language of civil religion and anti-Communism. Civil religious language relied on shared cultural assumptions about the Judeo-Christian foundations of the United States, the value of free exercise of religion, and the belief that the United States occupied a particular place in God's plan. Faced with an imposing Soviet threat and the specter of Communist revolutions worldwide, Americans—even many without a personal religious system—used the language of civil religion to define the foundations of the anti-Communist struggle. While there were significant variations in the ways religious groups thought the United States should confront a Communist enemy, the language of civil religion provided common tropes and images that papered over some of these differences.

Then, as American involvement in Vietnam expanded and as protest at home escalated, civil religious language was insufficient to unite Americans around a common cause, and deep disagreements about faith and war came to the fore. Chaplains, especially those from mainline and liberal denominations, experienced significant alienation from their denominational communities, which claimed that chaplains should act as prophetic voices within (and against) the military. Chaplains, former chaplains, and civilians engaged in debates about civilianizing the chaplaincy or at least stripping away the chaplain's military trappings of rank and uniform. Those who were opposed to the Vietnam War generally advocated a revamped and civilianized chaplaincy system, while those who supported its cause thought the established system produced the most beneficial outcomes. The debate over the Vietnam War and over the chaplaincy marked a significant point in the growing divide between liberals and conservatives in the United States. Liberal disillusionment with the chaplaincy, coupled with the military's new personnel policies, resulted in a sharp increase in the number of conservative and evangelical chaplains. Litigation that challenged the chaplaincy left it with a more limited mandate—to secure the right to free exercise of religion for all military personnel. And chaplains sought, and in some cases won, such free-exercise rights for themselves as well. This move toward conservatism and individualism in many cases destroyed or damaged the chaplain's position as a person in the middle.

After Vietnam, the institutional chaplaincy set out to correct its mistakes and to accommodate a diversifying military and a homogenizing Chaplain Corps. Due to a constant shortage of Catholic, Jewish, and liturgical Protestant chaplains, the Chaplain Corps abandoned the quota system that had been the basis for chaplain appointments for decades, opting instead to accept the best-qualified chaplains for available slots. They also altered the way chaplains were assigned to units, emphasizing long-term connections with smaller units rather than assigning chaplains for deployment overseas more randomly. The chaplaincy revamped its involvement with military character education programs, reducing the curriculum's religious content and undertones. In the late 1970s and 1980s, the chaplaincy shifted emphasis away from combat operations and toward garrison ministry, especially to military families. By the 1990s, the Chaplain Corps placed a new emphasis on its role in peacekeeping and nation-building operations, asserting that chaplains' education, intercultural training, and clerical authority could be an asset to the military in hostile areas. The changing demographics of the U.S. military would also prove a formidable challenge to the contemporary chaplaincy.[5]

Considered broadly, the chaplaincy offers a site for scholars to study civil-military relations and the church-state relationship in the United States. First, Vietnam-era trends in American religion, specifically in American Christianity, namely the move away from denominational alignment and toward alignment along political lines, deeply affected the Chaplain Corps' mission and individual chaplain's experiences.[6] The military relied on (and continues to rely on) civilian religious institutions to supply it with chaplain ministers, and this relationship deserves more consideration. Understanding chaplains' experiences also indicates some ways in which civilian religious culture and military culture enter into dialogue with one another—each providing language and images useful to the other. Second, the chaplaincy's shifting organizational culture and mission may be indicative of changes within the church-state relationship, in which religion and politics are inexorably intertwined with one another. By regulating the chaplaincy, the military—and therefore the federal government—is frequently in the position of commenting on or even regulating the religious practice of its members. The military provides an especially good site for testing the limits of the guarantee of the free exercise of religion.

Following the terrorist attacks on the United States in 2001, and the subsequent military operations in Afghanistan and Iraq, the relationship between religion and warfare has again come to the forefront of public discussion. Americans learned about jihad—at least superficially—and many painted the fight against terrorism in apocalyptic and cosmic terms.[7] As in Vietnam, chaplains became embroiled in these issues as they ministered to military personnel in the field and again became symbols for religious faith and practice in a time of war. In February 2003, the U.S. Army charged Muslim chaplain James Yee, a West Point graduate, who was providing spiritual care for detainees at the U.S. naval base at Guantanamo Bay, Cuba, with sedition, aiding the enemy, spying, espionage, and failure to obey a general order, after he was suspected of leaking classified information to the enemy. As a chaplain, Yee had almost constant, private access to detainees and was protected by pastoral privilege. The charges against Yee were dropped in 2004; he resigned and was granted an honorable discharge later that year.[8]

As the American wars in Iraq and Afghanistan began, and as they claimed thousands of lives, were protested, forgotten, surged, and eventually drawn down, the subject of religion in relation to the military mission and personnel retained an important place in public debate. Several chaplains who served in Iraq or Afghanistan published memoirs or collections of spiritual meditations soon after their return stateside.[9] A number of other chaplains have been interviewed by the mainstream or religious press.[10] The Internet only served to increase the amount of information available about the military chaplaincy and the Iraq war. The rapidity and democracy with which information and opinion is now disseminated and evaluated marked a significant change between the Vietnam War and the Iraq war, but the sides of the debate were largely the same, with one important exception: Liberal and mainline churches critical of the war were largely silent on the issue of chaplains being complicit in the immorality of war, reflecting the broad trend toward expressing "support" for American troops even if one is against the war. One of the few major criticisms of chaplains came from the organization Americans United for Separation of Church and State (AUSCS), which claimed that a Southern Baptist chaplain in Iraq was proselytizing and overstepping boundaries by offering soldiers food and fresh water in exchange for listening to a sermon and being baptized. Yet the AUSCS stopped well short of suggesting that federally funded chaplains had no place at all in war, instead emphasizing the chaplains' historical ecumenical responsibilities.[11] Even the *Christian Century*, which opposed the invasion of Iraq from the beginning and is traditionally antiwar, carried advertisements for military chaplain volunteers.[12] Chaplains' assertion of their pastoral role within the military had taken hold, even among vocal opponents of the war. Throughout the first decade of the twenty-first century, in fact, religious communities argued vociferously about the religious implications of the justifications for the two wars, American policies on torture and the treatment of prisoners and detainees, the killing of civilians with unmanned drone airstrikes, and the relationship between American service members, Muslim clerics, and local leaders. On the issue of military chaplains, however, the primary public debate was over the chaplain's methods, limits, and purpose rather than the legality or basic morality of having federally funded military chaplaincies.

Importantly, in the early twenty-first century, conservative and evangelical Christians voiced many of the same complaints about chaplains' ministries being muzzled that liberal and mainline groups did during the Vietnam era. But, whereas liberal and mainline groups couched the criticism in terms of questioning the chaplain's ability to faithfully practice a prophetic ministry that spoke out against the Vietnam War, conservative and evangelical critics of the chaplaincy during the wars in Afghanistan and Iraq framed it as an issue of restricting a chaplain's religious freedom. The fundamental questions, however, were the same—what was the primary role for chaplains? To whom did chaplains owe their primary allegiance? Did chaplains have to forsake religious beliefs in order to comply with military directives? And, finally, was it possible for chaplains to retain their own religious beliefs and integrity while faithfully executing the ecumenical and interfaith nature of their military assignment? For chaplains in the Vietnam War, the answer to this last question was a resounding "yes." Consistently, chaplains across the religious and political spectrum used their liminal position to cross cultural boundaries and to emphasize their role in caring for the spiritual needs of service members. Casting contemporary debates in this historical framework helps to clarify the fundamental issues at stake, as it seems that many conservative chaplains have reached different conclusions to the same questions, arguing that the requirements for diversity and inclusion in the contemporary military infringe on the particular requirements of their individual faiths.

In Vietnam, concern about the chaplaincy and chaplains' experiences reflected and even foreshadowed the national crisis over the Vietnam War and its memory. Religious Americans struggled over the proper role of military chaplains, and military chaplains, both during and after the war, wrestled with their involvement in Vietnam. In relating to war and politics, modern American religious communities and followers have had a broad range of responses available to them. Some have used the voice of religious authority to question and criticize the use of violence to solve political problems; they have stood in judgment of the United States and its actions abroad. Others have used religious ideas and language to justify full-throated support for American wars, foreign policy, and political maneuvering. Ultimately, though contradictory in their conclusions, both positions rely on a prophetic foundation for relating religious faith to the realm of war and politics. In the midst of these booming voices—broadcast loudly by national media, parachurch organizations, and public religious leaders—there have been (and are) other religious responses to war and politics as well. These voices are quieter, and more ambivalent—high-lighting both tensions and sympathies between religion and warfare. They reveal the complexity of religion as it is lived and practiced in people's day-to-day lives, and they illuminate the many ways in which private religious practice and beliefs can have significant institutional and widespread cul-tural consequences.

NOTES

Abbreviations Used in the Notes

CMH United States Center of Military History, Fort Leslie J. McNair, Washington, D.C.

NARA National Archives of the United States, Archives II, College Park, Md.

RG 247 Office of the Chief of Chaplains Central File

RG 472 Records of the United States Army Vietnam

USACHCS United States Army Chaplain Center and School Library, Fort Jackson, Columbia, S.C.

USMHI United States Military History Institute, Carlisle, Pa.

Introduction

1. The idea of certain groups or individuals operating in the literal and figurative space where two or more cultures meet is a common one in historical studies. Though several words are commonly used to express such ideas—"liminal," "frontier," "middle ground," "cultural mediator"—the ideas themselves are similar, namely that there are some spaces in which cultural exchange takes place more readily than others and there are certain people who facilitate such exchanges. For the sake of simplicity and clarity, I have chosen "people in the middle" to designate this concept. The idea, however, is informed by a general reading of global history literature and American history literature—particularly in the areas of civil rights and religious movements. Some important works that have informed my conceptualization of chaplains as people in the middle are Lepore, "Dead Men Tell No Tales"; Lepore, *The Name of War*; White, *Middle Ground*; Morris, *Origins of the Civil Rights Movement*; Robnett, *How Long? How Long?*; Dudziak, *Cold War Civil Rights*; and Nepstad, *Convictions of the Soul*. On the anthropological theoretical construct of liminality, see Turner, *Rites of Passage*; Turner "Liminality and Communitas"; Turner, "Passages, Margins, and Poverty"; and Karen J. Diefendorf, "The Military as a Ritual Society," *Army Chaplaincy* (Summer–Fall 1997).

2. The distinction between a "priest" and a "prophet" is originally Max Weber's. See Chapter 5 for an extended discussion of this framework. Anne Loveland has further argued that while mainline churches may have emphasized the prophetic role of the minister during war, chaplains viewed their roles as primarily pastoral, requiring them to minister to troops in Vietnam regardless of their personal attitudes toward the war. Toward the end of the war, Loveland claims, chaplains and the chaplaincy moved to a third model, one of institutional ministry, which made the military itself a primary focus for chaplain activities after the Vietnam War. See Loveland, "Prophetic Ministry."

3. For an extended discussion of role conflict and military chaplains, see Chapter 3.

4. See, for example, Kurzman, *No Greater Glory,* and The Immortal Chaplains Foundation, www.immortalchaplains.org (accessed 22 March 2013).

5. Official site for the Cause of Canonization of Servant of God Reverend Vincent Robert Capodanno, http://www.vincentcapodanno.org (accessed 22 March 2013). See also Mode, *Grunt Padre,* 77.

6. *Full Metal Jacket* (dir. Stanley Kubrick, Warner Bros., 1977).

7. "Praise the Lord and Pass the Ammunition," lyrics and music by Frank Loesser, Famous Music Corp., 1942. Later inquiries about the incident suggest that the chaplain in question, Howell Forgy, did not actually man the gun but instead had used the phrase to motivate the men along the firing line.

8. O'Neill, "True Story of the Patton Prayer."

9. *M*A*S*H* (dir. Robert Altman, Aspen Productions, 1970); Vea, *Gods Go Begging*; Melville, *Billy Budd.* The Father Mulcahy figure in the *M*A*S*H* television series is significantly more complicated, as his character develops over the course of eleven seasons to take on characteristics of all three archetypes. In this sense, the television version of the famous fictional chaplain may be as close to an "ideal type" as one might see in popular culture.

10. Bergen, introduction to *Sword of the Lord.*

11. Snape, *Royal Army Chaplains' Department.*

12. See especially Deuteronomy 20:2–4. In 2003, Muslim chaplain James Yee was arrested for sedition and charged with passing classified information to detainees at the U.S. naval base at Guantanamo Bay, Cuba. The charges were eventually dropped, and Yee gained an honorable discharge from the Army. See Yee and Molloy, *For God and Country,* and James Yee's official website, http://www.justiceforyee.com (accessed 22 March 2013).

13. On the Canadian Chaplain Corps' history, see "Canadian Forces Chaplain Branch" at http://www.cmp-cpm.forces.gc.ca/cfcb-bsafc/index-eng.asp (accessed 1 July 2013); on Royal Army chaplains, see Snape, *Royal Army Chaplain's Department*; on American Chaplain Corps' history, see Williams, "Chaplaincy in the Armed Forces of the United States," and Office of the Chief of Chaplains series, "The United States Army Chaplaincy," including Thompson, *From Its European Antecedents*; Norton, *Struggling for Recognition*; Stover, *Up from Handymen*; Gushwa, *The Best and the Worst of Times*; Venzke, *Confidence in Battle, Inspiration in Peace*; Ackermann, *He Was Always There*; and Brinsfield, *Encouraging Faith, Supporting Soldiers.*

14. See Bergen, introduction to *Sword of the Lord,* 4; and Slomovitz, *Fighting Rabbis,* 1–3.

15. Bergen, introduction to *Sword of the Lord,* 8; Slomovitz, *Fighting Rabbis,* 4.

16. On religion in the colonial and revolutionary eras, see Bonomi, *Under the Cope of Heaven*; Ahern, *Rhetoric of War*; Williams, *Soldiers of God*; and Cox, *Proper Sense of Honor.* On the American Civil War, see Brinsfield, *Faith in the Fight*; Miller, Stout, and Wilson, *Religion and the American Civil War*; Noll, *Civil War as a Theological Crisis*; and Corby, *Memoirs of Chaplain Life.* On the development of the American military chaplaincy, see Budd, *Serving Two Masters.*

17. On the lack of religion as a serious analytical category in histories of the twentieth-century United States, see Butler, "Jack in the Box Faith," and Schultz and Harvey, "Everywhere and Nowhere."

18. On the religious lives of American soldiers in the First World War, see Ebel, *Faith in the Fight*; on Woodrow Wilson's religious faith, see Tucker, *Woodrow Wilson*; on Progressivism, religion, and World War I, see Gamble, *War for Righteousness*; on the Peace Progressives, see Dawley, *Changing the World*; on religious pacifism from World War I to Vietnam, see Appelbaum, *Protestant Pacifist Culture*.

19. See Wuthnow, *Restructuring of American Religion*. The role of formal religious institutions, traditions, and practices on the Axis side is significantly more complicated. See Bergen, *Twisted Cross*; Faulkner, "Against Bolshevism"; and Syka, *Japan's Holy War*.

20. See Stittser, *Cautious Patriotism*.

21. The relationship between the American religious tradition and the Cold War is discussed at length in Chapter 1.

22. In his historiographical essay about religion and foreign relations in *Diplomatic History* Andrew Preston argued that scholars should look more closely at the links between the two and used the extensive scholarship on religious dissent for the Vietnam War as evidence of the possibilities. Preston even suggested that the most fruitful areas for research in this area lay outside of the "Truman, Eisenhower, and Vietnam War eras," because the literature on such dissent is extensive and persuasive. See Andrew Preston, "Bridging the Gap."

23. See, for example, Hall, *Because of their Faith*; Gill, *Embattled Ecumenism*; Gill, "Political Price of Prophetic Leadership"; Polner and O'Grady, *Disarmed and Dangerous*; Garrow, *Bearing the Cross*; Goldstein, *William Sloane Coffin, Jr.*; and Hulsether, *Building a Protestant Left*. On the antiwar movement in general, see Small, *Antiwarriors*, and Hall, *Rethinking the American Anti-War Movement*.

24. On the debate about Vietnam within the American Christian community, see Settje, *Faith and War*. For scholarly analysis of the religious aspect of the antiwar movement, see DeBenedetti and Chatfield, *American Ordeal*, and Friedland, *Lift Up Your Voice*. During the Vietnam War itself, religious groups and presses published a significant amount of dissenting literature. See, for example, Hamilton, *Vietnam War*, which includes antiwar sermons and essays from a variety of Christian preachers and leaders.

25. The specific case for "role conflict" as the primary paradigm for understanding chaplains' experiences is discussed in more depth in Chapter 3. The "two masters" dilemma stems from the Christian scripture that warns, "No slave can serve two masters; for a slave will either hate the one and love the other, or be devoted to the one and despise the other. You cannot serve God and wealth" (Luke 16:13). While the scripture refers specifically to wealth and God, theologians have interpreted it more widely and understand it to mean that humans cannot be faithful to both God and a secular entity or object.

26. Charles (Angelo) Liteky quoted in Michael Taylor, "A Matter of Honor: He Gave Back His Medal of Honor to Risk His Freedom in Protesting His Country's Policies," *San Francisco Chronicle*, 13 March 2000.

27. Ibid.

28. Liteky, "Congressional Medal of Honor Recipient Addresses U.S. Forces in Iraq."

29. Ibid.

30. Shy cited the brutality of the Second World War and the "surprising ferocity of the Civil War" as prime examples of when such approaches might be useful. See Shy, "Cultural Approach," 14.

31. Lynn, *Battle*.

32. Lee, "Mind and Matter."

33. Black, "Determinisms and Other Issues," 1218.

34. Lee, "Mind and Matter," 1118.

35. See, for example, Toews, "Intellectual History"; Scott, "Evidence of Experience"; Smith, "Paul Fussell's *The Great War and Modern Memory*"; White, "Telling More"; Klein, "On the Emergence of Memory"; Radstone, "Working with Memory"; Winter and Sivan, "Setting the Framework"; Bal, Crewe, and Spitzer, *Acts of Memory*; Struken, *Tangled Memories*; and Nord, "The Uses of Memory."

36. Louise White, writing about rumor, has argued that "historians could read in the inaccurate, the fantastic, and the constructed a world of . . . peoples we would not otherwise see." Memoirs allow historians to see those worlds "glimpsed through the fantastic and constructed accounts," and to come up with "a more specific version of events than we'd had before." White urges historians to move beyond the dichotomy of true and false, in which "false" accounts are simply discounted. "Fears and fantasies are situated in distinctive terrain," she wrote. "The power and importance of the made-up . . . are precisely that they are made up . . . they have to be constituted by what is credible. The imaginary and the fantastic must be constructed out of what is socially conceivable. . . . For historians, the invented account is at least as good as the accurate one." See White, "Telling More," 14.

Chapter One

1. Silk, "Notes on the Judeo-Christian Tradition in America"; Mazur, *Americanization of Religious Minorities*.

2. Bradley, *Imagining Vietnam and America*.

3. On the relationship between European democracies, American involvement in Indochina, and the Cold War, see Lawrence, *Assuming the Burden*.

4. See, for example, "Reds Step Up Support," *New York Times*, 24 January 1950, and "Reds in Control of Viet Minh," *New York Times*, 28 March 1950.

5. Tillman Durdin, "Quick U.S. Aid Held Vital to Vietnam," *New York Times*, 9 March 1950; CIA report, "Consequences to the U.S. of Communist Domination of Mainland Southeast Asia," 13 October 1950, quoted in Lawrence, *Assuming the Burden*, 6.

6. See Fall, *Hell in a Very Small Place*; Nordell, *Undetected Enemy*; and Giap, *Dien Bien Phu*.

7. On the relationship between the Americans and the South Vietnamese government, see Jacobs, *America's Miracle Man in Vietnam*, and Jacobs, *Cold War Mandarin*.

8. Historians of the 1950s have recently called to our attention the multiple ways in which the older story of the so-called liberal consensus falls apart under scrutiny. For example, see May, *Big Tomorrow*, and Sugrue, *Origins of the Urban Crisis*. On the issue of divergent civil religions, Robert Wuthnow has argued that a distinction has emerged since the 1960s between conservative and liberal Protestants; see "Divided We Fall: America's Two Civil Religions," *Christian Century*, 20 April 1988, 395–99.

9. Bellah, "Civil Religion in America"; Richey and Jones, *Civil Religion in America*; Hammond et al., "Forum: American Civil Religion Revisited."

10. Poll cited in Carroll, Johnson, and Marty, *Religion in America 1950 to the Present*.

11. See Miller, *Errand into the Wilderness*; Butler, *Awash in a Sea of Faith*; Bonomi, *Under the Cope of Heaven*; Miller, Stout, and Wilson, *Religion and the American Civil War*; Snay, *Gospel of Disunion*; and Wilson, *Baptized in Blood*.

12. See, for example, Ahlstrom, *Religious History of the American People*, and Albanese, *Sons of the Fathers*.

13. Bellah joined a long line of scholars interested in the "general" religion of the United States, naming more definitively what historian Sidney Mead called the "religion of the Republic" and theologian and sociologist Will Herberg called the "American Way of Life." But it was Bellah's term and conception that sparked the longest-lasting interest and debate, appearing as it did in the middle of the national crisis of Vietnam. Sidney Mead coined the phrase "religion of the republic" in his book *The Nation with the Soul of a Church*, 94; see also Herberg, *Protestant, Catholic, Jew*.

14. Bellah, "Civil Religion in America," 14.

15. Herberg, *Protestant, Catholic, Jew*, 35.

16. Ibid., 39.

17. Ibid., 75.

18. Ibid.

19. Richard Hutcheson identified this ideological makeup as "common denominator religion" in his book *Churches and the Chaplaincy*, 54.

20. Historian of religion Martin Marty has suggested four manifestations of civil religion in the United States. His typology included four combinations of characteristics, all of which are appropriately identified as expressions of civil religion. First, there are categories of civil religion: the "Under-God" type and the "transcendent nation" type. Within each of those categories, there existed two modes of expression—priestly and prophetic. These four categories of civil religion help explain how such divergent political, theological, scriptural, national, and ecclesiastical views could participate in a public culture that seemed to integrate discussions of "God" and "Country." Marty's typology challenged assumptions about a unified American "civil religion" or a shared American "religious culture" based on ill-understood ideas of a "Judeo-Christian" tradition. Marty suggested this typology in his essay "Two Kinds of Civil Religion."

21. See Herzog, *Spiritual-Industrial Complex*. For historical trends and contemporary data, see Gallup, "Religion," http://www.gallup.com/poll/1690/religion.aspx (accessed 1 July 2013). For an extended analysis of this poll question and the

likely over-reporting of church attendance, see Hadaway and Marler, "Did You Really Go to Church This Week? Behind the Poll Data," *Christian Century*, 6 May 1998, 472–75; Hadaway, Marler, and Chaves, "Overreporting Church Attendance in America"; and Hadaway, Long, and Marler, "What the Polls Don't Show." By way of comparison, no more than 20 percent of Britons surveyed with the same question said they had attended church in the last week.

22. Eisenhower quoted in *New York Times*, 23 December 1952.

23. Marty, *Under God, Indivisible*, 806.

24. Ibid., 302.

25. Carroll, Johnson, and Marty, *Religion in America*, 15, fig. 3. Other rates were United Presbyterian, +11 percent; Southern Baptist, +27.2 percent; Seventh-Day Adventist, +31.5 percent; Presbyterian U.S., +17.2 percent; Lutheran Church–Missouri Synod, +34.4 percent; Lutheran Church in America, +22.4 percent; Episcopal, +20.2 percent; Church of the Nazarene, +27.9 percent; and Roman Catholic, +38.5 percent.

26. Ibid., 19–20.

27. Hadaway and Marler, "Did You Really Go to Church This Week?"

28. The most explicit statement of this foundation came from Herberg in *Protestant, Catholic, Jew*.

29. For extended discourse analysis of how Christians debated the early Cold War, see Settje, *Faith and War*.

30. See, for example, Settje, *Lutherans and the Longest War,* 7–9.

31. Wald, "Religious Dimension of American Anti-Communism." The idea of "social sacralization" is a specific reference to Emile Durkheim's work on the social aspects of religious organization, practice, and belief.

32. Ibid.

33. Ibid.

34. Day, "Our Communist Brothers."

35. Marty, "Reinhold Niebuhr: Public Theology." Marty made the case for Niebuhr as a embodying both the religious and political strands of public theology, as he was well-known and well-respected in religious and political communities. Eric R. Crouse argued that conservative Protestants were more forceful in promoting their anti-Communist ideals than liberal Protestants and that the public rhetoric of ministers like Graham marked the popularly held "Christian" view during the early Cold War. See Crouse, "Popular Cold Warriors."

36. On Niebuhr, see especially Sizemore, "Reinhold Niebuhr"; Marty, "Reinhold Niebuhr and the Irony of American History"; Lovin, *Reinhold Niebuhr and Christian Realism*; Schlesinger "Reinhold Niebuhr's Role"; and Fox, "Reinhold Niebuhr."

37. Sizemore, "Reinhold Niebuhr," iii.

38. Craig, "New Meaning of Modern War," 687.

39. Graham, *Christianism vs. Communism*, 3.

40. Ibid.

41. Graham quoted in Marty, *Under God, Indivisible*, 330.

42. Matthews, "Reds and Our Churches," *American Mercury*, July 1953, 3–13.

43. "How Red is the National Council of Churches?," pamphlet cited in Settje, *Lutherans and the Longest War*, 67.

44. See Wuthnow, *Restructuring of American Religion*.

45. For a general history of Army chaplains in the post–World War II period, see Venzke, *Confidence in Battle*.

46. Harry T. Vaughn quoted in Venzke, *Confidence in Battle*, 5–6; for a later instance of a similar critique, see Mark A. Golub, "Some War-Like Chaplains," *Jewish Advocate*, 23 October 1969.

47. Until 1953, when it created a separate training program, Air Force chaplains trained at the Army Chaplain School. A formal Air Force Chaplain School was not established until 1960; the Navy established an independent chaplain school in 1951. All of the chaplain schools were consolidated in 2009 after the 2005 Base Realignment and Closure (BRAC) agreement, and the school is now located at Fort Jackson, S.C.

48. Office of the Chief of Chaplains Report to the Secretary of the Army, 25 October 1951, NARA RG 247, file 319.1.

49. Venzke, *Confidence in Battle*, 126–27.

50. Department of War, *Program for National Security*, 52–53.

51. Truman, "Address before a Joint Session of the Congress," 404–13.

52. For a more extended discussion of UMT proposals, see Hogan, *Cross of Iron*, 126–30; and Friedberg, *In the Shadow of the Garrison State*.

53. "Church Unit Bars Military Training," *New York Times*, 19 November 1947; What of UMT?," *United Evangelical Action*, 15 February 1952, 7. See also Loveland, *American Evangelicals*, and Gustafson, "Church, State, and Cold War." Some evangelical groups were more supportive of legislation that would provide for peacetime conscription, but most liberal groups opposed this measure as well, again citing their fear of militarism and militarization of the United States.

54. Committee on Religion and Welfare in the Armed Forces, "Military Chaplaincy," 19.

55. Loveland, "Morale Builders."

56. Ibid., 234.

57. Venzke, *Confidence in Battle*, 71–72.

58. Ibid., 73.

59. Department of the Navy, *History of the Chaplain Corps, United States Navy*, 2–3.

60. Ibid., 5.

61. See Chapter 2 for a more extended discussion of military chaplains' initial responses to the Vietnam War.

62. Venzke, *Confidence in Battle*, 72.

63. Ibid., 65–66.

64. Carl R. Hudson quoted in ibid., 68.

65. On the treatment of chaplains and POWs in North Korea and losing chaplains in combat, particularly after the Chinese intervention, see Venzke, *Confidence in Battle*, 83–86.

66. Frank Tobey, "Character Guidance Program," *Army Information Digest* 14 (October 1949), quoted in Loveland, "Morale Builders," 235.

67. See Loveland, *American Evangelicals*, for an extensive overview of the Evangelical mission to the military throughout the Cold War.

68. Lockerbie, *Man Under Orders,* 136.

69. Loveland, *American Evangelicals*, 42–43. For Harrison's full biography, see Lockerbie, *Man Under Orders*.

70. Phil Landrum, "Missionary to the Military," *United Evangelical Action*, July 1966, 8, and Orville McCormack, "Can a Man Serve God in the Military?," *Pentecostal Evangel*, 1 July 1962, 24–25, quoted in Loveland, *American Evangelicals*, 72.

71. Claude Chilton, *The Nazarene Serviceman* (Kansas City, Mo.), 1953, 14, quoted in Loveland, *American Evangelicals*, 4.

72. Loveland, *American Evangelicals*, 4; "Drafted to What?," *United Evangelical Action*, 1 November 1950, 9, quoted in ibid.

73. On mainline religious responses to the use of atomic weapons, see Hiebert, *Impact of Atomic Energy*, and Farrell, "Thomas Merton and the Religion of the Bomb."

74. For example, when leaders from the Lutheran World Federation (LWF), a left-leaning organization, planned a visit to the Soviet-satellite Baltic states, Soviet officials blocked their visit to Estonia at the last minute, claiming that the archbishop was seriously ill. This move by the Soviet Union intensified LWF commitment to battling Communism in Christian terms. See Settje, *Lutherans Longest War*, 35.

75. Moise, "Recent Accounts," 344.

76. A heated historiographical debate exists about the extent to which Diem's government was installed and propped up with the help of American politicians and over whether or not the regime was simply a puppet for American policies. See especially Catton, *Diem's Final Failure*; Lawrence, *Assuming the Burden*; Chapman, "Staging Democracy"; Miller, "Vision, Power and Agency"; Jacobs, *America's Miracle Man in Vietnam*; Jacobs, *Cold War Mandarin*; and Moyar, *Triumph Forsaken*.

77. See, for example, "Vietnam Controversy," *Commonweal*, 26 July 1963, 444–45; "Vietnam Repression," *Commonweal*, 6 September 1963, 524–25; "Brutality in Vietnam," *Christian Century,* 31 July 1963, 950; and "Diem Rebuked," *America,* 29 June 1963, 895. Mark Moyar offers a counterpoint to this assessment, arguing that Western protestations about religious freedom abuses were overblown and not common among the South Vietnamese. See *Triumph Forsaken*, 216–18.

78. See, for example, "More War or Less in Vietnam?," *Christian Century*, 11 March 1964, 326, and Reinhold Niebuhr, "President Johnson's Foreign Policy," *Christianity and Crisis*, 16 March 1964, 31–32.

79. "The Last Battle in Asia," *Christianity Today*, 19 June 1964, 23. See also Toulouse, "Christian Responses to Vietnam," 5.

80. Venzke, *Confidence in Battle*, 2; Bergsma, *Chaplains with Marines in Vietnam*, 1.

81. John A. Lindvall to Edward M. Mize, 12 April 1962, quoted in Venzke, *Confidence in Battle*, 146. Mize was the staff chaplain at the Ryuku Islands Headquarters.

82. Bergsma, *Chaplains with Marines*, 4.

83. Venzke, *Confidence in Battle*, 149.

84. Andrews, interview.

85. Ibid.

86. Ibid.

Chapter Two

1. Venzke, *Confidence in Battle,* 139; Summers, *Vietnam War Almanac.*

2. Venzke, *Confidence in Battle*, 139.

3. Moore, Bergsma, and Demy, *Chaplains with U.S. Naval Units*, 17–28.

4. The nature of Kennedy's legacy and plans for Vietnam are contested. Some have argued that Kennedy was looking to extricate the United States from direct involvement in Southeast Asia, while others argue that he was likely to continue on a path to escalation. See Kaiser, *American Tragedy;* Logevall, *Choosing War;* and Hunt, *Lyndon Johnson's War.*

5. Duiker, "Waging Revolutionary War."

6. The increased push from the North Vietnamese, the revolving door of Saigon governments, and the ominous warnings from Johnson's foreign policy advisers that the Kennedy-style programs were unlikely to work given the state of the ARVN prompted a reevaluation of Vietnam policy within the Johnson administration. On these issues, see Logevall, *Choosing War*, xvi. Logevall's argument runs counter to those expressed in books such as Gelb and Betts, *Irony of Vietnam*; Barrett, *Uncertain Warriors*; Kolko, *Anatomy of a War*; and Chomsky, *Rethinking Camelot*, which generally argue that beyond 1964, U.S. policy-makers faced a limited choices about Vietnam policy.

7. After the alleged attack on two American destroyers in the Tonkin Gulf by North Vietnamese vessels, Johnson ordered a strike on North Vietnamese naval bases and asked Congress to authorize the use of military force in Vietnam. On the Gulf of Tonkin incident, see Moïse, *Tonkin Gulf.*

8. Johnson's decision to escalate the war by sending American combat troops to Vietnam was not an easy one—especially given his desire to focus on realizing the Great Society promised by an aggressive and liberal domestic agenda. To fight a war in Vietnam might mean sacrificing the War on Poverty, which Johnson was eager to wage as much for his political reputation as for any societal benefit.

9. Bergsma, *Chaplains with Marines*, 4; and Moore, Bergsma, and Demy, *Chaplains with U.S. Naval Units.*

10. The battle of the Ia Drang Valley in November 1965 seemed to some to prove the operational potential of the basic concept of these large-unit operations. For an account of the battle, see Moore and Galloway, *We Were Soldiers*; on the Ia Drang Valley as a proof of the Army Operational concept, see Krepinevich, *Army in Vietnam*; for a counterpoint to Krepinevich, see Westmoreland, *Soldier Reports.*

11. Consistently, Westmoreland was given more resources but always less than he wanted, and build up in the rear—at large bases, such as those at Long Binh, Tan Son Nhut, or Qui Nonh—did not always result in greatly increased field strength.

12. Venzke, *Confidence in Battle*, 144.

13. Estes, *Paratrooper Chaplain*, 162–63.

14. In 1967, the United States moved to coordinate its nation-building and pacification efforts under one organizational umbrella, the Office of Civil Operations and Rural Development Support (CORDS). Additionally, the Marines formed Combined Action Platoons (CAP)—composed of a squad of Marines and local South Vietnamese Regional and Popular Forces—who would live and work in a single village to establish close ties with the local community in order to prevent Viet Cong infiltration and influence. On the CAP program, see Krepinevich, *Army in Vietnam*; on CORDS, see Daddis, *No Sure Victory*, 115–26.

15. Some claim that this was a fundamental strategic shift, while others argue that it was evidence that NVA and VC strength had been severely damaged after the Tet Offensive and were therefore biding their time and rebuilding their capabilities under Abrams's tenure. On the Tet Offensive and its consequences, see Spector, *After Tet*. For a laudatory account of Abrams's tenure as MACV commander, see Sorley, *A Better War*.

16. Johnson, interview.

17. William R. Goldie, interview by Henry Ackermann, cited in Ackermann, *He Was Always There*, 21.

18. "Program for Appointment and Ordering to Active Duty of Chaplains of Reserve Components of the Army," DA Circular 601, Department of the Army, Chief of Staff, NARA RG 247, General Correspondence 1962–1963, 201-45-1003-01, Folder 705-03, "Military Personnel Procurement Instructions Files (63) DA Cir 601-3, PERM COFF 31 Dec 63."

19. Ibid.

20. Dept. of the Army, *Office of the Chief of Chaplains Historical Review*, 1 July 1964–30 June 1965, 129.

21. In this context, the "mainline" denominations are those identified by Hutchison in *Between the Times*: American Baptist, Disciples of Christ, Congregationalist/United Church of Christ, Episcopalian, Lutheran, Methodist, and Presbyterian.

22. Ibid., 129–30.

23. Letter from Chief of Chaplains to Rabbi Henach Leibowitz and other addressees, 5 April 1966, quoted in *Office of the Chief of Chaplains Historical Review*, 1 July 1965–21 December 1966, 210.

24. Ibid., 212–13.

25. Ibid., 217.

26. Ibid., 234.

27. Johnson, interview; Day, interview.

28. Dept. of the Army, *Office of the Chief of Chaplains Historical Review*, 1 January 1967–30 June 1968, 121.

29. See, for example, "No Vietnam Choice for Chaplains," *Jewish Advocate*, 21 March 1968.

30. Dept. of the Army, *Office of the Chief of Chaplains Historical Review*, 1 July 1969–30 June 1970, 129.

31. Loveland, *American Evangelicals*, 26–27.

32. Duty rosters for MACV chaplains are available at USACHCS.

33. Kettler, *Chaplain's Letters*, 3 and 18.

34. Hopkins, *Chaplain Remembers Vietnam*, 81.

35. Keizer et al., "Overview of the Role of the Unit Ministry Team."

36. Gershen, *Destroy or Die*.

37. Kissinger, interview.

38. Dept. of the Army, *Office of the Chief of Chaplains Historical Review*, 1 January 1967–30 June 1968, 44–45.

39. Albert Hornblass, "Report on Jewish GI's in Vietnam," *Jewish Advocate*, 24 September 1970, A8.

40. David H. White, "GI's in Vietnam Plead for More Religious Aids," *Jewish Advocate*, 2 September 1965.

41. "The Jewish Chaplain," Jewish Welfare Board, February 1970, USACHCS, Vietnam Files, Box 7.

42. Albert Dimont, "Jewish Report," appended to After Action Report, USACHCS, Vietnam Files, Box 8, "Jewish Report"; Stegman, interview.

43. USARV/MACV SUPCOM Staff Chaplain Briefing, Bangkok, Thailand, 13–14 January 1973 (slide presentation transcript), 7, USACHCS, Vietnam Files, Box 8, "Briefing for Chief."

44. Stegman, interview.

45. Moore, Bergsma, and Demy, *Chaplains with U.S. Naval Units*, 41.

46. Ibid., 48.

47. John Senieur quoted in ibid., 42.

48. On the particular hopes and challenges of the ecumenical movement in the United States, see Gill, *Embattled Ecumenism*.

49. Ibid., 4–11. On the ecumenical movement in the United States, see Gill, *Embattled Ecumenism*. On the issue of Mormon chaplains and denominational services, see Newby, *It Took Heroes*, 46, 180, 396. On the *Midway* Seder, see David H. White, "GI's in Vietnam Plead for More Religious Aids," *Jewish Advocate*, 2 September 1965. For a discussion of the meaning of other such ecumenical acts, see Chapter 4.

50. Slomovitz, *Fighting Rabbis*, 12–18; Budd, *Serving Two Masters*, 39.

51. Budd, *Serving Two Masters*, 17.

52. O'Donnell, "Clergy in the Military," 222.

53. Dept. of the Army, *Office of the Chief of Chaplains Historical Review*, 1967–68, 156.

54. J. C. Lambert, Office of the Adjutant General, Department of the Army, "Professional Guidelines for Chaplains," 13 January 1964, NARA RG 247, Admin/Mgmt, General Correspondence 1954–1975, Box 4, Folder 721-01, "Religious Program Goals and Objectives (64)."

55. Drazin and Currey, *For God and Country*, 15.

56. "President Debases Chaplaincy Standards," *Christian Century*, 30 November 1966, 1465.

57. Ibid.

58. "Chaplaincy Agencies Defend High Standards," *Christian Century*, 25 January 1967, 101–2.

59. Newby, *It Took Heroes,* 22.

60. Ibid., 43–44.

61. Ibid., 244.

62. Ibid., 249.

63. Ibid., 396.

64. J. C. Lambert, Office of the Adjutant General, Department of the Army, "Professional Guidelines for Chaplains," 13 January 1964, NARA RG 247, Admin/Mgmt, General Correspondence 1954–1975, Box 4 Folder 721-01, "Religious Program Goals and Objectives (64)."

65. "USARV Religious Activities Reports (Consolidated)," NARA RG 472, HQ USARV, Chaplain Section, Religious Plans, Training, and Operations Div., Box 1.

66. Scharlemann, *Air Force Chaplains,* 36.

67. "Religious Activities and Character Guidance Reports, Quarter Ending 31 March 1971," NARA RG 472, XXIV Corps, Chaplain, Daily Journal 07May1968–19-MAR1972, "XXIV Corps Chaplain 722-01 Chaplain Activity Reporting File (FY 1972)."

68. Scharlemann, *Air Force Chaplains,* 122–23.

69. Dept. of the Army, *Office of the Chief of Chaplains Historical Review, 1967–68,* 47.

70. Johnson, interview.

71. Huggins, interview.

72. Dept. of the Army, *Office of the Chief of Chaplains Historical Review,* 1 July 1965–31 December 1966, 65.

73. James R. McClements, "The Chaplain and the Culture of Death: An Army Chaplain's Account of a Combat Ministry in the Highlands of South Vietnam," USMHI, 3–4.

74. Ibid.

75. Johnson, interview.

76. Anonymous, survey response, USACHCS, Vietnam Files.

77. Newby, *It Took Heroes,* 145.

78. Ibid., 152.

79. Bowers, *Forward Edge,* 75–76.

80. Albert M. Hansen, survey response, USACHCS, Vietnam Files.

81. Douglas E. Sowards, survey response, USACHCS, Vietnam Files.

82. Beasley, interview.

83. Loveland, "Prophetic Ministry." This topic is the subject of extended analysis in Chapter 5.

84. Ackermann, *He Was Always There,* 232.

85. John F. Kenny, "After Action Report: The Chaplaincy in Vietnam at the Time of Cessation of Hostilities," USARV/MACV SUPCOM, 12 February 1973, USACHCS, Vietnam Files.

86. Ibid.

87. Ibid.

88. Ibid.

89. On the treatment of Vietnam veterans returning home, see Lembke, *Spitting Image.*

90. Race, as an analytical category, or even a definitional category, is notably absent from many discussions by and about military chaplains. While the subject has received significant scholarly attention in the context of the Vietnam War, religious history, and midcentury American history, the historical record is nearly silent in this specific context. First, the records indicate that very few black chaplains deployed to Vietnam—often, black chaplains are identified by their affiliation with a historically black denomination (e.g., African Methodist Episcopal, AME-Zion, or the National Baptist Convention) or when they self-identify in a survey or other account, but these instances are few and far between. Likewise, white chaplains occasionally mentioned a general sense of racial tension but rarely discussed details or specific events.

91. Mode, *Grunt Padre.*

92. The reasons "padre" became the default name for many chaplains, regardless of their religious affiliation, are unclear. Some speculate that Catholic chaplains, due to their vows of celibacy, were more likely to take risks in combat because they did not have wives and children to return to. Catholic chaplains were also the largest group of chaplains from a single denomination or faith group, so nearly every unit would have some contact with a Catholic chaplain. Finally, Catholic chaplains were simply more likely to use their ecclesial title of "Father" than were other ministers, which would have made the informal "padre" a signal of both deference and respect for all chaplains.

93. Johnson, *Postmark,* 9.

94. Richard L. Heim, survey response, quoted in Ackermann, *He Was Always There,* 169.

95. Anonymous private (E-2), survey response, quoted in Ackermann, *He Was Always There,* 81–82.

96. Newby, *It Took Heroes,* 523.

Chapter Three

1. Paul N. Mitchell, "Army Chaplain Paul N. Mitchell Recalls His Duties during the Vietnam War," *Vietnam Magazine,* June 2005.

2. Samuel Hynes, in *The Soldiers' Tale,* suggests that war writing reflects "the need to report and the need to remember." This chapter explores the reporting function of war writing, whereas Chapter 6 analyzes the remembering function. Of course, as reports, first-person war writings come with significant attendant limitations, and chaplains' recollections are certainly not immune to these problems. For an extended discussion of the limitations of first-person accounts of war, see Vernon, "Introduction: No Genre's Land."

3. On the subgenre of twentieth-century (primarily) Anglo-American combat memoirs, see Hynes, *Soldiers' Tale.* The combat memoir frequently employs specific tropes and images that serve to relate the experience of combat to an unfamiliar audience. Chaplains' first-person writings have received scant scholarly attention: They have not usually been considered in compilations of combat memoirs because chaplains did not participate as combatants, and in other collections, such as those

that focused on gender, racial, or ethnic minorities' experiences in war, chaplains—mostly white and all male until the 1970s—were excluded as well. The significant exception is Bradley Carter's 2004 Ph.D. dissertation, "'Reverence Helmeted and Armored,'" which examines these accounts as a distinct subgenre of autobiographical writing in order to draw conclusions about chaplains' roles and attitudes in the twentieth-century United States.

4. Burchard, "Role Conflicts of Military Chaplains." For other examples of this argument, see Abercrombie, *Military Chaplaincy*; Leonard Ahrnsbrak, "Civil Religion and the Military: Are Chaplains Ministers of Two Religions?," *Christian Century*, 20 February 1974, 206–8; Jones, "Air Force Chaplain?"; Grun, "Military Chaplaincy"; Reaser, "Military Chaplain"; and Zahn, *Military Chaplaincy*.

5. "Clergy: Should Ministers Be Draft-Exempt?," *Time*, 7 April 1967. The decision to maintain the clerical and seminary exemption was widely condemned by religious critics of the war.

6. Abercrombie, *Military Chaplaincy*.

7. Ibid., 43; AR 635-20, "Personnel Separations: Conscientious Objection," 5 January 1966, Military Documents, Pentagon Library, Washington, D.C.; a similar provision for Reserve components was included in AR 132-25, 4 February 1966, Military Documents, Pentagon Library, Washington, D.C.

8. See Montgomery, "God, the Army, and Judicial Review," 379. The Air Force regulation is found in AF 35-24, 8 March 1963, and the Navy regulation is found in Navy Bureau of Naval Personnel Instruction 1616-6, 15 November 1962, Naval Publications and Forms Center, Philadelphia, Pa.

9. Dept. of the Army, *Office of the Chief of Chaplains Historical Review*, 1968–69, 35.

10. Letter from Chief of Chaplains to Robert Bird, 2 March 1967, NARA RG 247, Admin/Mgt., Box 5, Folder 721-01, "Conscientious Objectors (67)."

11. Letter from Alfred A. Miller to Office of Chief of Chaplains, 31 March 1967, NARA RG 247, Admin/Mgt., Box 5, Folder 721-01, "Conscientious Objectors (67)."

12. Letter from Chief of Chaplains to Alfred A. Miller, 31 March 1967, NARA RG 247, Admin/Mgt., Box 5, Folder 721-01, "Conscientious Objectors (67)."

13. American Friends Service Committee, "Are You a Conscientious Objector to War?," in ibid.

14. Dept. of the Army, *Office of the Chief of Chaplains Historical Review*, 1968–69, 40.

15. Ibid.

16. Evaluation Guide for Conscientious Objector, NARA RG 247, Admin/Mgmt, Box 5, Folder 721-01, "Conscientious Objector (67)."

17. "Policy Guidance Concerning the Interviewing of Conscientious Objector Applicants in the Armed Forces," NARA RG 247, Admin/Mgmt, Box 5, Folder 721-01, "Conscientious Objector (67)."

18. Chaplains are considered protected persons under the first Geneva Convention. They may not renounce these rights (Convention I, Article 7), and these rights may not be negotiated away (Convention I, Article 6). Chaplains who are captured

are not considered prisoners of war (Convention I, Article 28). The Additional Protocol I states again that chaplains are noncombatants and have no right to participate in hostilities (Article 43, Section 2).

19. Dept. of the Army, *Department of the Army Field Manual 16-5.*

20. Newby, *It Took Heroes,* 23–24; Venzke, *Confidence in Battle,* 64–100, esp. 82–83.

21. Venzke, *Confidence in Battle,* 149.

22. Letter from Chief of Chaplains Charles Brown to Theodore Koepke, MACV Staff Chaplain, 21 January 1966, NARA RG 247, Admin/Mgmt, 1954–1975, Box 5, Folder 721-01 "Chaplains, Non-Combatant."

23. Dept. of the Army, *Office of the Chief of Chaplains Historical Review,* 1 July 1965–31 December 1966, 65.

24. Al Arvay, interview by Henry Ackermann, USMHI.

25. Newby, *It Took Heroes,* 23–24.

26. Peter Brush, "Higher and Higher: American Drug Use in Vietnam," *Vietnam* 15 (December 2002): 46.

27. Prugh, *Law at War,* 106; see also Solis, *Marines and Military Law in Vietnam.*

28. Ackermann, *He Was Always There,* 200.

29. McCoy, *Politics of Heroin,* 113, 115, 222–23; and Prugh, *Law at War,* 107.

30. Musto, *American Disease.*

31. Norman E. Zinberg, "G.I.'s and O.J.'s in Vietnam," *New York Times Magazine,* 5 December 1971.

32. "Drug Abuse: The Chaplains' Ministry to the Drug Abuser," Instructor Pamphlet, 38, Chaplains and Chaplain Enlisted Assistants Supplemental Branch Training, 1972, USACHCS, Vietnam Files.

33. Ackerman, *He Was Always There,* 200–204.

34. "Drug Abuse: The Chaplains' Ministry to the Drug Abuser," Instructor Pamphlet, 38, Chaplains and Chaplain Enlisted Assistants Supplemental Branch Training, 1972, USACHCS, Vietnam Files.

35. Ibid., 41–42.

36. Llewellyn Murdock, survey response, USACHCS, Vietnam Files.

37. These should not be confused with the Marine Corps' Combined Action Program, which bore the same acronym. The Marine Corps program involved special units, Combined Action Platoons, composed of a squad of Marines and thirty-four South Vietnamese Popular Forces, living in South Vietnamese villages to combat Viet Cong and National Liberation Front activity. The program was operable between 1965 and 1971, primarily in the I Corps region, nearest the border with North Vietnam.

38. "Chaplain Orientation – RVN," U.S. Army Chaplain School, Fort Hamilton, N.Y., December 1968, 1–5, USACHCS, Vietnam Files, Box 5.

39. Ibid.

40. Ibid.

41. Chaplains were to use nonappropriated funds for nonofficial purposes, including donations to civic action projects and the purchase of denominationally

specific religious accessories, such as candlesticks or processional crosses. Frequently, however,chaplains misused appropriated funds for the purchase of denominational items.

42. Dept. of the Army, *Office of the Chief of Chaplains Historical Review*, 1965–66.

43. Scharlemann, *Air Force Chaplains*, 61.

44. Dept. of the Army, *Office of the Chief of Chaplains Historical Review*, 1967–68, 46.

45. *United Methodist Chaplain Newsletter*, Commission on Chaplains and Related Ministries, United Methodist Church, December 1971, 1, USACHCS, Vietnam Files, Box 7.

46. "Noteworthy News," *American Baptist Chaplain*, Department of Chaplaincy Services, American Baptist Convention, April 1969, USACHCS, Vietnam Files, Box 7.

47. Ibid.

48. "Mail Call," *Disciple Chaplain*, Committee on Military and Veterans Services, Disciples of Christ, July–September 1970, USACHCS, Vietnam Files, Box 7.

49. "Noteworthy News," *American Baptist Chaplain*, Department of Chaplaincy Services, American Baptist Convention, July 1968, vol. 11, USACHCS, Vietnam Files, Box 7.

50. Ibid.

51. Johnson, *Combat Chaplain*, v, 281; Johnson, interview.

52. "The Chaplaincy," TRADOC Issues, USACHCS, Vietnam Files.

53. Dulany, *Once a Soldier*, 41.

54. Hutchens, *Beyond Combat*, 81.

55. Bowers, *Forward Edge*, 60.

56. For responses to profanity, see Hopkins, *Chaplain Remembers*, 163, and Schumacher, *Soldier of God Remembers*, 57–60.

57. For responses to prostitution and other sexual activities, see Hopkins, *Chaplain Remembers*, 165–68; Falabella, *Vietnam Memoirs*, 135–36; and Hutchens, *Beyond Combat*, 55–57.

58. Burnham, *God's Squad*, 43–44.

59. Parker C. Thompson, survey response, quoted in Ackermann, *He Was Always There*, 181. Emphasis in original.

60. PBS *Frontline*, "Remember My Lai," 23 May 1989, transcript; Peers, *My Lai Inquiry*; Harry F. Rosenthal, "Reply to Chaplain: It's a Tough War," *Free Lance Star* (Fredericksburg, Va.), 11 December 1970.

61. Grossman, *On Killing*, 204.

62. Peers, *My Lai Inquiry*, 214–15.

63. Edward B. Fiske, "The Perils of Serving Two Masters," *New York Times*, 30 January 1972.

64. Newby, *It Took Heroes*, 30.

65. Zahn, *Military Chaplaincy*, 134.

66. Stephen Louden, "Chaplains as Whistle-blowers, You're Having a Laugh," quoted in Snape, *Royal Army Chaplains Department*.

67. The question was worded thusly: "Do you think the use of torture against suspected terrorists in order to gain important information can often be justified,

sometimes be justified, rarely be justified, or never be justified?" See Pew Research Center Publications, "The Religious Dimensions of the Torture Debate," 29 April 2009, http://www.pewforum.org/Politics-and-Elections/The-Religious-Dimensions-of-the-Torture-Debate.aspx (accessed 1 July 2013).

68. This issue is discussed in more depth in Chapter 5. See also Loveland, "Prophetic Ministry."

69. Ackermann, *He Was Always There*, 226.

70. Venzke, *Confidence in Battle*, 237–38.

71. Newby, *It Took Heroes*, 30.

72. Dulany, *Once a Soldier*, 73.

73. O'Donnell, "Clergy in the Military," 222; emphasis in original.

74. Ibid., 216.

75. Johnson, *Combat Chaplain*, 198–99.

76. Autry, *Gun Totin' Chaplain*, 144–45.

77. This incident was reported, using aliases, by Daniel Lang in "Casualties of War," *New Yorker*, 18 October 1969, 61. Lang later wrote a book, also titled *Casualties of War*, and the incident was the basis for Brian DePalma's feature film of the same name, *Casualties of War*.

78. For a detailed account of this story, see Newby, *It Took Heroes*, chap. 6.

79. Toulouse, "Christian Responses to Vietnam."

Chapter Four

1. Hutchens, *Beyond Combat*, 17. The first two verses of Romans 13 read, "Let every person be subject to the governing authorities; for there is no authority except from God, and those authorities that exist have been instituted by God. Therefore whoever resists authority resists what God has appointed, and those who resist will incur judgment." Exodus 20:13 reads, "You shall not murder" (New Revised Standard Version). The shorthand numbering of the commandments (the way in which individual verses are grouped together to derive a list of ten), however, is usually dependent on denomination and biblical translation. Thus, most Protestant and Eastern Orthodox Christians label this commandment as the sixth one, while Roman Catholics and some liturgical Protestants label it the fifth.

2. Bowers, *Forward Edge*, 34.

3. Ibid.

4. Johnson, *Postmark,* 49.

5. Ibid.

6. Caputo, *Rumor of War*, 171.

7. Ibid.

8. Des Champs, *Christian Soldier*, 121.

9. Richard D. Kemp, "A Chaplain Writes From Vietnam," *Activities* (Christian Science Chaplain Newsletter), April 1968, USACHCS, Vietnam Files, Box 7, "Christian Science Newsletters." Kemp was quoting Matthew 6:44.

10. Ibid.

11. Cherry, *From Thunder to Sunrise*, 26.

12. Ibid., 18.

13. This section responds, in part, to the call for historians of religion to study the lived experience of religion as it was practiced outside of the confines of the institutional church. Though such studies almost exclusively focus on lay practice, chaplains, as clergy, played a vital role in the way militaries experienced religion in war, a setting decidedly outside of the confines of the institutional church. Furthermore, the chaplains themselves each possessed a unique experience as they participated and served at the intersections of two cultures and institutions. Bradley Carter has argued that religious practices in combat constitute a new form of "vernacular religion" or "popular religion," which may or may not carry with it traditional, "official" meanings. Carter focused particularly on "foxhole faith," wherein common materials are reinvented as "holy hardware"; that is, objects of war that become objects of religion Chaplains, Carter argued, were surprisingly ambivalent or positive about these processes. See especially Hall, *Lived Religion in America*, and Carter, "'Reverence Helmeted and Armored,'" 170–211.

14. Michael McCormick uses the term "liturgy of war" to describe a particular wartime liturgy used by European armies from late antiquity until the Crusades. I adopt this term in its plural form in order to emphasize the multiple and dynamic worship practices that emerged over the course of the American war in Vietnam. See "Liturgy of War from Antiquity to the Crusades."

15. The focus in this section is necessarily on Christian liturgical traditions. In the decade of heaviest troop involvement in Vietnam only twenty Jewish chaplains served in-country, and at the time there were no provisions for Muslim, Buddhist, or Orthodox chaplains. The small number of Jewish chaplains renders substantial analysis of Jewish worship practices in the context of combat difficult; usually, Christian chaplains were charged with the spiritual welfare of the Jewish men in their units and were responsible for coordinating appropriate food, leave, or visitation to other units for services. Additionally, to my knowledge, no field-grade Jewish chaplains have left memoirs or other records of their service in Vietnam. Only one high-ranking Jewish chaplain, Saul Koss, has been interviewed under the Army's Senior Officer Oral History Program.

16. Herr, *Dispatches*, 58.

17. See, for example, Knight, "Supreme Six," 70.

18. National Lutheran Council Division of Service to Military Personnel, *Newsletter for Lutheran Chaplains* 6, no. 4 (1963).

19. Kettler, *Chaplain's Letters*, 3. All four corps areas had chaplains assigned to them, but units were often split apart and assigned to geographically disparate areas. In theory, chaplains were therefore responsible for providing religious services for men in a particular area, regardless of which unit they were a part of.

20. Venzke, *Confidence in Battle*, 238.

21. Johnson, *Combat Chaplain*, 125.

22. Schumacher, *Soldier of God*, 62.

23. Gary G. Baxter quoted in Ackermann, *He Was Always There*, 176.

24. Des Champs, *Christian Soldier*, 117.

25. Orris E. Kelly, interview by Henry Ackermann, 21 October 1985, quoted in Ackermann, *He Was Always There*, 183.

26. Ibid.

27. Dulany, *Once a Soldier*, 51.

28. Bowers, *Forward Edge*, 68.

29. Johnson, *Combat Chaplain*, 108.

30. O'Donnell, "Clergy in the Military," 220. The Catholic Sacrament of the Sick was called "Last Rites" or "Final Unction" prior to the Second Vatican Council (1968). Many Catholics continued to use the terms interchangeably.

31. Andrew Shimek, survey response, USACHCS, Vietnam Files, Box 5.

32. Anonymous chaplain, survey response, USACHCS, Vietnam Files, Box 5.

33. Bowers, *Forward Edge*, 68.

34. Newby, *It Took Heroes*, 253.

35. Emphasis added.

36. Knight, "Supreme Six," 70.

37. Wendell E. Danielson, "A Chaplain in Vietnam (As Inspired by the Psalmist)," *Chaplain*, July–August 1967, 4.

38. "Vietnam Songbook," USACHCS, Vietnam Files.

39. Scharlemann, *Air Force Chaplains*, 70.

40. Richard N. Donovan, "Mail Call: En-route to Vietnam; On Leave at Osawatomie, Kans.," *Disciple Chaplain,* Committee on Military and Veterans Services, Disciples of Christ, January–March 1971, USACHCS, Vietnam Files, Box 7.

41. Knight, "Supreme Six," 80–81.

42. Joseph Dulany also interpreted some of his experiences through Psalm 23. See Dulany, *Once a Soldier*, 41.

43. Stanley Beach quoted in Mode, *Grunt Padre*, 70.

44. On soldiers' religious interpretations of fate, Providence, divine will, and destiny in combat, see Kindsvatter, *American Soldiers*, 115–17.

45. Hopkins, *Chaplain Remembers*, 111.

46. Hutchens, *Beyond Combat*, 38.

47. Johnson, *Combat Chaplain*, 80.

48. Knight, "Supreme Six," 81–82. Psalm 91:3–8 reads, "Surely He will save you from the fowler's snare and from the deadly pestilence. He will cover you with His feathers and under His wings will you find refuge. His faithfulness will be your shield. . . .You will not fear . . . the arrow that flies by day . . . nor the plague that destroys at midday. A thousand may fall at your right side, ten thousand at your right hand, but it will not come near you. You will only observe with your eyes and see the punishment of the wicked."

49. Knight, "Supreme Six," 81–82.

50. Harry R. Jackson to Bill Brock, quoted in Dept. of the Army, *Office of the Chief of Chaplains Historical Review*, 1968–69, 45.

51. Wendell E. Danielson, "A Chaplain in Vietnam (As Inspired by the Psalmist)," *Chaplain*, July–August 1967, 4–8.

52. Ibid.

53. Ibid.

54. Baxter quoted in Ackermann, *He Was Always There*, 176.

55. Johnson, *Combat Chaplain*, 125.

56. Kettler, *Chaplain's Letters*, 201.

57. Robert Hess, survey response, USACHCS, Vietnam Files, Box 5.

58. Scharlemann, *Air Force Chaplains*, 55.

59. Dulany, *Once a Soldier*, 42.

60. It is important to distinguish this sort of "crisis-theology" from Karl Barth's neoorthodox "theology of crisis" See Barth, *The Holy Spirit and the Christian Life* and *The Epistle to the Romans*. For commentary on Barth, see Clough, *Ethics in Crisis*.

Chapter Five

1. On news writing and reading as a ritual, culturally constructed, significant act, see Carey, *Communication as Culture*, 20–21.

2. As part of a "General Offensive-General Uprising," and during this celebration of the Vietnamese New Year, Viet Cong and NVA forces conducted simultaneous, coordinated attacks on more than 100 American and ARVN installations, embassies, and cities. Though few of the attacks were ultimately conventionally successful—most of the places that were attacked were back in American or South Vietnamese control within a matter of hours—the audacity and tenacity of the attacks surprised Americans and began to sour them toward a war it appeared they might not win.

3. On media coverage of the Vietnam War, see Hammond, *Reporting Vietnam*; Hallin, *"Uncensored War"*; and Wyatt, *Paper Soldiers*.

4. On religious protest against the Vietnam War, see Hall, *Because of their Faith*; Carroll, *American Requiem*; Flipse, "To Save 'Free Vietnam'"; Friedland, *Lift Up Your Voice*; Quinley, "Hawks and Doves among the Clergy"; Heineman, "American Schism"; and Granberg and Campbell, "Certain Aspects of Religiosity."

5. Settje, "'Sinister' Communists"; Mark G. Toulouse, "Days of Protest: The *Century* and the War in Vietnam," *Christian Century*, 8 November 2000, 1154–57; and Toulouse, "Christian Responses to Vietnam."

6. These denominational debates have received significant scholarly attention in the last two decades. See Settje, *Lutherans and the Longest War*; Nutt, *Toward Peacemaking*; Gill, *Embattled Ecumenism;* Settje, *Faith and War*; Bogaski, "Swords and Plowshares"; and Alexander, *Peace to War*. These studies are immensely useful in understanding how these debates played out in specific religious communities, but the military chaplaincy is rarely included in the analysis.

7. Alexander, *Peace to War*, 31.

8. Plank, *Called to Serve*.

9. Southern Baptist Convention, "Resolution Concerning Peace," 1966; "Resolution on Peace," 1967; "Resolution on Peace," 1968; "Resolution on Peace and Justice for All Men," 1969; "Resolution on Peace," 1970; "Resolution on World Peace," 1971;

"Resolution on Achieving World Peace," 1972; "Resolution on Southeast Asia," 1973. The text of resolutions is available at sbc.net.

10. Baptist Press, "Pursue Vietnam War, Baptist Editor Says," *Western Recorder*, 13 February 1968, 29.

11. Bogaski, *Swords and Plowshares*, 201.

12. See, for example, Tim Dumont, "Army Panel Defends U.S. Role in Vietnam," *Hartford Courant*, 23 March 1971, 19.

13. Irving Spiegel, "Vietnam Protests Assailed by Rabbi: Returning Chaplain Cites Effect on Hanoi's Stand," *New York Times*, 7 May 1967.

14. Charles W. Cordray, "War Dissent Held Immoral by Chaplain," *Baltimore Sun*, 11 January 1968, A2.

15. Richard Homan, "Chaplain Says Antiwar Activity Has Not Harmed Morale of GI's," *Washington Post, Times Herald*, 8 January 1970, A3, ProQuest Historical Newspapers. See also Betty Medsger, "Chaplains' Chief Gives Insight on Viet War Role: 'Religion Is Life,'" *Washington Post, Times Herald*, 14 August 1971, B5, ProQuest Historical Newspapers.

16. Harry Trimborn, "GIs Turn to Religion," *Washington Post, Times Herald*, 2 August 1969, B6.

17. Richard E. Dryer, "An HUC-JIR Graduate, Now Chaplain In Vietnam, Believes Involvement There a Wise and Necessary One," *American Israelite*, 25 November 1965.

18. Betty Medsger, "Chaplains' Chief Gives Insight on Viet War Role: 'Religion Is Life,'" *Washington Post, Times Herald*, 14 August 1971, B5, ProQuest Historical Newspapers.

19. John Cogley, "Changed Atmosphere, Same Attitudes," *New York Times*, 21 August 1966.

20. See, for example, Edward B. Fiske, "Religion: The Clergy on Vietnam," *New York Times*, 7 January 1968; James Reston, "The Legal and Moral Issues of the War," *New York Times*, 7 January 1968; Edward B. Fiske, "Religion: Some Clergy Say 'No' on War," *New York Times*, 11 February 1968; Edward B. Fiske, "Antiwar Movement Makes Rapid Gains among Seminarians," *New York Times*, 3 March 1968; Fred C. Shapiro, "God and That Man at Yale: Chaplain Coffin," *New York Times*, 3 March 1968; and "Church Leaders Plan Day of Prayer on Christmas Eve to Widen War Protest," *New York Times*, 29 December 1969. Although these articles appeared in the *New York Times*, some of them were wire stories published widely in national newspapers. Other national newspapers reveal a similar bias.

21. Tracie Rozron, "60 Pray for Berrigan Group, Angela Davis," *Baltimore Sun*, 6 March 1972, C6.

22. Neuhaus, "War, the Churches, and Civil Religion." In the 1960s and early 1970s, Neuhaus was an active member of the religious Left, but his political leanings shifted to the right when *Roe v. Wade* was handed down. In 1990, Neuhaus converted to Catholicism and has since become a leading conservative voice in the religious community, where he speaks and writes broadly about conservative and ecumenical issues, particularly in his role as editor of *First Things*.

23. Ibid., 129.

24. Ibid., 130.

25. M. S. Handler, "Northeast Drive Urged on Baptists," *New York Times*, 26 May 1966.

26. Carl McIntire quoted in Pratt, "Religious Faith and Civil Religion," 167; Billy James Hargis, "How to Win the War," 1967, quoted in Allitt, *Religion in America*, 100.

27. William K. Harrison, "Is the United States Right in Bombing North Vietnam?," *Christianity Today*, 7 January 1966, 25–26; "Viet Nam: Where Do We Go from Here?," *Christianity Today*, 7 January 1966, 30–31.

28. "'National University' Proposed at NAE," *Christianity Today*, 13 May 1966, 47–48, quoted in Toulouse, "Christian Responses."

29. "Honesty in Government," *Christianity Today*, 26 March 1971, 25; "Editor's Note," *Christianity Today*, 7 May 1971, 3; "Vietnam: Continuing Impasse," *Christianity Today*, 6 August 1971, 25; "Plain Talk on Viet Nam," *Christianity Today*, 26 May 1972, 27; "The Indochina Fiasco," *Christianity Today*, 25 April 1975, 27; Toulouse, "Christian Responses," 21.

30. Hentoff, *John Cardinal O'Connor*.

31. "Mail Call," *Disciple Chaplain*, Committee on Military and Veterans Services, Disciples of Christ, July–September 1970, USACHCS, Vietnam Files, Box 7.

32. See Brinsfield, *Faith in the Fight*; Corby, *Memoirs of Chaplain Life*; Budd, *Serving Two Masters*; and Loveland, *American Evangelicals* and "Character Education."

33. Bonhoeffer, *Letters and Papers from Prison*, 360. On Christian and secular responses to the development of "secular theology" and the "Death of God" movement, see Allitt, *Religion in America*, 72–73.

34. Ellwood, *Sixties Spiritual Awakening*, 34–35.

35. Allitt, *Religion in America*, 13.

36. Newman and Halvorson, *Patterns in Pluralism*, 4.

37. Ibid., 4. In this assessment, the LDS Church is counted among evangelical groups because of its focus on proselytizing and because it is generally aligned with evangelical churches on conservative social and political issues.

38. Weber, *Economy and Society*, 425–38.

39. Ibid., 439–51. See also Turner, *Cambridge Companion to Weber*, and Swedberg, *Max Weber Dictionary*.

40. "Chaplains' Guidelines for Free and Responsible Expression of Conscience in the Military," *Chaplain*, May–June 1970, 3.

41. Coffman, "Constituting the Protestant Mainline."

42. William R. Miller, "Chaplaincy v. Mission," *Christian Century*, 2 November 1966, 1336.

43. Ibid. The *Link* and the *Chaplain* were periodicals published by the General Commission on Chaplains; they contained lively and thought-provoking debate, albeit geared toward a small and specific audience. The *Chaplain* served a professional audience, while the *Link* was directed toward enlisted personnel.

44. William R. Miller, "Chaplaincy v. Mission," *Christian Century*, 2 November 1966, 1337.

45. Norman MacFarlane, "Navy Chaplaincy: Muzzled Ministry," *Christian Century*, 2 November 1966, 1338–39.

46. Ibid., 1339.

47. Albert F. Ledebuhr, "Military Chaplaincy: An Apologia," *Christian Century*, 2 November 1966, 1332.

48. Ibid., 1334.

49. Richard S. McPhee, letter to the editor, *Christian Century*, 30 November 1966, 1476–77.

50. J. George Hilton, letter to the editor, *Christian Century*, 22 February 1967, 242.

51. Donald W. Shaner, letter to the editor, *Christian Century*, 30 November 1966, 1476.

52. William G. Sodt, letter to the editor, *Christian Century*, 30 November 1966, 1478.

53. Alfred P. Klausler, letter to the editor, *Christian Century*, 30 November 1966, 1478.

54. John Sayre, letter to the editor, *Christian Century*, 30 November 1966, 1478.

55. Carl Landes, letter to the editor, *Christian Century*, 30 November 1966, 1478.

56. W. Norman MacFarlane, letter to the editor, *Christian Century*, 4 January 1967, 18.

57. Robert E. Klitgaard, "Onward Christian Soldiers: Dehumanization and the Military Chaplain," *Christian Century*, 18 November 1970, 1379.

58. Ibid.

59. Thom Shepard, "Chaplains Held Too Military," *Boston Globe*, 19 January 1970, 11.

60. Roger L. Bradley, "Our Military Chaplains: A Plea for Prayer," *Standard* (Baptist General Conference), 29 December 1969, 8.

61. See, for example, Richard E. Dryer, "An HUC-JIR Graduate, Now Chaplain in Vietnam, Believes Involvement There a Wise and Necessary One," *American Israelite*, 25 November 1965; "Orthodox Soldier Opposing Vietnam War Gets Honorable Discharge," *Jewish Advocate,* 9 March 1967; D. H. White, "Report on Jewish Servicemen in Vietnam," *Jewish Advocate*, 28 October 1965; "Jewish Soldiers Ready for Vietnam Passover," *Jewish Advocate*, 20 August 1967; Constance Gorfinkle, "Letters: High Holidays in Vietnam," *Jewish Advocate*, 17 October 1968; and Selwyn D. Ruslander, "A Jewish Chaplain's Vietnam Journal," *Jewish Advocate*, 14 September 1967.

62. "No Vietnam Choice for Chaplains," JTA Wire Story, reprinted in *Jewish Advocate*, 21 March 1968.

63. Hayden Gilmore, "They Shall Jog and Not Faint," *Chaplain*, March–April 1971, 36–40.

64. Wendell T. Wright, "The Problems and Challenges of a Ministry in Vietnam," *Chaplain*, September–October 1970, 44–45.

65. Jack S. Boozer, "The Military Chaplaincy: One Calling, Two Roles," *Chaplain*, November–December 1970, 3.

66. Richard B. Cheatham Jr., "The Prophetic Role of the Military Chaplain," *Chaplain*, January–February 1971, 22–30.

67. Hedrick, "On Foreign Soil"; Budd, *Serving Two Masters*.

68. Wisconsin Evangelical Lutheran Synod, Topical Q&As, "Other Military Chaplains," http://arkiv.lbk.cc/faq/site.pl@1518cutopic_topicid70cuitem_itemidi875.htm (accessed 1 July 2013).

69. William E. Flood, "Maintaining a Pastoral Identity," *American Baptist Chaplain*, American Baptist Convention, July 1968, USACHCS, Vietnam Files, Box 7.

70. William Greider, "God, Government, and the Military Chaplains," *Washington Post*, 2 September 1969; reprinted in *Boston Globe*, 23 November 1969, and *Los Angeles Times*, 20 November 1969.

71. George Cornell, "Divided Allegiance of Chaplains Issue," AP Wire Story, printed in *Boston Globe*, 3 August 1968.

72. Martin Siegel, "Revamping the Military Chaplaincy," *Christian Century*, 8 August 1962, 959–60, 959.

73. Ibid.

74. Ibid., 959–60.

75. "Whither the Military Chaplaincy," *Christian Century*, 19 September 1962, 1119–20.

76. Ibid., 1120.

77. Quoted in Brinsfield, *Encouraging Faith, Supporting Soldiers*, 3.

78. Episcopal Church, General Convention resolution, quoted in ibid., 2.

79. George Cornell, "Divided Allegiance of Chaplains Issue," AP Wire Story, reprinted in *Boston Globe*, 3 August 1968.

80. Irving Spiegel, "Rabbi Supports Chaplain System: Head of Orthodox Council Disputes Jewish Congress," *New York Times*, 27 June 1968. For similar coverage on the debate within the Jewish community see eea number of earlier articles by Spiegel:: "Change Proposed for U.S. Chaplains: Rabbi Wants Clerics Taken Out of Military Control," *New York Times*, 24 March 1968; and "Jewish Congress Urges an End of Military Chaplaincy System," *New York Times*, 18 May 1968.

81. George Dugan, "Chaplains Urged to Doff Uniforms," *New York Times*, 4 June 1970.

82. "The Chopper Chaplains," *Time*, 11 February 1966.

83. Ibid.

84. "Honest to God—or Faithful to the Pentagon," *Time*, 30 May 1969. In 2006, Autry published his Vietnam memoir under the title *Gun-Totin' Chaplain*.

85. Ibid.

86. Ibid.

Chapter Six

1. Knight, "Supreme Six," 88.

2. Bradley Carter writes, "Perhaps the most significant rhetorical strategy of this subgenre is its quest to redefine combat in spiritual terms. This pervasive spiritualization does more than meet its audience's expectations of how a religious figure

should write. It also offers a sweeping resolution of conflicts identified in the chaplain problematic" "Reverence Helmeted and Armored".

3. Some of these accounts were published almost immediately after the Vietnam War ended, and others as recently as 2008; this chapter considers self-published memoirs, books published by trade, religious, and academic presses, as well as shorter accounts that were published in edited collections or periodicals. Henry Ackermann's official history of the Army chaplaincy in Vietnam, *He Was Always There*, is mostly based on the official survey responses and the published order of battle for Vietnam. More than 600 chaplains responded to the survey request, and the study included quantitative measures as well as open-ended questions.

4. The number of black chaplains serving on active duty in the Army during this period ranged from 17 in June 1963 to 55 in June 1971, comprising less than 3 percent of all chaplains. Furthermore, not all chaplains deployed to Vietnam, though it is unknown how many black chaplains did. See Ackermann, *He Was Always There,* 206.

5. Joseph Pronechen, "He Died with His Men – Sainthood Cause Begins for Vietnam Chaplain," *National Catholic Register* (Catholic Online), 26 May 2006, http://www.catholic.org/national/national_story.php?id=19983 (accessed 1 July 2013).

6. Letter from Amos F. Shumway to Henry Ackermann, 1 September 1985, USACHCS, Vietnam Files.

7. Philip K. Paulson, "I was an Atheist in a Foxhole," *The Humanist*, American Humanist Association (September/October 1989).

8. James May, "Chaplains," *Veteran* 30, no. 2 (Fall/Winter 2000).

9. Lembke, *Spitting Image.*

10. Jerry Lembke, "Recollections: 'Render Unto Caesar . . . ,'" *Veteran* 31, no. 1 (2001): 31.

11. Ibid.

12. Ibid.

13. Herr, *Dispatches*, 174–75.

14. Donald W. Shea, survey response, USACHCS, Vietnam Files.

15. Newby, *It Took Heroes*, ix–x.

16. Dulany, *Once a Soldier*, 4.

17. Ibid.

18. Autry, *Gun-Totin' Chaplain*, xviii–xiv.

19. Burnham, *God's Squad*, 1.

20. Hynes, *Soldiers' Tale*, 4.

21. On military memoirs and first-person narratives, see especially ibid. Hynes examines combat memoirs by English and American military personnel who fought in World War I, World War II, or Vietnam, as well as "survivor memoirs" of the Holocaust.

22. Ibid., 4. Hynes adds that this sort of isolation is reflected in the fact that war narratives have not generally conformed to "the literary fashions of their time. Tellers of Victorian wars have not been notably Victorian, narrators of modern wars have not been Modernists. Whatever their dates, they have nearly all been realists, adopting a common style that would come as close as language can to rendering

the things of the material world as they are" (ibid., 25–26). This goes equally well to the point that most combat memoirs were written without reference to other combat memoirs. One notable exception to this within the subgenre of chaplain memoirs is Autry's *Gun-Totin' Chaplain*, in which he writes, "They're good. Mine may be a little more philosophical. I've tried to convey the contributions chaplains make in war and peace" (p. xi).

23. See, for example, Johnson's *Combat Chaplain*.

24. See, for example, Ringnalda, *Fighting and Writing the Vietnam War*; Neilson, *Warring Fictions*; Jason, *Acts and Shadows*; Jason, *Fourteen Landing Zones*; Herzog, *Vietnam War Stories*; and Bates, *Wars We Took to Vietnam*.

25. Herr, *Dispatches*; O'Brien, *If I Die in a Combat Zone*; O'Brien, *The Things They Carried*.

26. Vernon, "Introduction: No Genre's Land," 3.

27. Jason, *Acts and Shadows*, 41–52.

28. Newby, *It Took Heroes*, vii–viii; emphasis in original.

29. Brown, *Another Side of Combat*, x; Winter, *Sites of Memory, Sites of Mourning*.

30. Dorsey, *Sacred Estrangement*, 9; see also Eakin, *American Autobiography*.

31. Dorsey, *Sacred Estrangement*, 9.

32. Des Champs, *Christian Soldier*, 7.

33. Ammerman, *Supernatural Events*, 17, 140.

34. Maguire, *Follies of a Navy Chaplain*; Estes, *Paratrooper Chaplain*; Itokazu, *Chaplain's Pilgrimage*.

35. Brown, *Another Side of Combat*, vii.

36. Ibid., ix.

37. Bowers, *Forward Edge,* 95.

38. Dulany, *Once a Soldier*; Schumacher, *Soldier of God Remembers*.

39. Newby, *It Took Heroes*, vii–viii.

40. See, for example, Bolton, *Therapeutic Potential of Creative Writing*; Baldwin, *Life's Companion*; Bolton, "Taking the Thinking Out of It"; and L'Abate, "Use of Writing in Psychotherapy."

41. Pennebaker, "Overcoming Inhibition," quoted in Bolton, *Therapeutic Potential of Creative Writing*, 199.

42. Ibid., 200.

43. Laufer, "War Trauma and Human Development," 40.

44. See Sonnenberg et al., *Trauma of War*.

45. Johnson, *Combat Chaplain*, 248.

46. Ibid., 3.

47. Bowers, *Forward Edge*, 131.

48. The "dark night of the soul" is a phase in one's spiritual life identified by St. John of the Cross, a Spanish mystic, in the late sixteenth century in which a person feels the total absence of light and hope; but the journey out of the dark night leads one to a higher level of consciousness. Thus, though in the midst of it, one would feel utter despair, the "dark night" experience is to be treasured. Many Christian authors have since used the term "dark night" to express any period in which a person feels deep separation from God. See Saint John of the Cross, *Dark Night of*

the Soul, and Reichardt, *Encyclopedia of Catholic Literature*, s.v. "Dark Night of the Soul, John of the Cross."

49. Mahedy, *Out of the Night*.

50. Ibid., 187.

51. Glen Van Dyne, introduction to Bowers, *Forward Edge*, 9–11.

52. Bowers, *Forward Edge*, 129.

53. See Autry, *Gun Totin' Chaplain*, and O'Brien, *Blessings from the Battlefield*. Since 2003, several other books about chaplains have also been published: Kittleson, *Meditations from Iraq*; Riddle, *For God and Country*; and Cash, *Table in the Presence*.

54. Autry, *Gun-Totin' Chaplain*, xi.

55. Ibid.

56. Ibid., xii.

57. Jim Marshall, foreword to Brown, *Another Side of Combat*, iv–v.

58. Hutchens, *Beyond Combat*, 127–28.

59. Ibid.

60. Johnson, *Postmark*, 96.

61. Day, "Vietnam Chaplain: Return to Vietnam 2004." Day's meditation is an example of theodicy, or a defense of God's goodness and omnipotence in response to/as a solution for the "problem of evil." This particular theodicy, which seeks to validate the existence of evil by limiting one of the primary attributes of God (in this case, Day places the limitation on "omnipotence"; other theodicies limit the omnipresence or omnibenevolence of God), is found most often in the schools of process theology. Day does not refer to either of these theological schools formally in his writing. On process theology, and its more contemporary variant, open theism, see Mesle, *Process Theology*, and Cobb and Griffin, *Process Theology*.

62. Day, "Vietnam Chaplain: Return to Vietnam 2004."

63. Day, interview.

64. Hutchens, *Beyond Combat*, 126.

65. Ibid., 126.

66. Falabella, *Vietnam Memoirs*, 154.

67. Hutchens, *Beyond Combat*, 128.

68. Gilbert, "Hard Tour in Vietnam Became Chaplain's 'Greatest Ministry.'"

69. Kiyo Itokazu, survey response, USACHCS, Vietnam Files.

70. Jan Friend, survey response, USACHCS, Vietnam Files.

71. David Kent, survey response, USACHCS, Vietnam Files.

72. Jan Friend, survey response, USACHCS, Vietnam Files.

73. Ibid.

74. Robert Hess, survey response, USACHCS, Vietnam Files.

75. Anonymous chaplain, survey response, quoted in Ackermann, *He Was Always There*, 231.

76. Charles E. LeClair, survey response, USACHCS, Vietnam Files.

77. Anonymous chaplain, survey response, quoted in Ackermann, *He Was Always There*, 231.

78. Marvin W. Trott, survey response, USACHCS, Vietnam Files.

79. James L. Juhan, survey response, USACHCS, Vietnam Files.

80. Hopkins, *Chaplain Remembers*, 2.

81. Charles E. LeClair, survey response, USACHCS, Vietnam Files.

82. Lloyd Kincaid, survey response, USACHCS, Vietnam Files.

83. Douglas E. Sowards, survey response, USACHCS, Vietnam Files.

84. Jack Moyar, survey response, USACHCS, Vietnam Files.

85. Donald W. Shea, survey response, USACHCS, Vietnam Files.

86. Lloyd Kincaid, survey response, USACHCS, Vietnam Files.

87. Larry R. Wedel, survey response, USACHCS, Vietnam Files.

88. David Kent, survey response, USACHCS, Vietnam Files.

89. Floyd Lacey, survey response, USACHCS, Vietnam Files.

90. Jack Brown, survey response, USACHCS, Vietnam Files.

91. Hopkins, *Chaplain Remembers*, 279.

92. Kiyo Itokazu, survey response, USACHCS, Vietnam Files.

93. Donald Robinson, survey response, USACHCS, Vietnam Files.

94. William P. Trotsauch, survey response, USACHCS, Vietnam Files.

95. Ackermann, *He Was Always There*, 228. By way of comparison, in a survey of soldiers about the same issues, only 33 percent of the respondents indicated their faith had been strengthened by their experiences in Vietnam.

96. Ackermann, *He Was Always There*, 242–43.

97. Kindsvatter, *American Soldiers*, 114.

98. Gray, *Warriors*, 116–21.

99. Hopkins, *Chaplain Remembers*, i.

100. Burkett, *Stolen Valor*.

Chapter Seven

1. O'Connor, *Chaplain Looks at Vietnam*; Cox, *Military Chaplains*; Zahn, *Military Chaplaincy*; Appelquist, *Church, State, and Chaplaincy*.

2. Gerhard W. Hyatt to Ray Strowser quoted in Brinsfield, *Encouraging Faith, Supporting Soldiers*, 26.

3. "U.S. Army Chaplain School Army '75 Workshop," USACHCS, Vietnam Files, 30.

4. Abercrombie, *Military Chaplaincy*. The book is based on quantitative survey data, rather than a qualitative study of chaplain behaviors and experiences.

5. Hutcheson, *Churches and the Chaplaincy*.

6. See Jonakait, "Abuses of the Military Chaplaincy"; and *Katcoff v. Marsh*.

7. Loveland, *American Evangelicals*, 111.

8. Dept. of the Army, *Office of the Chief of Chaplains Historical Review*, 1 July 1962–30 June 1963, 74–75.

9. Loveland, *American Evangelicals*, 112.

10. Jonakait, "Abuses of the Military Chaplaincy."

11. Ibid., A–B.

12. In 1979, Katcoff filed nine Freedom of Information Act (FOIA) requests with the Offices of the Chiefs of Chaplains of both the Army and the Navy. The Navy

requested advance payment of $192.50 for processing the request and supplying answers to the inquiries. Katcoff and Weider declined to pursue the matter further and instead focused their efforts on the Army, which complied with the FOIA requests at no charge. See Drazin and Currey, *For God and Country*, 46–47. While helpful for understanding the legal maneuvering (of both sides) involved in the case, Drazin and Currey's book often acts as an apologia for the military chaplaincy. Drazin was one of the primary chaplains involved in the legal defense of the chaplaincy, and the book lacks the critical analysis that a more detached scholar might bring to a study.

13. Ibid., 47. Katcoff and Weider's suit was the first to actually reach the courts; five others had been dismissed or decided on their merits. Ibid. 48.

14. Between 1963 and 1971, the Supreme Court determined that the establishment clause is violated when the government makes a law (1) whose purpose is to advance religion, or (2) whose primary effect is to advance religion, or (3) in which there is excessive entanglement between government and religion. Collectively, this three-pronged test became known as the *Lemon* test. See *Lemon v. Kurtzman*.

15. Drazin and Currey, *God and Country*, 53–54, 56.

16. Ibid., 65.

17. Ibid., 68–73.

18. Ibid., 126.

19. Ibid., 134–35.

20. Ibid., 146–47.

21. Ibid., 176–77.

22. Decision text, *Katcoff v. Marsh,* quoted in ibid., 180.

23. Drazin and Currey, *For God and Country*, 184.

24. Ibid., 197.

25. They did, however, request that the case be "dismissed without prejudice," which would retain their right to refile the suit in the future.

26. Drazin and Currey, *For God and Country*, 203.

27. The best works on conservative Christians' participation in politics and public issues are Martin, *With God on Our Side*; Loveland, *American Evangelicals*; Smith, *American Evangelicalism*; Marty, *Fundamentalism and Evangelicalism*; Jensen, "Culture Wars"; and Collins, "Liberals and Conservatives."

28. This was not a new characteristic of late-twentieth-century evangelicals. Christian Smith has argued that at least since the last third of the nineteenth century, one can "readily detect in [their] elite discourse a sense of crisis, conflict, or threat." As evidence of this phenomenon, Smith points to Josiah Strong's 1885 book *Our Country: Its Possible Future and Present Crisis*, Walter Clarke's *New Era* magazine article "Christians, Save the Christian Sabbath," Harold Ockenga's 1942 address to the National Conference for United Action among Evangelicals, and Carl Henry's 1986 book *Christian Countermoves in a Decadent Culture*. See Smith, *American Evangelicalism*, 121–23.

29. Edward E. Plowman, "Bibles in the Barracks: God and the Military," *Christianity Today* (31 March 1972): 32, quoted in Loveland, *American Evangelicals*, 174.

30. Loveland, *American Evangelicals*, 174.

31. Hutcheson, *Churches and the Chaplaincy*, 94; Loveland, *American Evangelicals*, 175.

32. Groh, *Air Force Chaplains*, 443–46. For discussion of the hymnal's development and analysis of the Protestant selections, see Carr, "Development of the Book of Worship."

33. Carter, "Context."

34. Groh, *Air Force Chaplains*, 448.

35. Hymnal Task Force quoted in ibid., 447.

36. Thomas M. Groome quoted in ibid., 450.

37. James W. Chapman, *Hello, Hymnal*, USAF Chaplain Board, quoted in ibid., 451.

38. Meade quoted in ibid., 451.

39. Groh, *Air Force Chaplains,* 449–50.

40. Tom Condon, "Chaplain sees U.S. Ruin in Volunteer Army Plan," *Hartford Courant,* 12 June 1971, 7.

41. "U.S. Army Chaplain School Army '75 Workshop," USACHCS, Vietnam Files, 34.

42. Appendix D, "Conclusions: The Chaplain, the Career Soldier, and His Family," in ibid., 9.

43. "U.S. Army Chaplain School Army '75 Workshop," USACHCS, Vietnam Files, 11.

44. Ibid., 1–3.

45. Ibid., 13.

46. Anonymous Air Force chaplain, quoted in Groh, *Air Force Chaplains*, 25.

47. Groh, *Air Force Chaplains*, 25.

48. Brinsfield, *Encouraging Faith, Supporting Soldiers*, 159.

49. Gordon Schweitzer quoted in ibid., 159.

50. Ibid.

51. Groh, *Air Force Chaplains*, 290.

52. Claims in the Navy that the Chaplain Corps maintained this quota system persisted well into the 2000s. There was no regulatory or evidentiary basis for the claim.

53. Bonnie Koppell, "Female Rabbis in the Military: A View from the Trenches," *Army Chaplaincy* (Winter–Spring 2000).54. Brinsfield, *Faith in the Fight,* 36–40.

55. Ibid., 41. 56. Chaves, "Symbolic Significance of Women's Ordination," 87. See also Chaves, "Ordaining Women."

57. Carolyn C. Wiggins, "Personal Reflections on Women in Naval Chaplaincy," *Navy Chaplain* 1 (Winter 1987): 4.

58. Keizer et al., "Overview of the Role of the Unit Ministry Team," 14.

59. USARV Chaplain Duty Rosters, USACHCS, CD-ROM.

60. Keizer et al., "Overview of the Role of the Unit Ministry Team," 15.

61. Ibid.

62. "White Letter #7, Sea Warrior Ministry Council: Operational Ministry Center/Regional Ministry Center," 1, U.S. Navy Chaplain Corps, www.chaplain.navy.mil (accessed 22 October 2006).

63. Wallace, "Fleet Religious Support Activity"; "White Letter #7, Sea Warrior Ministry." 64. Wallace, "Fleet Religious Support Activity."

65. Loveland, "Prophetic Ministry."

66. Zimmerman, interview, 55–56.

67. "Evolution of the Navy Chaplain Corps Seal," http://www.chaplain.navy.mil (accessed 24 October 2006).

68. In reality, chaplains of many faith groups are "over-represented" based on percentage because of the number of nonchaplain personnel who claim "no preference" as their religious affiliation.

69. Laurie Goodstein, "Evangelicals Are a Growing Force in the Military Chaplain Corps," *New York Times*, 12 July 2005; see also Alan Cooperman, "Military Wrestles with Disharmony among Chaplains," *Washington Post*, 30 August 2005; "By the Numbers: The U.S. Military Chaplaincy," *Christian Science Monitor*, http:// www. csmonitor.com/specials/chaplains (accessed 2 March 2008).

70. Brady, "Evangelical Chaplains Test Bounds of Faith; Donald E. Skinner, "Once a Rarity, UU Military Chaplains Increasing," Unitarian Universalist News, http://www.uuworld.org/news/articles/280936.shtml (accessed 1 July 2013).

71. See, for example, the 1987 "Religious Apparel Amendment" (10 U.S.C. §774), which allowed for military personnel to wear visible religious apparel provided it did not interfere with one's military duties or the operation of military equipment. The law effectively circumvented the 5-4 Supreme Court decision in *Goldman v. Weinberger*, which declared that the military had the right to prohibit deviations from the prescribed uniform, even if such deviations were religious in nature. Chaplain Arnold E. Resnicoff, a line officer in Vietnam and later a combat chaplain, lobbied for this amendment.

72. *Rigdon v. Perry*.

73. Larry Witham, "Military Chaplains' Role Disputed," *Washington Times*, 23 September 1996, USMHI, Chaplains, Bibliography File.

74. Stanley Sporkin, memorandum opinion, *Rigdon v. Perry*, 962, F. Supp. (D.D.C. 1997).

75. *Adair v. England*; *Chaplaincy of Full Gospel Churches v. England*. These two cases were consolidated by the U.S. District Court for the District of Columbia. In 2006, the case was remanded to district court, the appellate court having ruled that the plaintiffs had demonstrated the possibility of irreparable harm if the allegations of establishment were true.

76. *Adair v. England; Chaplaincy of Full Gospel Churches v. England.*

77. Dept. of the Air Force, Headquarters, U.S. Air Force, "Report of the Headquarters Review Group."

78. Memorandum, Melinda Morton to Michael Whittington, 30 July 2004, http://www.yale.edu/divinity/notes/050516/AFA_Report.7.04.pdf (accessed 1 July 2013). See also Gustav Spohn, "Professor Kristen Leslie Testifies at Congressional Hearing on Air Force Academy; Air Force Issues Guidelines against Promoting Any Particular Faith," Yale Divinity School, "Notes from the Quad," http://www. yale.edu/divinity/notes/050831/notes_050831_afa.shtml (accessed 1 July 2013). The full Yale Practicum Team report is also available there.

79. T. R. Reid, "Air Force Removes Chaplain from Post: Officer Decried Evangelicals' Influence," *Washington Post*, 13 May 2005.

80. John J. Lumpkin, "Intolerance Cited at Air Academy: Pentagon Probe Finds No Overt Religious Bias," *Associated Press*, 23 June 2005.

81. Carl Limbacher, "Chaplain Wants Christ Out of Air Force Academy," 12 May 2005, Newsmax.com, posted to FreeRepublic.com, http://www.freerepublic.com/focus/f-news/1401963/posts (accessed 1 July 2013).

82. Department of the Air Force, "Interim Guidelines."

83. Ibid.; emphasis added.

84. United States Air Force, Revised guidelines, http://www.af.mil/news/story.asp?id=123016168 (accessed 1 July 2013).

85. Associated Press, "Air Force Eases Religion Policy," 10 February 2006.

86. Leo Shane III, "Air Force Softens Rules on Religious Expression," *Stars and Stripes*, 10 February 2006.

87. National Defense Authorization Act of 2007, H.R. 5122, Sec. 590, 109th Cong., 2d sess.

88. Congressional Research Service, "The FY2007 National Defense Authorization Act."

89. Conference Report, H.R. Rep. No. 109-702, at 739, 30 September 2006.

Conclusion

1. Liteky, "Congressional Medal of Honor Recipient Addresses U.S. Forces in Iraq."

2. Liteky quoted in Michael Taylor, "Matter of Honor: He Gave Back His Medal of Honor to Risk His Freedom in Protesting His Country's Policies," *San Francisco Chronicle*, 13 March 2000.

3. Johnson, interview.

4. Day, interview.

5. On the question of diversity and the contemporary military chaplaincy, see Hansen, *Military Chaplains and Religious Diversity*.

6. Robert Wuthnow identified this realignment as the defining feature of American Christianity in the second half of the twentieth century. See Wuthnow, *Restructuring of American Religion*.

7. See Domke, *God Willing*; Zine, "Between Orientalism and Fundamentalism," 29; Juergensmeyer, *Terror in the Mind of God;* Anonymous (Michael Scheur), *Imperial Hubris*; Elshtain, *Just War against Terror*.

8. Eric Lichtblau, "Army Cleric Who Worked with Detainees Is Arrested," *New York Times,* 21 September 2003; Yee and Molloy, *For God and Country*; Yee's official website, http://www.justiceforyee.com (accessed 1 July 2013); Tim Golden, "Loyalties and Suspicions: The Muslim Servicemen; How Dubious Evidence Spurred Relentless Guantanamo Spy Hunt," *New York Times*, 19 December 2004.

9. See, for example, Kittleson, *Meditations from Iraq;* McCoy, *Under Orders*; Cash, *Table in the Presence*; Marrero, *Quiet Reality*; Benimoff and Conant, *Faith Under Fire*; Snivley, *Heaven in the Midst of Hell*; Bryan, *Memoirs from Babylon*; Russell,

Unvalidated Pain; Carroll, *Season in Baghdad*; Tyler, *War Zone Faith*; and Ristau, *At Peace with War*. These books—several of which have been published by small, religiously oriented presses—reveal many of the same patterns as the Vietnam-era memoirs: Chaplains interpret war through religious lenses and suggest a narrative of fulfillment and redemption even in the midst of war. They are convinced of God's presence on the battlefield, and they are also sure that they are God's representatives in these circumstances.

10. See, for example, "God & War: How Chaplains and Soldiers Keep the Faith Under Fire," *Newsweek*, 7 May 2007; Andrea Stone, "Military Copes with Shortage of Chaplains," *USA Today*, 5 February 2008; Deann Alford, "Faith, Fear, War, Peace: Snapshots of the Grim and 'Happy' Ministry of Today's Military Chaplains," *Christianity Today*, 1 December 2004; Kristin Henderson, "In the Hands of God," *Washington Post Magazine,* 30 April 2006.

11. Americans United for Separation of Church and State, "Military Should Rein in Baptizing Chaplain in Iraq, Americans United Urges," Americans United press release, May 2003, https://blog.au.org/church-state/may-2003-church-state/people-events/military-should-rein-in-baptizing-chaplain-in-iraq (accessed 1 July 2013).

12. "Saluting Chaplains, Reader Letters," *Christian Century,* 26 July 2003, 43–33; Glenn Palmer, letter to the editor, *Christian Century*, 14 November 2006, 53.

BIBLIOGRAPHY

Primary Sources
Archives

National Archives of the United States, Archives II, College Park, Md.
    Record Group 247, Office of the Chief of Chaplains Central Files
    Record Group 472, Records of the United States Army Vietnam
United States Army Chaplain Center and School Library, Fort Jackson, Columbia,
    S.C.
    Vietnam Files
United States Center of Military History, Fort Leslie J. McNair, Washington, D.C.
United States Military History Institute, Carlisle, Pa.

Oral History Interviews

Andrews, Joel Earl. Interview by Rodger Venzke. 1 December 1972, Senior Officer
    Oral History Program, United States Military History Institute, Carlisle, Pa.
Arvay, Alfred S. Interview by Henry F. Ackermann. Senior Officer Oral History
    Program, United States Military History Institute, Carlisle, Pa.
Beasley, Joseph. Interview by author. 13 September 2007, Chapel Hill, N.C.
Day, Jackson. Interview by author. 19 December 2007, Columbia, Md., Transcript
    in author's possession.
Huggins, Theodore. Interview by Henry F. Ackermann. 30 October 1985, United
    States Military History Institute, Carlisle, Pa.
Johnson, James. Interview by author. 17 January 2008, Fayetteville, N.C.,
    Transcript in author's possession.
Kissinger, Harry P. Interview by Rodger Venzke, n.d., transcribed by Patricia L.
    O'Conell, United States Military History Institute, Carlisle, Pa.
Stegman, Leonard F. Interview by Henry F. Ackermann, n.d., United States
    Military History Institute, Carlisle, Pa.
Zimmerman, Matthew. Interviewer unknown, n.d., Vietnam Files, United States
    Army Chaplain Center and School, Fort Jackson, Columbia, S.C.

Published Primary Sources

Ackermann, Henry F. *He Was Always There: The U.S. Army Chaplain Ministry
    in the Vietnam Conflict*. Washington, D.C.: Office of the Chief of Chaplains,
    Department of the Army, 1989.
Ammerman, Jim. *Supernatural Events in the Life of an Ordinary Man*. Enumclaw,
    Wash.: WinePress Publishing, 1996.
Autry, Jerry. *Gun Totin' Chaplain: A True Memoir*. San Francisco: Airborne Press,
    2006.

Benimoff, Roger, with Eve Conant. *Faith Under Fire: An Army Chaplain's Memoir*. New York: Crown Publishers, 2009.

Bonhoeffer, Dietrich. *Letters and Papers from Prison*. Edited by Eberhard Bethage, enlarged ed. New York: Macmillan, 1971.

Bowers, Curt. *Forward Edge of the Battle Area: A Chaplain's Story*. Kansas City, Mo.: Beacon Hill Press, 1987.

Brown, Jack E. *Another Side of Combat: A Chaplain Remembers Vietnam*. Nashville, Tenn.: Cold Tree Press, 2006.

Bryan, Jeff. *Memoirs from Babylon: A Combat Chaplain's Life in Iraq's Triangle of Death*. Combat Chaplain Ministries, 2011.

Burnham, James. *God's Squad: Pages from a Chaplain's Vietnam Diary, 1967–1968*. Self-published.

Caputo, Philip. *A Rumor of War*. Twentieth anniversary reprint edition. New York: Holt, 1996.

Carroll, Ernie. *A Season in Baghdad: Confessions of a Combat Chaplain*. Self-published, 2008.

Carroll, James. *An American Requiem: God, My Father, and the War that Came Between Us*. New York: Mariner Books, 1997.

Carter, Sydney. "Context." *Modern Liturgy* 7 (March/April 1980): 8–9.

Cash, Carey H. *A Table in the Presence: The Dramatic Account of How a U.S. Marine Battalion Experienced God's Presence Amidst the Chaos of War in Iraq*. Nashville, Tenn.: Thomas Nelson, 2004.

Casualties of War. Directed by Brian DePalma. RCA/Columbia Pictures Home Video, 1990.

Cherry, Corbin. *From Thunder to Sunrise: Reflections of Vietnam*. Paducah, Ky.: Turner Publishing Company, 1995.

Committee on Religion and Welfare in the Armed Forces. "The Military Chaplaincy" (a report to the president by the President's Committee on Religion and Welfare in the Armed Forces). Washington, D.C.: Government Printing Office, 1951.

Congressional Research Service. "The FY2007 National Defense Authorization Act: Selected Military Personnel Policy Issues," 21 July 2006, http://www.fas.org/sgp/crs/natsec/RL33571.pdf. 2 July 2013.

Corby, William, C.S.C. *Memoirs of Chaplain Life: Three Years with the Irish Brigade in the Army of the Potomac*. Edited by Lawrence Frederick Kohl. New York: Fordham University Press, 1992.

Day, Dorothy. "Our Communist Brothers." In *The Columbia Documentary History of Religion in America since 1945*, edited by Paul Harvey and Philip Goff, 35–40. New York: Columbia University Press, 2005.

Day, Jackson. "Vietnam Chaplain: Return to Vietnam 2004," http://www.vietnamveteransministers.org/chaplain/today.htm. 2 July 2013.

Department of the Air Force. "Interim Guidelines Concerning Free Exercise of Religion in the Air Force," http://www.af.mil/news/story.asp?id=123016168. 1 July 2013.

Department of the Air Force. Headquarters, U.S. Air Force. "Report of the Headquarters Review Group Concerning Religious Climate at the U.S. Air Force Academy," June 22, 2005, http://www.af.mil/pdf/HQ_Review_Group_Report.pdf#search= %22Headquarters% 20Review%20Group%20Concerning%20Religious%20Climate %20at%20the%20U.S.%20 Air%20Force%20Academy%22Department of the Air Force. 2 March 2008.

Department of the Air Force, Office of the Chief of Chaplains. *Air Force Chaplains*. Washington, D.C.: U.S. Government Printing Office, 1961.

Department of the Army. *Department of the Army Field Manual 16–5: The Chaplain*. Washington, D.C., August 1964.

———. *Office of the Chief of Chaplains Historical Review*, 1 July 1962–30 June 1963.

———. *Office of the Chief of Chaplains Historical Review*, 1 July 1964–30 June 1965.

———. *Office of the Chief of Chaplains Historical Review*, 1 July 1965–31 December 1966.

———. *Office of the Chief of Chaplains Historical Review*, 1966–67.

———. *Office of the Chief of Chaplains Historical Review*, 1 January 1967–30 June 1968.

———. *Office of the Chief of Chaplains Historical Review*, 1968–69.

———. *Office of the Chief of Chaplains Historical Review*, 1 July 1969–30 June 1970.

Department of the Navy. "White Letter #7, Sea Warrior Ministry Council: Operational Ministry Center/Regional Ministry Center." U.S. Navy Chaplain Corps, www.chaplain.navy.mil. 22 October 2006.

———. *History of the Chaplain Corps, United States Navy*. Vol. 4, 1946–52. Chaplains Division of the Bureau of Naval Personnel. Washington, D.C.: U.S. Government Printing Office, 1953.

Department of War. *A Program for National Security*. Washington, D.C.: U.S. Government Printing Office, 1947.

Des Champs, Thomas, with Phillip McGee. *Christian Soldier: The True Story of a Highly Decorated Vietnam-Era Chaplain*. Frederick, Md.: Publish America, 2004.

Dulany, Joseph. *Once a Soldier: A Chaplain's Story*. Self-published, 2002.

Estes, Arthur J. *Paratrooper Chaplain: The Memoirs of a Lifetime of Service to Military Personnel*. Victoria, B.C., Canada: Trafford Publishing, 2008.

Falabella, J. Robert. *Vietnam Memoirs: A Passage to Sorrow*. New York: Pageant Press International, 1971.

Friedstedt, Robert R. *The Circuit Riders of NAVSUPPACT*. San Francisco: n.p., 1967.

Giap, Vo Nguyen, with Huu Mai. *Dien Bien Phu: Rendezvous with History, a Memoir*. Translated by Lady Borton. Ha Noi, Vietnam: Gioi Publishers, 2004.

Graham, Billy. *Christianism vs. Communism*. Minneapolis, Minn.: Billy Graham Evangelical Association, 1951.

Hardman, Ric. *The Chaplain's Raid*. New York: Coward McCann, 1965.

Haworth, Larry. *Tales of Thunder Run: The Convoys, the Noise, the Ambushes . . . Stories of QL 13, the Route 66 of Viet Nam*. Eugene, Ore.: ACW Press, 2004.

Herr, Michael. *Dispatches*. New York: Knopf, 1977.

Hoard, Samuel L. *The Truth Will Set You Free*. St. Louis, Mo.: Concordia Publishing House, 2002.

Hopkins, Samuel. *A Chaplain Remembers Vietnam*. Kansas City, Mo.: Truman, 2002.

Hutchens, James. *Beyond Combat*. Chicago: Moody Press, 1968.

Itokazu, Kiyo. *A Chaplain's Pilgrimage: An Autobiography*. Lincoln, Neb.: iUniverse, 2007.

Johnson, James. *Combat Chaplain: A Thirty-Year Vietnam Battle*. Denton: University of North Texas Press, 2001.

Johnson, Raymond. *Postmark: Mekong Delta*. Westwood, N.J.: Fleming H. Revell, 1968.

Jonakait, Randolph. "The Abuses of the Military Chaplaincy." American Civil Liberties Union Report, 17 February 1973, USACHCS, Vietnam Files.

Kettler, Earl. *Chaplain's Letters: Ministry by "Huey," 1964–1965, The Personal Correspondence of an Army Chaplain from Vietnam*. Cincinnati: Cornelius Books, 1994.

Kimball, William R. *Vietnam: The Other Side of Glory*. Canton, Ohio: Daring Books, 1987.

Kittleson, Lance. *Meditations from Iraq: A Chaplain's Ministry in the Middle East, 2003–2004*. Lima, Ohio: CSS Publishing, 2005.

Klug, Eugene F. "Christianity, the Chaplaincy and Militarism." *Springfielder* 31 (1968): 24–29.

Knight, David E. "Supreme Six." In *Vietnam: The Other Side of Glory*, edited by William R. Kimball, 66–88. Canton, Ohio: Daring Books, 1987.

Lang, Daniel. *Casualties of War*. New York: McGraw-Hill, 1969.

Liteky, Charles (Angelo). "Congressional Medal of Honor Recipient Addresses U.S. Forces in Iraq," 7 May 2003, Military Families Speak Out, http://mfso.org/article.php?id=85. 3 March 2008.

Lockerbie, D. Bruce. *A Man Under Orders: Lieutenant General William K. Harrison, Jr.* New York: Harper and Row, 1979.

Maguire, Connell J. *Follies of a Navy Chaplain*. Maywood, N.J.: ChiChi Press, 2003.

Mahedy, William P. *Out of the Night: The Spiritual Journey of Vietnam Vets*. New York: Ballantine Books, 1986.

Marrero, Emilio. *A Quiet Reality: A Chaplain's Journey into Babylon, Iraq, with the First Marine Expeditionary Force*. Grand Haven, Mich.: FaithWalk Publishing, 2009.

McCoy, William. *Under Orders: A Spiritual Handbook for Military Personnel*. Ozark, Ala.: ACW Press, 2005.

Mole, Robert L. "Unit Leader's Personal Response Handbook." Washington, D.C.: U.S. Government Printing Office, 1968.

Newby, Claude D., with Lucille Johnson. *It Took Heroes: A Cavalry Chaplain's Memoir of Vietnam*. New York: Ballantine Books, 2003.

O'Brien, Thomas R., ed. *Blessings from the Battlefield*. Huntington, Ind.: Our Sunday Visitor, 2002.

O'Brien, Tim. *If I Die in a Combat Zone: Box Me Up and Ship Me Home*. New York: Delacorte Press, 1973.

———. *The Things They Carried: A Work of Fiction*. Boston: Houghton Mifflin, 1990.

O'Connor, John. *A Chaplain Looks at Vietnam*. Cleveland, Ohio: World Publishing, 1968.

O'Donnell, Joseph. "Clergy in the Military—Vietnam and After." In *The Sword of the Lord: Military Chaplains from the First to the Twenty-First Century*, edited by Doris Bergen, 215–32. Notre Dame, Ind.: Notre Dame University Press, 2004.

Peers, W. R. *The My Lai Inquiry*. New York: W.W. Norton, 1979.

Plank, David W. *Called to Serve*. Springfield, Mo.: Gospel Publishing House, 1967.

Ristau, Harold. *At Peace with War: A Chaplain's Meditations from Afghanistan*. Eugene, Oreg.: Wipf and Stock Publishing, 2012.

Rose, Ben Lacy. *Memoirs of a Chaplain in Combat in World War II*. Richmond, Va.: QA Press, 2002.

Russell, Melinda. *Unvalidated Pain: A Chaplain's Journey to Iraq and Back*. Bloomington, Ind.: AuthorHouse, 2013.

Schumacher, John W. *A Soldier of God Remembers: Memoir Highlights of a Career Army Chaplain*. Winona Lake, Ind.: Grace Brethren North American Missions, 2000.

Snively, Sheri. *Heaven in the Midst of Hell: A Quaker Chaplain's View of the War in Iraq*. Riverside, Calif.: Raven Oaks Press, 2009.

Truman, Harry S. "Address before a Joint Session of the Congress on Universal Military Training," 23 October 1945. *Public Papers of the Presidents, Harry S. Truman (1945)*. Washington, D.C.: U.S. Government Printing Office, 1961.

Tyler, George. *War Zone Faith: An Army Chaplain's Reflections from Afghanistan*. Boston, Mass.: Skinner House Books, 2013.

United States Congress, Senate, Committee on Foreign Relations. 90th Cong., 1st sess., *Background Information Relating to Southeast Asia and Vietnam*. 3d rev. ed. Washington, D.C.: U.S. Government Printing Office, 1967.

Walker, Conrad, with J. Walker Winslow. *The Leapin' Deacon: The Soldier's Chaplain*. Austin, Tex.: Lang Marc Publishing, 2004.

Wallace, Stephen O. "The Fleet Religious Support Activity." U.S. Navy Chaplain Corps. Washington, D.C., 1985.

Westmoreland, William C. *A Soldier Reports*. New York: Doubleday, 1976.

Newspapers and Periodicals

Activities (Christian Science)	*The Boston Globe*
America	*The Chaplain*
American Baptist Chaplain	*Christian Century*
The American Israelite	*Christianity and Crisis*
American Mercury	*Christianity Today*
The Army Chaplaincy	*Christian Science Monitor*
The Baltimore Sun	*Commonweal*

The Disciple Chaplain	The New Yorker
Free Lance Star (Fredericksburg, Va.)	New York Times
The Hartford Courant	San Francisco Chronicle
The Humanist	The Standard
The Jewish Advocate	Stars and Stripes
The Los Angeles Times	Time Magazine
The Link	United Evangelical Action
National Catholic Register	The Veteran
The Navy Chaplain	Vietnam Magazine
Newsletter for Lutheran Chaplains	Washington Post, Times Herald
Newsweek	

Court Cases and Decisions

Adair v. England, 183, F. Supp. 2d 31, 34, n. 1 (D.D.C. 2002)

Chaplaincy of Full Gospel Churches v. England, 276, F. Supp. 2d 79 (D.D.C. 2003)

Goldman v. Weinberger, 475 U.S. 503 (1986)

Katcoff v. Marsh, 755 F.2d 223, 225–29 (Calif. 2 1985)

Lemon v. Kurtzman, 89, 310 F. Supp. (1971)

Rigdon v. Perry, 962, F. Supp. (D.D.C. 1997)

United States v. Seeger (1964)

Secondary Sources
Books and Articles

Abercrombie, Clarence. *The Military Chaplaincy*. Beverly Hills, Calif.: Sage Publications, 1997.

Ackermann, Henry F. *He Was Always There: The U.S. Army Chaplain Ministry in the Vietnam Conflict*. Office of the Chief of Chaplains. Washington, D.C.: U.S. Government Printing Office, 1989.

Ahern, Marie L. *The Rhetoric of War: Training Day, the Militia, and the Military Sermon*. New York: Greenwood Press, 1989.

Ahlstrom, Sydney. *A Religious History of the American People*. New Haven, Conn.: Yale University Press, 1972.

Albanese, Catherine. *Sons of the Fathers: The Civil Religion of the American Revolution*. Philadelphia: Temple University Press, 1976.

Alexander, Paul. *From Peace to War: Shifting Allegiances in the Assemblies of God*. Telford, Pa.: Cascadia Publishing House, 2009.

Alkula, Charles J. "Out of Many, One: The Formation of a Community of Faith in the Sea Services." D.Min. dissertation, Drew University, 2005.

Allitt, Patrick. *Religion in America since 1945: A History*. New York: Columbia University Press, 2003.

Anderson, David L., ed. *The Columbia History of the Vietnam War*. New York: Columbia University Press, 2011.

Anonymous (Mark Scheur). *Imperial Hubris: Why the West is Losing the War on Terror*. N.p.: Brassey's, 2004.

Appelbaum, Patricia. *Protestant Pacifist Culture between World War I and the Vietnam Era*. Chapel Hill: University of North Carolina Press, 2009.

Appelquist, A. Ray. *Church, State, and Chaplaincy: Essays and Statements on the American Chaplaincy System*. Washington, D.C.: General Commission on Chaplains and Armed Services Personnel, 1969.

Bal, Mieke, Jonathan Crewe, and Leo Spitzer. *Acts of Memory: Cultural Recall in the Present*. Hanover, N.H.: University Press of New England, 1999.

Baldwin, Christina. *Life's Companion: Journal Writing as a Spiritual Quest*. New York: Bantam, 1991.

Barrett, David M. *Uncertain Warriors: Lyndon Johnson and His Vietnam Advisors*. Lawrence: University Press of Kansas, 1993.

Barth, Karl. *The Epistle to the Romans*. Translated by Edwyn C. Hoskyns. 1922. New York: Oxford University Press, 1968.

———. *The Holy Spirit and the Christian Life: The Theological Basis of Ethics*. Louisville, Ky.: Westminster/John Knox Press, 1993.

Bates, Milton J. *The Wars We Took to Vietnam: Cultural Conflict and Storytelling*. Berkeley: University of California Press, 1996.

Bellah, Robert. *The Broken Covenant: American Civil Religion in Time of Trial*. New York: Seabury Press, 1975.

———. "Civil Religion in America." *Daedalus* 96 (Winter 1967): 1–21.

Berg, Thomas C. "'Proclaiming Together?' Convergence and Divergence in Mainline and Evangelical Evangelicalism, 1945–1967," *Religion and American Culture* 5 (Winter 1995): 49–76.

Bergen, Doris. *Twisted Cross: The German Christian Movement in the Third Reich*. Chapel Hill: University of North Carolina Press, 1996.

———, ed. *The Sword of the Lord: Military Chaplains from the First to the Twenty-First Century*. Notre Dame, Ind.: University of Notre Dame Press, 2004.

Bergsma, Herbert. *Chaplains with Marines in Vietnam, 1962–1971*. Washington, D.C.: United States Marine Corps, 1985.

Black, Jeremy. "Determinisms and Other Issues." *Journal of Military History* 68 (October 2004): 1217–32.

Bogaski, George A. "Swords and Plowshares: American Protestants and the Vietnam War." Ph.D. dissertation, University of Oklahoma, 2010.

Bogle, Lori Lynn. *The Pentagon's Battle for the American Mind: The Early Cold War*. College Station: Texas A&M, 2004.

Bolton, Gillie. "Taking the Thinking Out of It: Writing, a Therapeutic Space." *Journal of the British Association for Counselling* 6 (1995): 215–18.

———. *The Therapeutic Potential of Creative Writing: Writing Myself*. London: Jessica Kingsley Publishers, 1999.

Bonomi, Patricia. *Under the Cope of Heaven: Religion, Society, and Politics in Colonial America*. Updated ed. Oxford: Oxford University Press, 2003.

Bradley, Mark P. *Imagining Vietnam and America: The Making of Postcolonial Vietnam, 1919–1950*. Chapel Hill: University of North Carolina Press, 2000.

Brady, Jeff. "Evangelical Chaplains Test Bounds of Faith in Military," National Public Radio, *All Things Considered*, 27 July 2005.

Brinsfield, John W. *Encouraging Faith, Supporting Soldiers: The United States Army Chaplaincy, 1975–1995.* Washington, D.C.: U.S. Government Printing Office, 1997.

———. *Faith in the Fight: Civil War Chaplains.* Mechanicsburg, Pa.: Stackpole Books, 2003.

Brown, Robert McAfee, Abraham Heschel, and Michael Novak. *Vietnam: Crisis of Conscience.* New York: Association Press, 1967.

Budd, Richard. *Serving Two Masters: The Development of American Military Chaplaincy, 1860–1920.* Lincoln: University of Nebraska Press, 2002.

Burchard, Waldo W. "Role Conflicts of Military Chaplains." *American Sociological Review* 19 (October 1954): 196–210.

Burkett, B[ernard] G. *Stolen Valor: How the Vietnam Generation was Robbed of Its Heroes and Its History.* Dallas, Tex.: Veracity Press, 1998.

Butler, Jon. *Awash in a Sea of Faith: Christianizing the American People.* Cambridge, Mass.: Harvard University Press, 1990.

———. "Jack in the Box Faith: The Religion Problem in Modern American History." *Journal of American History* 90, no. 4 (March 2004): 1357–78.

Canipe, Lee. "Under God and Anti-Communist: How the Pledge of Allegiance God Religion in Cold War America." *Journal of Church and State* (2003): 305–23.

Capps, Walter. *The Unfinished War: Vietnam and the American Conscience.* Boston: Beacon Press, 1982.

Carey, James W. *Communication as Culture.* Boston: Unwin Hyman, 1989.

Carr, Gary W. "The Development of the Book of Worship for United States Forces." Mdiv. thesis, Duke University Divinity School, 1996.

Carroll, Jackson W., Douglas W. Johnson, and Martin E. Marty. *Religion in America: 1950 to the Present.* San Francisco: Harper and Row, 1979.

Carter, Bradley L. ""Reverence Helmeted and Armored': A Study of Twentieth-Century United States Military Chaplain Memoirs." Ph.D. diss., University of Kansas, 2004.

Catton, Philip E. *Diem's Final Failure: Prelude to America's War in Vietnam.* Lawrence: University Press of Kansas, 2002.

Chapman, Jessica M. "Staging Democracy: South Vietnam's 1955 Referendum to Depose Bao Dai." *Diplomatic History* 30 (September 2006): 671–703.

Chaves, Mark. "Ordaining Women: The Diffusion of an Organizational Innovation." *American Journal of Sociology* 101 (January 1996): 840–73.

———. "The Symbolic Significance of Women's Ordination." *Journal of Religion* 77 (January 1997): 87–114.

Chomsky, Noam. *Rethinking Camelot: JFK, the Vietnam War, and U.S. Political Culture.* Cambridge, Mass.: South End Press, 1993.

Clough, David. *Ethics in Crisis: Interpreting Barth's Ethics.* Burlington, Vt.: Ashgate Publishing, 2005.

Cobb, John, and David Griffin. *Process Theology: An Introductory Exposition.* Philadelphia: Westminster Press, 1976.

Coffman, Elesha. "Constituting the Protestant Mainline: The *Christian Century,* 1908–1947." Ph.D. diss., Duke University, 2008.

Collins, Randall. "Liberals and Conservatives, Religious and Political: A Conjuncture of Modern History." *Sociology of Religion* 54, no. 2 (1993): 127–46.

Cox, Caroline. *A Proper Sense of Honor: Service and Sacrifice in George Washington's Army*. Chapel Hill: University of North Carolina Press, 2007.

Cox, Harvey G. *Military Chaplains: From a Religious Military to a Military Religion*. New York: American Report Press, 1971.

Craig, Campbell. "The New Meaning of Modern War in the Thought of Reinhold Niebuhr." *Journal of the History of Ideas* 53, no. 4 (October–December 1992): 687–701.

Crouse, Eric R. "Popular Cold Warriors: Conservative Protestants, Communism, and Culture in Early Cold War America." *Journal of Religion and Popular Culture* 2 (Fall 2002): 1–18.

Daddis, Gregory A. *No Sure Victory: Measuring U.S. Army Effectiveness and Progress in the Vietnam War*. New York: Oxford University Press, 2011.

Dawley, Alan. *Changing the World: American Progressives in War and Revolution*. Princeton, N.J.: Princeton University Press, 2005.

DeBenedetti, Charles, and Charles Chatfield. *An American Ordeal: The Antiwar Movement of the Vietnam Era*. Syracuse, N.Y.: Syracuse University Press, 1990.

Domke, David. *God Willing: Political Fundamentalism in the White House, the "War on Terror," and the Echoing Press*. Ann Arbor: University of Michigan Press, 2004.

Dorrien, Gary. *Soul in Society: The Making and Renewal of Social Christianity*. Minneapolis, Minn.: Fortress Press, 1995.

Dorsey, Peter A. *Sacred Estrangement: The Rhetoric of Conversion in Modern American Autobiography*. University Park: Pennsylvania State University Press, 1993.

Drazin, Israel, and Cecil B. Currey. *For God and Country: The History of a Constitutional Challenge to the Army Chaplaincy*. Hoboken, N.J.: KTAV, 1995.

Dudziak, Mary L. *Cold War Civil Rights: Race and the Image of American Democracy*. Princeton, N.J.: Princeton University Press, 2000.

Duiker, William J. *Sacred War: Nationalism and Revolution in a Divided Vietnam*. New York: McGraw Hill, 1995.

———. "Waging Revolutionary War: The Evolution of Hanoi's Strategy in the South, 1959–1965." In *The Vietnam War: Vietnamese and American Perspectives*, edited by Jayne S. Werner and Luu Doan Huynh, 24–36. Armonk, N.Y.: M. E. Sharpe, 1993.

Eakin, Paul John, ed., *American Autobiography: Retrospect and Prospect*. Madison: University of Wisconsin Press, 1991.

Ebel, Jonathan. *Faith in the Fight: Religion and the American Soldier in the Great War*. Princeton, N.J.: Princeton University Press, 2010.

Ellis, Richard. *To the Flag: The Unlikely History of the Pledge of Allegiance*. Lawrence: University Press of Kansas, 2005.

Ellwood, Robert S. *The Sixties Spiritual Awakening: American Religion Moving from Modern to Postmodern*. New Brunswick, N.J.: Rutgers University Press, 1994.

Elshtain, Jean Bethke. *Just War against Terror: The Burden of American Power in a Violent World*. New York: Basic Books, 2003.

Fall, Bernard. *Hell in a Very Small Place: The Siege at Dien Bien Phu*. Philadelphia: Lippincott, 1967.

Farrell, James J. "Thomas Merton and the Religion of the Bomb." *Religion and American Culture* 5 (Winter 1995): 77–98.

Faulkner, Lauren. "Against Bolshevism: Georg Werthmann and the Role of Ideology in the Catholic Military Chaplaincy." *Contemporary European History* 19, no. 1 (January 2010): 1–16.

Fiol, J. R. "A Goodly Heritage: The Making of a Military Chaplain." *Presbyterion* 14 (1988): 123–27.

Flipse, Scott. "To Save 'Free Vietnam' and Lose Our Souls: The Missionary Impulse, Voluntary Agencies, and Protestant Dissent against the War, 1965–1971." In *The Foreign Missionary Enterprise at Home: Explorations in North American Cultural History*, edited by Daniel H. Bays and Grant Wacker, 206–22. Tuscaloosa: University of Alabama Press, 2003.

Fox, Richard W. "Reinhold Niebuhr and the Emergence of the Liberal Realist Faith, 1930–1945." *Review of Politics* 38 (April 1976): 244–65.

Friedberg, Aaron. *In the Shadow of the Garrison State: America's Anti-Statism and Its Cold War Grand Strategy*. Princeton, N.J.: Princeton University Press, 2000.

Friedland, Michael Brooks. *Lift Up Your Voice Like a Trumpet: White Clergy and the Civil Rights and Antiwar Movements, 1954–1973*. Chapel Hill: University of North Carolina Press, 1998.

Gamble, Richard. *The War for Righteousness: Progressive Christianity, the Great War, and the Rise of the Messianic Nation*. Wilmington, Del.: Intercollegiate Studies Institute, 2003.

Garrow, David J. *Bearing the Cross: Martin Luther King, Jr., and the Southern Christian Leadership Conference*. New York: Harper Collins, 1986.

Gelb, Leslie, and Richard Betts. *The Irony of Vietnam: They System Worked*. Washington, D.C.: Brookings Institute, 1978.

Germain, Aiden. *Catholic Military and Naval Chaplains, 1776–1914*. Washington, D.C.: Catholic University of America Press, 1929.

Gershen, Martin. *Destroy or Die: The True Story of Mylai*. New Rochelle, N.Y.: Arlington House, 1971.

Gheddo, Piero. *The Cross and the Bo-Tree: Catholics and Buddhists in Vietnam*. Translated by Charles Underhill Quinn. New York: Sheed and Ward, 1970.

Gilbert, Kathy. "Hard Tour in Vietnam Became Chaplain's 'Greatest Ministry.'" United Methodist Church. Interview with Billy Whiteside, 27 May 2005, http://archives.umc.org/interior.asp?ptid=2&mid=7985. 25 February 2008.

Gill, Jill K. *Embattled Ecumenism: The National Council of Churches, the Vietnam War, and the Trials of the Protestant Left*. DeKalb: Northern Illinois University Press, 2012.

———. "'Peace Is Not the Absence of War, but the Presence of Justice': The National Council of Churches' Reaction and Response to the Vietnam War, 1965–1972." Ph.D. dissertation, University of Pennsylvania, 1996.

———. "The Political Price of Prophetic Leadership: The National Council of Churches and the Vietnam War." *Peace and Change* 27, no. 2 (2000): 271–300.

Goldstein, Joseph, Burke Marshall, and Jack Schwartz. United States Department of the Army. *The My Lai Massacre and Its Cover-up: Beyond the Reach of Law?: The Peers Commission Report*. New York: Free Press, 1976.

Goldstein, Warren. *William Sloane Coffin, Jr.: A Holy Impatience*. New Haven, Conn.: Yale University Press, 2004.

Granberg, Donald, and Keith E. Campbell, "Certain Aspects of Religiosity and Orientations toward the Vietnam War among Missouri Undergraduates." *Sociological Analysis* 34, no. 1 (Spring 1973): 40–49.

Gray, J. Glenn. *The Warriors: Reflections on Men in Battle*. 1959. Lincoln: University of Nebraska Press, 1998.

Griggs, Walter S., Jr. "The Selective Conscientious Objector: A Vietnam Legacy." *Journal of Church and State* 21 (1979): 91–107.

Groh, John E. *Air Force Chaplains, 1971–1980*. Air Force Chaplains, vol. 5. Washington, D.C.: Office, Chief of Air Force Chaplains, 1986.

Grossman, Dave. *On Killing: The Psychological Cost of Learning to Kill in War and Society*. New York: Back Bay Books, 2009.

Grun, Margaret Kibben. "The Military Chaplaincy: Defining the Tension, Discovering the Opportunity." D.Min. dissertation, Princeton Theological Seminary, 2002.

Gushwa, Robert L. *The Best and Worst of Times, 1920–1945*. Office of the Chief of Chaplains, The United States Army Chaplaincy. Vol. 4. Washington, D.C.: U.S. Government Printing Office, 1977.

Gustafson, Merlin. "Church, State, and Cold War, 1945–1952." *Journal of Church and State* 8 (1966): 49–63.

Hadaway, C. Kirk, Penny Long Marler, and Mark Chaves. "Overrepresenting Church Attendance in America: Evidence that Demands the Same Verdict." *American Sociological Review* 63, no. 1 (February 1998): 122–30.

———. "What the Polls Don't Show: A Closer Look at U.S. Church Attendance." *American Sociological Review* 58, no. 6 (December 1993): 741–52.

Hale, Wallace. "Religious Education in the Armed Forces." *International Journal of Religious Education* 36 (1960): 17–18.

Hall, David G., ed. *Lived Religion in America: Toward a History of Practice*. Princeton, N.J.: Princeton University Press, 1997.

Hall, Mitchell K. *Because of Their Faith: CALCAV and Religious Opposition to the Vietnam War*. New York: Columbia University Press, 1990.

———. *The Vietnam War*. New York: Longman, 2000.

Hall, Simon. *Rethinking the American Anti-War Movement*. New York: Routledge, 2012.

Hallin, Daniel. *The "Uncensored War": The Media and Vietnam*. New York: Oxford University Press, 1986.

Hamilton, Michael P. ed. *The Vietnam War: Christian Perspectives*. Grand Rapids, Mich.: Eerdmans, 1967.

Hammer, Ellen J. "Geneva, 1954: The Precarious Peace." In *Light at the End of the Tunnel: A Vietnam War Anthology*. Rev. ed., edited by Andrew J. Rotter, 47–56. Wilmington, Del.: SR Books, 1999.

Hammond, Philip E., Amanda Porterfield, James G. Moseley, Jonathan D. Sarna. "Forum: American Civil Religion Revisited." *Religion and American Culture* 4, no. 1 (Winter 1994): 1–23.

Hammond, William M. *Reporting Vietnam: Media and Military at War.* Lawrence: University Press of Kansas, 1998.

Hansen, Kim Philip. *Military Chaplains and Religious Diversity*. New York: Palgrave Macmillan, 2012.

Hedrick, Charles. "On Foreign Soil: The Tragedy of a Civilianized Chaplaincy during the Mexican-American War." *Military Chaplains' Review* (Winter 1992): 61–85.

Heineman, Kenneth J. "American Schism: Catholic Activists, Intellectuals, and Students Confront the Vietnam War." In *The Vietnam War on Campus: Other Voices, More Distant Drums*, edited by Marc Jason Gilbert, 89–118. Westport, Conn.: Praeger, 2001.

Hentoff, Nat. *John Cardinal O'Connor: At the Storm Center of a Changing American Catholic Church*. New York: Scribner, 1988.

Herberg, Will. *Protestant, Catholic, Jew: An Essay in American Religious Sociology*. Garden City, N.Y.: Doubleday, 1955.

Herring, George C. *America's Longest War: The United States and Vietnam, 1950–1975*. 2d ed. New York: Knopf, 1986.

Herzog, Jonathan P. *The Spiritual-Industrial Complex: America's Religious Battle against Communism in the Early Cold War*. New York: Oxford University Press, 2011.

Herzog, Tobey C. *Vietnam War Stories: Innocence Lost*. London: Routledge, 1992.

Hess, Gary *Vietnam: Explaining America's Lost War*. Malden, Mass.: Blackwell, 2009.

Hiebert, Erwin N. *The Impact of Atomic Energy: A History of Responses of Government, Scientific, and Religious Groups*. Newton, Kans.: Faith and Life Press, 1961.

Hogan, Michael. *A Cross of Iron: Harry S. Truman and the Origins of the National Security State, 1945–1954*. Cambridge, UK: Cambridge University Press, 1998.

Hornsby, Benny Jackson. "A Design for Equipping Chaplains for Ministry in Combat and Crisis Situations in the United States Navy." D.Min. dissertation, Fuller Theological Seminary, 1989.

Hulsether, Mark. *Building a Protestant Left: Christianity and Crisis Magazine, 1941–1993*. Knoxville: University of Tennessee Press, 1999.

Hunt, Michael H. *Lyndon Johnson's War: America's Cold War Crusade in Vietnam, 1945–1968*. New York: Hill and Wang, 1996.

Hutcheson, Richard. *The Churches and the Chaplaincy*. Atlanta, Ga.: John Knox Press, 1975.

Hutchison, William R. *Between the Times: The Travel of the Protestant Establishment in America.* New York: Cambridge University Press, 1989.

Hynes, Samuel. *The Soldiers' Tale: Bearing Witness to Modern War*. New York: Viking, Penguin Press, 1997.

Jacobs, Seth. *America's Miracle Man in Vietnam: Ngo Dinh Diem, Religion, Race, and United States Intervention in Southeast Asia, 1950–1957*. Durham, N.C.: Duke University Press, 2004.

———. *Cold War Mandarin: Ngo Dinh Diem and the Origins of the Vietnam War, 1950–1963*. Lanham, Md.: Rowman & Littlefield, 2006.

Jason, Philip K. *Acts and Shadows: The Vietnam War in American Literary Culture*. Lanham, Md.: Rowman and Littlefield, 2000.

———, ed. *Fourteen Landing Zones: Approaches to Vietnam War Literature*. Iowa City: University of Iowa Press, 1991.

Jenkins, Robert John. "Collective Protestant Worship: Accommodation in Form." D.Min. dissertation, Drew University, 1995.

Jensen, Richard. "The Culture Wars, 1965–1995: A Historian's Map." *Journal of Social History* 29, Social History and the American Political Climate (1995): 17–37.

John of the Cross. *Dark Night of the Soul*. Translated by Mirabi Starr. New York: Riverhead Books, 2002.

Johnstone, Tom, and James Hagerty. *The Cross on the Sword: Catholic Chaplains in the Forces*. London: Geoffrey Chapman, 1996.

Jones, Michael T. "The Air Force Chaplain: Clergy or Officer?" Air War College Student Paper. Maxwell Air Force Base, Air War College, Air University, 1996.

Juergensmeyer, Mark. *Terror in the Mind of God: The Global Rise of Religious Violence*. Rev. ed. Berkeley: University of California Press, 2003.

Kaiser, David. *American Tragedy: Kennedy, Johnson, and the Origins of the Vietnam War*. Cambridge, Mass.: Belknap Press, 2000.

Keizer, Herman, Kenneth A. Seifried, David L. Howard, and Joseph E. Miller. "An Overview of the Role of the Unit Ministry Team (UMT) in Operation Desert Shield/Desert Storm with a Critical Evaluation of Religious Support Activities and Technical Doctrine and Command Team Assessment of UMT Actions, Capabilities and Effectiveness." Army War College Student Paper, U.S. Army War College, Carlisle Barracks, 1992, USMHI AWC Student Papers 1991/1992—Jones to Roach, filed under Keizer.

Kindsvatter, Peter S. *American Soldiers: Ground Combat in the World Wars, Korea, and Vietnam*. Lawrence: University of Kansas Press, 2003.

Klein, Kerwin Lee. "On the Emergence of Memory in Historical Discourse." *Representations* 69 (2000): 127–50.

Kolko, Gabriel. *Anatomy of a War: Vietnam, the United States, and the Modern Historical Experience*. New York: Pantheon, 1985.

Krepinevich, Andrew F., Jr. *The Army in Vietnam*. Baltimore, Md.: Johns Hopkins University Press, 1986.

Kurzman, Dan. *No Greater Glory: The Four Immortal Chaplains and the Sinking of the Dorchester in World War II*. New York: Random House, 2004.

L'Abate, Luciano. "The Use of Writing in Psychotherapy." *American Journal of Psychotherapy* (1991): 45, 87–91.

LaCapra, Dominick. *Rethinking Intellectual History: Texts, Contexts, Language.* Ithaca, N.Y.: Cornell University Press, 1983.

Laufer, Robert S. "War Trauma and Human Development: The Viet Nam Experience." In *The Trauma of War: Stress and Recovery in Viet Nam Veterans*, edited by Stephen M. Sonnenberg, Arthur S. Blank Jr., and John A. Talbott, 31–56. Washington, D.C.: American Psychiatric Press, 1985.

Lawrence, Mark A. *Assuming the Burden: Europe and the American Commitment to War in Vietnam.* Berkeley: University of California Press, 2005.

Lee, Wayne E. "Mind and Matter—Cultural Analysis in American Military History: A Look at the State of the Field." *Journal of American History* 93 (March 2007): 1116–42.

Lembke, Jerry. *The Spitting Image: Myth, Memory, and the Legacy of Vietnam.* New York: New York University Press, 1998.

Lepore, Jill. "Dead Men Tell No Tales: John Sassamon and the Fatal Consequences of Literacy." *American Quarterly* 46 (December 1994): 479–512.

———. *The Name of War: King Philip's War and the Origins of American Identity.* New York: Knopf, 1998.

Logevall, Fredrik. *Choosing War: The Lost Chance for Peace and the Escalation of War in Vietnam.* Berkeley: University of California Press, 1999.

Loveland, Anne C. *American Evangelicals and the U.S. Military, 1942–1993.* Baton Rouge: Louisiana State University Press, 1996.

———. "Character Education in the U.S. Army, 1947–1977." *Journal of Military History* 64 (July 2000): 795–818.

———. "From Morale Builders to Moral Advocates: U.S. Army Chaplains in the Second Half of the Twentieth Century." In *The Sword of the Lord: Military Chaplains from the First to the Twenty-First Century*, edited by Doris L. Bergen, 233–50. Notre Dame, Ind.: University of Notre Dame Press, 2004.

———. "Prophetic Ministry and the Military Chaplaincy during the Vietnam Era." In *Moral Problems in American Life: New Perspectives on Cultural History*, edited by Karen Halttunen and Lewis Perry, 245–60. Ithaca: Cornell University Press, 1998.

Lovin, Robin W. *Reinhold Niebuhr and Christian Realism.* Cambridge, UK: Cambridge University Press, 1995.

Lynn, John. *Battle: A History of Combat and Culture, from Ancient Greece to Modern America.* Boulder, Colo.: Westview Press, 2003.

Martin, William. *With God on Our Side: The Rise of the Religious Right in America.* New York: Broadway Books, 1996.

Marty, Martin E. "Reinhold Niebuhr and the Irony of American History: A Retrospective." *History Teacher* 26, no. 2 (1993): 161–74.

———. "Reinhold Niebuhr: Public Theology and the American Experience." *Journal of Religion* 54 (October 1974): 332–59.

———. "Two Kinds of Civil Religion." In *Civil Religion in America*, edited by Russell E. Richey and Donald G. Jones, 139–57. New York: Harper and Row, 1974.

———. *Under God, Indivisible, 1941–1960.* Vol. 3 of *Modern American Religion.* Chicago: University of Chicago Press, 1986.

————, ed. *Fundamentalism and Evangelicalism: Modern American Protestantism and Its World*. Munich, Germany: K.G. Saur, 1993.

May, Larry. *The Big Tomorrow: Hollywood and the Politics of the American Way*. Chicago: University of Chicago Press, 2000.

Mazur, Eric Michael. *The Americanization of Religious Minorities: Confronting the Constitutional Order*. Baltimore, Md.: Johns Hopkins University Press, 1999.

McCormick, Michael. "The Liturgy of War from Antiquity to the Crusades." In *The Sword of the Lord: Military Chaplains from the First to the Twenty-First Century*, edited by Doris L. Bergen, 45–67. Notre Dame, Ind.: University of Notre Dame Press, 2004.

McCoy, Alfred W. *The Politics of Heroin*. Chicago, Ill.: Lawrence Hill, 1991.

McCoy, William. *Under Orders: A Spiritual Handbook for Military Personnel*. Ozark, Ala.: ACW Press, 2005.

Mead, Sidney. *The Nation with the Soul of a Church*. New York: Harper and Row, 1975.

Melville, Herman. *Billy Budd, Sailor: An Inside Narrative Reading Text and Genetic Text*. Edited by Harrison Hayford and Merton M. Sealts. Chicago: University of Chicago Press, 2001.

Mesle, C. Robert. *Process Theology: A Basic Introduction*. St. Louis, Mo.: Chalice Press, 1993.

Miller, Edward. "Vision, Power and Agency: The Ascent of Ngô Đình Diêm, 1945–1954." *Journal of Southeast Asian Studies* 35, no. 3 (October 2004): 433–58.

Miller, Perry. *Errand into the Wilderness*. Cambridge, Mass.: Harvard University Press, 1956.

Miller, Randall M., Harry S. Stout, Charles Reagan Wilson, eds. *Religion and the American Civil War*. New ed. New York: Oxford University Press, 1998.

Mode, Daniel. *The Grunt Padre: The Service and Sacrifice of Father Vincent Robert Capodanno, Vietnam 1966–1967*. Oak Lawn, Ill.: CMJ Marian Publishers, 2000.

Moïse, Edwin. "Recent Accounts of the Vietnam War—A Review Article." *Journal of Asian Studies* 44 (February 1985): 343–48.

————. *Tonkin Gulf and the Escalation of the Vietnam War*. Chapel Hill: University of North Carolina Press, 1996.

Montgomery, Robert E. "God, the Army, and Judicial Review: The In-Service Conscientious Objector." *California Law Review* 56, no. 2.

Moore, Deborah Dash. "Jewish GIs and the Creation of the Judeo-Christian Tradition." *Religion and American Culture* 8 (Winter 1998): 31–53.

Moore, Harold G., and Joseph L. Galloway. *We Were Soldiers Once . . . and Young*. New York: Random House, 1992.

Moore, Richard G. "The Military Chaplaincy as Ministry." MA thesis, Duke University, 1993.

Moore, Withers M., Herbert L. Bergsma, Timothy Demy. *Chaplains with U.S. Naval Units in Vietnam, 1954–1975: Selected Experiences at Sea and Ashore*. Vol. 9, *History of the Chaplain Corps, United States Navy*. Washington, D.C.: U.S. Government Printing Office, 1985.

Morris, Aldon. *The Origins of the Civil Rights Movement: Black Communities Organizing for Change.* New York: Free Press, 1984.

Moyar, Mark. *Triumph Forsaken: The Vietnam War, 1954–1965.* Cambridge, UK: Cambridge University Press, 2006.

Musto, David F. *The American Disease: Origins of Narcotic Control.* 3rd ed. New York: Oxford University Press, 1999.

Neilson, Jim. *Warring Fictions: American Literary Culture and the Vietnam War Narrative.* Jackson: University Press of Mississippi, 1998.

Nepstad, Sharon Erikson. *Convictions of the Soul: Religion, Culture, and Agency in the Central America Solidarity Movement.* Oxford: Oxford University Press, 2004.

Neuhaus, Richard John. "The War, the Churches, and Civil Religion." *Annals of the American Academy of Political and Social Science,* The Sixties: Radical Change in American Religion, 387 (January 1970): 128–40.

Newman, William M., and Peter L. Halvorson. *Patterns of Pluralism: A Portrait of American Religion, 1952–1971.* Washington, D.C.: Glenmary Research Center, 1980.

Niebuhr, Reinhold. *Christian Realism and Political Problems.* New York: Scribner, 1953.

Noll, Mark. *The Civil War as a Theological Crisis.* Chapel Hill: University of North Carolina Press, 2006.

Nord, David Paul. "The Uses of Memory: An Introduction." *Journal of American History* 85, no. 2 (September 1998): 409–10.

Nordell, John R., Jr. *The Undetected Enemy: French and American Miscalculations at Dien Bien Phu 1953.* College Station: Texas A&M University Press, 1995.

Norton, Herman A. *Struggling for Recognition, 1791–1865.* Office of the Chief of Chaplains, The United States Army Chaplaincy. Vol. 2. Washington, D.C.: U.S. Government Printing Office, 1977.

Nutt, Rick. *Toward Peacemaking: Presbyterians in the South and National Security, 1945–1983.* Tuscaloosa: University of Alabama Press, 2007.

O'Neill, James H. "The True Story of the Patton Prayer." *Review of the News,* 6 October 1971.

Park, Richard Louis. "A Program to Clarify Role Expectations of the Military Chaplain." D.Min. dissertation, Southern Baptist Theological Seminary, 1978.

Peers, W. R. *The My Lai Inquiry.* New York: W.W. Norton, 1979.

Pennebaker, J[ames] W. "Overcoming Inhibition: Rethinking the Roles of Personality, Cognition, and Social Behavior." In *Emotion, Inhibition and Health,* edited by Harald C. Traue and J[ames] W. Pennebaker, 100–115. Seattle: Hogrefe and Huber, 1993.

Polner, Murray, and Jim O'Grady. *Disarmed and Dangerous: The Radical Lives and Times of Daniel and Philip Berrigan.* New York: Basic Books, 1997.

Prados, John, and Ray W. Stubbe. *Valley of Decision: The Siege at Khe Sanh.* Boston: Houghton Mifflin, 1991.

Pratt, Andrew Leroy. "Religious Faith and Civil Religion: Evangelical Responses to the Vietnam War, 1964–1973." Ph.D. dissertation, Southern Baptist Theological Seminary, 1988.

Preston, Andrew. "Bridging the Gap between the Sacred and the Secular in the History of American Foreign Relations." *Diplomatic History* 30, no. 5 (November 2006): 783–812.

Prugh, George S. *Law at War: Vietnam, 1964–1973*. Washington, D.C.: Department of the Army, 1975.

Pusateri, Richard. "A Basis for Military Chaplains' Moral and Ethical Advisory to Commands." D.Min. dissertation, Princeton Theological Seminary, 2004.

Quinley, Harold E. "Hawks and Doves among the Clergy: Protestant Reactions to the War in Vietnam." *Ministry Studies* 3, no. 3 (1969): 5–20.

Radstone, Susannah. "Working with Memory: An Introduction." In *Memory and Methodology*, edited by Susannah Radstone, 1–22. New York: Berg, 2000.

Reaser, Clarence L. "Military Chaplain: God's Man or the Government's?." *Princeton Seminary Bulletin* 62, no. 3 (1969): 70–73.

Reichardt, Mary R., ed. *Encyclopedia of Catholic Literature*. Westport, Conn.: Greenwood Press, 2004.

Richey, Russell E., and Donald G. Jones, eds. *Civil Religion in America*. New York: Harper and Row, 1974.

Riddle, John. *For God and Country: Four Stories of Courageous Military Chaplains*. Uhrichsville, Ohio: Barbour Publishing, 2003.

Ringnalda, Don. *Fighting and Writing the Vietnam War*. Jackson: University Press of Mississippi, 1994.

Robnett, Belinda. *How Long? How Long? African-American Women in the Struggle for Civil Rights*. New York: Oxford University Press, 1997.

Rodrigues, Jose A. "Ethics and the Army Chaplain." MS thesis, Duke University, 1997.

Scharlemann, Martin H. *Air Force Chaplains, 1961–1970*. Office of the Chief of Air Force Chaplains. Air Force Chaplains. Vol. 3. Washington, D.C.: U.S. Government Printing Office, 1972.

Schlesinger, Arthur M., Jr. "Reinhold Niebuhr's Role in American Political Thought and Life." In *Reinhold Niebuhr: His Religious, Social, and Political Thought*, edited by Charles W. Kegley and Robert W. Bretall, 125–50. New York: MacMillan, 1956.

Schultz, Kevin M., and Paul Harvey. "Everywhere and Nowhere: Recent Trends in American Religious History and Historiography." *Journal of the American Academy of Religion* 78, no. 1 (2010): 129–62.

Scott, Joan W. "The Evidence of Experience." *Critical Inquiry* 17 (Summer 1991): 773–97.

Settje, David E. *Faith and War: How Christians Debated the Cold and Vietnam Wars*. New York: New York University Press, 2011.

———. *Lutherans and the Longest War: Adrift on a Sea of Doubt about the Cold and Vietnam Wars, 1964–1975*. Lanham, Md.: Lexington Books, 2007.

———. "'Sinister' Communists and Vietnam Quarrels: The Christian Century and Christianity Today Respond to the Cold and Vietnam Wars." *Fides et Historia* 32, no. 1 (2000): 81–97.

Shy, John. "The Cultural Approach to the History of War." *Journal of Military History* 57, no. 5 (October 1993): 13–26.

Sigler, David Burns. *Vietnam Battle Chronology: U.S. Army and Marine Corps Combat Operations, 1965–1973.* Jefferson, N.C.: McFarland, 1992.

Silk, Mark. "Notes on the Judeo-Christian Tradition in America." *American Quarterly* 36, no. 1 (1984): 65–85.

Sizemore, Russell Yost Foster. "Reinhold Niebuhr and the Rhetoric of Liberal Anti-Communism: Christian Realism and the Rise of the Cold War." Ph.D. dissertation, Harvard University, 1987.

Skya, Walter. *Japan's Holy War: The Ideology of Radical Shinto Ultranationalism.* Durham: Duke University Press, 2009.

Slattery, Den. *From the Point to the Cross: One Vietnam Vet's Journey Toward Faith.* Kirkwood, Mo.: Impact Books, 1992.

Slomovitz, Albert. *The Fighting Rabbis: Jewish Military Chaplains and American History.* New York: New York University Press, 1999.

Small, Melvin. *Antiwarriors: The Vietnam War and the Battle for Hearts and Minds.* Wilmington, Del.: Scholastic Record, 2002.

Smith, Christian. *American Evangelicalism: Embattled and Thriving.* Chicago: University of Chicago Press, 1998.

Smith, Leonard V. "Paul Fussell's *The Great War and Modern Memory*: Twenty-Five Years Later." *History and Theory* 40, no. 2 (May 2001): 241–60.

Snape, Michael. *The Royal Army Chaplains' Department, 1796–1953: Clergy Under Fire.* Rochester, N.Y.: Boydell Press, 2007.

Snay, Mitchell. *The Gospel of Disunion: Religion and Separatism in the Antebellum South.* Chapel Hill: University of North Carolina Press, 1997.

Solis, Gary D. *Marines and Military Law in Vietnam: Trial by Fire.* Washington, D.C.: Headquarters, U.S. Marine Corps, 1989.

Sonnenberg, Stephen M., and Arthur S. Blank Jr., and John A. Talbott, eds. *The Trauma of War: Stress and Recovery in Viet Nam Veterans.* Washington, D.C.: American Psychiatric Press, 1985.

Sorley, Lewis. *A Better War: The Unexamined Victories and Final Tragedy of America's Last Years in Vietnam.* New York: Houghton Mifflin, 1999.

Spector, Ronald. *After Tet: The Bloodiest Year in Vietnam.* New York: Free Press, 1993.

Statler, Kathryn C. *Replacing France: The Origins of American Intervention in Vietnam.* Lexington: University Press of Kentucky, 2007.

Stittser, Gerald Lawson. *A Cautious Patriotism: The American Churches and the Second World War.* Chapel Hill: University of North Carolina Press, 1997.

Stone, Ronald H. *Christian Realism and Peacemaking: Issues in U.S. Foreign Policy.* Nashville, Tenn.: Abingdon Press, 1988.

Stover, Earl F. *Up from Handymen, 1862–1920.* Office of the Chief of Chaplains. The United States Army Chaplaincy. Vol. 5. Washington, D.C.: U.S. Government Printing Office, 1977.

Struken, Marita. *Tangled Memories: The Vietnam War, the Aids Epidemic, and the Politics of Remembering.* Berkeley: University of California Press, 1997.

Sugrue, Thomas. *The Origins of the Urban Crisis: Race and Inequality in Postwar Detroit*. Princeton, N.J.: Princeton University Press, 1996.

Summers, Harry G. *Vietnam War Almanac*. Rev. ed. Novato, Calif.: Presidio Press, 1999.

Swedberg, Richard, ed. *The Max Weber Dictionary: Key Words and Concepts*. Stanford, Calif.: Stanford University Press, 2005.

Thompson, Parker C. *From its European Antecedents to 1791*. Office of the Chief of Chaplains, The United States Army Chaplaincy. Vol. 1. Washington, D.C.: U.S. Government Printing Office, 1978.

Toews, John E. "Intellectual History after the Linguistic Turn: The Autonomy of Meaning and the Irreducibility of Experience." *American Historical Review* 92 (October 1987): 879–907.

Tomlin, Gregory Dale. "Hawks and Doves: Southern Baptist Responses to Military Intervention in Southeast Asia, 1965–73." Ph.D. dissertation, Southwestern Baptist Theological Seminary, 2003.

Toulouse, Mark G. "Christian Responses to Vietnam: The Organization of Dissent." Religion and Culture Web Forum (June 2007), http://martycenter.uchicago.edu/webforum/ 062007/vietnam.pdf. 1 July 2013.

Tucker, Robert W. *Woodrow Wilson and the Great War: Reconsidering America's Neutrality, 1914–1917*. Charlottesville: University of Virginia Press, 2007.

Turley, William S. *The Second Indochina War: A Concise Political and Military History*. 2d ed. Lanham, Md.: Rowman and Littlefield, 2009.

Turner, Stephen, ed. *The Cambridge Companion to Weber*. New York: Cambridge University Press, 2000.

Turner, Victor. "Liminality and Communitas." In *The Ritual Process: Structure and Anti-Structure*. Chicago: Aldine, 1969.

————. "Passages, Margins, and Poverty: Religious Symbols of Communitas." In *Dramas, Fields, and Metaphors: Symbolic Action in Human Society*. Ithaca, N.Y.: Cornell University Press, 1974.

————. *The Rites of Passage*. Translated by Monika B. Vizedom and Gabrielle L. Caffee. Chicago: University of Chicago Press, 1960.

Vea, Alfredo. *Gods Go Begging*. New York: Penguin, 1999.

Venzke, Rodger. *Confidence in Battle, Inspiration in Peace: The U.S. Army Chaplaincy, 1945–1975*. Office of the Chief of Chaplains, The United States Army Chaplaincy. Vol. 6. Washington, D.C.: U.S. Government Printing Office, 1977.

Vernon, Alex. "Introduction: No Genre's Land: The Problem of Genre in War Memoirs and Military Autobiographies." In *Arms and the Self: War, the Military, and Autobiographical Writing*, edited by Alex Vernon, 1–40. Kent, Ohio: Kent State University Press, 2005.

————, ed. *Arms and the Self: War, the Military, and Autobiographical Writing*. Kent, Ohio: Kent State University Press, 2005.

Vickers, Robert Clayton. "The Military Chaplaincy: A Study in Role Conflict (Clergy, Role Expectations)." Ed.D. dissertation, Peabody College for Teachers of Vanderbilt University, 1984.

Wald, Kenneth D. "The Religious Dimension of American Anti-Communism." *Journal of Church and State* 36, no. 3 (1994): 483–506.

Weber, Max. *Economy and Society: An Outline of Interpretive Sociology*. Edited by Guenther Roth and Claus Wittich. Translated by Ephraim Fischoff et al. 1922. Reprint, New York: Besminster Press, 1968.

Wells, Tom. *The War Within: America's Battle over Vietnam*. Berkeley: University of California Press, 1994.

White, Louise. "Telling More: Lies, Secrets, and History." *History and Theory* 39, no. 4 (December 2000): 11–22.

White, Richard. *The Middle Ground Indians, Empires, and Republics in the Great Lakes Region, 1650–1815*. New York: Cambridge University Press, 1991.

Williams, Eugene Franklin. *Soldiers of God: The Chaplains of the Revolutionary War*. New York: Carleton Press, 1975.

Williams, George H. "The Chaplaincy in the Armed Forces of the United States of America in Historical and Ecclesiastical Perspective." In *Military Chaplains: From a Religious Military to a Military Religion*, edited by Harvey G. Cox, 11–58. New York: American Report Press, 1971.

Wilson, Charles Reagan. *Baptized in Blood: The Religion of the Lost Cause, 1865–1920*. Athens: University of Georgia Press, 1983.

Winter, Jay. *Sites of Memory, Sites of Mourning: The Great War in European Cultural History*. New ed. Cambridge, UK: Cambridge University Press, 1998.

Winter, Jay, and Emmanuel Sivan, eds. "Setting the Framework." In *War and Remembrance in the Twentieth Century*. Cambridge, UK: Cambridge University Press, 1999.

Wuthnow, Robert. *The Restructuring of American Religion: Society and Faith since World War II*. Princeton, N.J.: Princeton University Press, 1988.

Wyatt, Clarence R. *Paper Soldiers: The American Press and the Vietnam War*. New York: W. W. Norton, 1993.

Yee, James, with Aimee Molloy. *For God and Country: Faith and Patriotism Under Fire*. New York: Public Affairs, 2005.

Young, Marilyn B. *The Vietnam Wars, 1945–1990*. New York: Harper, 1991.

Zahn, Gordon H. *The Military Chaplaincy: A Study of Role Tension in the Royal Air Force*. Toronto: University of Toronto Press, 1969.

Zine, Jasmin. "Between Orientalism and Fundamentalism: Muslim Women and Feminist Engagement." In *(En)Gendering the War on Terror: War Stories and Camouflaged Politics*, edited by Krista Hunt and Kim Rygiel, 27–50. Burlington, Vt.: Ashgate Publishing, 2006.

INDEX

34–35; deployment of chaplains, 13, 40, 44, 45–46; directives on chaplains, 47–49, 59, 62–63, 82–85, 87, 92–93, 163, 200; duties of chaplains, 64–65; changes after Vietnam, 208–9, 213, 222–23

Army Chaplain School, 31–32, 83, 90, 170, 198, 208, 211, 239 (n. 47); survey by, 67, 70, 91, 102, 167, 168, 170, 173, 189, 190, 192, 193

Army chief of chaplains, 36, 49, 51, 59, 80, 83, 86, 87, 92–93, 138, 162, 172, 198, 200, 213

Army Office of the Chief of Chaplains. *See* Office of the Chief of Chaplains

Army of the Republic of Vietnam (ARVN), 38, 46, 47, 93, 100, 141, 241 (n. 6), 252 (n. 2)

Army War College, 32, 54, 213, 226

Arvay, Al, 87

Assemblies of God (AOG), 26, 52, 135

Associated Press, 157, 219

Association of Jewish Chaplains in the Armed Forces, 153–54

Atheists, 68, 82, 162, 170–71, 193, 215, 263 (n. 68)

Atomic bomb, 8, 20, 30, 36, 37, 99

Atrocities. *See* War crimes and atrocities

Autry, Jerry, 104–5, 163, 174, 183–84

"Back in the world" (Vietnam-era slang for the United States), 15, 17, 90, 114, 117, 119, 123, 128, 131, 225

Baldwin, Charles, 215

Bao Dai (Nguyen Phuc Vinh Thuy), 21

Baptism, 109, 119, 130, 202, 229; "Baptism by fire," 115–16, 119, 165

Baptist General Conference, 153

Baptists, 36, 136, 140, 156–57, 192, 215, 229; numbers of, in chaplaincy, 52, 53, 217; as mainline denomination, 53, 242 (n. 21); first-person accounts of, 167, 189, 190–91. *See also* American Baptist Convention; National

Baptist Convention; Southern Baptist Convention

Bastogne, battle of, 4

"Battle Hymn of the Republic" (song), 121, 122, 186–87

Baugham, Billy, 219–20

Baxter, Gary, 117, 252 (n. 54)

Beach, Stanley, 124

Beasley, Joseph, 69–70

Bellah, Robert, 22, 23, 24–25, 237 (n. 13)

Bergen, Doris, 5–6

Berrigan, Daniel and Philip, 8, 134, 139

Bible, 26, 122, 202. *See also* Scripture

Bible Presbyterian Church, 140

Bien Hoa Air Force Base, 93, 149

"Big Unit War," 44–45

Billy Budd (Melville), 5

Binh Tuy Air Base, 89

Bonhoeffer, Dietrich, 134–35, 143

Book of Worship (Armed Forces Hymnal), 196, 205–7

Bowers, Curtis (Curt), 69, 86, 95, 109, 110, 119, 121, 179, 181–82, 183

Bradley, Roger, 153

"Bring God to men and men to God" (motto), 70, 96–97, 127

Brown, Charles, 86–87, 162

Brown, Jack, 177, 178–79, 184, 192

Buddhists, 39, 134, 215, 250 (n. 15)

Burchard, Waldo, 79–80

Burchell, Francis, 93

Burnham, James, 97, 175

CALCAV. *See* Clergy and Laymen Concerned about Vietnam

Calley, William, 104–5

Cambodia, 37, 45, 141, 170

Camp Pendleton (California), 205

Cam Ranh Bay, 65, 89, 129

Capodanno, Vincent, 4, 72–73, 124, 169–70

Caputo, Philip, 111–12, 172

Carter, Bradley, 246 (n. 3), 250 (n. 13), 256–57 (n. 2)

Carter, Sydney, 196, 205, 207

Department of the Army, U.S., 32, 48–49, 84

Des Champs, Thomas, 112, 117–18, 178

Diem, Ngo Dinh, 21, 38, 39, 40, 44, 240 (nn. 76, 77)

Dien Bien Phu, Battle of, 21, 37, 39

Dimont, Albert, 56

Disciples of Christ, 52, 192, 242 (n. 21)

Dorchester, USS, 4

Draft, exemptions from, 80, 246 (n. 5)

Draft resistance, 37, 74, 134, 139, 188

Drawdowns, military: after World War II, 34, 35; in Vietnam, 56–57, 64, 70, 155, 210

Drazin, Israel, 202

Drugs, illegal, 15, 18, 71, 72, 77, 88–91, 107, 209, 210; detoxification programs, 89–90

Dryer, Richard, 138

Duc, Thich Quang. *See* Thich Quang Duc

Dulany, Joseph, 95, 100, 102–3, 109, 119, 129–30, 174, 187, 251 (n. 42)

Easter, 121, 123, 124, 129

Eastern Orthodox Church, 49, 211, 249 (n. 1)

Easter Offensive, 47

Ecumenism, 14, 43, 51, 58, 60, 61, 116–17, 122, 123, 143–44, 148, 158; of combat, 16, 17, 24, 116–17, 131, 189; in post-Vietnam chaplaincy, 17, 197, 200, 205, 207, 214, 215–16, 230; tradition of, in chaplaincy, 58–60, 196–97, 207, 216, 220, 226, 229

Eisenhower, Dwight D., 25–26, 38

Episcopal Church (Protestant Episcopal Church of the United States of America), 81, 160–61, 212, 238 (n. 25)

Episcopalians, 58, 78, 167, 182, 217, 242 (n. 21)

Episcopal Peace Fellowship, 139, 150

Estes, Arthur, 45–46, 178

Evangelicalism, 14–15, 19, 26, 28, 31, 53, 94–95, 101, 153, 221, 226; and

Cold War, 29–30, 33, 136–37, 143–44; opposition to liberalism, 37, 204, 261 (n. 28); Southern Baptist Convention, 50, 52, 94, 136, 140, 143, 161; responses to Vietnam War, 108, 135–42, 164, 167; criticism of chaplaincy, 230; defined, 254 (n. 37). *See also* National Association of Evangelicals

Evangelicals, 58, 78, 115, 215–16, 219–20, 227, 239 (n. 53); witnessing within military, 36, 126, 196, 205, 217–18, 229, 240 (n. 67)

Falabella, Robert, 187–88, 248 (n. 57)

Finnegan, Terence P., 208

First Amendment, 9, 36, 196, 199, 200–203, 216–18; free exercise clause, 27, 204, 220, 226, 227, 228, 230; establishment clause, 221

1st Cavalry Division, 97–98

Forgy, Howell, 4, 234 (n. 7)

Fort Benning, 222

Fort Bragg (North Carolina), 61

Fort Hamilton, 211

Fort Jackson, 239 (n. 47)

Fort Leavenworth, 178, 188

Fort Lewis, 99

4th Infantry Division, 118

France, 20–21

Friend, Jan, 189

Fuller, Charles, 143

Full Metal Jacket (film), 4

Fundamentalism, 26, 139

Fundamentalists, 140, 170

Garetts, Francis, 140

General Commission on Chaplains and Armed Forces Personnel (GCCAFP), 31, 60, 145, 154, 161, 254 (n. 43)

General Commission on Churches and the Chaplaincy, 198

Geneva Accords (1954), 37–38

Geneva Conventions, 35, 86, 87, 88, 99, 246–47 (n. 18)

Kennedy, Robert Francis, 191
Kenney, John, 71
Kent, David, 189, 192
Kentucky Baptist Convention, 136
Kettler, Earl, 53, 128
Kincade, Lloyd, 191, 192
King, Martin Luther, Jr., 191
Kissinger, Harry, 54–55
Klausler, Alfred, 149–50
Klitgaard, Robert, 152
Knight, David, 122, 124, 125–26, 165
Koepke, Theodore, 86
Koppell, Bonnie, 211
Korean War, 20, 31, 34–36, 42, 86, 93, 148, 239 (n. 65)

Lacy, Floyd, 192
Landes, Carl, 150–51
Laos, 37, 45
LDS Church. *See* Church of Jesus Christ of Latter-day Saints
LeClair, Charles, 189–90, 191
Ledebuhr, Albert F., 147–49, 160
Lembke, Jerry, 171–72
Lemieux, Earnest S., 40
Lemon v. Kurtzman (Supreme Court case), 201, 203, 261 (n. 14)
Lester, Elmore, 40
Lewis, Francis, 99–100
Liberalism, religious, 14–15, 30, 33, 58, 210, 239 (n. 53); within chaplaincy, 16, 17, 52, 205, 227; critique of chaplaincy, 16, 36, 60, 139, 145–52, 160, 196–204, 220–21, 229, 230; responses to Vietnam War, 18, 84, 101, 136–43, 154, 164, 167, 215–16; and anti-Communism, 20, 27–29, 37, 39, 42, 238 (n. 35); defined, 27–28
Libraries, 65, 92, 93, 142, 147, 201, 202
Liminality. *See* People in the middle
Lincoln, Abraham, 58
Lindvall, John, 40
Linebacker I & II, Operations, 47
Liteky, Angelo (AKA Charles Liteky), 10–12, 222, 223

Little, Gene, 170
Liturgies of war, 16, 109–10, 114–30 passim, 130–31, 224, 250 (n. 13); defined, 114, 250 (n. 14)
Long Binh Post, 55, 69–70, 89
Loveland, Anne, 52, 207, 233 (n. 2)
Lutheranism, 30, 242 (n. 21); Lutheran Chruch–Missouri Synod, 50, 116; Wisconsin Evangelical Lutheran Synod, 156; Lutheran Church of America, 212; Lutheran World Federation, 240 (n. 74)
Lutherans, 78, 116, 139, 167, 217–18

MacFarlane, Norman, 147–51, 160
MACV. *See* Military Assistance Command, Vietnam
Maguire, Connell J., 178
Mahedy, William, 182
Mainline denominations, 19, 24, 26, 33, 95, 115, 143, 210; within chaplaincy, 16, 50, 141, 227; responses to Vietnam War, 18, 84, 101, 134, 140–41, 142, 167, 215–16, 233 (n. 2); and anti-Communism, 37, 39, 42; defined, 53, 242 (n. 21); critique of chaplaincy, 60, 145–52, 160, 164, 196–204, 220–21, 229, 230; ordaining women, 211–12
Marijuana, 88, 89, 90
Marine Corps, U.S., 4, 45, 72–73, 109, 111–12, 120, 124, 159, 169–70, 205; deployment of chaplains, 40, 45; duties of chaplains, 48; historical records of, 77, 168; Combined Action Platoons (CAP), 242 (n. 14), 247 (n. 37)
Marty, Martin E., 26, 237 (n. 20), 238 (n. 35)
*M*A*S*H* (film), 5
*M*A*S*H* (television series), 234 (n. 9)
May, James, 171
McCarter, Calvin W., 129
McCarthy, Joseph, 14–15, 30
McClements, James, 66–67
McIntire, Carl, 140

McLaughlin, Joseph M., 202, 203
McPhee, Richard, 149
Meade, Henry J., 207
Medal of Honor, 4, 10, 169, 222
Mekong Delta, 46
Memoirs, 16, 165, 194, 222, 225–26, 229, 264–65 (n. 9); use of, as sources, 14, 77–78, 166–67, 173–84 passim, 236 (n. 36), 245–46 (n. 3), 257 (n. 21), 257–58 (n. 22); by nonchaplains, 115, 193–94, 195
Memory, 14, 78, 173–75
Methodist Church of America, 212
Methodists, 40, 52, 53, 93, 167, 188, 217, 242 (n. 21). *See also* African Methodist Episcopal Zion Church; United Methodist Church
Midway, USS, 58
Military Assistance Command, Vietnam (MACV), 159; historical records of, 13; operational history, 38, 44–47; chaplaincy under, 40, 44, 53, 56–57, 86, 93, 168
Military Chaplain, The (Abercrombie), 81, 199
Miller, Richard, 63
Miller, William R., 146–47, 148, 149, 160
Mishler, Jacob, 202
Mitchell, Paul, 76
Morale, 112, 127, 137; chaplains' effect on troops', 7, 41, 43, 66, 68, 97, 142, 204; chaplains', 56, 71, 74, 111–12
Mormons, 58, 59–61, 68, 88, 116, 167, 207, 243 (n. 49). *See also* Church of Jesus Christ of Latter-day Saints
Morton, MeLinda, 217–18
Moyar, Jack, 191–92
Murdock, Llewellyn, 91
Music, as part of religious practices, 122–23, 209. See also *Book of Worship*; Songs
Muslims, 6, 215, 228–29, 230, 234 (n. 12), 250 (n. 15)
My Lai incident, 54–55, 98, 99–100, 104, 134, 141

National Association of Evangelicals, 50, 60, 141
National Baptist Convention, 49, 192, 245 (n. 90)
National Council of Churches, 8, 30, 134, 140
National Guard, 32, 35, 48, 49, 81, 186
National Jewish Welfare Board (NJWB), 55, 59, 211
National Liberation Front (NLF), 38, 46
Navy, U.S., 48, 103, 147, 148, 149, 158, 160, 164, 169, 205; historical records of, 13, 77, 167–68, 178; in Korea, 34–35; deployment of chaplains, 40, 44; area coverage in, 57; civic action programs (CAPS), 93; changes in, after Vietnam, 212, 213–15; directives on chaplains, 216; quota system in, 217, 262 (n. 52); training of chaplains, 239 (n. 47)
Navy chief of chaplains, 137
Nazarenes, 167, 238 (n. 25)
Neo-pagans, 215
Neuhaus, Richard John, 139–40, 142, 163, 253 (n. 22)
Newby, Claude, 60–61, 72, 74–75, 173, 177, 179; relations with commanders, 68–69, 88; responds to atrocities, 100, 102, 105–6; leading services, 121, 129
New York Times, 99, 134, 137, 138–39, 161, 215
Nguyen Phuc Vinh Thuy. *See* Bao Dai
Nicaragua, 10, 222
Niebuhr, Reinhold, 19, 28–29, 135, 238 (n. 35)
9th Infantry Division, 126
Nixon, Richard, 46–47, 72, 139
North Vietnamese Army (NVA), 44, 45, 46, 47, 97, 112, 169, 242 (n. 15), 252 (n. 2)
Nuclear weapons. *See* Atomic bomb

O'Connor, John, 141, 198
O'Donnell, Joseph, 103, 109, 119–20

Office of the Chief of Chaplains (OCCH), 62, 83, 86, 172, 201, 208, 260 (n. 12); historical records of, 13; directives issued by, 49–52, 62, 85, 87

101st Airborne Division, 178

Orphanages, 76, 92, 93

Orthodox denominations, 250 (n. 15). *See also* Eastern Orthodox Church

Pacifism, Christian, 134–35

"Pacifist critique," 6, 79–80, 100–101, 146–47, 166

"Padre," as generic name for chaplains, 72–73, 245 (n. 92)

Paulson, Philip, 170–71

Pearl Harbor, 4

Pennebaker, James W., 179–80

Pentagon Papers, 134

Pentecostalism, 26, 135

Pentecostals, 167, 217

People in the middle, 1–2, 16, 99, 107–8, 165, 194, 230; officer/enlisted, 1, 66–67; sectarian/ecumenical, 1, 132, 133, 149, 197, 216, 227; soldier/clergy, 15, 43, 72, 74–75, 78–81, 91, 94, 99, 107–8, 145, 153; defined, 233 (n. 1)

Plank, David, 135

Pleiku Air Base, 55, 123

Post-traumatic stress disorder (PTSD), 17, 179, 180–82, 186, 210, 222–23

POWs (prisoners of war): American, 86, 210; Vietnamese, 96, 100, 111

"Praise the Lord and Pass the Ammunition" (song), 4, 234 (n. 7)

Prayer, 120, 122, 128, 136, 153, 171, 182, 192; Patton prayer, 4; soldier's, 115; public, by chaplains, 218–20

Predestination, 124–25

Presbyterianism, 143, 242 (n. 21); Presbyterian Church, 81, 161; Presbyterian Church in the United States, 81, 143; United Presbyterian Church, 157; Presbyterian Church (USA), 160, 212

Presbyterians, 26, 31, 53, 58, 78, 167, 189, 215, 217

Privilege, pastoral, 103, 105, 229

Profanity, 15, 71, 94, 95, 107

Project Life Postcard Campaign, 216–17

Prostitution, 71, 95–96

Protestant Episcopal Church of the United States of America. *See* Episcopal Church

Protestantism, 23, 58, 78, 139–40, 237 (n. 8); and anti-Communism, 30; influence on chaplaincy, 34, 154; Liturgical, 78, 117, 196, 217, 227. *See also* Conservatism, religious; Evangelicalism; Liberalism, religious

Protestantism, mainline. *See* Mainline denominations

Protestants, 31, 73, 94, 95, 126, 143, 193, 206–7, 217; attending services, 26; Vietnamese, 38, 94; numbers of, in chaplaincy, 45, 49, 196, 211; services held by, 58, 76, 118; and LDS Church, 59, 61, 68; donations collected by, 92, 93, 139; "low-church," 115; responses to Vietnam War, 150–51, 160

PTSD. *See* Post-traumatic stress disorder

Public theology, 238 (n. 35); and Cold War, 25–30; defined, 26–27

Puritans, 23, 177–78

Quakers (Religious Society of Friends), 83–84

Quota system, 49–52, 55, 78–79, 211, 217, 227, 272 (n. 52)

Race: relations, among troops, 72, 210; of chaplains, 77–78, 167–68, 245 (n. 90)

Radio Church of God (Worldwide Church of God), 83

Rape, 105–6

Reagan, Ronald, 10, 183

Religious autobiographies. *See* Spiritual autobiographies

Religious Right, 196, 197, 204, 221
Religious Society of Friends. *See* Quakers
Reserves, U.S. Armed Forces, 32, 48, 51, 81, 206, 246 (n. 7)
Retreats, religious, 40, 60–61, 65, 182, 201
Rich, Donald, 93–94
Rigdon v. Perry (court case), 216–17
Robinson, Donald, 193
Rohr, John A., 164
Role conflict, 15, 100–101, 106–7, 108, 165–67, 194, 224–25; defined, 2–3; in scholarship on chaplaincy, 9, 76–77, 79–82, 198–99, 235 (n. 25)
Roles, of chaplains, 77, 127, 144–55, 157, 223, 224–25, 226, 230
—defined, 144
—evangelical/missionary, 153
—institutional ministry, 233 (n. 2)
—pastoral, 233 (n. 2); as duty, 2, 43, 133, 139, 160–61, 164; as choice, 17, 70, 102, 106, 162, 197, 225, 229
—prophetic, 233 (n. 2); as duty, 2, 101, 112, 133, 160–62, 164, 172, 196, 227, 230–31; as choice, 17, 70, 102, 106, 225
Rolling Thunder, Operation, 45, 47
Roman Catholic Church. *See* Catholic Church
Royal Air Force (RAF), 100–101, 198
Rumor of War, A (Caputo), 111–12, 172

Sacramental rites, 43, 61, 64, 109, 114, 116–19, 130, 176; Sacrament of the Sick, 109, 119–20; defined, 115. *See also* Baptism; Communion
Saigon (Ho Chih Minh City), 40–41, 44, 46, 55, 56, 119, 123, 134, 163
Sale, Lyman, Jr., 157
Sampson, Francis, 80
Schlesinger, James, 196, 206
School of the Americas, 11, 222
Schumacher, John, 117, 248 (n. 56)
Schweitzer, Gordon, 210–11

Scripture, 73, 110–11, 113, 130; I Corinthians 13 ("Love never fails"), 127; Deuteronomy, 6; Exodus 14 (Moses and the Red Sea), 124; Exodus 20:13 ("you shall not kill"), 9, 79, 97, 110, 249 (n. 1); Galatians 6:7 ("as ye sow, so shall ye reap"), 97; Jeremiah, 101; Luke 6:31 ("do unto others as you would have them do unto you"), 97; Luke 16:13 ("No slave can serve two masters"), 9, 235 (n. 25); Matthew 5:44 ("love your enemies"), 113; Matthew 6:9–13 (Lord's Prayer), 73; Psalm 46 ("God is our refuge and strength"), 126, 127; Psalm 91:3–8 ("He will save you from the fowler's snare"), 125, 251 (n. 48); Psalm 91:5 ("you will not fear the terror of the night"), 125; Romans 13 (submission to authorities), 110, 141, 172, 249 (n. 1)
Seeker, Philip, 164
Senieur, John, 57
September 11, 2001, 183, 228
Services, by chaplains, 43, 45, 68, 98, 109, 110, 119, 213, 219; field, 35, 54, 55, 69, 116–17, 118, 121, 126, 128, 229; memorial, 35, 57, 120, 191; denominational, 61, 76; numbers held, 62–63, 162; attendance at, 62–64, 70–71, 123, 148, 162; importance of, 102, 114, 175–76, 250 (n. 19); holiday, 121, 123, 124, 128, 129; healing, 182; for retired service members, 202
Sexual activity, 15, 71, 94, 95–96, 209
Shaner, Donald, 149
Shea, Donald, 70, 173, 192
Shimek, Andrew, 120
Shumway, Amos, 170
Siegel, Martin, 158–60
Sodt, William, 149
Songs, 4, 121–22, 130, 186–87, 196, 197, 205–7, 224. *See also* Music
Sources, problems of, 13–14, 77–78, 133, 166, 167–73, 245 (n. 92)

Southern Baptist Convention, 50, 52, 94, 136, 140, 143, 161
Soviet Union. *See* Union of Soviet Socialist Republics
Sowards, Douglas, 69, 191
Space, sacred, 128–30
Special Forces (U.S. Army), 38
Speiser, Lawrence, 199–200
Spellman, Francis, 49
Spiritual autobiographies, 16, 68, 177–79
Sporkin, Stanley, 217
Stars and Stripes (periodical), 219–20
Staudt, William, 40
Stegman, Leonard, 56–57
Stevenson, Adlai, 25–26
Supreme Court of the United States, 82–83, 261 (n. 14)

Tan Son Nhut Airfield, 40, 55, 56, 183, 241 (n. 11)
Task Force Barker, 54, 98
Tet Offensive, 46, 112, 134, 242 (n. 15), 252 (n. 2)
Therapeutic writing. *See* Trauma writing
Thich Quang Duc, 134
Thompson, James, 141
Thompson, Parker, 97–98
Thurmond, Strom, 196, 206
Time magazine, 162–64
Tobey, Frank, 36
Torture, use of, 96, 100, 101, 229, 248–49 (n. 67)
Trauma of war, 18, 73–74, 104, 172, 175, 180, 182–83, 187, 188, 195, 209. *See also* Post-traumatic stress disorder
Trauma writing, 16, 166, 179, 181, 194
Trinitarianism, 207
Trotsauch, William, 193
Trott, Marvin, 190
Truman, Harry S., 29, 31, 32–33
Tuy Hoa Air Base, 64, 92

20th Infantry Division, 54
24th Infantry Division, 35

Union of Soviet Socialist Republics (USSR), 37, 38, 39, 42, 45, 183, 227, 240 (n. 74)
Unitarians, 26, 58
United Church of Christ, 26, 146, 242 (n. 21)
United Methodist Church, 26, 93, 188
United Presbyterian Church, 157
United States Army, Vietnam (USARV). *See* Army, U.S.
United States v. Seeger, 82–85
Unit Ministry Teams (UMT), 213
Universal military training (UMT), 20, 30, 32–33, 239 (n. 53)

VanLandingham, Ralph, 93
Vavrin, Frank, 162
Viet Cong (VC), 38, 45, 46, 100, 101, 104, 109, 163, 242 (n. 15), 252 (n. 2)
Viet Minh, 20, 21
Vietnam: history of U.S. involvement in, 20–21, 44–47, 184; sovereignty of, 37–38; religious responses to U.S. involvement in, 37–41, 133–42; in popular U.S. media, 189–90, 195, 225
Vietnamese civilians, interactions with, 93–94, 107, 112–13, 123
"Vietnamization," 47, 72
"Vietnam syndrome," 2, 230
Vietnam Veteran Ministers, 186, 223
Vietnam Veterans Against the War, 171, 186, 223
Vo Nguyen Giap, 44

War crimes and atrocities, 15, 77, 96–107, 108, 225, 226
Warriors, The (Gray), 193–94
Washington, George, 7, 142
Washington Post, 138, 157
Weber, Max, 144
Weddings, 202
Wedel, Larry, 192